THE TROUBLE WITH GOVERNMENT

THE TROUBLE WITH GOVERNMENT

DEREK BOK

HARVARD UNIVERSITY PRESS
Cambridge, Massachusetts and London, England
2001

Printed in the United States of America

Library of Congress Cataloging-in-Publication Data

Bok, Derek Curtis.

The trouble with government / Derek Bok.

p. cm.

ISBN 0-674-00448-5 (alk. paper)

1. Political planning—United States. 2. United States—Politics and government—1989–

3. United States—Social policy. I. Title.

JK468.P64 B66 2001

306′.0973—dc21   00-063476

To Paul Jellinek

PREFACE

THIS IS THE SECOND and final volume in a project begun in 1992 at the behest of the Robert Wood Johnson, Rockefeller, and MacArthur foundations. The invitation came as a complete surprise at a meeting in my office shortly before I retired as president of Harvard University. What the foundations wanted was a book on why our government was not working better and how it could be improved—surely a daunting assignment.

My first reaction was that the project was simply too vast and unwieldy. Besides, I thought, innumerable books and articles have already been published on every aspect of American government. What more could one hope to say on the subject? Any university library contains masses of material marshaling facts and testing hypotheses about how our government actually works. The shelves groan under the weight of books propounding theories about how an ideal government ought to function, not to mention countless monographs on specific problems in the public sphere and the mischief they cause.

On further reflection, however, I was struck by how hard it was to find a comprehensive work that drew upon all the individual studies to try to discover whether our federal government was in fact performing badly, what its most important problems were, why they existed, and whether they could be remedied. At a time of such intense dissatisfaction with Washington, such a book might help to sort out all the criticisms and search for positive ways to respond. With that thought in mind, I decided, somewhat to my surprise, to undertake the project.

It soon occurred to me that before I plunged ahead to analyze the government's weaknesses, I should study its performance to try to ascertain how well the enterprise was actually working. This inquiry led to the publication of *The State of the Nation* (1996), a book that examined the progress of the United States over the past forty years in seventeen different fields of activity, ranging from economic growth and productivity to health care and housing to personal responsibility and the arts. In each field, I described the development of government programs and policies and then compared the results with those of six other advanced industrial democracies: Britain, Canada, France, Germany, Japan, and Sweden. This study confirmed, at least for me, that our government was indeed performing less effectively than it should be in helping the society progress toward many of the goals affirmed by large majorities of the people.

The present volume builds on the earlier study to explore why the federal government's policies have often failed to achieve what most Americans profess to want, and whether there are reforms that would help to improve its performance. In the course of this work, I consider the role played by the various participants in the public arena—notably politicians, bureaucrats, the media, and interest groups—that are most often blamed for all that Americans dislike about government and politics. I also spend considerable time examining the influence of the public itself, an influence that turns out to be more substantial than many writers seem to believe.

The title of the book is adapted from Alfred Hitchcock's dark comedy *The Trouble with Harry*. Harry's trouble, of course, was that he was dead. Only a few stubborn libertarians and anarchists would say the same about government in the United States. While people differ about how sick our government is, almost everyone believes that it is very much alive. Most people also think there are remedies that could help to nurse it back at least to somewhat better health. These sentiments underlie the chapters to follow.

The entire project has taken longer than I—or my sponsors—anticipated when we initially agreed to undertake the work in 1991.

Throughout, the foundations have been remarkably patient and supportive. I could not have asked for greater understanding and encouragement, especially from Paul Jellinek, vice president of the Robert Wood Johnson Foundation, who was a principal force in launching the effort in the first place. In completing this volume, I was also privileged to spend eight uninterrupted weeks at that most magical of scholarly retreats, the Rockefeller Center in Bellagio, Italy. For all this help and support, I am enormously appreciative.

In the course of my work, I have received invaluable research assistance from a large number of Harvard students, too many to list individually here. To all of them, I acknowledge most gratefully their good work in helping me to understand a wide range of government policies and programs.

In addition, numerous colleagues have kindly read portions of the manuscript and offered helpful comments. I owe particular thanks to Robert Blendon, Sheila Burke, Cary Coglianese, Jane Fountain, Charles Fried, Marshall Ganz, Philip Heymann, David King, Pippa Norris, Richard Parker, Phil Sharp, John Simon, and Malcolm Sparrow.

I can never adequately express my gratitude to Connie Higgins for her extraordinary loyalty and patience in typing, retyping, cutting, and pasting more drafts of this manuscript than either of us wants to remember.

To Michael Aronson, my editor, I owe a debt for valuable advice about how to make the manuscript more readable.

Finally, as always, my family has been exceptionally helpful—Victoria, in commenting on parts of the study having to do with urban problems; Hilary, in reading the entire manuscript at an early stage when much candid advice was needed and freely given; and Sissela, who has read and reread chapters with unfailing patience and given innumerable useful comments.

CONTENTS

IV. *The Role of the People*

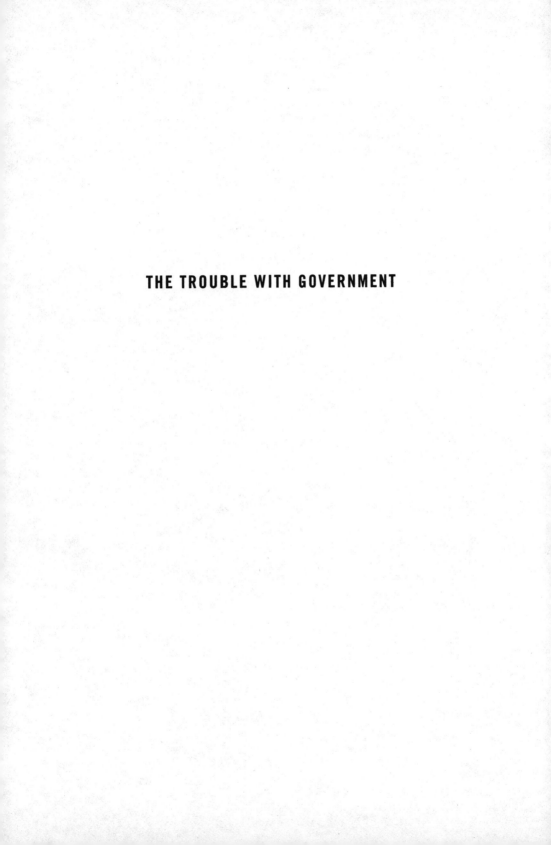

THE TROUBLE WITH GOVERNMENT

INTRODUCTION

O N A WARM SPRING DAY in 1985, late in the afternoon, I found myself in Washington seated in the office of that quintessential Irish politician, Boston's own Speaker of the House, Thomas P. "Tip" O'Neill. I had just spent the best part of a week talking to members of Congress about student aid, trying to counter President Reagan's annual assault on federal scholarships and loans. It had been slow, painstaking work. Now that I had finished my rounds, it was time to report on my activities to the lawmaker who happened not only to lead the House but to represent the district in which my university stood.

Thinking back on what I had seen and heard, I could not help being struck by how engaged and articulate all of the legislators had seemed, and how informed they were about the arcane details of student aid. Surely these people were a far cry from the prevailing image of Washington politicians, an image that provoked such disapproval from the public. Thus, having finished my business with the Speaker, and noting that he had just lit a cigar and settled back in his chair, I felt moved to ask a question that had nothing to do with the purpose of my visit. "You have been in this building for over thirty years, Mr. Speaker," I began. "Looking back, do you believe that the quality of people elected to Congress has gotten better, gotten worse, or stayed the same?" Without a moment's hesitation, Mr. O'Neill replied, "The quality is clearly better, much better." He paused, puffed on his cigar, and added ruefully: "But the results are definitely worse."

I've often wondered about the Speaker's reply. In fact, the questions that his words evoke form the central themes of this book. Has the federal government's performance truly declined over the past few decades, and in what respects has it fallen short? If the abilities of our lawmakers have increased, why has their effectiveness diminished? Finally, are there ways to improve the government's performance without producing results that could make the cure even worse than the disease?*

Different people answer these questions in different ways, depending on their vantage point. Large majorities of the public have harsh words to say about politics, politicians, and the policymaking process. But these unflattering views are not necessarily shared by those who make their living keeping a close watch on events in Washington. As one might expect, most members of Congress have a much better opinion of their colleagues than does the general public, and feel surprisingly positive about the operations of the federal government as a whole. Journalists are much more critical than politicians, but they often disagree with the public and with one another about exactly what has gone wrong. To confuse matters further, political scientists who try to test empirically how the system actually works frequently reach results that contradict impressions held by all the other interested groups.

---

* Most of what is said about government in these pages will be about the *federal government*. But other levels of government will enter the story at various points, and much of the discussion will be relevant to state governments, which typically resemble the federal government in their institutional structure. Local governments, however, have a much different structure and vary so greatly from one to another that it is difficult to generalize about them.

   Although the book will touch on many fields of government activity, all of them involve issues of domestic policy. These are the areas that have provoked the greatest dissatisfaction among rank-and-file Americans. Foreign policy is a separate subject, with its own peculiar dynamic. Its goals are harder to define and its results much more difficult to measure and evaluate, not least because there is strong disagreement over whether and how to take account of the consequences for inhabitants of other countries. For reasons of space, therefore, this subject must remain beyond the purview of this book.

The Views of the Public

Throughout most of the 1990s, large majorities of the public felt that the country was headed in the wrong direction and that Washington deserved much of the blame.[1] Although Americans continue to believe overwhelmingly that their *system* of government is the best in the world, most of them have a low opinion of the work of public officials in Congress and the Executive Branch. Sunshine laws and other steps to open the political process to public view have not helped to restore people's confidence. Instead, Americans have responded much like the well-known theater critic who began one review by stating, "I have seen this play at a disadvantage: the curtain was up." The number of people who trust the federal government to do the right thing all or most of the time plummeted from 76 percent in 1964 to only 21 percent in 1994, before rebounding modestly toward the end of the millennium after several years of unbroken economic prosperity.[2] A strong plurality currently regard the federal government as the greatest domestic threat America faces, far outnumbering those who chiefly fear organized labor or big business.[3]

A closer look reveals that not everything about government has fallen into such disfavor. The major *institutions* of our national government (not their performance) continue to enjoy firm support. Huge majorities express approval or strong approval of Congress, the presidency, and the Supreme Court.[4] Among occupational groups, both public and private, two of the four that currently enjoy the highest popular esteem actually work for the federal government—the armed forces and members of the Supreme Court—while a third group, the police, works for state and local governments.[5] (The fourth category comprises leaders of the church.) Even career civil servants enjoy a modestly favorable reputation, despite considerable doubts about their energy and efficiency.[6] Apparently, then, it is not the federal government as a whole, nor its principal institutions, nor even many of its members that have lost the confidence of the public. The chief culprits, by a wide margin, are elected politicians.

While most Americans are satisfied with the work of their own representative in Congress, more than three-fourths believe that "our leaders are more concerned with managing their images than with solving the nation's problems."[7] A survey rating the honesty and ethical standards of twenty-six different professions showed members of Congress winding up near the bottom.[8] In the eyes of the public, politicians in Washington do not serve the needs of voters but dance instead to the tune of powerful organizations that contribute money to their campaigns. According to one survey in 1995, 86 percent of Americans agreed that Congress is too heavily influenced by interest groups in making its decisions.[9] Most people believe that politicians running the country don't care what ordinary Americans think.[10] Even larger majorities feel that "elected officials in Washington lose touch with the people pretty quickly."[11]

To the public, federal lawmakers seem to spend more time attacking each other in petty, partisan ways than working together to solve the nation's problems. When officials do act, the results are widely viewed as disappointing. Almost 70 percent of Americans believe that when the national government tries to address an issue, it generally "creates more problems than it solves."[12] In repeated polls, the median respondent has estimated that the federal government wastes almost half of every tax dollar it receives.[13] By virtually every measure, then, the people have come to have a disturbingly low opinion of their political leaders in Washington.

The Opinions of Journalists

Television commentators and newspaper reporters rarely pass sweeping judgments on subjects as vast as the quality of the federal government. What they do talk about at length is politics and politicians. In private, their views on this subject are more nuanced than those of the public. Old Washington hands will generally agree with Speaker O'Neill that the average ability of legislators has improved substantially since World War II.[14] Journalists who cover Congress first-hand are also less inclined than their editors back home to rank well-heeled lobbyists as the government's biggest problem.[15]

However much they differ in their personal views, reporters manage, wittingly or not, to convey a fairly clear consensus about what they think is wrong in the nation's capital. The answer is politics, as it is currently practiced. To the Washington press corps, almost every decision, almost every speech and pronouncement by government leaders is a calculated move in a great political game. Officials rarely mean what they say; they act not so much to serve the people or the national interest but to further their own political ambitions or the fortunes of their party. According to reporters, therefore, the key to covering national affairs is not merely to record what politicians do and say but to discover their real motives and to speculate on the political consequences.

Newspaper columnists tend to probe more deeply than reporters. Over the years, many of them have published books about politics and government. They do not always agree, however, on precisely what has gone wrong. For example, those that have written about Congress are divided on whether lawmakers are out of touch with the American people. William Greider believes that members of Congress gradually drift apart from their constituents and that interest groups, especially those with money, absorb too much of the average legislator's attention.[16] E. J. Dionne blames politicians in both major parties for adopting extreme positions that offer unsatisfactory choices to a centrist, pragmatic public.[17] On the other hand, George Will and Alan Ehrenhalt portray members of Congress as exceptionally ambitious people who care so much about reelection that they pay *too much* attention to the views of their constituents.[18] According to these authors, most lawmakers are so lacking in courage that they rely on focus groups and opinion polls to guide their votes, even when good judgment should cause them to steer an independent course that would better serve the national interest.

Other books that columnists have written about Washington contain almost as many theories to explain the government's performance as there are authors. Jonathan Rauch puts the blame on organized groups that rally their members to block any reform which threatens their special interests.[19] David Broder has stressed the decline of political parties and their diminished ability to mobilize consensus in support of sound public policies.[20] Hedrick Smith has pointed to the separation of powers under the Constitution, which often leaves the White House and Congress under the control of different parties, thus causing recurrent gridlock and confusion.[21] As explanations accumulate, the only point uniting almost all these authors is that the enterprise of government is not faring well.

The Impressions of Politicians

Politicians have a more sympathetic view of themselves and their work. This would hardly be surprising, were it not for the fact that during reelection campaigns members of Congress often go out of their way to denigrate the federal government and to portray themselves as outsiders eager to sally forth to Washington to help "clean up the mess." Apparently, much of this talk is meant only to curry favor with disgruntled voters. According to a recent poll, 63 percent of members of Congress have a "mostly favorable" or "very favorable" view of the federal government, whereas only 38 percent of the public shares such a positive opinion.[22] In sharp contrast to the average voter, most lawmakers in Washington also have a high regard for the ability, idealism, and dedication of their colleagues.[23] Former state legislators (of whom there are a goodly number in Congress) frequently assert that only the very best state representatives tend to make it to Washington. When asked what has impressed them most favorably about Congress, many members of the House and Senate reply that it is the chance to work with such outstanding people.

Although legislators are aware of how much the public distrusts Congress and politicians, members of the House and Senate also know that almost all of them enjoy a high approval rating from their own constituents. They know that more than 90 percent of House incumbents win reelection. Few of them even face a serious opponent. If so many of the sitting members are held in such high esteem, lawmakers argue, how seriously can one take the public's low regard for Congress and politicians?

Members also feel that they make far greater efforts than most people realize to stay in touch with the views of their constituents. Representatives speak of traveling home several times each month to meet with voters, often in open forums where they can respond to any questions on the minds of the audience. Some even try to show how close they are to their constituents by continuing to reside in their home district, journeying to Washington for three days each week to conduct their legislative business. Almost all members of Congress routinely answer a huge volume of constituent mail, send periodic newsletters to everyone in their district, and assign a large part of their staff to solving problems great and small that individual voters encounter in their dealings with the federal government.

Most lawmakers will admit that they do not always manage to explain to citizens their stand on current public questions. But they are quick to point out how difficult it is to translate complex issues into language that voters will understand. The problem is not that constituents are stupid but that so few of them are interested enough to take the time to study the details of healthcare policy, welfare reform, or other important policy questions. Besides, politicians must often communicate with the public through the media, which tend to abbreviate and distort their message. Many lawmakers can recall occasions on which they have made repeated attempts to speak to voters about important issues, only to be ignored by reporters. When they do appear on television, they are often restricted to ten-second sound bites. Small wonder, they declare, that politicians so often strike voters as superficial and manipulative. How can anyone talk thoughtfully about international trade policy or environmental regulation in such a cramped, unnatural format?

With the media so fixated on scandal and the opportunities for meaningful discussion so limited, few members of Congress are surprised that citizens have such a jaundiced view of the legislative process. Many legislators even share the public's concern about the effect of money on politics and policy. But most of them think that voters exaggerate the impact of lobbyists and their campaign contributions. As they see it, lawmakers are rarely influenced in the way they vote by the few thousand dollars that an interest group can legally give to an incumbent's campaign. Besides, with powerful vested interests typically arrayed on both sides of important policy issues, legislators often remark that they feel relatively free to cast their votes as they think best; either way, they will please some lobbyists and anger others.

While defending their actions and those of their colleagues, most members of Congress do agree that the process of making policy for the nation is not working smoothly. According to seasoned legislators, however, the public underestimates the problems involved in trying to pass important pieces of legislation. Whereas individual citizens may have firm opinions about important policy issues, they forget that other voters often have sharply different views that vastly complicate efforts to forge a consensus. What strikes most people as political maneuvering or obstructionist tactics may actually reflect an agonizingly difficult search for a reasonable compromise that will solve a problem in ways that do not unfairly burden any interested group. Many lawmakers are fond of quoting Bismarck's celebrated remark that watching a legislature make laws is much like watching a butcher make sausages. It is not a pretty sight. But in a country with many different points of view, there is no other way to proceed if the interests of democracy are to be served.

The Findings of Social Scientists

Professors of politics are not nearly as likely as the general public to blame politicians for what ails the government. Their business is to explain, not to pass judgment. The generalizations they seek will not come easily if they dwell too long on the endless variety of individual personality and behavior. Accordingly, unlike journalists, with their constant speculation about the hidden motives of government leaders, they tend to look upon public officials as a homogeneous set of rational actors who pursue their interests by responding in predictable ways to the opportunities and incentives they encounter. If there are problems in Washington, therefore, scholars will tend to find them in the institutions and procedures that shape the environment in which officials have to function.

Instead of passing sweeping judgments, political scientists spend their time collecting data and looking for ways to test hypotheses about the operations of government. The writings that result can seem narrow and technical. Yet piece by piece, this empirical work may create a more reliable picture of how Washington works than the ad hoc opinions and assertions freely offered in more popular accounts. On a number of important points, the research casts a revealing light on views about the federal government commonly held by media commentators and the general public.

For example, contrary to what most citizens believe, scholars who have studied the effects of public opinion on policy find that officials usually act in accordance with public opinion.[24] Political scientists also differ from the public in their views about organized interest groups. While most Americans look upon these "special interests" as selfish entities that tempt legislators to neglect the public interest, most professors of government credit such organizations with playing a useful role in explaining the needs and desires of a large, heterogeneous society to the members of Congress. Many scholars who study the legislative process are not even convinced that the campaign contributions lobbyists shower on lawmakers have much effect on how the latter vote, at least on matters of substantial national importance.[25]

Political scientists are likewise far from convinced that America suffers as much from gridlock, divided government, and weak political parties as many journalists seem to believe. Researchers who have looked closely at the effects of having one party control Congress and the other preside over the Executive Branch do not find that the number of bills passed differs significantly from the number passed in periods during which the same party controls both branches.[26] Investigators who have compared the experience of several advanced democracies have also found that our supposedly feeble Republican and Democratic parties have managed to translate their platforms into policy at a rate that equals or exceeds that of most other countries—including some, like Britain, where the party in power normally enjoys a comfortable majority of loyal supporters in the legislature.[27]

In short, many scholars see a political process quite different from the one described by other participants in the drama. While citizens perceive the problems of government in human terms by blaming politicians, lobbyists, bureaucrats, and other political actors, scholars are more likely to look for explanations in institutions and other impersonal forces. Whereas journalists often convey the impression that things are bad and getting worse, political scientists tend to speak in a manner so detached that it is easily mistaken for complacency. Professors will reply that they are not in the business of passing judgment; they are scholars devoted to finding facts and explaining why political institutions work as they do. Nevertheless, as they continue to produce empirical studies that refute popular complaints about the way the government behaves, they can easily convey an impression that things are not as bad as most people think and that the familiar culprits are not so obviously to blame. As Montaigne long ago observed, "Tout comprendre, c'est tout pardonner."

The Importance of Evaluating How the Government Performs

Clearly, the several groups just described offer different perspectives on how well the government is functioning and who or what is at fault. Resolving these differences is important, for the performance of public officials at all levels matters much more to the nation than it did when the twentieth century began. Over the past sixty years, Americans have come to ask more and more of their government as newer concerns for economic security, the environment, access to health care, racial and gender equality, and consumer protection have joined more traditional demands for national defense and essential services. Now that citizens have come to depend on the State to meet so many of their needs, their welfare depends more than ever before on how well their government performs.

The multiple responsibilities of the federal government give it exceptional opportunities to serve the people and fulfill their aspirations, especially now that America has amassed such impressive wealth and power. As President Clinton observed in his final State of the Union speech: "Never before has our nation enjoyed, at once, so much prosperity and social progress with so little internal crisis or external threats. Never before have we had such a blessed opportunity—and, therefore, such a profound obligation—to build the more perfect union of our founders' dreams."[28]

At the same time, the government also has exceptional capacities to frustrate and disappoint its citizens. Now that its programs and policies affect so many lives in such important ways, people suffer more acutely when the results fall short of expectations. In practical terms, a shoddy performance by public officials today can mean inadequate schooling for children, hunger for needy families, sluggish growth or even a recession for the economy, useless training for workers seeking job skills, substandard health care, polluted air, and a host of other misfortunes.

These consequences are sobering enough, but they are not the only reason for concern. Eventually, persistent disappointment over the government's performance could deepen and solidify the public's loss of trust and confidence in its officials and in their capacity to help people achieve their goals. Distrust of government, of course, is not a new phenomenon in this country; it was widespread even at the time the Constitution was drafted, when America was blessed with statesmen of the stature of George Washington, Thomas Jefferson, and James Madison. What is unique about the past quarter-century is that for the first time in our history, citizens combine a profound distrust of the federal establishment with a set of ambitious national objectives that no society on earth has achieved without the active leadership of the State.

Although a measure of skepticism toward government can be healthy for any democracy, suspicion can easily become excessive. Whereas too much trust allows officials to grow complacent and irresponsible, severe distrust can make it impossible to muster the support needed to act effectively when circumstances require. Voters may be unwilling to accept additional taxes and quick to condemn the most enlightened proposals to deal with pressing national problems. Administrators may react defensively by exercising tighter control over subordinates and adhering rigidly to established rules and procedures. Courts may respond by imposing more elaborate procedural safeguards to protect citizens against the threat of official mistakes. Cooperation may suffer if officials lack the confidence to work closely with one another. Compromise will become more difficult. In all these ways, excessive distrust may cause the government to become more cautious, more indecisive, more bureaucratic, and less capable of responding effectively to people's needs.

A common belief in the Constitution and in the system of government it provides has long been the strongest bond uniting America's highly diverse society. Now that Communism has been discredited, however, and memories of the Soviet Union have faded, Americans could conceivably lose sight of just how precious our political system is. If election after election yields results dissatisfying to the people, voters might gradually come to suspect that it is not just officials who are creating a problem but the institutions in which they serve.

The immediate risk for this country is not a repudiation of the system; support for our constitutional framework is overwhelming and is likely to remain so, at least as long as the economy does tolerably well and most Americans continue to be content with their own personal circumstances. The dangers come in a quieter, more passive form. Amid the welter of separate interest groups, religious denominations, advocacy organizations, and associations of all kinds, government is the one authoritative agency that can define, enunciate, and validate a set of common moral standards and obligations for all the people.[29] In a country without an established Church, a traditional monarchy, or even a respected, apolitical head of state, there is no other institution that can perform this function. It is in this sense that Louis Brandeis described the government as "the potent, the omnipresent teacher," as it has clearly proved to be in articulating the essential framework of our social order: our basic liberties, our fundamental standards of fairness, our equality of rights enjoyed by different races, genders, and ethnic groups.[30] Continued lack of confidence in public officials and diminished respect for the work they do could eventually weaken the moral authority of the State and thus hamper it in carrying out a role that is essential to any society, especially one as diverse as ours.

Persistent distrust can also corrode the foundations of government in yet another way. A healthy democracy requires the active involvement of substantial numbers of citizens. Persistent doubts about the way the government is working, the value of politics, and the relevance of elections could accentuate the political apathy that has already driven voting turnouts and participation in civic affairs to uncomfortably low levels. For almost half a century, each new generation has participated less in politics and public affairs than its predecessor. Eventually, these trends could reach a point that would threaten the legitimacy of the political process and weaken the cohesion of the society itself.

These dangers are clearly important enough to warrant a careful look at how well our government is performing and how it might be helped to perform better. To explore these questions, I attempt in Part I to review the record of the United States during the past several decades. This analysis reveals that even though the public's concerns are often exaggerated, serious problems do exist with the performance of the federal government and critics do have plausible grounds for complaint. Part II begins by examining some of the principal reasons given by the public to explain why the government does not function better. Since none of these explanations turns out to be especially helpful, the remaining chapters in Part II try to pinpoint the most important failings that hamper the work of government and explain the reasons that account for each of these weaknesses. Part III then examines a variety of remedies to determine which hold the greatest promise of helping to improve the government's performance.

A word of caution is in order. The chapters that follow will not disclose some undiscovered flaw that allegedly explains all of the trouble and frustration in Washington. Nor will these pages reveal a single all-purpose remedy to resolve our problems. In anything as vast and complicated as a national government, there will be many factors at work and many reforms worth considering. If there is any persistent theme that emerges from this book, it is that many of the government's failings are not primarily the result of scheming politicians, incompetent bureaucrats, or selfish interest groups; they have their roots in attitudes and behaviors that are widely shared among the people themselves. Much of the fault, in other words, lies not in Washington but in ourselves.

Because citizens are so important to our democracy, the last section of the book explores their role in some detail. Of particular concern is the current tendency of many Americans to proceed down two contradictory paths. On the one hand, voters currently have more influence over their government than at any time in recent memory, and they would like even greater control by deciding more policy issues by referendum, devolving more authority to local officials, and replacing professional politicians with people like themselves through the use of term limits. On the other hand, while wishing to exert more influence, Americans are devoting decreasing amounts of time to politics and public life—voting less, attending fewer political meetings, reading less about events in Washington, even listening less to speeches by the President.

This is an ominous trend. As the following pages seek to demonstrate, the public's growing lack of interest in civic affairs contributes in important ways to all the deficiencies and frustrations that trouble people most about their government. Ignoring this fact merely causes us to pin our hopes on ineffective remedies, leading eventually to even more frustration and finger pointing. Until we are prepared to take our role as citizens more seriously, there is little prospect that institutional tinkering and election reforms can accomplish enough to ease our current discontent.

I

Is Anything Wrong?

I

IS AMERICA ON THE WRONG TRACK?

Toward the end of the millennium, signs of prosperity were evident everywhere in the United States. The economy continued its prolonged expansion, with the Gross Domestic Product (GDP) growing by more than 3 percent per year. Unemployment reached its lowest level in more than two decades, yet inflation continued to lie mercifully dormant. Consumer confidence rose steadily while the stock market climbed even faster, to the delight of the many tens of millions of Americans fortunate enough to own shares. Even the inner cities started to benefit from greater access to capital and growing numbers of jobs.

Buoyed by this abundance, Americans seemed to have every reason to feel positive about their country. But that was far from the case.[1] When people were asked in a 1997 survey how they thought the nation was progressing, 57 percent replied that "things have gotten pretty seriously off on the wrong track."[2] Still more gloomy were the results of another survey, conducted the year before, in which Americans were asked whether the country was improving or declining in seventeen separate areas of national life, ranging from crime and health care to the standard of living and prevailing levels of morality.[3] A majority of the respondents replied that the nation was strongly or moderately declining in eleven areas, and a plurality reported a decline in three others. More startling still, in none of the seventeen areas did as many as one-fourth of the respondents feel that the country was enjoying strong or moderate improvement.

Why have Americans been so pessimistic about the state of the country throughout most of the past thirty years? Granted, efforts to reform the healthcare system broke down. Years of enacting welfare programs have not eradicated poverty. Drugs are an ever-present problem. Inner-city schools continue to have heavy dropout rates and depressingly low student test scores. At the same time, the United States remains the wealthiest industrial democracy on earth and the world's only superpower. No other country enjoys more freedom or inspires greater loyalty in its citizens. Technological breakthroughs occur at a dizzying pace. Crime rates have been falling over most of the past twenty years, and the environment is improving. America may have problems, but every country has problems. By what calculus, then, can the public conclude that the nation has been heading in the wrong direction?

This is an important question for a book about government. Public policy plays such a pervasive role in advanced societies that examining what has gone well or badly for the country as a whole is bound to hold important clues about the way the government has performed. If the society is progressing well in almost all respects, it is likely that the government is also functioning well. If the society is encountering difficulty in a number of important fields in which the government is active, the nature of these problems will probably throw light on weaknesses in official policies and in the administration of public programs.

At first glance, however, trying to decide how well America has been doing or how much it has progressed seems a hopeless enterprise. How can one attempt such a task without making judgments so subjective that different people will inevitably come to widely varying results? What looks like progress to liberals such as Gloria Steinem or Bill Clinton may well seem disheartening to conservatives such as William Bennett or Robert Bork. What consumer advocate Ralph Nader counts as success will often seem wrongheaded to the National Association of Manufacturers.

Fortunately, there is one foundation on which to base a more objective evaluation. Americans often differ about the proper policies that their government or other major institutions should pursue. But large majorities tend to agree, at least in a general way, on the goals the country should be trying to achieve in most major fields of activity, such as health care, housing, education, and job training. With respect to the economy, for example, there is a broad consensus that America needs to attain as high and as constant a growth rate as possible consistent with full employment and reasonably stable prices. In the case of health care, most Americans want a high quality of medicine available to everyone at the lowest reasonable cost. By examining a variety of fields to determine how much headway the country has made toward widely accepted ends, it should be possible to render a rough judgment on the nation's progress over the past few decades—not by feminists' standards, conservatives' standards, or environmentalists' standards, but according to objectives endorsed by most Americans.

Not everyone will agree with using majority opinion—even the opinion of large majorities—as a valid basis for evaluating a nation's progress. In particular, critics will argue that any list of goals established by majority opinion could slight legitimate minority concerns and thus be open to serious question on grounds of fairness.* Fortunately, however, majority opinion in the United States is quite sensitive to legitimate minority interests, even if Americans do not always live up to their professed ideals. In any case, the aim of this exercise is not to try to demonstrate conclusively whether and how much the United States has "improved" but simply to test the judgment of a majority of Americans that the society has been "going downhill" or

---

* For example, if most Americans did not consider abolishing poverty or racial discrimination to be a proper goal of the society, there would be an obvious conflict between the public's standards for evaluating its government and those of virtually every moral philosopher. In fact, however, it is hard to think of important instances in which the public's goals conflict with those of a substantial body of moral thought in the United States. The most likely example involves attitudes toward equality of result. Many philosophers, notably John Rawls, would argue for substantially more equality in the distribution of income than would a majority of Americans. See David Miller, "Distributive Justice: What the People Think," *Ethics*, 102 (1992): 555. This difference of opinion, however, does not affect the consensus on any of the goals used in this study.

has been "headed in the wrong direction." The goals established by Americans themselves seem the most appropriate basis for making this assessment.

The method used here to evaluate America's record is open to one further objection. Having recorded the advances made in a large number of different fields, one cannot combine the results into a single, comprehensive measure of progress, since there is no consensus on the relative importance of health care, education, housing, crime prevention, and all the other areas of activity measured. Even so, if America has moved ahead toward a large majority of its goals (including such important objectives as increased prosperity and the preservation of freedom), most people will agree that the country has made progress overall. Conversely, most will acknowledge that the nation has declined if our society has lost ground in pursuing a large preponderance of its aims. As a result, a look at the nation's progress in pursuing a wide variety of goals may well provide a serviceable test of whether the public has been right in thinking that America has been "heading in the wrong direction."

The impossibility of constructing a single composite index of progress is even less consequential to the ultimate purpose of this book. If we wish to determine how the government is functioning, trying to measure the nation's overall progress is much less useful than evaluating the progress made toward each of a number of different goals that matter to the public. The latter approach is the one most likely to reveal the kinds of tasks public officials do well and the things they consistently do badly. In this way, we can pinpoint the most fundamental and characteristic strengths and weaknesses of federal policies and programs and thereby lay a useful foundation for much of the later analysis of how our government has performed and why it has not been more successful.

The Record since 1960

In an earlier volume, I gave a detailed account of America's record over the past several decades in seventeen different fields of activity, including the economy, education, crime, housing, health care, employment relations, environmental quality, poverty, science and technology, race relations, individual freedom, and the arts.[4] The seventeen fields were chosen to include activities that concern young and old, blacks and whites, suburbanites and city dwellers, rich and poor. One or more of the fields bear on each of the broad societal goals that matter most to large majorities of Americans: achieving economic growth and prosperity, enhancing the quality of life, gaining security from the major hazards of everyday living, providing opportunities for all to develop according to their abilities and effort, and promoting basic values—notably, individual freedom, personal responsibility, and compassion toward those less fortunate than oneself.

Table 1 summarizes the progress made since 1960 toward seventy-five specific objectives taken from these seventeen fields of activity. It turns out that since 1960 the United States has made substantial progress in more than two-thirds of the cases. Contrary to all the pessimism about the condition of our society, only in less than a fourth of the goals could one conclude that our situation has actually deteriorated.

The progress of the economy exemplifies the gains America has made in the past several decades. Since 1960, the Gross Domestic Product (in constant dollars) has more than tripled. Almost all families now have automobiles, kitchen appliances, television sets, and other possessions that only a minority could afford just after World War II. Unemployment levels have edged up only slightly over this period, while rates of inflation have not shown any long-term tendency to increase.

The quality of life in America, at least in its more tangible aspects, has likewise improved over the past several decades. Aided by government-backed mortgages, tax benefits, and federal highway programs, Americans have moved to the suburbs in great numbers, increasing their rates of homeownership and gaining the living space, privacy, and quieter neighborhoods that many seemed to covet. After the passage of federal legislation, air pollution declined and contaminated rivers and lakes were opened once again to swimming and fishing. After 1965, with support from newly established federal and state subsidy programs, the arts flourished, with audiences doubling and redoubling and the number of symphony orchestras, dance companies, operas, and theaters multiplying several-fold.

Table 1. U.S. record on seventy-five objectives that are of concern to Americans: mid-1990s compared with early 1960s.

Policy area	Improved	About the same	Worse
I. PROSPERITY			
1. *The economy*			
a. Per capita income	x		
b. Productivity per worker	x		
c. Rate of productivity increase			x
d. Controlling inflation		x	
e. Minimizing unemployment		x	
f. Net investment in plant and equipment (percent of GDP)	x		
2. *Research and technology*			
a. Number of scientists and engineers per 100,000 people	x		
b. Number of articles per year in refereed journals	x		
c. Number of patents per year issued to Americans	x		
d. Share of GDP devoted to civilian R&D	x		
e. Share of worldwide high-tech exports			x
3. *Education*			
a. Percent graduating from high school	x		
b. Percent graduating from college	x		
c. Student achievement in reading		x	
d. Student achievement in math and science		x	
4. *Labor market policy*			
a. Percent of workforce trained by employer	x		
b. Range of vocational courses available in high school and college	x		
c. Amount of government-sponsored training	x		
II. QUALITY OF LIFE			
1. *Housing*			
a. Percent of dwellings with serious defects	x		
b. Percent of population owning home	x		
c. Affordability for renters			x
2. *Neighborhoods*			
a. Concentration of poverty in urban neighborhoods			x
b. Degree of segregation by race	x		

Table 1 (continued).

Policy area	Improved	About the same	Worse
c. Percent of population living in a neighborhood of choice (city, suburb, exurb)	x		
d. Fear of crime			x
3. Environment			
a. Amount of air pollution	x		
b. Amount of water pollution	x		
c. Percent of drinking water purified	x		
4. The arts			
a. Number of arts organizations	x		
b. Size of audience for plays, concerts, etc.	x		
c. Public and private funding for arts (other than ticket sales)	x		
d. Consumer spending on the arts (percent of disposable income)	x		
III. OPPORTUNITY			
1. Children's well-being			
a. Rate of infant mortality	x		
b. Availability of childcare	x		
c. Extent of prenatal care	x		
d. Percent of children living in poverty	x		
e. Parental leave policy	x		
f. Percent of infants vaccinated	x		
2. Racial equality			
a. Voting rights	x		
b. Housing discrimination	x		
c. Segregation in schools	x		
d. Quality of education for blacks	x		
3. Equality of opportunity			
a. Access to preschool	x		
b. Access to universities	x		
c. Extent of racial discrimination in employment	x		
d. Extent of gender discrimination	x		
e. Overall equality of opportunity	x		

Table 1 (continued).

Policy area	Improved	About the same	Worse
IV. PERSONAL SECURITY			
1. *Health care*			
a. Technical quality	x		
b. Life expectancy	x		
c. Percent of population covered by health insurance	x		
d. Cost as percent of GDP			x
2. *Job security*			
a. Percent of workforce with some form of legally sanctioned representation			x
b. Protection from arbitrary discharge		x[a]	
c. Retraining and other help in case of layoffs	x		
d. Unemployment insurance (percent of unemployed receiving)	x		
3. *Violent crime*			
a. Incidence of homicide per 100,000 people			x
b. Rapes and assaults per 100,000 people			x
c. Success in solving violent crimes (clearance rates)			x
4. *Old age*			
a. Average retirement income (as percent of prior wages)	x		
b. Percent of elderly living in poverty	x		
c. Percent covered by healthcare insurance	x		
d. Financial assistance for long-term care	x		
5. *Likelihood of accidental death*			
a. All accidental deaths (per 100,000 people)	x		
b. On the highway (per 100,000 people)	x		
c. At work (per 100,000 workers)	x		
V. VALUES			
1. *Personal freedom*			
a. Degree of freedom guaranteed by law	x		
2. *Personal responsibility*			
a. Violations of criminal laws (per 100,000 people)			x
b. Percent of children born out of wedlock			x
c. Percent of income given to charity			x
d. Community service (1977–1997)	x[b]		x[b]
e. Voting rates			x
f. Cheating on exams			x

Table 1 (continued).

Policy area	Improved	About the same	Worse
3. *Providing for the poor and disadvantaged*			
a. Incidence of poverty	x		
b. Severity of poverty (aggregate poverty gap as percent of GDP)	x		
c. Effectiveness of government transfer programs	x		

a. While safeguards against unreasonable discharges have increased because of antidiscrimination laws and recent judicial doctrines in some states, the number of workers protected against such discharges by collective bargaining contracts has substantially decreased.

b. The evidence is confused on this point, with "volunteering" having increased and "worked on community project" having declined. See Robert D. Putnam, *Bowling Alone: The Collapse and Rivival of American Community* (2000), pp. 127–133.

Meanwhile, opportunities have increased for many Americans. To help all children get a good start in life, the federal government has taken steps to ensure adequate nutrition for infants in poor families, guarantee parental leave for many working mothers, immunize children, establish preschool programs for low-income youngsters, and provide tax subsidies for childcare. Having enacted the GI Bill after World War II, Congress followed it with massive federal programs for scholarships and subsidized loans to make college accessible to millions of young people. Antidiscrimination and affirmative action programs have helped, at least to some extent, to break down barriers and expand the access of women and minorities to universities and to careers in management, the professions, and other coveted occupations.

Americans have also gained added protection since 1960 from several of the greatest hazards of everyday life. Social Security benefits and private pensions have expanded to the point that persons over sixty-five years of age enjoy a standard of living that is virtually equal to that of younger generations. The quality of health care has likewise improved substantially, adding an estimated five years to the average life-span of Americans. Medicare, Medicaid, and the growth of private health insurance have extended medical coverage to more Americans: from fewer than 50 percent in 1960 to roughly 85 percent today. Even the incidence of poverty, notwithstanding the numbers of homeless and the persistence of blighted urban ghettos, has declined from more than 40 percent of the population in 1960 to less than 13 percent today.

Finally, the courts and Congress have greatly expanded the scope of individual freedom in the United States. The Supreme Court has guaranteed a black citizen's right to vote, a family's right to use contraception, a company's right to advertise, a newspaper's right to comment on public figures, a woman's right to have an abortion, and a minority child's right to attend an all-white school, to mention only a few. Congress has increased the options available to handicapped persons, to minorities seeking to vote and buy homes, to women applying to college. Homosexuals, suspected criminals, and indigent families all enjoy greater rights and freedoms than they possessed several decades ago.

Granted, not everything in America has improved since 1960. Healthcare costs have risen much faster than the cost of living, causing medical bills to consume ever-larger shares of many people's income. Poor neighborhoods in our large cities, especially in the North and East, suffer from greater concentrations of poverty and unemployment than they did in 1960. Despite improvements in the 1990s, levels of violent crime still exceed those of forty years ago. Although the data leave something to be desired, cheating in school, drug use, out-of-wedlock births to teenagers, and serious child abuse also seem to have increased significantly. Troubling as they are, however, these scattered instances of decline are greatly outnumbered by all the examples of progress toward goals that most Americans hold dear.

Not everyone will come away feeling positive about the nation's performance on the basis of these figures. Anyone who believes that pathologies such as crime, drugs, and inner-city poverty matter more than anything else could look at the record and insist that the country has gone downhill in recent decades. But most Americans have a more balanced view of the nation's progress and do not give overriding importance to a few specific goals. As a result, considering all the fields of activity that concern the people of this country, critics would have a hard time arguing that our society has suffered an overall decline since 1960. On the contrary, in most respects Americans seem to have come much closer to achieving the goals that they consider most important.

Skeptics may still ask whether the pace of progress has not diminished or even reversed itself in the past twenty years, citing such items as the decline in real wages for low-skilled male workers, the lack of progress in integrating our schools, and the increase in official rates of poverty, especially among young children. From 1970 to 1996, the percentage of children under the age of six who were living in poverty rose from 16.6 to 22.7, while the percentage of children in "extreme poverty" doubled; average weekly earnings for production workers fell from $298 to $256; and the percentage of Americans without healthcare insurance rose from 10.9 to 15.6.[5]

If progress has faltered in some respects, however, it has quickened in others. For example, crime and most other forms of personal irresponsibility have either stopped growing or have declined since the mid-1970s. The environment has improved substantially, after deteriorating for decades prior to the 1970s. Unemployment and inflation receded in the 1980s and 1990s, after rising substantially during the preceding decade. Job-related injuries are no longer increasing. Test scores in public schools have stopped declining, and some have even risen modestly since 1980.

Whether one concludes that progress has slowed, therefore, depends very much on one's point of view. Those who believe that a nation's record is chiefly determined by the growth rate of its Gross Domestic Product will conclude that America's progress has slackened since the early 1970s. Those who care passionately about violence and crime may reach the opposite conclusion. Considering the full range of objectives that Americans view as important, however, one can find no convincing evidence that progress in the United States has even decelerated appreciably, let alone gone into reverse, in the past twenty-five years.

Comparisons with Other Leading Democracies

Although the record suggests that Americans are far too pessimistic in thinking that the United States is "headed in the wrong direction," there are limits to what one can learn from historical trends. They will indicate whether a country is making progress toward its basic goals, but they are of little help in judging whether the nation and its government are making *satisfactory* progress. Almost every advanced democracy makes *some* headway over long periods of time in promoting the welfare of its citizens. The truly important question to ask is not merely whether a country has progressed but whether it has progressed rapidly enough.

There is no way of arriving at a definitive answer to such a question. But it is possible to shed some light on the matter by comparing America's progress with that of other major democracies. Such comparisons are treacherous, of course, since nations differ in so many ways. Still, if we have advanced as rapidly as most countries that share our goals, there should be *some* presumption that our society is functioning reasonably well. If we have not progressed as fast toward a variety of important goals, our failure to do so should at least raise serious questions about our performance as a nation.

Comparisons of this kind are aided by the fact that advanced democracies such as Britain, Canada, France, Germany, Japan, and Sweden all seem to share our belief in the same basic social goals. Only one important difference exists. To the chagrin of many liberals, Americans seem to care less than most people in those other countries about achieving greater equality in the material conditions of life. But large majorities of citizens in all leading democracies want to achieve economic prosperity, a better quality of life, equal opportunity for everyone, reasonable security from the basic hazards of life, individual freedom, and high standards of personal responsibility. Not only do people in all those nations subscribe to the same general social goals; they hold similar objectives in a wide variety of specific policy areas, such as housing, education, health care, and the environment. Moreover, reasonably good data exist regarding developments in all those countries during the past thirty to forty years. As a result, it is possible to compare America's progress in a wide variety of fields with that of countries quite similar in their development and their social goals.

On the positive side, the data show that the United States is preeminent in several important fields of endeavor. Our economy currently enjoys the highest overall rate of productivity, and our standard of living continues to exceed that of any other major democracy.

Throughout the 1990s, no major country rivaled America in starting entrepreneurial ventures and adapting quickly to the new imperatives of global competition. Apart from the economy, the quality of our scientific research, the progress of U.S. technology, and the standard of medical care available in our leading academic healthcare centers are still unequaled in the world. No nation enjoys more individual freedom (although other major democracies have now come to have much the same basic liberties). No other people are so willing to give to worthy causes or to devote their time to community endeavors.

In some respects, America's lead has even been widening over its principal competitors. As our economy prospered in the 1990s, other advanced democracies were encountering serious economic problems, including high unemployment, overextended welfare states, and sluggish rates of economic growth. Many of those countries had budget deficits and jobless levels well above ours. As evidence of these difficulties has accumulated, a triumphal note has begun to enter the discourse of many American political leaders, business executives, and financial analysts. Commentator after commentator has waxed eloquent about our record of job creation, our prolonged prosperity, our technological and entrepreneurial dynamism. As President Clinton declared in his final State of the Union address: "The state of our union is the strongest it has ever been."[6]

Such praise could easily suggest that the United States leads the world in all important respects. But America has other objectives beside prosperity that concern its citizens—objectives such as equal opportunities for everyone, adequate security from the major hazards of life, reasonable standards of personal responsibility, and human compassion. When one examines our comparative performance with respect to this larger array of common goals, the picture changes substantially. Indeed, it is hard to compare the full range of our accomplishments since 1960 with the record of other leading democracies without feeling some dismay. The conclusions are summarized in Table 2. *Although the results are mixed, as Table 2 reveals, with respect to seventy-five separate objectives the progress made by the United States from 1960 to the mid-1990s has been below average in roughly two-thirds of the cases and at or near the bottom of the list in approximately half.*

Table 2. U.S. record in seventy-five areas, compared with that of six other industrial democracies (Britain, Canada, France, Germany, Japan, and Sweden).

Policy area	Most successful[a]	Above average	Average	Below average	Least successful[a]
I. Prosperity					
1. *The economy*					
a. Per capita income	x				
b. Productivity per worker	x				
c. Growth rate of per capita income (1960–1995)					x
d. Growth rate of productivity (1960–1995)					x
e. Productivity growth (1990s)			x		
f. Controlling inflation (1960–1995)		x			
g. Minimizing unemployment (1960–1995)				x	
h. Minimizing unemployment (1980–1995)		x			
i. Average hourly compensation of production workers				x	
j. Net investment in plant and equipment as percent of GDP (1960–1995)					x
2. *Research and technology*					
a. Number of scientists and engineers per 100,000 people	x				
b. Percent of articles in refereed journals	x				
c. Number of citations per scientific article	x				
d. Percent of patents issued	x				
e. Share of world trade in high-tech goods	x				

3. *Education*
   a. Percent graduating from high school
   b. Percent graduating from college   x
   c. Literacy (ages 18–64)   x
   d. Student achievement in math (13-year-olds)   x
   e. Student achievement in science (13-year-olds)   x

4. *Labor market policy*
   a. Percent of GDP spent on training (public and private)   x
   b. Percent of workforce receiving training   x
   c. Effectiveness of employment service   x
   d. Effectiveness of school-to-work programs   x

II. QUALITY OF LIFE

1. *Housing*
   a. Quality of housing   x
   b. Percentage of population owning home   x
   c. Affordability for entire population   x

2. *Neighborhoods*
   a. Reducing segregation by income   x
   b. Reducing segregation by race   x
   c. Minimizing fear of crime   x
   d. Variety of choice in neighborhoods   x
   e. Length of commute to work   x

Table 2. (continued)

Policy area	Most successful[a]	Above average	Average	Below average	Least successful[a]
3. Environment					
a. Reduction in air pollution (1970–1990)				x	
b. Reduction in water pollution (1970–1990)			Impossible to compare		
c. Percent of population with waste-water treatment			x		
d. Percent of waste recycled					x
4. The arts					
a. Total audience for performances and exhibitions				x	
b. Total support (public and private) other than ticket sales				x	
c. Rate of growth in public and private support for the arts 1970–1990)	x				
III. OPPORTUNITY					
1. Children's well-being					
a. Reducing infant mortality					x
b. Percent of children vaccinated				x	
c. Percent enrolled in preschool				x	
d. Reducing percent living in poverty					x
e. Providing parental leave					x
3. Career opportunities					
a. Rate of upward mobility			x		
b. Reducing gender gap in earnings				x	
c. Women in high-status jobs		x			

1. *Health care*
   a. Technical quality
   b. Life expectancy
   c. Patients' evaluation of their own care
   d. Containing cost as percent of GDP
   e. Coverage by health insurance
   f. Public evaluation of system

2. *Job security*
   a. Percent of workforce with some form of legally sanctioned representation
   b. Protection from arbitrary discharge
   c. Assistance in case of layoffs

3. *Violent crime*
   a. Incidence per 100,000 people
   b. Success in solving crime
   c. Minimizing fear for personal safety

4. *Old age*
   a. Average retirement income after taxes (as percent of previous wages)
   b. Reducing percent of elderly living in poverty
   c. Access to affordable long-term care

Table 2. (continued)

Policy area	Most successful[a]	Above average	Average	Below average	Least successful[a]
5. *Likelihood of accidental death*					
a. Reducing accidental deaths from all causes					x
b. At work			x[b]		
c. On the highway		x[c]			x[c]

V. VALUES

Policy area	Most successful[a]	Above average	Average	Below average	Least successful[a]
1. *Individual freedom*					
a. Degree of freedom guaranteed by law		x			
2. *Personal responsibility*					
a. Obeying criminal laws					x
b. Not having children out of wedlock			x		
c. Minimizing number of children born out of wedlock to teenage mothers					x
d. Voting in elections					x
e. Percent of income given to charity	x				
f. Community service	x				
3. *Providing for the poor and disadvantaged*					
a. Lowering incidence of poverty					x
b. Minimizing severity of poverty (aggregate poverty gap as percent of GDP)					x
c. Effectiveness of government transfer programs					x

a. For purposes of this table, "Most successful" includes cases in which the United States is close to the very best among the seven countries compared, while "Least successful" includes cases in which the U.S. is close to the very worst.

b. Comparisons are questionable because of differences in methods of reporting.

c. The United States has the worst record when computed by deaths per 100,000 people, but an above-average record when measured by deaths per 100 million vehicle-miles.

What the Comparisons Reveal

These findings cannot be dismissed as a mere reflection of America's reluctance to emulate the European welfare state or some other model over which reasonable people differ. Table 2 measures results rather than policies. It compares our success as a society with that of other advanced democratic societies in achieving a broad array of goals, such as minimizing violent crime, vaccinating children, curbing pollution, and educating young people—goals shared by large majorities of citizens in all the societies involved, including our own. It is also unlikely that the results reflect an arbitrary choice of goals to compare. Each objective was chosen because of its intrinsic importance and its connection with even more fundamental aspirations of the society, such as opportunity, security, or freedom. In most cases, the goals were selected without any prior knowledge of what international comparisons would reveal.

These tabulations are sobering. While identifying some areas of great strength, they reveal many points of weakness. Even in the economy, where America's performance has been strongest, the record is not ideal in all respects. Although our industry emerged from World War II with an immense comparative advantage and although our economy performed exceptionally well in the 1990s, average rates of growth, productivity increase, and unemployment over the entire period from 1960 to the present are all below the levels achieved by most of our principal rivals. Even in the most recent period studied, from 1989–1998, per capita rates of growth in productivity and GDP have been only average or below average for advanced industrial democracies.[7] If the United States continues to enjoy higher living standards than other leading nations, it is not so much because of superior productivity growth but because higher proportions of our adult population hold jobs and because they work more hours per year than people in any other highly developed country.[8] Achieving prosperity this way is hardly an unmitigated blessing for everyone, especially women, many of whom would prefer not to work such long hours or even to work at all. (The *Wall Street Journal* reported in 1996 that 62 percent of parents "believed their families had been hurt by changes they had experienced at work, such as more stress and longer hours.")[9]

As one moves from the economy to other important social goals, the U.S. record is much weaker. Consider the effort to provide opportunity for all. Americans have always stressed the importance of giving everyone a chance to get ahead. We have traditionally referred to the United States as "the land of opportunity," as it clearly has proved to be for countless citizens and immigrants. In keeping with these sentiments, more than 90 percent of the public believes that every reasonable effort should be made to ensure that all Americans receive an adequate chance to succeed according to their talents and aspirations.[10] Yet our progress toward this goal has hardly been exceptional. Most experts on the subject do not find that people in the United States can climb the social ladder more rapidly than citizens of several Western European nations.[11] In fact, a recent comparative survey of eight highly developed countries even found that the United States had the *lowest* proportion of employees in the bottom earnings quintile who succeeded over a five-year period in moving up to the next quintile or into the top 60 percent.[12]

Comparative studies also reveal that America has consistently lagged behind other industrial nations in creating an environment in which all children can have a healthy start and develop to the best of their ability.[13] Infant mortality rates are higher and access to prenatal care is lower in the United States than in other leading nations. Higher proportions of children live in severe poverty. Opportunities for parents to take time from work to be with a newborn child are more limited. Vaccination rates are only average at best. Access to quality childcare and enrollment in preschool educational programs are lower than in other industrial democracies, such as France and Sweden. American students leave high school less proficient in basic subjects, especially math and science, than their counterparts in many advanced democracies.[14] Job training and school-to-work programs are likewise less effective than in several other highly developed economies.[15]

The United States has also been relatively unsuccessful in protecting its citizens from the basic hazards of everyday life. Rates of violent crime are much higher than in other advanced democracies.[16] Access to quality health care is more limited; in fact, the United States is the only major democracy in which a substantial fraction of citizens still lacks basic health insurance of any kind.[17] Critical job interests are likewise more at risk than they are in other leading industrial nations.[18] Workers who are fired unjustifiably have more limited rights of redress; employees who are laid off receive less advance warning, less training, and lower relocation benefits; and rates of industrial accidents are average at best. As for the perils of old age, elderly Americans do enjoy incomes that (relative to prior earnings) are as high as, or higher than, those in other advanced nations. Nevertheless, poverty rates among Americans over sixty-five are greater, and assistance in the event of chronic illness and long-term hospitalization is more limited.[19]

Although Americans are more generous than citizens of other countries in giving their money to charity, much higher proportions are poor in the United States than in other democracies. Poverty rates are especially high among young children, reaching levels approximating 20 percent. Among adults, several million Americans have been unable to escape from poverty even though they work full-time throughout the year.[20]

The poor are not simply a statistical artifact culled from some arbitrary government definition of poverty. According to the Department of Housing and Urban Development, 5.3 million households in 1995 consisted of "very low-income renters" who received no federal housing assistance and either lived in severely substandard housing or paid half or more of their reported income for rent.[21] One-third of all adults between eighteen and sixty-four earning less than $20,000 annually had a medical problem during the preceding year but could not afford to see a doctor.[22] According to findings by the Department of Agriculture and the Community Childhood Hunger Identification Project, 4.1 million households and approximately 4 million children under the age of twelve go hungry because of insufficient funds during some part of the year.[23] In the words of Doug O'Brien of Second Harvest (a major distributor of food to the needy), "We have a hunger problem. And other Western industrialized nations do not have a hunger problem. And that is just not acceptable when we have such abundance."[24]

Finally, the United States has made less progress than other leading nations in several other areas involving the quality of life. Despite much regulation and large expenditures of money, America appears to have accomplished less in reducing air pollution than most other leading industrial democracies.[25] Moreover, notwithstanding its success in creating attractive housing in pleasant suburbs for tens of millions of Americans, the United States still contains many inner-city neighborhoods that are exceptionally burdened with crime, drugs, high unemployment, and dilapidated housing. Indeed, to one team of visiting experts from abroad, many of these neighborhoods displayed conditions "to be expected in a poverty-stricken third-world country, not in one of the earth's richest nations."[26]

Questioning the Verdict

Comparisons of the kind just described are fraught with difficulty, and skeptics will doubtless wish to question the conclusions or interpret them in more reassuring ways.[27] Some will point out that the United States must be more successful than these findings suggest, else America would not continue to be the preferred destination of millions of would-be immigrants around the world. Others will observe that much of the rapid progress Europe and Japan have made in the past few decades is only a temporary result of catching up after the ravages of World War II. Still others will dispute the very suggestion that America's record has been any less impressive than that of other nations. Rather, they will say, our experience simply reflects the special values and priorities of the American people, who prefer to maximize freedom and prosperity rather than offer handouts to the poor or coddle the sick, the elderly, and the working classes to protect them from dangers they could guard against themselves.

On closer inspection, none of these arguments is especially persuasive.* Although more people migrate to the United States than to any other country, immigration is a dubious measure of a nation's performance; after all, the three countries with the next highest number of immigrants are India, Russia, and Saudi Arabia. Moreover, while the United States offers especially attractive opportunities and rewards for individuals of exceptional talent, relatively few people continue to move to this country from other advanced democracies, and the numbers have fallen substantially since 1960. Total immigration

---

* The arguments are treated in greater detail in Derek Bok, *The State of the Nation* (1997), ch. 19.

from the Dominican Republic is now above that of France, Britain, and Germany *combined*, while legal immigration from Mexico is six times greater.

America is still the country of choice for millions of people seeking to emigrate from poorer nations around the world. For them, life in this country may be a vast improvement. Nevertheless, it is doubtful that their decision to come to America results from an informed judgment that we surpass other industrial nations in the success of our healthcare system, the quality of our schools, or other aspects of life compared in these pages. Rather, their choice probably reflects the prevalence of English as a second language throughout the world, the images of wealth and opportunity projected globally by our dominant film and television industries, and the easier access provided by our immigration laws. None of these explanations negates the findings summarized in this chapter.

The fact that other countries had the benefit of emulating America's economic and technological advances after World War II fares no better as an explanation for our modest comparative record. Catching up undoubtedly gave Europe and Japan an advantage in economic growth rates for a few decades. But catch-up cannot account for areas in which other countries have surpassed the United States. It hardly explains why their job training programs work better, why their parental leave, daycare, and preschool programs are more ample, why their infant mortality rates and healthcare costs are lower and their health insurance coverage broader, why fewer of their people are poor, why their environmental regulations are often more effective, or why they are more likely to offer adequate protection from the crippling expense of long-term illness.

Can one argue, finally, that America's record merely reflects a difference in the balance Americans choose to strike among the basic goals of their society—a special set of tradeoffs among competing values that is unique to this country? Actually, this explanation seems unlikely, since there are few basic conflicts between the principal social goals that require any serious tradeoffs. Individual liberty is generally thought to promote economic prosperity and vice versa. Equality of opportunity favors growth and enhances freedom. Even efforts to overcome poverty will increase equality of opportunity and may also stimulate growth by building human capital.

The greatest potential conflict among the goals involves the tension between economic growth and protection against the familiar hazards of everyday life, particularly protection against the threat of losing one's job. It is possible that elaborate employment safeguards and expensive social protection programs can hamper economic growth and efficiency. The question that remains, then, is whether the comparative results in Table 2 merely reflect the tradeoffs that Americans have chosen to make between these two sets of values.

At first glance, the evidence might appear to support this interpretation. In recent years, America's growth rates have been higher, its unemployment levels have been lower, and its productivity has continued to be greater than in any major democracy. At the same time, some economists have cited the generous social welfare programs and restrictive employment laws in many European countries as an important reason for their lagging growth rates and high jobless rates in the 1990s.

Of course, one should not read too much into comparative performance over only a decade or less, remembering how different the world looked only a generation ago, when much of Western Europe was growing faster with less unemployment than the United States and when Japanese industry seemed all-powerful. Overall, from 1960 to 2000, several other advanced nations enjoyed a better economic performance than the United States *and* more ample social and protective legislation. Nevertheless, now that Japan is struggling to fix its faltering economy and countries such as France and Germany try to cope with severe unemployment and overextended welfare states, American policies have undoubtedly come to look more promising than they did in the 1980s. Profiting from our example, other countries are beginning to trim their social benefits and to rely more on the free market.

A close look at the results in Table 2, however, suggests that a desire for rapid growth cannot explain many of the cases in which America's performance falls below that of other advanced democracies. It cannot account for our lackluster record in achieving universal access to health care, holding down medical costs, curbing pollution, lowering infant mortality rates, eliminating hunger, or reducing poverty. Nor can it excuse our ineffective job training and labor market policies, mediocre school performance, inadequate provision for long-term care, high rates of pregnancy among teens, or limited availability of preschool programs.

It is even doubtful whether more generous social welfare provisions in other countries have led to lower growth rates. According to a leading scholar of the welfare state, "the studies of the aggregate relationship between economic performance and the size of the welfare state . . . do not yield conclusive evidence. The results of econometric studies of the relationship between social transfer spending and growth rates are mixed: some find that high spending on social transfers leads to lower growth; others find the reverse."[28] As a massive set of studies by the McKinsey Global Institute concludes, a more persuasive explanation for America's continued lead in productivity and per capita GDP is that the United States has been more inclined than other leading democratic nations to expose all sectors of the economy to domestic and foreign competition.[29]

When and how Europe and Japan can overcome their current economic troubles is impossible to foretell. They may well need to go further in relaxing some employment restrictions, trimming some welfare benefits, and even reducing payroll taxes and entry-level wages. But no one is predicting that the imperatives of growth will require these countries to scale back social programs to U.S. levels, let alone restrict the benefits to only some of those who need them.[30] Nor would any sensible person argue that America's current lead in productivity and per capital GDP productivity is in some way attributable to lower test scores in math and science, more expensive health care, higher infant mortality, more dilapidated inner cities, higher rates of crime, or greater poverty, homelessness, and hunger. On the contrary, it is more plausible to suppose that our economic success has been achieved in spite of these problems. Thus, the evidence simply does not support the theory that our overall record can be explained satisfactorily as a conscious, necessary tradeoff to achieve greater prosperity.

In any case, if the United States has succeeded in attaining the people's goals and accurately balancing their priorities, most Americans don't seem to know it. According to recent surveys, two-thirds or more of the public believe that the country should give a "high" or "very high" priority to achieving objectives in which our performance has lagged behind that of many other countries, such as protecting the environment, reducing poverty, and ensuring that every American has access to affordable health care.[31] More generally, if the U.S. record truly reflected popular values and priorities, a majority of the public would hardly have concluded throughout most of the past quarter-century that "the country is headed in the wrong direction" and that "things have gotten pretty seriously off on the wrong track." Nor would majorities of the people have so little confidence not only in their political leaders but in the leaders of almost all of the nation's major institutions.

Overall, therefore, the figures in Table 2 appear to paint a reasonably accurate picture. They point to some major successes, notably in achieving high levels of prosperity and productivity. But they also reveal a nation with only an average or below-average record in accomplishing most of the other items on a long list of goals and priorities that large majorities of citizens claim to share. Although our society has progressed, our progress relative to other nations is mediocre enough to justify considerable frustration and disappointment despite America's wealth and prosperity. The critical question for this study is what role the government has played in bringing about these lackluster results.

2

THE ROLE OF GOVERNMENT

THE AMERICAN PEOPLE have not hesitated to blame Washington for the country's sluggish progress toward many widely cherished goals. Just 31 percent agreed in 1998 that the federal government had a positive effect on the nation.[1] In a poll two years earlier, 56 percent felt that the way the government and the political system are working is "one of the most important problems facing this country," with another 33 percent ranking it as "an important problem" (though "not one of the most important problems").[2] A strong plurality responded in 1997 that the federal government is more of a hindrance than a help in pursuing the American Dream.[3]

As the millennium came to a close, years of prosperity coupled with reports of falling crime rates seemed at last to raise the spirits of Americans. Pollsters reported a modest upturn in public confidence in Washington and the society as a whole. Even so, a majority of the people continued to feel that the country was on the wrong track, while more than two-thirds of the people did not trust the federal government to do the right thing all or even most of the time.[4]

The nation's relatively meager success in achieving the goals most Americans hold dear might seem enough to justify the public's dour assessment. A disappointing record for the society, however, does not necessarily mean that the *government* has been performing badly. This is especially true in this country, where the State is typically assigned a more limited role than in most major democracies. Is there any way of telling, then, how much the government has contributed to the nation's mediocre record?

Looking back at Table 2, which compares America's performance in seventy-five separate endeavors with that of other leading nations, one quickly discovers a striking fact. In virtually every case, government policies—and especially federal policies—play an important part, often the decisive part, in explaining how the nation has fared since 1960.[5]

The government's role is just as prominent in areas in which America has done comparatively well as it is in fields where we have lagged behind. Our programs of public funding for science and higher education have had much to do with our continued leadership in research and technology. Federal support has been crucial to the excellence of our academic health centers. Federal judges and lawmakers are even more responsible for our unsurpassed achievement in enlarging the outer limits of individual freedom.

Less often acknowledged are the contributions of public policy to economic growth and prosperity. According to an exhaustive recent study by the McKinsey Global Institute, whatever success America has achieved in maintaining its position as the world's most productive economy is chiefly due not to the exceptional skills of our workforce or to the entrepreneurial talents of our managers, but to the willingness of the national government to expose the economy to the rigors of competition, both foreign and domestic.[6] Countries like Japan, Germany, and France, however efficient they may be in certain sectors, have allowed large parts of their economy to remain heavily subsidized, protected from foreign imports, or sheltered from domestic competition. Thus, even economic growth and productivity, which seem so much the province of private initiative, turn out to depend heavily on a public policy enlightened enough to resist the continuous pressures to grant various forms of relief from the rigors of the market.

By the same token, the national government has also played a prominent role in most of the fields in which our performance has been disappointing. Congress has been the principal architect of a hugely expensive healthcare system that still leaves many millions of

Americans uninsured and many more without adequate long-term care. Federal programs have been the principal means for helping the poor, yet when it comes to eliminating hunger or lifting people out of poverty, government policies have proved less successful in the United States than in any other leading democracy. Because of our employment legislation, employees here are more vulnerable to lay-offs and arbitrary firing, less able to find good job training, and less likely to be covered by unemployment insurance than workers in any of our principal competitors. The content and enforcement of our national labor laws help account for the fact that so few American workers have any form of collective representation in dealing with their employers.

Government must also shoulder much of the responsibility for our disappointing record in protecting children and giving them a decent start in life. Federal programs are heavily involved in the nation's lagging efforts to immunize children, lower infant mortality, prevent low birthweight, guarantee parental leave, and expand effective pre-school programs. Public schools contribute to the failure of American children to perform as well in science and math as their counterparts in many other nations, while publicly supported vocational study and school-to-work initiatives fall short of what countries such as Germany, Sweden, and Japan have accomplished to prepare young people for productive jobs.

Finally, government policies have much to do with many of the problems encountered in improving the quality of life for all Americans. State and federal programs lie at the heart of the nation's efforts to reduce pollution, which have achieved only modest success in comparison with the programs of other advanced countries. Housing laws, zoning requirements, public-transportation subsidies, and assorted policies toward racial discrimination, drugs, and crime have all contributed to the economic and racial segregation in urban areas and to the persistence of decaying inner-city neighborhoods.

The only cases of lagging performance in which the role of public policy seems somewhat tenuous and problematic are instances involving personal responsibility, such as violent crime, drug consumption, and voting rates. Here as well, however, the government has had an impact. Law enforcement clearly has an effect on crime rates, though how much is a matter of dispute. Registration requirements and other election laws have an important influence on voting turn-outs. Even in the case of drug consumption, where the impact of public policy is more debatable, programs of deterrence and prevention presumably have *some* substantial effect on levels of use.

In short, not only has America's progress in many areas of importance to the people lagged behind the achievements of other leading democracies; in virtually every case, official policies and programs have been heavily involved. More often than not, the government's role has been predominant. With such a record, one can understand why Americans might be dissatisfied with the way their government has performed in serving the needs and aspirations of its citizens.

By itself, however, the fact that government is prominently involved in many endeavors where our performance is poor still does not demonstrate that public officials are responsible. No two countries are exactly alike. They vary in countless ways that may affect the work of government. As a result, it is possible that public officials in the United States have faced unusual challenges rarely met by their counterparts in other nations. Can one imagine, then, any special handicaps that could have hampered the performance of our government and caused it to lag behind other leading democracies in many areas of endeavor?

One possibility is the sheer size of the country. Small nations may be easier to govern because there are fewer regional differences to accommodate and simpler problems of administration and supervision. As d'Alembert observed in his paean to eighteenth-century Geneva, "It is perhaps only in little states that one can find the model for a perfect political administration."[7]

But is small size necessarily such an advantage? If so, why would the countries of Western Europe go to such lengths to create a political union, despite far greater language and cultural barriers than those of the United States? Moreover, if size could truly account for the modest record of our government, one would expect America to excel in fields where local governments play the principal role, such as public education, law enforcement, housing, and urban affairs. Yet our accomplishments even in these areas fall below those of other major democracies and do not seem any greater, relatively speaking, than our achievements in other fields of endeavor.

Another handicap our government has had to bear is the special responsibility of leadership that America has assumed both during and after the Cold War. Since the 1950s, the United States, in comparison to most leading democracies, has generally devoted 2–5 percent more of its GDP to national defense. These outlays are undoubtedly a burden. They make it more difficult to find the money for many domestic programs. Yet they cannot explain our record in fields such as public schooling, health care, and environmental regulation, where America spends *more* than most other advanced democracies but achieves less impressive results. Nor can defense costs be the real reason we have spent less than other countries on so many other social programs. Since our rates of taxation are substantially *below* those of almost all our leading competitors, our decision as a society not to spend more on social welfare is clearly a matter of political choice, not an economic necessity brought on by huge national-security expenditures.

Apart from external, objective handicaps, such as geographic size or the Cold War, Americans could conceivably possess subtler, more subjective attitudes or values that make it peculiarly difficult for public officials to succeed. For example, our high rates of violent crime may result not from any fault of the police or the criminal laws but from the special desire of many Americans to own guns. Similarly, the larger audiences in Europe for concerts and operas may simply reflect a difference in popular taste rather than a greater willingness of foreign governments to subsidize the arts. Such explanations seem plausible. Still, looking back over the long list of goals in which America's performance is weak, it is hard to imagine that specific differences of values such as those just mentioned could account for enough of the cases to alter the overall picture significantly. To make a substantial difference, one would have to point to a more pervasive set of attitudes that distinguish Americans in ways that could affect a wide variety of government policies and programs.

It will be important to consider this possibility in the subsequent chapters that seek out reasons for our government's performance. For the moment, however, the only pervasive set of attitudes that readily comes to mind involves the troubling problem of race. Without doubt, race is a major factor in American life. The prejudice and

discrimination of earlier times have left their mark on many government policies and created a legacy that contributes to America's lagging achievements in a number of fields, such as crime, life expectancy, infant mortality, and school performance,. In subtler forms,
racial prejudices linger to this day, creating handicaps that continue
to slow the progress of minority groups.

Serious as they are, however, racial problems do not offer an adequate explanation for America's modest overall performance. They
have little or nothing to do with many of the areas in which we compare poorly with other nations, such as the heavy cost of health care,
the lack of protection given to basic interests of workers in their jobs,
or our mediocre record in curbing pollution and reducing workplace
injuries. Moreover, in other fields of endeavor where race has a more
obvious impact on the nation's progress, the United States—as
Table 3 makes clear—has a poorer record than other advanced nations even if one calculates the figures for whites alone.

Of course, race in America has become intertwined with a series of
other problems—urban poverty, crime, and drugs, to name a few—
that combine to create a formidable challenge for anyone seeking to
reform inner-city schools, lower crime rates, improve public housing,
or reduce pregnancy among teens. Doesn't this complex of issues
constitute an unusually heavy burden for America in addressing
many of the items in which its performance compares poorly with
that of other leading countries?

Once again, the argument fails under close analysis. As with race
itself, though urban problems undoubtedly affect our record ad-
versely, our relative position in most areas of endeavor would not
change significantly if inner cities were deleted from the calculations.
Besides, it is hardly fair to use race, or the inner city, or the
"underclass" as reasons to excuse the government's performance,
since all these problems are in large part a product of government
policies, be they segregation laws, zoning restrictions, public housing
programs or a host of other measures. It is even a bit of a stretch to
argue that the complex of issues bound up with race and poverty
represents a peculiarly difficult problem. After all, Japan has had to
cope with the devastation of World War II; Britain faces the subtle
barriers of class; Germany must try to absorb an entire new country
that labored for forty years under a totalitarian regime. All in all,

Table 3. International comparisons on a range of social problems in the mid-1990s.

Problem	Canada	France	Germany	Japan	Sweden	U.K.	U.S. (whites only)
1. Infant mortality (per 1,000 births)	6.9	6.6	6.5	4.3	5.7	7.2	7.3
2. Life expectancy (in years)	78.1	78.2	76.3	79.3	78.3	76.8	76.5
3. Percent of children in poverty	9.3	4.6	2.8	Not available	1.4	6.9	13.2
4. Health insurance coverage (percent of population)	100	99	99	100	100	100	86.4
5. Homicides (per 100,000 people)	2.0	1+	1+	0.5	1+	0.5	5.3

Source: Statistical Abstract of the United States, 1994 (1994), pp. 87, 91, 119, 475, 855.

therefore, neither race nor the underclass nor any other burdens unique to America offer a convincing rationalization to excuse or explain away the government's modest performance.

Looking back at the record, then, what can one make of the government's performance over the past four decades? Clearly, the balance sheet is not as dismal as many Americans seem to think. The United States is a wealthy and successful country, and the government has done much to help make it so. In the vast majority of fields in which public policy plays a prominent role, the nation has moved ahead since 1960, often in substantial ways. It is simply preposterous to assert, as majorities of the public have said in several polls, that "every problem the federal government touches gets worse."

With good reason, however, Americans have high expectations for their country. They believe that their system of government is the best in the world. They know that the United States has unequaled material resources with which to address its problems and fulfill its goals. They have great confidence in themselves. As a result, they expect their government not only to make progress but to do at least as much as other advanced nations to accomplish goals that matter to the people.

By these high standards, Americans do seem to have good cause for feeling disappointed with their government.[8] Their concerns are neither trivial or theoretical. Based on the accomplishments of other leading democracies, it is not unreasonable to suppose that more enlightened public policies in the United States could have given all citizens guaranteed access to quality health care at a cost per person of several hundred dollars less than what Americans are currently paying. A more effective government could likewise have provided opportunities for all parents to enroll their small children in well-run, affordable preschool and childcare programs; a chance for everyone to enjoy cleaner air and water at a lower cost than the country is now paying; substantial reductions in the number of small children and elderly persons who experience hunger or live below the poverty line; greater assurance for employees in small and medium enterprises that their employers would abide by the rules regarding minimum pay, overtime, racial discrimination, and other safeguards; not to mention protection for everyone from being fired without reasonable cause. Better yet, the savings achieved from more efficient health care and environmental regulation might even have paid for these benefits and more without the need to raise taxes.

Responding to the public's frustration with Washington, two recent presidents of the United States have uttered widely quoted statements about the role of government. Ronald Reagan, in his inaugural address of 1981, delivered his now-famous remark: "Government is not the solution to our problems. Government *is* the problem."[9] Sixteen years later, after proclaiming that "the era of big government is over," Bill Clinton declared that "government isn't the solution and it isn't the problem either."[10]

Of the two remarks, Mr. Clinton's is the hardest to comprehend. Surely, government has been a major problem. The record over the past forty years contains too many examples in which public policies have failed to accomplish as much as those of other democratic governments in pursuing goals shared by most citizens. Nothing that has occurred during Mr. Clinton's tenure suggests that government is no longer a problem. Despite the prosperity of the 1990s, the failures of public policy revealed in Table 2 remain pretty much in place: the poverty, the weak performance of American high school students, the deficiencies of the healthcare system, and many more. A handful of afflictions, such as violent crime and pregnancy among teens, seem to have abated somewhat, but they remain more serious than in other major democracies, and few close observers give public policy most of the credit for bringing about the recent declines or feel that the underlying problems are close to being resolved.

Just as odd is Mr. Clinton's declaration that "government is not the solution." All of his major initiatives have involved extensive and demanding government intervention. His healthcare plan is the most spectacular example; it failed in large part because most Americans came to doubt that the federal government was even capable of making such a complicated plan work. The crime bill of 1996 called for 100,000 more policemen and substantially enlarged the federal role in a field traditionally reserved primarily for state and local authorities. The Welfare Reform Act of 1996 is no exception to this pattern. Moving many thousands of single mothers from welfare into productive jobs will clearly require much more demanding, enlightened efforts on the part of state officials than earlier programs for aiding the poor.

President Reagan's remark is more thought-provoking. He rightly points out that government *is* a problem. But the question he did not answer is how the government can avoid being a major part of the solution. How else can the nation achieve such widely supported goals as providing reasonable opportunities for everyone to get ahead; overcoming poverty, at least among those who cannot help themselves; giving every American adequate security against the principal hazards of life; and protecting them against pollution, false advertising, unsafe products, and other common features of the free market? No industrialized country on earth has managed to make impressive progress toward objectives such as these without major involvement by the State.

What Mr. Reagan must have meant is that America would have a better chance of achieving these goals (while interfering less with individual freedom and prosperity) if the market did more and the government did less.[11] This is a promising idea that has already borne fruit in a wide range of initiatives to privatize public services, deregulate industries, and utilize taxes and other market-based mechanisms (rather than mandatory rules and inspections) to achieve environmental goals. These efforts have shown that a more effective government does not have to mean a larger bureaucracy or more elaborate, intrusive regulations. What is often overlooked, however, is that all of the new initiatives, while providing a less ambitious role for government, still require a high quality of official policymaking and administration.

Deciding when to rely on markets and when to resort to government intervention is itself a difficult challenge that calls for much wisdom and imagination. Many countries have paid a high price for the mistakes their governments have made in addressing this question. Once policymakers have chosen to rely on free markets, the role of government does not cease. On the contrary, maintaining competition demands a continuing effort by legislators to withstand the pressures for protection that constantly arise from one industry or another. Successful markets also require a network of laws and courts to enforce agreements, prevent anticompetitive behavior, and protect the public against a host of undesirable practices. A private securities market can function effectively only so long as extensive regulations guard investors against fraud and manipulation. A food manufacturer must comply with rules that protect consumers against impurities and guarantee them accurate information about the contents of the goods they purchase. Every company has to obey a variety of laws to ensure truthful advertising, prevent discrimination in hiring, and maintain reasonable safeguards for the safety of employees. All of these rules need to be wisely conceived and skillfully administered to protect the public interest without hobbling corporate managers or burdening them with unnecessary costs.

Much the same is true of newer schemes to make more use of competition and market forces in carrying out public functions. Congress can sometimes replace direct regulation of the environment by creating a market of tradable permits that will determine how much waste companies can discharge into the air or water. But public officials are still needed for many tasks, such as determining how to allocate the permits, organizing the market for trading, making sure that it operates fairly, deciding how much polluting material can be discharged, and checking to see that each participating firm emits no more of the pollutants than it is authorized to do by the permits it holds. Experience to date suggests that these functions are much more extensive and difficult to execute than many enthusiasts anticipated when they first proposed such schemes. Other market-based proposals, such as school vouchers, present public officials with similar problems.

President Reagan has recently been joined by another group of critics who maintain that national governments will grow less and less important as global economic forces increasingly determine what political leaders can and cannot do. This is not a wholly new idea. During the past one hundred years, economists have repeatedly argued that government policymakers cannot or should not resist the dictates of the free market. Global marketeers have simply added a new set of imperatives, in the form of multinational firms that can escape regulation or bond traders who will punish any government seeking to violate their sense of sound economic principles.

While global markets have unquestionably altered the calculations of officials everywhere, their impact on government is easily exaggerated. They are likely to have little effect on most traditional government functions, such as developing an effective healthcare system, reducing poverty, or minimizing violent crime. If anything, global competition underscores the long-standing need for governments to create better systems of education and job training. Even in the domain of monetary and fiscal policy, American officials will retain more discretion than policymakers in most other countries because of America's importance in world markets and its influence in helping to set the rules of the new international economy. More important, to the extent that global competition and international capital flows do influence policy, they are not fundamentally different from the many other external factors that have always shaped the decisions and limited the discretion of public officials. The eternal challenge for political leaders is how to make wise choices that take full account of forces beyond their control in order to make whatever progress they can toward important policy goals. During World War II, for example, and later on during the Cold War, America's options were heavily affected in all kinds of ways first by Germany and Japan and then by the Soviet Union. Nevertheless, no one would argue that these external forces diminished the federal government's role; if anything, they magnified the scope and importance of decisions made in Washington.

Whatever pundits say about the role of the State, substantial majorities of the American people seem convinced that a large and active federal government will continue and should continue in the future. According to opinion surveys taken just after President Clinton delivered his remark about the end of big government, almost no one took him seriously.[12] Other pollsters have consistently found that large majorities of Americans believe that the federal government should go on spending as much as it currently does, or even more, on a wide variety of major domestic programs. For example, in 1999 a public-opinion survey by Albert and Susan Cantril found that more than 70 percent of Americans favored increasing or maintaining current funding for job training, medical research, teachers' salaries, student aid for higher education, clean air, Head Start programs, safe work environments, consumer product regulation, Medicaid, and low-income housing.[13] Support for such mammoth programs as Social Security and Medicare runs even higher.

In short, the lesson to draw from America's performance over the past forty years is not simply that official programs and policies have had a lot to do with the nation's problems (along with its achievements). Of equal importance is the fact that government must continue to play an important role—though possibly a different one—if the country is to arrive at viable solutions. There is little in the record of the past forty years to inspire confidence that our government in its current form will be able to perform to the public's satisfaction.

The disappointments of the past do not necessarily mean that legislators and other top leaders have been solely at fault. Just who or what is to blame is still unexplained. In a democracy, interest groups, media, intellectuals, and the citizenry as a whole all share with public officials a responsibility for the government's performance. The chapters that follow will pay attention to all these groups in trying to find the reasons for America's record over the past four decades. At this point, all one can say is that the way in which our public policies have been conceived and carried out seems to have had a lot to do with our problems as a society in achieving the goals that most Americans profess to share. The vital question is why these failings have occurred. Only if we can be clear about what has gone wrong can we hope to identify the causes and eventually find the remedies that will help the government perform better in the future.

II

LOOKING FOR REASONS

AT THE BEGINNING of the twenty-first century, the United States enjoys the dubious distinction of having the highest healthcare costs in the world while remaining the only major democracy with a substantial fraction of its population lacking basic medical insurance. On several occasions in the past hundred years, Congress seriously considered plans to provide for universal health coverage. In each case, determined opposition led by physicians, business organizations, and conservative lawmakers barred the way. With the election of President Clinton, however, all of the auguries seemed to favor major reform. Rising health costs threatened to put American business at a disadvantage in world markets and thus made corporate executives receptive to any proposal that might shift health costs to the government. Growing segments of the medical community expressed a desire to consider reforms; even hospitals seemed intrigued by the prospect of a plan that would relieve them of the heavy burden of having to give free medical care to the uninsured. Most important of all, large majorities of the public rated healthcare reform among the most urgent problems facing the nation and voiced support for a plan that would provide medical insurance for all Americans.

Moved by these favorable signs, Clinton made healthcare reform a centerpiece of his campaign. His election seemed to present him with an excellent chance to translate his promises into law. True to his word, he moved quickly to address the issue by announcing early in 1993 that he would assemble a taskforce of experts to review the subject and draft a proposal that he could submit to Congress. To underscore his commitment to reform, he even took the unprecedented step of naming his wife, Hillary, to head the effort.

Months later, after deliberating under a cloud of secrecy, the taskforce produced its report. More than 1,300 pages long, the final document detailed a complicated plan guaranteeing a defined, comprehensive package of healthcare benefits to all Americans. Under this scheme, everyone would have a choice among different healthcare providers ranging from prepaid health plans to individual doctors. Employers would pay most of the health insurance premiums for their employees, employees would pay the rest, and the government would subsidize the costs for individuals of limited means. The proposal guaranteed that no one would have to pay more than a stipulated percentage of income for health care and that companies would not pay more than a fixed percentage of their total payroll. New bureaucratic entities, called regional healthcare alliances, would act as intermediaries between individuals and employers and competing health plans. All companies with fewer than 5,000 employees would be required to offer healthcare coverage through an alliance. In turn, alliances would make sure that providers did not raise prices excessively or omit essential benefits, or engage in adverse selection by refusing to enroll members with higher-than-average health risks. In addition, alliances would see to it that individuals and families received enough information about alternative healthcare providers to enable them to make enlightened choices.

President Clinton announced the plan to Congress in a widely acclaimed speech on September 22, 1993. In forceful tones, he urged the lawmakers "to fix a health care system that is badly broken, . . . giving every American health security—health care that is always there, health care that can never be taken away."[1] In the days that followed, Mrs. Clinton went to Capitol Hill to respond to detailed inquiries from congressional committees. Pictures of the First Lady sitting alone before a battery of lawmakers coolly answering questions on a subject of extraordinary complexity won her widespread applause. Moved by all the favorable publicity and eager for reform, large majorities of the public expressed support for the President's plan. According to TV analyst William Schneider, "The reviews are in and the box office is terrific."[2]

At that moment, the chances for sweeping reform seemed greater than they had ever been over the long, trying history of healthcare legislation. But appearances proved deceiving. After a year of constant committee hearings, reports, negotiations, trial balloons, and arguments from every quarter, Senate Leader George Mitchell announced on September 26, 1994, that healthcare legislation was dead, at least for that session of Congress. After all the publicity and all the talk, the failure to produce even limited reform seemed to epitomize the breakdown in government that many Americans feared.

Poking through the wreckage, analysts found plenty of likely culprits for the demise of healthcare reform. Many blamed the President and his advisers. His plan was too ambitious for a divided, suspicious public, and too complicated for ordinary people to understand. His choice of Hillary to lead the effort was an error, since it made it difficult for others in the Executive Branch to criticize the proposal. In retrospect, almost everyone condemned the decision to rely on experts working for months in secrecy from the media. Such a procedure aroused needless suspicion, froze out influential Administration officials whose support was vital, and produced a plan that was impractical and highly vulnerable to political attack.

Public-opinion specialists had another theory for the downfall of the Clinton plan. They pointed out that support for reform was always more precarious than many commentators had assumed. Although most Americans favored universal coverage in principle, they divided sharply on how this goal might best be achieved. A large segment favored managed competition, but many others supported a single-payer system, while still others preferred a plan to make insurance affordable for everyone by giving vouchers to low-income individuals.[3] In view of these divisions, pollsters were less disposed to regard the failure of the Clinton plan as a breakdown in the political process and more inclined to consider it a casualty of the public's ambivalence on the issue. If a breakdown had occurred, they believed, it was due to the failure of many Americans to educate themselves enough about the details of the competing proposals so that they could work their way intelligently toward consensus. As several observers pointed out, large majorities of the public remained woefully ignorant on such fundamental points as the meaning of managed competition or the total cost of health care in America.[4]

Reacting to these findings, several critics attacked the media for not doing a better job of informing the people about the choices before Congress. By examining the content of articles and broadcasts during 1993 and 1994, analysts found that reporters soon began to concentrate on legislative tactics, political infighting, and personalities in the congressional debates while devoting less and less attention to the substance of the alternative plans being considered.[5] Journalists never made clear that a great deal of consensus did exist on certain aspects of reform, such as the need to allow employees to keep their coverage when they changed jobs and the need to prevent insurance companies from refusing to enroll individuals with pre-existing health problems. Some critics argued that if this consensus had been communicated and widely publicized, Congress might have felt under pressure to pass at least a limited reform package containing the points of general agreement.

According to other commentators, interest groups were the real reason for the demise of President Clinton's plan, just as they had been in earlier reform efforts. In their lengthy book on the healthcare campaign, *The System* (1996), Haynes Johnson and David Broder described in detail the efforts of the Health Insurance Association of America and the National Federation of Independent Business to defeat the Clinton plan. By the time the proposal finally died, special interests had spent more than $100 million on a national campaign replete with television commercials and other massive efforts to drum up grassroots support. To some observers, these tactics were critical in generating enough confusion among the public to persuade many legislators that it was safe to oppose reform.

At the same time, more than economic interest must have been involved to elicit opposition from some of the powerful groups that lobbied against the Clinton proposal. Large corporations, for example, had much to gain from a national plan that would reduce their healthcare cost burdens. Why, then, did the Business Roundtable, composed of the leading American corporations, come out in opposition, much to President Clinton's dismay? One plausible explanation is that ideology triumphed over immediate self-interest. The prospect of heavier government involvement in a sector making up almost 15 percent of the entire national economy simply cut too sharply against the grain of free-enterprise executives. Similar feelings led many Republican lawmakers to mount an all-out fight against any attempt by the government to intervene further in the healthcare field. In this sense, health care may simply have been the latest casualty in a long series of inconclusive battles between liberal and conservative elites.

However potent ideological conflicts may have been, it would be difficult to give a complete account of the fate of President Clinton's bill without emphasizing the role of America's distinctive system of government. If the United States had a parliamentary system with strong political parties able to discipline their members, Mr. Clinton could presumably have pushed legislation through. True, such systems do not give heads of government as much power as might appear at first glance. Had a British prime minister proposed an elaborate health plan, much internal negotiation would have occurred among party leaders behind closed doors, and many adjustments might have been made before the plan was presented to Parliament. In the end, however, in view of the public support for reform and its prominent place in the ruling party's platform, party discipline would have probably allowed some form of universal coverage to win out. Not so in America. With a separate legislative branch filled with independent lawmakers lacking strong party loyalties, several Democrats in Congress quickly produced radically different plans of their own, and the President could not muster the authority to rally his party behind a single program.

While all of the preceding explanations seem plausible, the fact remains that Congress failed to respond to the clear and emphatic wish of the people to have some system of health care that would guarantee access to everyone at a reasonable cost. To ordinary Americans, it scarcely mattered whether the President or his experts made mistakes or whether their elected representatives acted as they did because of interest group pressures or ideological convictions. The final result simply confirmed their suspicion that elected politicians do not really care what voters want and quickly lose touch with their constituents after they arrive in Washington.

In sum, the great healthcare debate lends support to many different theories as to why our government has failed to do a better job of fulfilling the needs and hopes of the American people. But how much substance is there to these theories? Are some of them largely without merit? Are some more important than others? Do any provide a reasonably complete explanation of why the federal government has so often failed in the past forty years to live up to the public's expectations? The chapters that follow try to answer these questions.

3

THE USUAL SUSPECTS

IN THE LINEUP OF POSSIBLE culprits, three suspects are often held chiefly responsible for the failings and frustrations associated with government. The list was confirmed as recently as 1999 in an opinion survey sponsored by the Council for Excellence in Government. Conducted by Republican pollster Robert Teeter and Democratic pollster Peter Hart, the survey found that 38 percent of the respondents put the greatest blame on special interests, 29 percent on the media, and 24 percent each on elected officials and the political parties to which they belong.[1] What have the accused done to deserve such condemnation? Are they truly responsible for the government's failings or only the usual suspects rounded up by a restless public seeking to hold someone accountable for all that seems distasteful in the nation's capital?

Politicians

The simplest explanation for the problems of government is that the elected leaders are incapable of carrying out their duties effectively. That appears to be the verdict most Americans have reached. Two-thirds of the respondents in a 1996 survey stated that our system of government was good but that "the people running it are incompetent."[2] Not all public servants have earned this harsh judgment; judges and military officers enjoy greater confidence than civil servants, who in turn command much greater esteem than politicians. The latter are in a class by themselves. They have aroused such negative feelings that a poll conducted in late 1995 revealed that in a list of fourteen occupations, Americans ranked U.S. senators, members of Congress, and politicians at the very bottom—below even lawyers, labor leaders, and advertising executives.[3]

Those who criticize politicians often exclaim that the quality of leadership in the country has slipped markedly. Time and again, one hears that recent presidents are not made of the same stuff as Franklin Roosevelt or Abraham Lincoln, not to mention George Washington and Thomas Jefferson. Critics regularly complain that statesmen are leaving Congress and being replaced by politicians of lesser ability and stature. If these charges are true, one need hardly look further for a reason to explain the disappointing performance of our government.

In fact, however, there is very little evidence to support such a verdict. Granted, few historians will rank any recent president among the most distinguished occupants of the Oval Office. But such comparisons are treacherous. The range of tasks that modern presidents must perform and the number of programs for which they are responsible have multiplied several-fold over the past fifty years. The scrutiny that the media give to every aspect of their lives has increased tremendously. Voters rarely give the party in the White House control over both houses of Congress. In short, the challenges presidents face have changed so much that no one can be sure how well the giants of yesteryear would have fared in today's political environment.

It is also worth noting that few if any other leading democracies today seem blessed with widely admired chief executives; much the same is true of major American corporations, universities, and other institutions. The dearth of highly respected figures at the helm of so many countries and organizations suggests that any leadership deficit in Washington has not come about because of a weakness on the part of our elected officials or even through a defect in our political procedures and institutions. The more likely explanation is that current conditions in advanced nations have changed in ways that make successful leadership unlikely everywhere. The record of those on top seems to depend at least as much on the surrounding circumstances as on their qualities of character and personal dynamism. That is why most great statesmen have emerged when the people were unified in pursuit of an urgent common goal (such as winning a war or staving off some other pressing danger), not in times like the present. Even Winston Churchill enjoyed an indifferent political career until the menace of Adolf Hitler forced Britons to turn to him and gratefully accept his direction.[4]

The evidence of decline in Congress is no more convincing than the case for deteriorating leadership in the White House. Of course, there can be no proof one way or the other, since no reliable yardstick exists to measure the quality of a legislature. But such scraps of evidence as do exist hardly suggest a growing incompetence. Measured by educational attainment, Congress has improved dramatically from the middle of the nineteenth century, when Tocqueville could remark: "In a country in which education is very general, it is said that the representatives of the people do not always know how to write correctly."[5] Today, virtually every member of Congress has a college diploma. The attainments of the members have continued to increase, with considerably higher proportions holding advanced degrees than one would have found three or four decades ago.[6] As for other qualities, political scientists Allen Hertzke and Ronald Peters echo the sentiments of Tip O'Neill: "Contemporary members of Congress . . . are on average brighter, better motivated, harder working, and better suited for public service than any previous generation."[7] Agreeing with this appraisal, long-time political reporter Adam Clymer declares: "Any veteran observer of Congress . . . would say that the typical member is better educated and harder working than whoever held the seat thirty-five years ago."[8]

Like presidents, however, lawmakers today have to contend with serious burdens and obstacles that limit their chances for distinguished service. The growing cynicism and distrust among the public make it difficult for elected officials to win support for ambitious new programs. A prying press feeds the public's suspicions with a steady diet of petty scandals and allegations that would have probably gone unreported forty years ago. A government frequently divided along ideological lines succumbs to stubborn disagreements that reduce bold proposals to half-hearted compromises or mire them indefinitely in acrimonious gridlock. Under these trying conditions, without the benefit of some overarching crisis to unify the people, politicians find it increasingly difficult to supply the impressive leadership that so many people feel is missing.

A closer look at the current political environment reveals several other changes that have influenced the types of politicians elected to high positions and their subsequent behavior in office. One such trend is the sharp decline in the number of incumbent officials who have to face the test of running against challengers with substantial political experience, stature, or accomplishment. During the 1970s and 1980s, more and more congressional elections were virtually uncontested. Fewer and fewer challengers seemed worthy enough to the public to receive more than 30 percent of the vote, and most had no significant record of public service. By 1990, only 10 percent of all the candidates running against congressional incumbents had ever held a political office of any kind.[9]

How can one account for the dwindling number of experienced challengers? The most likely explanation is that worthy candidates exist; they simply do not think they have a sufficient chance of defeating an incumbent to justify leaving their jobs and making the effort required to run for Congress.[10] After all, throughout the past several decades, more than 90 percent of all sitting members seeking reelection to the House of Representatives have won, most of them by large margins.

There are many reasons incumbents are so hard to beat. Despite the popular dislike of Congress, a majority of Americans approve of the job their own representative is doing (another reason to be suspicious of sweeping allegations of decline).[11] In addition, incumbents have many built-in advantages: ready access to television, free mailings to constituents, opportunities to help individual voters with their problems.

If that were all that could be said on the matter, there would be nothing worth discussing. No one can object if sitting politicians make the most of their position and do a good job of pleasing their constituents. But challengers face another obstacle quite apart from an incumbent's good performance. The obstacle is money. Today, the costs of mounting a serious campaign for Congress run to several hundred thousand dollars or more. Unless would-be candidates are personally wealthy, even the most capable of them may be unable to raise such a sum except when incumbents have retired or shown themselves to be noticeably vulnerable. Fortunately, the stiff competition for most open seats helps ensure that able people win these elections most of the time, and winners who turn out to be inept or unpopular will usually attract capable, well-funded opponents. Still, the difficulty that even the worthiest challenger faces in soliciting funds to run against a sitting member limits the options available to voters and lowers their chances of choosing a representative who truly reflects their values and aspirations.

Another factor affecting the kinds of people elected to Congress is the encouragement our system gives candidates to run for office on their own initiative, raise their own money, organize their own campaigns, and rely very little on help from their political party. Such lawmakers are no longer the exception but the rule. Because parties in most states choose their nominees by primary elections, those who decide to run do not require the endorsement or the assistance of their party organization. With the aid of television and direct-mail techniques, they need not rely on party volunteers. Since political parties no longer command the loyalty from voters that they once did, candidates do not even depend so heavily on the Democratic or Republican label to win elections.

There are benefits to using primaries rather than conventions. During earlier times, in districts where one party had an overwhelming advantage, convention delegates did not need to choose the ablest, most attractive candidates in order to win. Now that primaries are in wide use, therefore, one rarely encounters the party hacks of bygone years who were sent to Washington to do the bidding of a powerful state or local political boss. This is undoubtedly one reason Speaker O'Neill could say with such conviction that the quality of his fellow legislators had improved since World War II.

Overall, however, independence may well produce as many problems as it solves. Increasingly, Congress has become a collection of strong-minded individualists, each intent on having an impact, gaining recognition, expanding personal influence, and, above all, staying in power or winning an even higher office. While a legislature composed of such people can generate a wealth of new ideas, it can also be a body in which compromise is difficult and jockeying for power and influence is intense. This problem may explain Speaker O'Neill's additional comment that as the quality of individual lawmakers increased, the quality of legislation declined.

The third worrisome trend that may affect the kind of legislators who win office grows out of the arduous work they do and the life they have to lead. The demands of office have clearly grown much heavier in the past few decades. Legislative sessions last longer and leave less time for family and friends.[12] The sums of money politicians must amass to wage a competitive race grow constantly larger and take increasing amounts of time to raise. Public distrust has steadily risen, collegiality in Congress has waned, and campaigning has become more negative, threatening to rob political careers of many of their psychological rewards.

Surprisingly, these burdens do not seem to be troubling most current members of Congress. According to a 1998 survey, 57 percent of incumbents are *very* satisfied with their jobs, and none admit to being mostly or very dissatisfied.[13] Fifty-six percent report that they find the job more satisfying than when they first took office, while only 16 percent consider their work less rewarding.[14]

Of course, these results reflect only the opinions of incumbents and do not reveal how many able people decide not to run because of the strains of a political career. Close observers continue to worry that the pressures of the job may at last be starting to take a toll on the quality of people willing to stand for election. When many of Congress' most respected members announced their retirement in the 1990s, veterans of both political parties expressed the fear that the new members were not the equal of those who had departed.[15] As yet, however, there is still no hard evidence that fewer intelligent, capable people are prepared to accept the trials and tribulations of a political career. Most studies of the political process have found an ample supply of talented people willing to run when their chances seem promising.[16]

Whether or not the burdens of office have diminished the quality of legislators entering Congress, they presumably affect the motivations of people who serve there. National politics is hardly a vocation for amateurs, however talented. Few candidates could contemplate raising all the necessary money, campaigning ceaselessly for months on end, and working under pressure for sixty or seventy hours every week unless they possessed an almost unnatural desire for power.

Professional politicians driven by such ambition bring important assets to public life. Their striving often comes from a genuine desire to improve the world and make a positive difference. Their determination to stay in office means that they will heed the views of their constituents. The stamina and energy required to raise the money and win a contested election may serve the public well by virtually guaranteeing that those who win will bear up under the sheer physical demands of a career in Congress.

At the same time, ambition makes most politicians excessively concerned with holding on to their jobs. When politics is no longer part-time work (as it was only a few generations ago) but a full-time career to which its practitioners are passionately drawn, incumbents can become too willing to "do whatever it takes" to win elections. Fewer and fewer principles seem important enough to justify sacrificing a political career or even running a moderate risk of losing a campaign. Otherwise decent public servants will go to indecent lengths to try to redraw district lines or resist campaign finance reforms to protect their chances to stay in office. Elected officials may feel increasingly tempted to slight the larger interests of nation or party rather than risk displeasing voters or major contributors.[17] At times, ambition can even lead to the chicanery of a Richard Nixon, the Faustian bargain on race of a George Wallace, or the evasions and untruths of a William Clinton.

Extreme personal ambition can also make it difficult for individual legislators to speak frankly with their constituents. As retaining office becomes more and more important, politicians begin to calculate everything they say and do, relying extensively on consultants. Spontaneity diminishes as every policy proposal and pronouncement is pretested with focus groups and artfully designed to attract the attention of the media. In an effort to exploit the cynicism of their constituents, incumbents not only attack their opponents but disparage the very Congress in which they serve. Increasingly, politics takes on the appearance of a distasteful, negative, artificial game in which candidates try to do in their opponents while marketing themselves like breakfast cereals.[18]

Where does all this leave the harsh complaints often leveled against politicians? There are surely tendencies afoot that give legitimate cause for worry. Too many congressional races are essentially uncontested, and too many legislators seem excessively ambitious and independent. Nevertheless, it is doubtful that these problems are more serious than those of earlier times, when many lawmakers were undistinguished lackeys sent to Washington by some political machine or powerful interest group. By every objective standard, the levels of intelligence and education in Congress and the amounts of time and energy that legislators devote to their jobs are impressive. Whatever else they may be, members of Congress and other top political leaders are surely not incompetent. On the contrary, the true puzzle of our politics is not how such inept individuals come to power but why such able, energetic people have not done a better job of fulfilling the aspirations of the voters who elected them.

If Americans judge politicians too harshly, perhaps they have a stronger case for criticizing the media. After all, few people catch more than an occasional glimpse of their representative in Congress, and fewer still have first-hand dealings with the President or the top congressional leadership. But almost everyone has looked at television or read a newspaper enough to evaluate the work of reporters and news commentators. As the next section makes clear, the verdict of the public is far from favorable.

Are the Media Damaging Democracy?

Thomas Jefferson once remarked that "were it left to me to decide whether we should have a government without newspapers, or newspapers without a government, I should not hesitate a moment to prefer the latter."[19] That was before he became President of the United States. After enduring the "splendid misery" of that high office, he had less complimentary things to say about the press. To Abigail Adams, he wrote complaining of "the overwhelming torrent of slander which is confounding all vice and virtue, all truth and falsehood in the United States."[20] And referring to certain outspoken newspaper editors, Jefferson observed to the governor of Pennsylvania: "I have therefore long thought that a few prosecutions of the most eminent offenders would have a wholesome effect in restoring the integrity of the presses."[21]

Most politicians and high government officials share Jefferson's ambivalence about the media. The public, too, is becoming more dissatisfied. Although most people still claim to have at least "some" confidence in television and newspapers, the share of the public expressing "a great deal of confidence" dropped from approximately 20 percent in 1973 to 10 percent in 1996, while the fraction feeling "hardly any confidence" doubled from roughly 20 percent to 40 percent.[22] A majority now regards newspapers and television as one-sided and unfair in presenting the news, and growing numbers believe that the media interfere with the ability of officials to do their job.

Even journalists have started to complain. Prominent commentators, such as David Broder and James Fallows, have raised serious questions about the role of the media and its effect on the political process.[23] In books and speeches, they have claimed that the media have undermined political parties, trivialized political discourse, and made citizens unduly cynical and negative about public affairs. Rather than concentrate on important current issues, they say, journalists have turned increasingly to celebrity watching, sensationalism, and the petty drama of political infighting in Washington.

These are serious charges. Newspaper reporters and television commentators play an indispensable role in helping to inform the public and hold politicians accountable for their actions. If the charges against the media are even half true, the consequences for democratic government could be grave. Still, the question remains: Are the criticisms valid?

The Impact of Television on Political Behavior

Taken together, newspapers, television programs, radio broadcasts, and now the Internet reach almost everyone in the United States. Television has become such a powerful force that the entire political process has had to adapt to conform with the medium. Now that producers present the news in soundbites averaging less than ten seconds, officials have learned to convey their message in short, attention-grabbing "one-liners." Official announcements are timed and White House schedules carefully arranged to make the evening news.

Media coverage has also had an effect on elections, sometimes catapulting political neophytes with an arresting message into public prominence, as Larry King did for Ross Perot. Thanks to television, candidates can run effective campaigns on their own, thus minimizing their dependence on political parties for publicity and campaign workers. At the same time, the sheer expense of television has greatly increased the cost of campaigns, forcing candidates to spend more time raising money and to rely more on contributions from wealthy donors and interest groups.

While these effects are significant, the impact of newspapers and television is easily exaggerated. Media coverage is important to lesser-known candidates who need to become better known to voters. Even so, candidates can purchase their own TV spots to put their name before the public. By the time of the final election, many analysts find that the principal effect of television has been to reinforce previously held opinions rather than to change voters' minds. Factors such as the income, education, and age of voters and the party to which they belong are much more potent than TV exposure in explaining how people vote.

As for weakening political parties, television is hardly the only force involved. The rise of the Civil Service and the resulting decline in patronage played an early part. The tendency of voters to pay less attention to party labels and more to candidates began years before TV sets became ubiquitous.[24] Because citizens wanted a larger part in the selection process and felt that party leaders were too ingrown and too insensitive to their needs, almost all states stopped nominating candidates by convention and adopted a primary system. As a result, both the Democratic and Republican organizations ceased to have a decisive role in choosing and electing candidates and thereby lost much of their leverage over their members in Congress.

The effect of television costs on the election process is also open to question. If television disappeared, would candidates respond by spending less money? Or would they continue to raise the same amounts and use the funds for other purposes, such as direct mailing, websites, billboards, newspaper ads, and grassroots organizing? No one knows. So long as money can be used to help persuade additional voters, however, one suspects that candidates will go on raising as much of it as they can to gain an edge over their opponents. And even if television costs turn out to have uniquely potent effects, the obvious answer is not to blame the medium but to give all candidates free or discounted TV time.

In short, while television has undoubtedly altered the nature of political campaigns, there is little reason to hold it responsible for the demise of strong parties, loyal precinct workers, and modestly priced campaigns. Nor would the election process necessarily improve by curtailing a medium that has permitted candidates to communicate directly to so many constituents. While television has led to attack ads and abbreviated newsbites, it has also allowed millions of citizens to watch debates and speeches that explore election issues. Although much of its coverage seems superficial, it has stimulated many Americans to take an interest in political campaigns. If television has aggravated the burdens of campaign financing, encouraged negative campaigning, and inhibited grassroots organizing, the remedy surely lies in confronting these problems directly rather than condemning the medium that has brought them into clear view.

Charges of Bias

Many critics have attacked the media over the years for the way they present the news. Conservatives insist that most reporters are liberal politically and are therefore biased in their coverage of politics and public affairs. Liberals reply that the media are controlled by large corporations and wealthy advertisers and that the content of reporting must be influenced accordingly.[25]

Fortunately, most efforts to search news columns and TV programs for systematic political bias have come up empty.[26] Studies of reporting on presidential elections have seldom found convincing evidence of persistent favoritism for either side. It is true that publishers sometimes try to influence newspaper stories or to interfere with editorial policy.[27] In the main, however, such interventions have sought to further the commercial interests of advertisers, as tobacco interests seem to have done in discouraging articles about the health hazards of smoking. Only rarely have advertisers tried to use their leverage to force reporters to promote a political candidate or support an ideological point of view.

Critics such as Noam Chomsky and Ralph Nader sometimes make a different point, claiming that the media are much too inclined to feature mainstream values and orthodox ideas instead of encouraging those daring enough to challenge the status quo. Whether or not the allegation is true, so long as the media are largely made up of private companies in a highly competitive business, the themes and viewpoints expressed, at least on the major networks, are bound to reflect what large numbers of people are interested in hearing. Producers will often give coverage to someone outside the mainstream who does something exciting and provocative, such as Louis Farrakhan, David Duke, or even Ralph Nader himself. What the media will not do is make room for pronouncements from any quarter that promise to be dull, hectoring, or unpopular. The remedy, if one exists, will come from lowering the cost of access through the growth of the Internet and the proliferation of new TV channels. By themselves, of course, added channels, websites, or new political magazines will not guarantee a large national audience for new and challenging radical ideas. But that is something no democracy can deliver. All that one can legitimately expect is that unconventional ideas will find a foothold. Thereafter, it is up to those who hold such beliefs to expand their audience through a gradual process of persuasion.

Spreading Cynicism

The most frequent attacks on the media in recent years have not claimed deliberate bias or manipulation but have criticized the tendency of newspapers and TV analysts to denigrate public officials and minimize their accomplishments.[28] Though negativism about government and politics is hardly new, it has greatly increased since the 1960s. One content analysis of TV news revealed that the proportion of negative stories during presidential campaigns rose from 25 percent in 1960 to 42 percent in 1972 and then to 60 percent in 1988.[29] In 1992, 63 percent of all news stories about Bill Clinton were negative; the figures for George Bush and Ross Perot were 69 percent and 54 percent, respectively.[30] The trend in the coverage of Congress is much the same. In 1972, three of four stories about Congress were predominantly unfavorable. In 1982, the fraction grew to seven out of every eight stories, and in 1992, to nine out of every ten.[31]

There is something troubling about the growing preponderance of negative stories in the media. Journalists in the United States pride themselves on being accurate and unbiased in their reporting. But even if each story they write about politics and public affairs is entirely accurate and fair, the overall impression will be seriously distorted and misleading if the share of stories devoted to scandal, conflict, and official bumbling is far greater than the actual incidence of these problems in the real world. With such a depressing diet, the worry is that citizens may gradually become more cynical, while sinking into the role of passive spectators, much like fans watching a football game.[32]

On the surface, at least, the prevailing trends in public opinion and voter behavior seem to confirm these fears. With the content of news reporting becoming increasingly negative, attitudes toward government have indeed grown more cynical. As the media's fixation on polls, campaign tactics, and the "horse-race" aspects of politics has increased, voting rates have gradually declined. Now that reporters are devoting more and more attention to scandal, the public has come to regard politicians as scoundrels who enrich themselves in office and put the interests of lobbyists above the needs of the country.

These parallels are disturbing. But how much hard evidence is there that the media are at fault? How do we know that the increasing negativism of the media is not a reflection of growing public cynicism rather than the other way around?

One way of finding out is to look for opinion polls about politics and public affairs that also contain questions about the reading and viewing habits of the respondents. With such surveys, one can compare the attitudes toward government of those who regularly read papers and watch TV news with the attitudes of those who don't. If the media are influencing their audience, the results should show up in these comparisons.

Interestingly, such inquiries reveal little difference in attitude between those who regularly watch television news and those who don't.[33] There are also no significant differences between those who do and do not read newspapers, once extraneous factors such as education are held constant. Only radio talk shows seem to attract listeners with feelings about government that vary significantly from those of nonlisteners, and here the differences are not what most people would suspect. Regular listeners turn out to be *less* alienated from government (less inclined to feel that politicians don't listen and that ordinary voters don't count), even after controlling for differences in income and education. Studies of this kind undoubtedly need to be replicated and refined. Because the media reach so many people, those who do not read, listen, or watch regularly may still be affected by the negative reactions of those who do. Nevertheless, as matters now stand, suspicions abound, but the available evidence does not bear them out.

Who Is Responsible?

Allegedly, the trend toward negativism began when a new breed of journalist entered the newsrooms in the 1960s, especially those of leading papers such as the *New York Times* and the *Washington Post*. These reporters were much more likely than their predecessors to come from comfortable middle-class families and Ivy League universities. Like many others in their generation, they were quick to question authority and highly critical of much going on in the society, especially persistent racism and the Vietnam War. Distorted government reports about the war heightened their suspicions about the truthfulness of public officials. Watergate confirmed their worst fears. In this environment, the exposés by *Washington Post* reporters Bob Woodward and Carl Bernstein seemed to exemplify journalists' finest response to all the manipulation and deception practiced by people in high places. Before long, so it is alleged, reporters were outdoing one another in rooting out scandal and ascribing base or self-interested motives to all manner of public officials.

This account is accurate up to a point. But there is something unreal about the story line. Newspapers and TV news organizations are more than collections of autonomous Ivy League reporters. There are other significant actors, such as owners and publishers, who are interested in making a profit from the enterprise—not to mention editors, who often decide which stories to cover, what prominence to accord each item, and how the stories should be portrayed. One can hardly assign responsibility for the quality of news reporting, let alone think about how to improve matters, without asking who in the typical news organization actually makes the key decisions and for what reasons.

The 1960s and 1970s were golden years for reporters, when professional values had a preferred place and commercial considerations were muted. Newspapers were prospering and were often owned by publishing families animated by motives other than maximizing returns. Television networks did not face competition from cable, their news departments did not operate as profit centers, and news chiefs at the major networks had a relatively free hand to spend and cover what they wanted.

As the 1970s wore on, however, competitive pressures intensified. Newspaper editors became uncomfortably aware that readership was eroding at the rate of approximately 1 percent per year just when more and more papers were passing from family ownership into the control of large commercial chains that were preoccupied with the bottom line. Meanwhile, a new breed of owner was taking control of the television networks. General Electric bought NBC; Loew's acquired CBS; Capital Cities took over ABC. These corporate owners quickly sensed that they were confronting stiffer competition from cable outlets. Before long, their cost accountants looked at the figures, saw that news organizations were a losing operation, and concluded that there was no good reason for this. Quickly, heads began to roll, budgets came under sharper scrutiny, and expense accounts grew leaner.[34]

During the 1980s, as newspaper readership slowly fell and cable television made deep inroads into network audiences, newspaper publishers and TV moguls invited market researchers to study their audiences and advise them on how to stop the decline. For newspapers, the answer seemed to call for shorter stories, more sports and local news, more photos and graphics, more human interest, and less coverage of politics. For television, the prescription was much the same, adapted to the special nature of the medium: briefer soundbites, simpler presentations, more emphasis on visual presentation over substantive content. As one newsman put it, "We were ordered to add glitz. We were told to feature a celebrity interview at least every half hour."[35] The prevailing wisdom was that audiences wished to be entertained rather than informed.

News departments felt increasing pressure to feature more conflict, drama, and scandal, with an emphasis on emotion rather than analysis. From 1976 to 1992, sensational and human-interest stories increased their share of TV news from 12 percent to 41 percent.[36] Emphasizing crime proved to be a particularly effective way of attracting audiences, especially for local television news.[37] Stations sought to attract younger male viewers by using much faster-paced stories and increased coverage of violence, focusing not on crime statistics or explanations for lawlessness but on the lurid details of murders and other acts of mayhem.

National network news and large metropolitan papers have not placed as much emphasis as local stations on catastrophe and crime. Yet they, too, have responded to their audience by devoting less time to politics and public affairs. As Doug Underwood observes, "In a period of shorter stories and shrunken newshole, it's probably fair to assume that publishers will use public alienation as an excuse to cut government coverage."[38] Quoting another media specialist, he notes that "editors have paid close attention to polls that show that readers (and particularly young readers) don't 'connect' with government news."[39]

Some critics resist the notion that market forces are primarily responsible for the trend toward negativism, crime, and entertainment. They point to opinion polls suggesting that viewers would actually like more hard news and serious discussion and less attention to gossip, conflict, political maneuvering, and an endless series of preelection polls. In a 1995 survey, 70 percent of the respondents agreed that "journalists are more interested in sensational stories about politicians than about policy issues or the problems facing the country."[40] In the same poll, 72 percent replied that "journalists underestimate the public by assuming that they want stories about scandals instead of stories about policy issues and the country's major problems."[41]

Such surveys doubtless reflect the values and preferences that respondents believe they have and would like to have. It is much less clear that they reveal how people actually behave when they flip the pages of their newspaper or punch the buttons of their television set. But it is what people do, not what they say, that affects the bottom line. Newspaper publishers look closely at how various format changes affect circulation. Television networks monitor even more precisely not only what is happening to their ratings but how viewers respond to different segments of a single broadcast. It is hard to believe that editors and publishers, armed with elaborate ratings and circulation figures, would alter the content of the news as they have if they did not believe that the changes were in line with the actual responses of their audiences. Even public TV broadcasters notice similar trends. The PBS show *Frontline* does not seek profits and has little need to worry about ratings. Yet according to executive producer Michael Sullivan, "when we do something about drugs, sex, or violence, the ratings go up."[42]

In this environment, news reporters are not entirely free to write as they choose about public affairs, and it is pointless to criticize them as if they were. Rather, they are professionals in a business enterprise that is trying to maximize its profits in a highly competitive market. At times, the economic constraints are implicit rather than imposed heavy-handedly. Depending on their status and the organization they work for, journalists will have varying degrees of discretion in choosing what they write about and how they present their material.[43] But even the best-known television anchors can find their jobs in jeopardy if their ratings drop significantly, as John Chancellor and Roger Mudd discovered in the early 1980s. According to former *Chicago Tribune* editor James Squires, "almost no editor or news director today has the authority to alter or add content to newspaper or broadcast formats unless it fits into a preconceived and approved marketing plan."[44] Michael Fancher, executive editor of the *Seattle Times,* is even more blunt: "Some editors resist getting involved in the business of newspapering, fearing that they will be tainted by filthy lucre. I believe those editors are doomed. Sooner or later their journalistic options will be prescribed by someone else's bottom line."[45]

The Media in Perspective

The fact that the market determines the way journalists portray politics and public affairs hardly means that current news reporting is ideal. Nor does it necessarily mean that people are getting the kind of coverage they want. Americans are of two minds about the news they receive. It may well be that at the end of a long day, the average family will choose a visual diet of crime, political infighting, and human-interest stories rather than a serious discussion of important topics. But Americans do not thank the media for pandering to their appetite for drama, scandal, and entertainment masquerading as news. On the contrary, according to a 1997 poll, 64 percent of the public believes that the news is too sensationalized.[46] In shaping the news as they do, therefore, media executives may be responding to what their audience actually reads and watches, but this does not prove that their decisions serve the nation's interests or even reflect the only true desires of the people.

The public's ambivalence about the kind of news it wants is merely one of several reasons for refusing to use the market as the test of whether newspapers and television broadcasters are adequately serving democracy's need for an informed citizenry. The content of public-affairs reporting in a market system reflects the wishes of advertisers as much as the interests of the people, perhaps even more. Most corporate sponsors want to avoid issues which are controversial enough that they might alienate a significant body of consumers. Above all, they dislike stories that seem critical of the products they sell. Rather than appealing to all Americans evenhandedly, they prefer to concentrate on reaching the most promising consumer audiences, which generally include people of means, especially those between the ages of eighteen and forty-five. From a marketing perspective, low-income families are rarely attractive. As a Bloomingdale's executive allegedly remarked to the *New York Post* in explaining why the store did not advertise in that paper: "Your readers are our shoplifters." Responding to these preferences, some newspapers actually discourage readership in the inner city to improve the demographic profile of their circulation base in the eyes of advertisers.

The economics of the marketplace also lead media owners to underinvest in serious public-affairs programming, because they cannot capture an important part of the value created by such coverage—namely, the value in a democracy of educating the public about political issues of importance to their welfare. In view of the crucial need for a well-informed citizenry, therefore, a healthy democracy should never simply accept the dictates of the marketplace. Rather, it should always invest more in disseminating news and information about public affairs than commercial considerations would allow.

But it is one thing to show that the market cannot fully meet the information needs of a democracy and quite another to blame the media for the results. So long as newspapers and TV producers compete as enterprises in a commercial market—and it is hard to conceive of a serious alternative—they will be driven to act much as they do today. Continued exhortation or criticism may help a bit, but it will hardly bring about a substantial change in media behavior. Even if television broadcasters were somehow persuaded to increase the depth and seriousness of their news coverage, it is likely that many viewers would simply switch to other channels, leaving them even less informed about public affairs than they are at present.

Rather than browbeat the media, therefore, it would be wiser to look for some other way to help meet the information needs that democratic government requires. More public television might help, along with subsidies to make serious public-affairs programming more attractive to commercial producers.* Even these measures, however, cannot guarantee that the added programs will attract substantial audiences. In the end, unless some way is found to alter the choices the public makes about what to watch and read, the prevailing diet of news and information will continue to provide less diversity of ideas and expose fewer people to a serious treatment of important issues than one would like to see in a thriving democracy.

Do Interest Groups Control Policy?

For all the criticism they attract, journalists are generally credited with trying to serve the public. The same cannot be said of interest groups and those who work in their behalf. Lobbyists are avowedly

---

* In this regard, it is interesting to note that the average market share of public TV broadcasting among all OECD countries is 42 percent (compared to an average market share of only 3 percent for public television in the United States). News and current affairs make up 25 percent of what is broadcast on public television in OECD countries.

engaged in trying to promote the private interests of their clients. That is what they are paid to do. This self-serving behavior may account for their unenviable status as the suspects most often accused of subverting the work of government.

The very mention of lobbyists conjures up images of overweight influence peddlers in Gucci shoes tucking cash-filled envelopes into the pockets of corruptible legislators. To most Americans, there is no mystery about the way the process works. The root of the problem is money. During 2000, interest groups and wealthy individuals gave close to half a billion dollars to the Democratic and Republican parties for use in election campaigns. People naturally assume that the donors get a lot in return for these massive contributions. By very large majorities, the American people have come to believe that special interests control most of the important policies decided by the federal government.

The Impact of PAC Contributions

After the sweeping campaign finance laws that Congress passed in 1974, political action committees (PACs) became the vehicle of choice for business, labor, and other well-financed interest groups to make political contributions. Under the law, donations to political candidates were closely regulated so that no PAC could give more than $10,000 to anyone running for Congress ($5,000 each for the primary and the general election). In addition, Congress required disclosure of all PAC contributions and forbade lobbyists from currying favor with lawmakers by offering cash or expensive gifts for their personal use.

Many investigators have tried hard to ascertain the impact on policy of these PAC contributions.[47] Since all donations to candidates are a matter of public record, it is easy to examine the recorded votes of House and Senate members to determine what link, if any, exists between PAC money and policymaking in Congress. Such work has shown a strong correlation between political contributions and the voting records of legislators receiving such gifts. For example, members of Congress who receive donations from the dairy industry are much more likely than those who don't to vote in favor of milk price supports. The crucial question, however, is whether the lawmakers vote for price supports because they have received donations or whether they receive donations because they are already committed advocates of price supports (perhaps because they have a lot of dairy farmers in their district).

Further research on this question has unearthed some surprising facts. If contributions truly influenced votes, one would think that most PACs would give the maximum to many legislators. Yet the average PAC donation to congressional campaigns has not been much above a thousand dollars, far below the legal limit. In 1990, fewer than 5 percent of all PAC contributions (and only 2 percent of all corporate PAC donations) exceeded $5,000, half the total amount allowable by law.

Another curious fact has to do with how interest groups decide which legislators should receive their support. If money "bought" votes, one would expect lobbyists to avoid giving much to members of Congress who were already committed supporters; they would be more likely to make their gifts to "swing voters" whose help would be critical for enacting needed legislation. But this is not the usual pattern. Most lobbying efforts and interest group donations are directed at staunch supporters who would be likely to remain so even if no donation were forthcoming.[48]

In view of these findings, it is not surprising that studies to determine the impact of interest group donations on votes in Congress have discovered only a slight connection at best.[49] Many researchers cannot detect any significant influence.[50] Even those who find that PAC contributions do produce statistically significant changes in voting report that the effects are much more modest than most popular accounts suggest.[51]

Why do interest groups bother contributing money to lawmakers if their gifts have so little impact on policy? The usual answer is that donations buy access—the chance to meet with members of the Congress or their staff and present information and arguments on important issues. One can imagine why access would be well worth the money. After all, a few thousand dollars is a small price to pay for being able to talk face-to-face on important issues with those having the ultimate power to decide. But it would be a mistake to make too much of buying access. Lawmakers and their staffs talk to many individuals and groups that do not give money. Moreover, if access were truly critical and money were the key, contributors should have a significant impact on policy decisions. But this is precisely what researchers have failed to show.*

Some investigators have suggested a more intriguing reason for interest groups' donations to legislators. Perhaps such contributions do not influence votes. Perhaps they are not even intended to do so. What they may accomplish instead is to influence what lawmakers do *before* legislation reaches the floor. Giving money may help interest groups persuade supportive legislators to introduce a friendly amendment, delay committee consideration until lobbyists have time to marshal their data, or insert a helpful clause into a committee report that may be useful later in arguing to judges about the interpretation of a statute.[52] This could explain why PACs give so heavily to their friends. It is not an extra vote that lobbyists want; they can count on that in any case. What they hope for is some added effort by lawmakers who already support them but who might be persuaded to go the extra mile to intervene and protect their interests at some strategic moment in the legislative process.

Although this explanation seems plausible, no one yet knows how much success contributors have had persuading friendly lawmakers to work harder in their behalf. Nor is anyone sure whether the effect they have comes from campaign donations or from actions of a more innocent kind. When lobbyists from the American Association of Retired People (AARP) or the National Rifle Association (NRA) talk to lawmakers, it is far from clear that financial contributions speak as loudly as the fact that these organizations have thousands of dedicated supporters across America who might not only vote against legislators they regard as unfriendly but could also work hard to defeat them in the next election.

---

* It is often hard to tell whether interest groups are giving money to buy access and influence or responding to implicit threats from influential politicians and their supporters. Lobbyists and business executives may feel they have to give in order to make sure that they are not penalized for failing to contribute or kept from getting contracts they deserve on the merits in favor of competitors who were more willing to donate handsomely. Anecdotal evidence suggests that many business executives and their representatives do in fact believe that they are being "shaken down" in this fashion.

Advantages to Incumbents

If the only danger from PAC donations was the threat of influencing the votes of individual lawmakers, Americans might not need to worry. But such contributions may also affect elections to Congress by giving incumbent legislators a critical advantage over would-be opponents. Together, PACs contribute a large fraction of the money incumbents spend on their campaigns. Some members of Congress obtain more than half of their campaign funds from this source. Because sitting members are almost always heavily favored to win re-election, corporate lobbyists have found it sensible to support them (if they are not too unfriendly) rather than contribute to challengers, even if the latter are more sympathetic to business. On the strength of such calculations, PAC donations benefit incumbents by a ratio of 10 to 1 over their campaign rivals.[53] That is a major reason the average House incumbent spent \$733,731 in the 1998 election campaign, while the average challenger managed to spend only \$184,357.[54]

It is still not entirely clear how much difference PAC contributions make to the reelection rates of sitting lawmakers. Incumbents have many advantages besides PAC support—so much so, that they were almost always reelected even in the days before PACs began to make political donations.[55] At the very least, however, PAC contributions tend to reinforce the incumbent's natural advantage and help discourage able challengers by creating an image of invulnerability. By so doing, they may make Congress less responsive to changes in public sentiment and deprive the public of the chance to elect individuals with the greatest ability and the most attractive ideas.

Soft Money

In recent years, campaign contributions have begun to take new forms that pose even greater dangers than PAC money to the integrity of the political process. Aided by a series of rulings by the Federal Elections Commission, contributors can now give unlimited amounts of so-called soft money to the Democratic and Republican parties to finance their "party building" activities. Such contributions were modest through most of the 1980s but mushroomed in the 1990s. Donors began to give many millions of dollars of soft money, which parties increasingly used to help fund specific election campaigns. In 1996, Philip Morris alone gave $2.5 million to the Republican Party, while R. J. R. Nabisco contributed $1.2 million. In the same year, the Communications Workers of America and the American Federation of State, County, and Municipal Employees gave more than $1 million each to the Democrats.[56]

Business organizations must expect to exert *some* influence on government decisions in return for such large contributions. Certainly, leaders in the House and Senate cannot help being aware of the hefty sums that come to their parties from particular industries and special interests. They are unlikely to forget these contributions when they decide which legislative priorities to pursue. It strains common sense to think that party leaders will press their colleagues in Congress to enact legislation that offends major funding sources, save in rare cases where popular support is so strong that failing to act would carry grave political risks.

At the very least, the existence of such large donations creates a suspicion that public officials can be bought. What else can Americans think when newspapers repeatedly carry stories of large soft-money contributions (accounting for a total of approximately one-half billion dollars in the 2000 presidential campaign alone)? By all indications, such gifts are a major cause of the corrosive cynicism that so many Americans currently feel toward their government and its elected officials.

Independent Expenditures and Issue Advocacy Ads

Another problem that has emerged in recent years is the large amount of money spent in election campaigns by interest groups acting independently of candidates or political parties. Sponsors use such funds either for TV ads and other communications that expressly support or attack a specific candidate by name (in which case contributors must disclose the source) or for "issue advocacy" ads addressing important questions in a political campaign without explicitly taking sides. The line between these two categories has become extremely blurred. For example, during the 1996 congressional elections, organized labor spent more than $30 million on issue advocacy ads that were plainly intended to persuade people to vote for specific Democratic candidates. So long as the ads do not expressly advocate the election or defeat of a specific candidate, however, they do not violate current campaign finance laws and sponsors are not required to reveal their identity.

It is difficult to estimate the impact of such expenditures. They are probably less effective than direct contributions for gaining influence with candidates. As for their ability to harm candidates, the jury is still out. Such tactics can easily backfire, because voters will often resent the efforts of outsiders to influence elections. Almost none of the Republican lawmakers targeted by organized labor in 1996 lost their seats. Word that the AFL-CIO was making major efforts to defeat the designated candidates simply caused business to respond by contributing large sums of its own. On the other hand, not every candidate threatened by issue advocacy ads will have supporters wealthy enough to come forward with large offsetting expenditures. Nor will incumbents welcome the prospect of having a well-heeled interest group spend substantial amounts of money to defeat them. The mere threat of independent expenditures may lead some lawmakers to refrain from taking positions that might antagonize powerful organizations.

Grassroots Lobbying

Apart from the growth of soft money and issue advocacy, recent developments have brought about one further change in the way that conventional interest groups go about trying to influence legislation. With the growth of subcommittees and the declining authority of committee chairs, power in Congress has become more diffuse, so that lobbyists find it harder to have an impact simply by talking to a few key senators or House members. In addition, as public disaffection with politics has increased, lawmakers seem to be paying closer attention to the views of their constituents. Opinion polls count more heavily. Editorials and other communications from influential constituents have more weight these days, when voters seem so restive and dissatisfied. Observing these trends, interest groups have increasingly turned to grassroots efforts to mobilize popular support for their legislative agendas.

The use of grassroots lobbying has grown enormously in recent years.[57] At times, lobbyists will mount such campaigns to show how many voters support their position. More often, they seek to dramatize the intensity of the support. As one commentator has reported, quoting a trade association lobbyist: "A lot of members of Congress are nervous, and they know that everyone who's going to pick up the phone, or take the trouble to write a letter, is not only going to be a knowledgeable voter, and an active voter, but an active person who's going to go out and change people's minds."[58]

In the hands of skillful practitioners, grassroots campaigns can achieve considerable size and sophistication. The American Association of Retired People, the National Education Association, and other well-funded organizations with large national constituencies can use electronic means to produce thousands of letters to Congress in a matter of days. Telephone banks allow interest groups to contact supporters, explain an issue to them, and switch their calls automatically to telephones in the White House or in legislative offices on Capitol Hill. High-powered organizations, such as the National Federation of Independent Business (NFIB), which has more than 600,000 members in every part of the country, can buy time to attack any bill they oppose on TV stations in the districts of key members of Congress, while placing Op-Ed pieces and even editorials in supportive local newspapers. Aggressive interest groups can mobilize influential friends and supporters of a key member of Congress, getting them to write personal letters or make telephone calls. Pressure of this kind is often the most effective method of all because it uses the resource that is most important to legislators: their base of voter support.

The real problem with grassroots lobbying is the same one raised by political contributions. Both methods give undue power to organizations that possess enough money and sophistication to develop the contacts, the key supporters, and the advanced technology to carry out effective mobilizing efforts. Grassroots campaigns can have greater influence only as more interest groups begin to involve themselves in elections and use their money, members, and organizing skills to back candidates sympathetic to their needs. Such tactics could have an even greater impact on political elections than they do in the legislative process. If only 10–20 percent of all eligible voters go to the polls in primary elections, an interest group with money, organizing skill, and a strong base of local support can have an effect far beyond the size of its actual membership in the general population.

There is no telling how far this new grassroots politicking will go. The Christian Coalition made considerable progress for a time in gaining control of state Republican organizations and electing delegates to the Republican convention.[59] Consider the words of Jack Faris, describing what he calls the "endgame" of his organization, the National Federation of Independent Business:

> Our goal for the year 2000 for the election of the President of the United States is to have candidates of both parties who are sold out for small business and free enterprise. That's our goal. In the Senate, our goal is to have at least sixty members that either own small businesses or who have proven by their voting records that they understand what's good for small business. We want two hundred fifty votes in the House of Representatives either to be small-business owners and/or those who supported small-business owners. That's our goal. And we don't care whether they're D's [Democrats] or R's [Republicans].[60]

According to veteran reporters David Broder and Haynes Johnson, the NFIB had a major part in seeing to it that more than half the new Republican House members in the sweep of 1994 had small-business backgrounds. The "endgame," it appears, is more than just a game.

The Effects of Countervailing Power

The fact that money and organizing power count heavily in the American political system would scarcely have surprised the grand architect of the U.S. Constitution, James Madison. Even in 1789, Madison feared the rise of selfish factions that could gain enough power in the government to impose their will on others. His hope, explained in Federalist Paper 10, lay in creating a larger national polity with enough factions that none would have the strength to dominate. Building on this notion, pluralist scholars two centuries later talked of a nation with so many competing interest groups that each would be countered by others, leaving lawmakers free to cast their votes in the interests of the country as a whole.

These hopes have come to pass to a degree that would have amazed Madison. By the early 1990s, the number of PACs had grown to almost 5,000, and the ranks of Washington lobbyists had swelled to more than 23,000.[61] While most of the new organizations represent business, many are public advocacy groups that champion a wide range of interests, including those of consumers, children, poor people, and ethnic minorities.

Today—just as the pluralists hoped—when important measures come before Congress, powerful organizations often joust with one another, diminishing the risk that any single group will exert decisive influence. As Representative Barney Frank observed, remarking on the effect of PAC contributions on policymaking in Congress: "There's money any way you vote."[62] Major business interests confront a formidable array of advocacy groups representing consumers, environmentalists, women, minorities, public health concerns, and many more. These public-interest organizations are often far from insubstantial. A recent survey of twenty-four public-advocacy groups found that the average size of staff was 132 and the average annual budget $14 million.[63] Although few of them feature active members and strong grassroots organizations, they have certainly made their voice heard in Washington. Whereas many of them were treated as radical upstarts twenty-five years ago, they are now regarded as credible sources by the media and appear regularly to testify and submit information to Congress.[64] Indeed, they have become the most frequently cited sources on policy issues by national television reporters.[65]

The existence of so many countervailing organizations undoubtedly helps keep powerful interests from influencing policy in harmful ways. At the same time, competition among rival interest groups will not consistently yield constructive results even if our society becomes more thoroughly organized than it is already. As former President Jimmy Carter once explained, "The national interest is not always the sum of all our single and special interests."[66]

One reason for Carter's remark is that the prospect of losing existing benefits will normally arouse voters and the interest groups that represent them much more than the prospect of gaining equivalent benefits not yet enjoyed. Similarly, the few who profit from a special tax break or subsidy usually care a lot about preserving their benefits, while the multitude of taxpayers who share the cost are hardly aware of the burden, let alone willing to organize to escape it. For these reasons, as Jonathan Rauch points out, "driven by the demands of the organized lobbies, the government struggles desperately to keep going everything it ever tried for every group it ever aided. And so, lacking any better option, Washington just piles new programs on top of old programs. Laws are passed, policies adopted, programs added or expanded—things 'get done'; but as layer is dropped upon layer, the whole accumulated mass becomes gradually less rational and less flexible."[67] Eventually, the system becomes clogged by vested interests, defending all manner of special subsidies and corporate welfare provisions. Their cumulative weight threatens to retard progress by leaving the government with too little money for new initiatives that promise greater benefits for the public.*

Another flaw in the pluralist vision is that even in a political system as crowded as ours with organized groups, effective countervailing pressures do not exist in every case. More than 40 percent of all interest groups cannot identify any organized opposition, according to one national survey.[68] Corporate and industry PACs often proceed unopposed when they are seeking not to change some major policy or law but simply to gain special tax preferences or other narrow advantages. In such cases, their natural adversaries may be individual taxpayers who are far too dispersed to mount any serious opposition.

It is equally clear that some important interests are not nearly as well mobilized as others. A few, such as children, cannot vote even though they have a large stake in many policy decisions being taken today. Others, notably the poor and the chronically unemployed,

---

* Some authors suggest that interest groups will eventually bring government to a standstill; see, for example, Jonathan Rauch, *Demosclerosis: The Silent Killer of American Government* (1994). Such predictions seem a bit extreme. In fact, careful research indicates that Congress does manage to kill a large number of old programs every year, though not as many as the new programs it creates. See Robert M. Stein and Kenneth N. Bickers, *Perpetuating the Pork Barrel: Policy Subsystems and American Democracy* (1995), who report that Congress killed an average of thirty-six programs per year from 1971 to 1990 while creating an average of fifty-seven, and that the vast bulk of increased public spending came from a few well-established entitlement programs such as Social Security and Medicare. Moreover, Rauch's analysis does not give sufficient weight to the effects of economic growth in bringing new resources to the government. Thus, his diagnosis seemed more telling in the early 1990s, when growth was sluggish and huge deficits put a ceiling on government expenditures, than it did in 2000, when deficits turned to surpluses and the economy grew more rapidly.

have the right to vote and organize politically but lack the will and the resources to do so. Much the same is true of workers in low-wage jobs. Compared with Americans with incomes over $75,000, individuals with incomes under $15,000 are barely one-third as likely to be active members of any organization, little more than half as likely to vote in elections, and only one-tenth as likely to make a political contribution.[69] In one survey of interest groups in Washington, 80 percent represented business and the professions, while only 5 percent were citizen advocacy organizations and only 3 percent represented the poor and disadvantaged.[70] With such unequal resources, poorly organized interests are bound to lose out to more powerful, well-financed organizations.

Interest Groups in Perspective

In an ideal democracy, all citizens should have an equal opportunity to influence public policy, whether they happen to be rich or poor. But guarding the political process from the uneven influence of money is no simple task, as the discussion above attests. On balance, what does the record tell us about how much advantage wealth and organization give to powerful special interests?

Several groups of social scientists have dogged the footsteps of legislators through the entire process of getting particular bills through Congress to determine the role that special interests play.[71] By and large, their findings are reassuring. The investigators have consistently found that organized groups have much less impact than most Americans assume. More often than not, the authors report that lobbyists spend much of their time communicating with their own constituents, keeping them informed, and seeking their approval of positions to place before Congress. When lobbyists do go to the Hill, they tend to meet with lawmakers (or their aides) who are already reliable supporters. They devote surprisingly little time to trying to persuade neutral legislators whose votes are likely to be crucial to the bill in question.

Other scholars have looked at entire fields of legislative activity to determine the success of special interests in shaping federal policy to suit their purposes. In a recent work of this kind, Gary Mucciaroni studied the impact of producer groups on developments over several decades in the fields of foreign trade, agriculture, deregulation of industry, and tax policy.[72] During this period, lobbyists clearly won some victories. In the end, however, Mucciaroni concludes: "Although producer-group fortunes vary greatly across time and policy areas, on balance these groups now find themselves on the short end of the public policy stick as often as not. In only one of the four policy areas examined in this book—agriculture—does the persistent, entrenched clientelism of old still hold sway. . . . Even in the case of agriculture [where producer groups were most influential], it is not at all clear that the ability of farm interests to capture parts of the government was more important for the maintenance of agricultural programs than were public sympathy for family farmers and party competition in the Senate."[73]

The scattered evidence available also suggests that strong interest groups have *less* influence in the United States than in other industrialized countries.[74] For example, farmers in Europe and Japan have generally managed to obtain larger government subsidies and to receive more trade protection than is true in America. Environmental restrictions in Europe appear to be no more strict, and in some cases are even less so, than in the United States. Japanese businessmen have often extracted greater concessions from politicians in return for their campaign contributions than firms in this country. Similarly, American industries have generally failed to do as well as their European counterparts in obtaining import protections, while retail establishments abroad have managed to secure many more government restrictions to shield them from competition than have merchants in the United States.

Overall, therefore, well-financed interest groups do not seem to have been as much of a threat over the past few decades as popular legend would suggest. They have been much more successful at obtaining small favors and limited concessions than at altering important policies in major ways. They have been better at blocking changes in the status quo than at getting new proposals enacted. Many of their victories have been only temporary, and few have succeeded for very long against the force of aroused public opinion. When they have had substantial influence, as in the case of the farm organizations, the American Association of Retired People, or the

National Rifle Association, their power has often come more from the large number of active voters they represent than from the money they contribute to political parties and candidates.

While these conclusions are reassuring up to a point, they in no way justify complacency. Well-financed organizations representing business, labor, the professions, parts of agriculture, and other special interests have still had much more influence than they deserve. Even if interest groups cannot control major policies for long, the cumulative effect of countless small concessions and special benefits can add up to many billions of dollars and bring about a host of compromises that hamper the effectiveness of government programs. The tendency of interest groups to support sitting legislators has discouraged able challengers by further increasing the formidable advantages of incumbency. In addition, the presence of powerful interests in so many areas of society has made the unorganized more vulnerable than they would otherwise be by raising the odds that, in straitened times, any necessary sacrifices will fall disproportionately on the weak.

The dangers posed by interest groups have recently become much greater still, with the recent surge of soft-money contributions, independent expenditures, and expensive grassroots efforts to influence public opinion. Most studies of interest group influence come from an earlier era, when political action committees could give only a few thousand dollars to any legislator. No one knows the impact of six- and seven-figure donations to political parties, but the prognosis can hardly be encouraging. Whatever their actual influence on policy, the mere existence of such massive political donations is enough to provoke widespread suspicion that elected officials are corrupt and impervious to the wishes of ordinary citizens. For all these reasons, the threat of interest groups and their campaign contributions to our political system has become serious enough to warrant a determined effort to level the playing field by minimizing the power of money in public affairs.

False Arrests

Having reviewed the evidence, what can one make of the serious charges the public has leveled against politicians, the media, and interest groups? The choice of suspects is understandable. The accused are the most visible participants in a game the public heartily dislikes. Yet once the facts are carefully sorted through, the case is weaker than most people think. Politicians are rarely incompetent; in fact, they tend to be very well educated, highly intelligent, and remarkably energetic. The media have not seriously damaged the political process, nor are they principally to blame for the negativism and triviality of much reporting on civic issues. Of the three suspects, lobbyists appear to be the most culpable, but even their influence was greatly exaggerated until recently, when their campaign contributions and grassroots lobbying began to reach a size sufficient to merit serious concern.

Some critics will still insist that political leaders are at fault for lacking the vision to inspire citizens and restore their flagging confidence in government. Others will claim that the media have failed us by not finding reporters who can write with sufficient verve and imagination to lure the public away from sitcoms and quiz shows long enough to attend to politics and public affairs. But arguments of this kind are hardly fair. Now and then, politicians or journalists may appear on the scene with the rare ability to light up the sky and lift the standards of their craft. But it is difficult to imagine any political system or media enterprise producing such paragons more than very occasionally. As a result, to assume that such a high standard is possible or to blame politicians or the media for failing to achieve it seems unrealistic in the extreme. No democracy in recent times has consistently managed to produce political leaders or journalists who can perform at such a level.

Rather than blame our political leadership or our television producers and newspaper publishers, the American people should assume some responsibility themselves for much of what distresses them about politicians, lobbyists, and the media. Their lack of interest and short attention span have a lot to do with the shallow, sensational, scandal-ridden coverage of the media. Their cynicism and distrust encourage the negative tactics that crop up in so many political campaigns. The apathy of middle-of-the-road Americans and their unwillingness to vote magnify the impact of "astroturf" lobbying and help lobbyists to win more victories than they deserve.

The final flaw in the case against the usual suspects is that the charges against them are not linked convincingly to the failures of the federal government to achieve the goals most Americans affirm. If political leaders in other democracies seem no more accomplished than our own, if their media are equally negative, and if business, labor, and farm groups abroad are at least as powerful as their American counterparts, how can incompetent leadership, cynical journalists, or scheming special interests explain why other nations so often surpass us in attaining goals that command wide popular support? If legislators can sometimes seem unresponsive, columnists excessively carping and shallow, and lobbyists devious and self-serving, what do these failings have to do with the shortage of quality childcare, or the persistence of hunger in America, or the inadequacies of our public schools? The public's accusations leave these problems unexplained. Yet it is such problems that most need explaining, since it is their continued existence that reveals most clearly how the government has failed to meet the hopes and expectations of the American people.

4

WHAT DO WE NEED TO EXPLAIN?

ASKING PEOPLE WHAT AILS the federal government is a bit like asking Boston Red Sox fans why their team isn't doing better. There are plenty of ideas—some ingenious, some helpful, some bizarre—but none offers a fully adequate explanation for the team's performance. Much the same is true of government. As the fate of President Clinton's healthcare bill so aptly revealed, pundits have offered many theories to explain why the government does not work better. Most of them help account for some of the disappointments. Nevertheless, remembering all the different fields of activity summarized in Chapter 1, how is one to know which of the theories are most useful in explaining the many instances in which America's performance lags behind that of other leading nations?

Thinking further about the Red Sox may help to answer this question. In evaluating a baseball team, analysts would never try to explain its record by trying to figure out in detail exactly what went wrong in each and every game the club has lost. Such an effort would soon break down under the unmanageable weight of particulars. But seasoned observers would hardly propose theories about the team's performance without first looking at its record carefully enough to spot the recurrent weaknesses that seem to account for most of the defeats. Have the losses resulted from a repeated failure to hold a lead in the late innings? Or an inability to hit for extra bases? Or a series of errors by a porous infield?

As Chapter 1 makes clear, our government, like the Red Sox, has had some notable successes, but it has also suffered a number of setbacks. Before conjuring up more theories, we would do well to think back on these examples and try to discover what kinds of institutional problems, legislative errors, or administrative difficulties occur most frequently in the many instances and areas of activity in which America's policies have fallen short of what other leading nations have achieved. To this end, the pages that follow describe four basic weaknesses that crop up repeatedly in the fields in which America's performance has lagged. Explaining the reasons for these weaknesses will go a long way toward understanding why our government has failed so often to accomplish as much as other advanced democracies in helping to fulfill the wishes of its citizens.

The Design of Legislative Programs

No one can study government programs in the United States without being struck by the frequent clumsiness in their design. Some federal programs, such as our healthcare system, consist of many parts that seem disjointed and badly put together. Other government initiatives, such as urban development and food safety, are divided into scores of duplicate programs that cause much confusion and unnecessary administrative expense. Often, federal expenditures seem wildly extravagant—building hospitals that are not really needed, aiding "disadvantaged" students in affluent suburban schools, subsidizing large businesses with ample profit margins. At other times, programs contain goals and timetables that are much more ambitious than the funding they receive, or implementation bogs down in procedures so cumbersome and slow as to seem almost willfully clumsy and inefficient.

Because these flaws take so many forms, one could easily fail to notice a common underlying theme. The principal problem is not that Washington bureaucrats are unable to administer the laws effectively, although examples of administrative incompetence undoubtedly exist. Nor is it that judges are too quick to interfere or interest groups too skillful in blocking implementation, though these things can also happen. Rather, the thread that runs most prominently through the deficiencies of federal programs is a singular lack of sound legislative design.

Good legislative design has four important characteristics. *Objectives* should be clear, consistent, and realistic. Programs should embody a *strategy* properly conceived to achieve their intended goals. The *administrative machinery* should be of a kind well suited to carrying out the strategy. Finally, the legislature should provide enough *resources* to implement the strategy effectively without undue waste. Unfortunately, important legislation in the United States is repeatedly marred by failures to live up to these standards.

Federal statutes often lack clear objectives and thus fail at the outset to give adequate direction to those who must administer the laws. Occasionally, Congress has even pursued conflicting aims in addressing the same subject. For example, lawmakers regulating savings-and-loan banks relaxed controls over the kinds of investments these institutions could make while continuing to insure depositors against any losses that occurred. Eventually, many savings-and-loans took excessive risks and went bankrupt, leaving the government to pay the bills. In the case of tobacco, Congress has taken a number of steps to discourage smoking while still maintaining generous subsidies to sustain tobacco growers.

More often, the announced objectives are simply not feasible. In regulating the environment, for example, Congress has repeatedly established deadlines described by scholars as falling "somewhere between the merely unrealistic and the wholly fantastic."[1] Clean-air laws have frequently set standards that many cities could not possibly achieve, such as a requirement in the 1970 act that big cities lower their levels of carbon monoxide, hydrocarbons, and ozone by 90 percent before 1978. The Clean Water Act of 1972 proclaimed that *all* pollutants into waterways must be eliminated by 1985. The notorious "Delaney clause" in the 1958 amendments to the Pure Food and Drug Act required the Food and Drug Administration to prohibit additives containing any carcinogens whatsoever, regardless of how insignificant the risk.

At a pettier level, many bills emerging from Congress are larded with provisions to achieve purposes unrelated to those of the main body of legislation—a new training program for displaced workers, a special tax dispensation for some group of companies, even a new post office or courthouse for the district of a key member of the legislative committee. Congress, as a body, rarely considers these items individually or attempts to weigh their costs and benefits against other possible uses of public funds. Often, some well-placed lawmaker inserts a special benefit at the last minute or hides it deep in a thick statute so that it will escape rigorous scrutiny by colleagues.

The methods lawmakers use to achieve their legislative goals also leave much to be desired. In some fields, Congress has enacted laws containing several strategies that conflict with one another. For example, in the National Affordable Housing Act of 1990, interested committees introduced three separate proposals embodying radically different theories about the nature of the problem and how it could be solved. One advocated an increase in existing programs, another called for new programs of construction, and the third sought to distribute rental vouchers to the needy. Instead of debating these approaches and deciding which seemed best, Congress responded by including all three in the final bill. At other times, legislators have prescribed different methods to achieve the same goal even though the methods clearly contradict one another. In the Clean Air Act of 1990, for example, one provision established a cost-benefit criterion for regulation by the Environmental Protection Agency (EPA), while another imposed on companies a strict—and highly inefficient—requirement to use the best available technology. On other occasions, Congress enacts laws containing strategies that are at odds with the announced goals. For example, in establishing price supports for agriculture, lawmakers repeatedly emphasized the aim of saving the family farm while providing benefits and supports that directed 75 percent of the payments to the 15 percent of farms grossing more than $100,000 per year.

Periodically, the legislative strategy breaks down because Congress enacts rules but attaches remedies so mild that companies and individuals find it advantageous to break the law. Under the Fair Labor Standards Act, for example, penalties were kept so low for many years that calculating employers stood to gain by deliberately ignoring the minimum-wage requirement. In the regulation of television programming, the only remedy provided was the revocation of a television station's license, a penalty so drastic and so difficult politically that the Federal Communications Commission had no effective sanction at all with which to enforce its standards.

In other instances, Congress has imposed agency requirements that are obviously unrealistic. In several environmental laws, for example, Congress has stipulated that the EPA take no account of costs in setting standards. Such a provision contradicts human nature and defies good sense. The practical result is to force regulators to impose excessively onerous rules or resort to various subterfuges to disguise their use of cost data.

In still other legislative programs, lawmakers have created administrative machinery so complicated that effective implementation becomes all but impossible. In reconstituting public television, for example, Congress did not establish a single national entity, as virtually every other advanced democracy has done. Instead, it created "a hydra-headed structure of competing authorities: the Corporation for Public Broadcasting to hold the money; the Public Broadcasting Service to gather and deliver the programming, and the American Public Television Stations to lobby Congress and protect the interests of the stations."[2] The result, according to a former public-television executive, was a "bureaucratic nightmare of competing entities and overlapping functions, which are wasteful of human, financial, and technical resources, sap creative energy, blur the lines of responsibility, and divert the medium's attention from its principal mission of providing quality programming."[3]

Having enacted new programs and created administrative machinery to carry them out, Congress frequently provides insufficient funding to achieve its stated purposes. The Housing Act of 1949 announced a goal of building 675,000 to 810,000 new units in the next four years, but provided so little money that the goal was not achieved for nearly fifteen years. In the case of environmental regulation, according to economist Paul Portney, "Congress has consistently given the EPA more assignments than resources," thus contributing to repeated failures by the agency to meet the deadlines Congress itself prescribed.[4] At times, needed funds are withheld even though larger investments would save money. For example, the Special Supplemental Nutrition Program for Women, Infants, and Children (WIC) has repeatedly received insufficient funding to cover all eligible persons, despite independent studies finding that each dollar invested returns more than three dollars in lower medical costs and other savings.[5] Similarly, tens of billions of dollars are lost each year to healthcare fraud, yet programs of detection and prevention received only minimal support until recently.

One might ask whether inadequate funding merely reflects the tendency of Americans to want more programs than they are willing to pay for. This is only partly correct. Although many initiatives are underfunded, legislators often insist on expanding programs to benefit many more people than those truly in need. Thus, in providing funds to supplement the education of disadvantaged children, Congress allowed so much aid to flow to relatively prosperous school districts that communities in genuine need of help ended up with too little money to do a proper job. Similarly, President Clinton's promise to put 100,000 more policemen on the streets did not result in carefully allocating new patrolmen to the high-crime areas where they could do the most good. Instead, Congress spread the money widely enough to include many localities in which the need was much less acute.

If the problems described here were simply a matter of inelegant draftsmanship or minor administrative confusion, they would scarcely bear repeating. But faulty legislative design is hugely expensive both in money and results. For example, through the gradual accumulation of ad hoc initiatives, Congress has built an ungainly healthcare system that annually costs at least $1,000 per person more than the next most expensive system in the world, yet still manages to leave more than 40 million Americans without any medical insurance.[6] In seeking to protect citizens from accidents and disease, federal lawmakers have enacted so many separate programs and divided responsibility for them among so many different legislative committees that money is spent with little regard to relative risk. As a result, the government allocates tens of billions of dollars more each year than it needs to spend to preserve the number of lives currently saved under existing programs.[7] In regulating the workplace, Congress has appropriated so much less than it would cost to enforce its rules effectively throughout the economy that many laws, such as antidiscrimination statutes and work-safety requirements, have very little practical effect for the hundreds of thousands of smaller firms that officials never find time to inspect. In all these ways, faulty legislative design emerges as the principal cause of the ineffectiveness and waste that anger so many taxpayers.

Poorly crafted legislation occurs in such a wide variety of programs that it is tempting to stop the discussion at this point. If the reasons for shoddy design were understood, could there be anything left to explain to account for the deficiencies of government? As it happens, there *is* more that warrants explanation. In several important areas of government activity, the weaknesses of design consistently take such a special form that further analysis is called for. One such case is the broad field of regulation.

Regulating the Economy

Among the industrial nations of the world, the United States is exceptional for the anger and resentment stirred up by official efforts to regulate the economy. Small-business owners and corporate executives are often virulent in their complaints. Most Americans have declared quite consistently over the years that they would prefer less regulation of business and that government intervention usually creates more problems than it solves.[8] Such sentiments echo an even wider body of opinion that the federal government has become too powerful and exercises too much control over the lives of ordinary people.

Despite these criticisms, it is hard to come up with a list of specific regulations that Americans would agree to repeal or even to cut back. Busing would doubtless qualify, but busing was a creature of the courts rather than a product of Congress and has, in any event, been largely discontinued. Affirmative action is often criticized, but a close reading of opinion polls suggests that what Americans truly dislike are racial preferences in awarding jobs or contracts rather than affirmative action as originally conceived by Congress (that is, setting nonbinding goals and making special efforts to identify promising female and minority candidates without resorting to quotas or basing the final hiring decision on race or gender).

Except for a few examples of this kind, Americans clearly support most specific types of regulation. Opinion polls show strong, persistent approval for such staple items as environmental protection, health and safety regulations (even seatbelts), antitrust and labor laws, truth-in-advertising requirements, and other consumer safeguards.[9] Why are people so critical if they cannot point to a list of unnecessary laws that they would like to do without? Perhaps their complaints merely reflect a general suspicion of government. Perhaps they object to the *way* the government regulates rather than the existence of regulations per se. Opinion surveys do not give a clear answer.

Throughout much of the twentieth century, most close observers agreed on the principal weakness of American regulatory policy: too often, officials were "captured" by the industries they were supposed to control, so that federal law became an instrument for stifling competition and keeping out potential rivals.[10] However, with the deregulation that has occurred since the late 1970s in industries such as airlines, trucking, and telecommunications and with the growth of interest groups representing consumer and environmental concerns, this charge has lost much of its force.

Critics today are more likely to complain that regulations are wasteful. Either they cost more than any benefits they bring, or they misallocate resources by spending too much on problems that are hard to remedy and too little on problems that could be eliminated or reduced more cheaply. For example, one survey of water projects by the Environmental Protection Agency revealed that actual cleanup costs for rivers and harbors were often *several times* greater than the minimum amounts required to accomplish the same result.[11] Studies on allocating regulatory resources have arrived at equally startling findings. Analysts report huge variations among government agencies and individual programs in the cost-effectiveness of their programs. Thus, the EPA regulates benzene emissions at a cost of $19 million per life saved, while efforts to provide regular mammograms for the 70 percent of women who do not currently receive them could save additional lives for a rate per life of less than $17,000.[12]

The potential benefits of improved allocation are quite substantial. For example, one recent review of 185 federal programs claimed that redistributing existing resources could save more than 60,000 additional lives per year without spending any more money.[13] Alternatively, the government could save more than $30 billion per year and still preserve as many lives as are currently saved merely by adopting the simple rule of investing the available funds only in interventions costing less than $16,500 for each life preserved.

Of course, estimates of this kind are somewhat misleading, because there are practical limits to the efficiency attainable in a democracy. Without a massive program of reeducation, people will not necessarily approve of moving money from programs attacking highly visible risks to programs involving less publicized dangers, even if such shifts would make it possible to save more lives for the same amount of money. Still, the existing misallocations are sufficiently serious and widespread that considerable gains in efficiency could undoubtedly be made without seeking changes that would encounter popular resistance of this kind.

The second principal weakness of America's regulatory system has to do with the procedures by which rules are enacted and enforced. Simply put, the process costs too much, takes too long, is far too rigid, and antagonizes too many people in return for results that rarely exceed and often lag behind those of other leading democracies. Looking further, one can discern at least four important differences that distinguish America's approach to regulation and give rise to many of the vociferous complaints that critics level against the system.*

A prime distinguishing feature of America's regulatory process is, first of all, that officials rely heavily on methods of "command and control"—issuing rules, conducting inspections, citing violations, and imposing fines. Typically, congressional committees and regulatory agencies allow interested groups to present evidence and submit comments before promulgating rules. Unlike officials in most other advanced democracies, however, American lawmakers usually decide what requirements should apply without making serious efforts to broker an agreed result through patient negotiations among the interested parties. Once the rules are in place, inspectors tend to en-

---

* In recent years, the federal government has been making efforts to experiment in ways that depart from the distinctive regulatory style described in these pages. But such efforts—tradeable emissions permits, negotiated rulemaking, and so on—are as yet utilized in too small a proportion of regulatory actions to alter fundamentally what is said below. The new initiatives are considered in some detail in Chapter 12, along with other possibilities for regulatory reform.

force them unilaterally rather than working cooperatively with individual firms to solve problems, share innovative ideas, or search for solutions that take account of circumstances unique to particular plants. In most other industrial nations, inspectors try harder to achieve voluntary compliance through informal agreement, using penalties only as a last resort.

Another special characteristic of the U.S. system is the rigidity with which rules are applied. Since the late 1960s, regulatory statutes have become much more specific, prescribing standards, deadlines, procedures, and methods of operation in much greater detail. Legislative committees have monitored the work of administrative agencies more closely. Judicial review has tended to be more searching, permitting judges to look more carefully at the reasons agencies give for their decisions and to defer less readily to administrative judgments. Agency heads in turn have been more reluctant to delegate authority to inspectors in the field. Instead, Washington issues detailed rules and prescriptions that inspectors must enforce without much room for deviation or accommodation at the plant level. In all these respects, the United States has departed from the tendency in other advanced democracies to enact more general legislative rules and to subject executive officials to less exacting oversight.

The third important difference distinguishing our regulatory system from those of most other industrial nations is its exceptionally fragmented nature. At the national level, many overlapping programs frequently coexist, each with its own bureaucracy and its own set of rules and procedures. Often, state and even local agencies regulate the same activity. Thus, there are dozens of separate laws and administrative units that attempt to ensure pure food, or provide a clean environment, or protect Americans against carcinogens.

The fourth and final hallmark of our system is the extensive opportunity it provides to contest unwelcome rulings. Disgruntled parties can seek redress from higher authorities in Congress, the White House, the regulatory agency, and above all the judiciary. Over the past few decades, rights of appeal to the courts have been extended to parties other than companies and individuals directly harmed by regulatory actions. As a result, environmental groups, consumer organizations, and other public-interest advocates can now bring suit to force government agencies to abide by legislative guidelines and timetables. In most other countries the right to sue is more strictly limited, the permissible grounds for complaint are much narrower, and efforts to overturn administrative decisions are much less frequent.

On the surface, the American style of regulation seems quite straightforward and effective. Experienced regulatory specialists issue rules to carry out the will of Congress after receiving evidence and arguments from interested parties. Inspectors go forth to visit firms and secure compliance with the regulations, issuing fines or injunctions to those who do not behave as the law requires. Ample opportunities exist for aggrieved parties to appeal official decisions in order to correct errors and prevent arbitrary actions.

In practice, however, the results have been far from satisfactory. The rules developed for virtually every field of regulation have become more and more intricate and hard to understand. At times, they make no practical sense when applied to the specific conditions of individual companies that have to comply. Not surprisingly, they also provoke a great deal of litigation. Rather than diminishing as the applicable rules grow more familiar, the volume of lawsuits often continues to rise. Thus, the entire regulatory system turns out to be very slow and extremely expensive to administer, incurring legal costs far above those of other leading democracies.

These difficulties might be easy enough to bear if the system produced impressive results in reducing accidents, curbing pollution, or accomplishing other regulatory goals. Alas, success of this kind is rare. Labor laws in the United States have not been nearly as effective as those of countries such as Japan, Sweden, or Germany in avoiding intimidation and other forms of interference with the right of workers to organize. A series of studies have found that the Occupational Safety and Health Administration (OSHA) has reduced the incidence of job injuries very little during the past thirty years.[14] Environmental regulation has made considerable progress but still has not achieved as much as authorities have accomplished in Japan and several West European countries.[15] Laws requiring employers to make reasonable efforts to accommodate the handicapped have had little if any effect on the percentage of Americans with disabilities in the workforce.[16] Traffic safety regulators have been much slower than their opposite numbers in Europe to enact some of the most basic safeguards.[17]

Although the more consensual modes of regulation practiced abroad seem harmonious by comparison, they are not without drawbacks of their own.[18] In other countries, business and labor have often succeeded in persuading the government to enact restrictions that hamper competition and keep out new rivals that might bring better quality and lower prices. Because appeals to the courts are limited, mistakes are not as likely to be corrected (although the more collaborative, consensus-based process abroad makes mistakes less likely to occur). Groups that have organized in recent decades to protect the environment, consumer interests, and women's rights are not always invited to participate in government-sponsored consultations and thus have a hard time making their voices heard. Because legislatures in other countries are much more thinly staffed than congressional committees in the United States, they cannot readily conduct effective oversight over highly technical forms of regulation, such as the control of toxic waste.

These weaknesses are not trivial. At the same time, it is clear that regulation overseas has tended to be more sensitive to local company conditions, more expeditious, and less costly by far than the lawyer-ridden, document-laden procedures common in the United States. The cooperative methods used abroad have also created much less hostility and elicited more voluntary compliance. As one American business school professor declared after a comprehensive study of British environmental policy, "In scores of interviews that I conducted with corporate executives in Great Britain, including several with the subsidiaries of American-based multinationals, not one could cite an occasion when his firm had been required to do anything it regarded as unreasonable."[19] A similar statement would be inconceivable in the United States.

Such harmony would come at a stiff price if it meant that companies abroad could do pretty much as they pleased. But on the whole, there is little indication that the regulatory process in other leading democracies has been coopted and undermined by industry in areas such as consumer protection, healthcare quality, job safety, or the environment. Most scholars who have studied regulation overseas report that standards are usually as strict in Europe and Japan as in America and that companies are at least as scrupulous in seeking to comply.[20] More important, comparative data seem to show that other advanced nations have frequently accomplished more than the United States in curbing pollution, promoting collective bargaining, aiding the handicapped, protecting consumers, and reducing workplace injuries.[21] Hence, it is not at all clear just what we have gained for all the costs and aggravations of our contentious, adversarial form of regulation.

Protecting the Interests of Working People

Like their counterparts in other advanced countries, working people in the United States would like to enjoy certain basic forms of security.* They want to earn enough to free themselves and their families from poverty when they work full-time on a regular basis. Like other Americans, they need reasonable access to health care when they or their family members fall ill and adequate income after their retirement. By large majorities, they would also like the *opportunity* to join a union (or some organization to represent their interests) if they wish to do so.[22] They seek protection from arbitrary treatment by employers, including redress if they are fired unjustifiably from their job. (That is why virtually all collective bargaining agreements include prohibitions against termination without just cause.) They would like to have a reasonably safe working environment, unemployment insurance to tide them over if they are laid off for reasons beyond their control, and training and advice to help them find a new job. These aspirations have grown keener as the uncertainties of the contemporary global economy increase and opportunities for secure lifetime employment diminish. As President Reagan's chief pollster Richard Wirthlin recently declared, "Ameri-

---

* It is impossible to give a precise definition of "working people" for the purposes of this book. The term should not include those who are prosperous enough that they can readily take care of their own critical needs (adequate pensions, healthcare benefits, and so on) or consistently hold jobs that routinely provide adequate pensions, health coverage, even severance pay. Nor does it include those who do not normally have regular work. In general, those to whom this section applies tend to have below-average yearly earnings, modest work skills, and something less than a college degree. Households headed by persons answering this description make up at least half of the population under sixty-five years of age.

cans are seeking reassurance for their own peace of mind and per-sonal security. One of the most dominant values is: I want to feel secure."[23]

In light of these aspirations, a close look at America's record over the past forty years reveals a striking fact. In comparison to employ-ees in other advanced industrial democracies, working people in America consistently receive much less protection against the princi-pal threats to their security and well-being. Instead of enacting com-prehensive laws to give everyone access to health care, or job train-ing when they are laid off, or safeguards against being fired without good cause, policymakers in the United States are more inclined to let people fend for themselves. Americans are expected to take care of their own security, either individually or by working for compa-nies that give pensions and other benefits to their employees.

This approach is quite suitable for higher-income Americans with college degrees who can readily manage to buy insurance, negotiate severance agreements, and take other prudent steps to guard against familiar risks. It does not work nearly as well for Americans with less education, fewer skills, and lower-paying jobs. Several million work-ers cannot even earn enough to rise above the official poverty line, al-though they work full-time throughout the year.* Many others are hard-pressed financially. In 1999 more than half of all families with incomes below the median reported that they had "just enough" or "not enough" money to pay for basic living expenses; in the mid-1990s 18.5 percent of all households actually reported negative wealth.[24] Many of these families find that there are simply too many urgent bills to pay to leave room to buy insurance against serious ill-ness and other dangers that may never materialize. Even workers earning above-average wages find it hard to save in a culture where the pressures to consume are so great.

All too often, therefore, working families put off taking steps to ensure that they are adequately protected against risk. When adver-sity strikes, their fate typically depends on whether they happen to work for an employer who offers benefits that cover their situation.

---

* In recent years, Congress has taken steps to improve the lot of the working poor by increas-ing the Earned Income Tax Credit and expanding Medicaid coverage to include more children. Yet even these benefits only partially offset the decline in real wages for men between 1979 and 1997.

The net result is that working people in the United States are much more vulnerable to the basic hazards of life than their counterparts in other industrialized nations.

For example, although almost all American workers are covered by Social Security and thus enjoy a guaranteed minimum income in old age, they must rely more than citizens of other industrialized nations on receiving a private pension from their employer in order to secure a comfortable retirement. If they happen to work for an employer who does not provide such benefits, they must often make do with a Social Security check less generous than the benefits available in most other leading democracies.

Similarly, while large majorities of Americans believe in universal health insurance, workers who are not elderly, poor, or disabled will be insured only if their employer is willing to provide such protection. As the economy has grown more competitive, fewer firms offer these benefits. Less-educated, lower-paid employees are especially likely to go unprotected.[25] Nearly one-fourth of all working-age adults with incomes of $20,000 to $35,000 have no health insurance, and nearly 30 percent went without needed medical services during the past year because they could not afford them.[26] For those with incomes under $20,000, the figures rise to more than 40 percent. In contrast, among working-age Americans earning more than $60,000, only 3 percent lack medical insurance.[27]

In the current environment, therefore, a long-term job with good benefits is particularly valuable. Yet employment of this kind seems to be another casualty of the modern global economy. Increasingly, employees in their twenties must expect to work for several different employers in the course of their careers. Even in the prosperous 1990s, the odds of having to change jobs went up by more than one-third for young people, in comparison to similar cohorts of workers in earlier decades.[28]

In an economy like ours, the consequences of losing a job are often severe. Two years after being laid off, more than 60 percent of employees in the mid-1990s were earning less than in their previous job, and more than one-third suffered a reduction in income of more than 20 percent.[29] Moreover, workers in this country are especially vulnerable when they are let go, because they can lose important benefits that the State guarantees to everyone in other advanced democracies. For example, of all Americans laid off in 1997 who found other work, almost 30 percent did not receive health benefits from their new employer.[30]

Despite the importance in the United States of keeping a job with benefits, American workers enjoy much less employment security than their counterparts in other major industrial democracies. The United States is virtually the only leading country in which most employees who are wrongfully terminated have no adequate means of seeking redress.[31] True, workers dismissed because of race, religion, gender, or sexual orientation can file a complaint with the Equal Employment Opportunity Commission, and courts in several states have been more willing to intervene on one ground or another to protect employees who are fired unjustly. Nevertheless, antidiscrimination cases are only a small fraction of all unjust dismissals and often take more than a year to be heard. In states where employees can go to court, litigation is expensive, and many attorneys do not consider it worth their while to take a case from a low-income worker, even on a contingent-fee basis. Overall, therefore, the protection given to American employees is much more limited than in other industrial nations, where workers can typically complain at little cost to a special administrative tribunal and obtain a reasonably prompt hearing if they believe that they were fired unjustly.

American workers also receive much less protection when they lose their jobs for economic reasons. Congress has enacted legislation requiring advance notification of impending layoffs, but this law applies only to firms employing over 100 workers and is reportedly only casually enforced.[32] In contrast, throughout much of Western Europe, employers are not only obliged to notify workers in advance of layoffs; they must exhaust other alternatives, such as reassignment or cutting the working hours of all employees, before letting anyone go.

In many industrialized countries, when employees are laid off, they typically receive extensive retraining and are entitled to many months of unemployment benefits amounting to a high proportion of their prior wages.[33] In contrast, programs for displaced workers in the United States exist only for limited categories, such as those laid off because of foreign trade, and even these efforts have had only limited success in helping people find new jobs. In the case of unemployment insurance, benefits in America last for shorter periods, cover fewer workers, and make up a smaller fraction of previous wages than is true throughout Western Europe.

Even the safeguards that the law does provide are often vitiated through inadequate enforcement caused by limited funding. For example, the Fair Labor Standards Act prescribes a forty-hour week and requires premium pay for overtime. But insufficient funding has limited Labor Department inspections to such a degree that employers can disregard the laws with little chance of getting caught, often by hiring people and calling them "supervisors" (who are exempt from the law) although they perform the same duties as ordinary employees. The losses to the workers involved are not trivial. Using conservative assumptions, the Employer Policy Foundation concluded in a 1996 study that illegally denied overtime pay amounted to at least $19 billion per year.[34] Similar charges of inadequate enforcement could be leveled against several other protective laws, such as antidiscrimination legislation or workplace safety regulation.

Working parents in the United States also receive less government assistance than their counterparts in other industrial democracies to help them reconcile the demands of their job with their responsibilities to their children. Even though Americans work more hours per year and have fewer vacation days than employees in almost any other major democracy, Congress could not pass a parental leave law until 1993. As enacted, the legislation covers fewer workers and guarantees shorter periods of leave than comparable laws in other countries; it is also virtually unique in failing to require that the leaves be paid. Other laws to assist parents are similarly modest. Childcare receives relatively little government subsidy and is often of low quality. Preschools enroll a smaller fraction of the population than in most other advanced democracies and are available for less than half of all families with incomes low enough to qualify them to attend at government expense.[35]

Some critics argue that workers who want more protection are free to join a union and seek appropriate safeguards through collective bargaining. Compared to employees in other advanced democracies, however, American workers face substantial obstacles in seeking to organize to protect their interests. Unlike most employers overseas, American managers still tenaciously resist efforts to unionize their workers. In principle, the National Labor Relations Act protects the right to organize and, if a majority of employees so choose, requires employers to bargain collectively over wages, hours, and conditions of employment. In practice, however, the law has not stopped many companies from resorting to flagrant methods of intimidation to keep their workers from choosing a union. In more than 25 percent of organizing campaigns, employers flout the law by illegally firing one or more employees for exercising their right to persuade their fellow workers to vote for the union.[36]

The result of such weak social and employment legislation in the United States is a much more precarious existence for American workers than employees in other leading countries enjoy. The consequences go well beyond those unlucky enough to lose their jobs. As one would expect, countless people who are employed worry about the risks they run, especially during periods when the economy is not booming. According to a November 1995 poll, 51 percent of Americans admitted to being troubled by the fear of losing their job, 77 percent were concerned about not having enough money for their retirement, and 83 percent were worried about being unable to afford needed health care.[37]

Although these anxieties have eased somewhat after a long period of unbroken prosperity, a majority of Americans indicated in 1999 that they were "very concerned" about whether they could afford health care if a family member fell ill and whether they would have enough money for their retirement.[38] Even with unemployment at its lowest level in years, the percentage of workers who thought it likely that they would lose their jobs in the next year actually increased from 1990 to 1996, while the proportion who thought that it would be "very easy" to find a new position with equivalent pay and benefits fell sharply.[39]

Many employers will defend the limited employment safeguards in this country, arguing that the United States has simply chosen to strike a wiser balance between the desire for personal security and the demands of a rapidly growing economy. By enacting fewer protective laws, they maintain, America has been able to achieve greater prosperity and a more dynamic, flexible economy.

Whatever the merits of this argument, there is little evidence that Americans prefer to have less protection and lower benefits in order to achieve greater prosperity. Substantial majorities believe in the right to join a union. Majorities (though not so large as in Europe) also favor unemployment insurance, universal access to good health care, parental leave, and other protective measures that are either missing or inadequately funded in the United States.

Moreover, the desire to maximize productivity and growth cannot adequately explain the modest efforts in the United States to help workers and protect their essential job-related interests. Efficiency does not require that health care or a decent retirement income be dependent on holding a job with a company that happens to provide such benefits. Nor does efficiency explain why childcare assistance is less generous in America than in other countries, or why job training and relocation assistance for laid-off workers are less extensive, or why conscientious enforcement of employment legislation is often limited to firms of substantial size. All these benefits and safeguards can be organized and paid for without pushing up payroll taxes or keeping employers from managing their enterprises efficiently. It is even possible to have procedures to prevent unjustified job terminations that do not unduly hamper operations; many unionized companies have long had grievance procedures without demonstrable losses of productivity.

Many critics point to Europe's restrictions on layoffs as a substantial deterrent to growth. Even here, however, the truth of the matter is unclear. According to a detailed investigation by the McKinsey Global Institute, "while many [European] employers complained about inflexibility in interviews, when companies were forced to react to dramatic changes in the marketplace, they were able to overcome these barriers."[40] Other analysts have come to similar conclusions.[41] The fact that productivity has risen faster in France, Sweden, and Germany than it has in America over most of the past several decades raises doubts about how much Europe has suffered from its restrictive employment legislation.

The most questionable employment policies in Europe are the extremely generous jobless benefits and the high payroll taxes and entry-level wages common in France and Germany. Such requirements probably contribute to the heavy and protracted unemployment that has plagued both countries in the 1990s. But high minimum wages and unemployment allowances are only two of many protective measures denied American workers. Moreover, while one may legitimately criticize these benefits for being too generous, American policies can be attacked for moving too far in the opposite direction. If government programs have aggravated unemployment abroad, policies in the United States have allowed several million Americans to work full-time and still earn too little to lift their families out of poverty.

All in all, therefore, America's peculiar approach to protecting basic employment-related interests has achieved results that fall well short of what most American workers would prefer and what most industrial democracies have achieved. If foreign governments have sometimes gone too far in protecting their workers, the United States has consistently done too little, even making due allowance for productivity, economic growth, and other important national interests. The result has been a set of employment safeguards and benefits that impose more hardship and create more personal insecurity than working people in this country needed to endure.

Policies Toward the Poor

In comparison with the achievements of other advanced democratic states, the record of the U.S. government in coping with the problems of poverty has been conspicuously unsuccessful. In 1999, after years of unprecedented prosperity, 11.8 percent of Americans were officially classified as poor, including almost 20 percent of all children. This result does not appear to reflect the will of the people. For decades, substantial majorities of Americans have felt that federal officials should do more to help people in poverty who cannot help themselves. In 1996, for example, 67 percent of the public believed that the federal government was not trying hard enough to serve the needs of the poor, while only 14 percent felt that it was making too much of an effort.[42] Despite this support, government programs consistently do less to lift people out of poverty than those of any other advanced industrial democracy.

Welfare payments to mothers of dependent children fall below the poverty line in almost every state (even when food stamps and other benefits are included), and the amounts provided have shrunk significantly in the past twenty-five years. Housing programs are plainly insufficient to the need, with only 30 percent of ostensibly eligible households actually receiving rent vouchers, subsidized apartments, or any other form of federal assistance. Public housing projects have been largely restricted to inner-city locations, where they have often been highly segregated, infested with crime, and far removed from areas with substantial employment opportunities.

The impact of poverty in the United States is revealed most starkly by the plight of its poor children. More than 80 percent of Americans have expressed a willingness to pay more in taxes if the money is used to feed needy children and ensure their access to decent medical care.[43] Yet several million children live in households that experience hunger, while millions more remain without adequate access to health care. These figures are much higher than those for any other advanced democracy.

An overwhelming 94 percent of Americans believe that the government should make every reasonable effort to make certain that all children have an equal chance to succeed according to their abilities.[44] Yet no objective observer would agree that the United States has yet come close to achieving this goal for young people growing up in poverty. For virtually every form of assistance to children, America ranks below the average for advanced, industrial democracies, and on most counts it stands at or near the bottom of the list.[45] Prenatal care is often inadequate for mothers in poverty; infant mortality rates are higher than those of twenty other nations; supplemental nutrition is funded for only 80 percent of officially eligible poor mothers and infants; and preschool programs are available to only a fraction of all poor families, allowing more than one-third of all American children to arrive at school in a state of unpreparedness to learn.[46] Once in school, children from poor neighborhoods rarely receive much effective help to prepare them for the world of work. Job training programs for high school dropouts are seldom successful, and vocational education in the high schools is notoriously ineffective. By international standards, the United States spends fewer dollars on training, and its schools are less connected to the world of work than in most other advanced nations.

The brightest spot in America's antipoverty efforts is its record with respect to the elderly.[47] As a result of Social Security and Medicare, official poverty rates among Americans over age sixty-five have fallen dramatically, from 35 percent in 1960 to less than 10 percent in the mid-1990s. Even so, the current level is still the highest of any major democracy. Among widows over sixty-five, the rate approaches 20 percent; among blacks, the rate is approximately 25 percent. Since the elderly are often unable to supplement their Social Security pensions by working, falling into poverty can often mean genuine privation. According to a 1993 Urban Institute study, one-third of all elderly households with incomes below the poverty line reported that during the past few months they had gone without food or had had to choose between buying food or paying their rent or medical bills.[48] Further problems afflict those who are chronically ill. Because the United States lacks a comprehensive plan for financing long-term care, elderly people who need to move to a nursing home must either spend their resources or transfer them to relatives so that they can claim to be in poverty and thereby qualify for financial help under Medicaid.

Legislative debates about poverty programs regularly provoke partisan battles resulting in compromises that fail to deal effectively with the underlying problem.[49] A typical resolution is to announce an ambitious program for the poor but allow states to restrict coverage to only a portion of those in need. For example, Congress enacted Medicaid to provide access to health care for those who could not afford it. But federal lawmakers gave the states responsibility for deciding who would be eligible for such assistance. Although Congress has subsequently mandated coverage for certain categories, notably young children, eligibility for most poor people runs a wide gamut: in 1995, Connecticut defined as eligible all those with incomes equal to 132 percent of the official poverty level, whereas Alabama restricted eligibility to persons with incomes below a level set at only 34 percent of the poverty line.

Another familiar compromise for resolving legislative battles over the poor is to approve a program but appropriate funds sufficient to reach only a fraction of those for whom assistance was ostensibly intended. For example, housing legislation purports to grant subsidies so that poor families will not have to pay more than 30 percent of their income in rent. In practice, however, less than one-third of all poor families actually receive assistance, and many of the rest pay much more than 30 percent of their reported income for housing.

The same pattern has been repeated in preschool programs, such as Head Start, where less than half of all poor children are accommodated, and in nutritional supplements for mothers and small children, which reach only 80 percent of all supposedly eligible families.

Inadequate funding forces officials to adopt various strategies to make do with meager resources. One method is to avoid publicizing benefits adequately so that many eligible people never apply. Another approach is to tighten eligibility requirements and make greater efforts to weed out fraudulent claimants, malingerers, and other undeserving applicants. Such reforms typically bring some reduction in abuse, with accompanying savings. Unfortunately, they can also result in eligibility procedures so complex and unfriendly that deserving applicants are either turned away improperly or discouraged from trying to enroll. Thus, according to a 1990 report of the General Accounting Office, only 44 percent of households eligible for food stamps actually received them.[50] Among those not served, 62 percent were either unaware that they were eligible, or were incorrectly told that they were ineligible, or were frustrated by procedures that seemed too complicated or demeaning.*

Often, even strict enforcement of eligibility standards does not save enough money to allow the government to help all eligible individuals. In this case, the first response is usually to stretch available funds so far that the quality of services declines and the program no longer produces the hoped-for results. This process has frequently undermined efforts to take successful human-services initiatives and replicate them on a broad scale. For example, the promising Perry Pre-School experiment that helped inspire Head Start was soon translated into federal programs, many only half a day in length, that were too thinly staffed to offer the services given by the original Perry project.[51] It is easy to destroy the effectiveness of social programs in this way. Working with drug-addicted parents, helping troubled children, or giving single mothers the training, counseling,

---

* In 1998, 48 percent of all people officially classified as poor had no food stamps. General Accounting Office reports continued to stress reasons such as tightening of eligibility requirements, confusion over the requirements, and erroneous application of the law by state officials. *Food Stamp Program: Various Factors Have Led to Declining Participation*, GAO 99-185 (July 1999).

and childcare needed to move them off welfare are expensive, labor-intensive activities. When funding is inadequate, the results are at best far less than anticipated and at worst almost totally ineffective.

If officials cannot stretch the available funds to reach all of the intended beneficiaries, their normal response is to limit assistance to the poorest of the poor. Many public housing projects have allotted most of their units to single mothers on welfare, just as training programs have given priority to high school dropouts and the chronically unemployed. While these recipients have the greatest need, they are also the hardest to help. As a result, by concentrating its efforts on the most difficult cases, the government makes it very difficult to succeed, and the results are typically disappointing.

Unfortunately, repeated experiences of this kind seldom lead to greater understanding about how to make social programs succeed. Instead, failures leave both sides to the debate feeling vindicated. Opponents claim that federal programs do not work, just as they predicted, while supporters insist that inadequate funding brought about the disappointing results. While both sides argue, Congress has continued to enact a series of patchwork solutions, awkward compromises, and underfunded programs that have appeared to give something to everyone while almost invariably promising more than they deliver.

Why These Four Chronic Problems Need Explaining

Thinking back over the several persistent failings just described—the neglect of the poor, the meager protection given to the interests of working people, the prevalence of wasteful, contentious, often ineffective regulation, and the many imperfections of legislative design—some readers may come away wondering why these particular problems have been plucked from the long list of disappointing international comparisons set forth in Chapter 1. Since this question is fundamental to much that follows, it deserves a thoughtful answer.

Of the four principal failings, the easiest to justify is faulty legislative design, since this problem plays a prominent role in virtually all the cases in which America's performance is comparatively weak. Again and again, in field after field, the operative legislation is burdened by unrealistic objectives, inadequate funding, clumsy implementing machinery, and poor targeting of funds. The costs in terms of waste, frustrated expectations, and harmful side effects are virtually incalculable.

As previously noted, the evidence of clumsy legislative design is so pervasive that one is tempted to ask why it is necessary to add any other failings to the list of problems to be explained. Certainly, many disappointing programs for poor and working people and many controversial efforts to regulate the economy suffer from this malady. But there is more to the matter than that. In creating programs to alleviate poverty or to provide employment safeguards, Congress has not simply passed badly constructed laws; the results are also consistently less generous to working people and the poor than similar programs in other leading democracies. Similarly, regulation in America is not only marked by insufficient funds, unrealistic goals, and cumbersome administrative machinery; it has a distinctive adversarial, legalistic style that leads to exceptional expense and irritation. These characteristic patterns strongly suggest that government programs would continue to be plagued by neglect of the poor, by inadequate provision for working people, and by contentious, wasteful regulation even if Congress could somehow change its ways and consistently produce coherent, well-constructed legislation. For this reason, each of these three specific failings requires explanation in its own right.

But why, the persistent reader may ask, should one choose these three failings from the long list of potential candidates? The inclusion of poverty is probably the most obvious. By virtually every measure, the United States consistently ranks below other advanced democracies in its provisions for the poor. The consequences are apparent in many areas of American life, including nutrition, housing, schools, the safety of the streets, and the economic segregation of many urban neighborhoods. The numbers of people affected exceed 30 million, including roughly 20 percent of all children under the age of six. This record persists in spite of continuing public support to do more to alleviate poverty.

The neglect of working people also underlies many of the instances in which our performance falls below that of most other leading democracies. Such cases include ineffective job training, vocational education, and school-to-work programs; the spotty protection afforded to vital job interests, such as safeguards against being fired or laid off without good reason; the frequent lack of reasonable security from other major hazards, such as unemployment and limited access to health care; and the government's failure to deal effectively with a number of basic family needs, such as parental leave, vaccinations for children, access to preschool, and the availability of affordable childcare, among others. These weaknesses affect the welfare of scores of millions of lower-skilled, lower-income Americans who cannot easily afford to make private provision for the needs and hazards that government-sponsored programs neglect.

Contentious, often ineffective regulation is the last and perhaps most problematic of the basic failings identified. It is directly reflected in only four of the areas included in the international comparisons set forth in Chapter 1: work safety, highway safety, worker representation, and environmental protection. Moreover, regulators in the U.S. are not consistently unsuccessful; they have outdone their counterparts in other leading democracies in avoiding the use of laws to suppress competition. Nevertheless, the failings of our regulatory system affect almost everyone in the United States. The aggravations caused by petty requirements and intrusive inspections may seem to weigh only on corporations, but the waste of complying with unnecessary rules inflates the prices paid by all consumers. Similarly, the harm produced by inadequate regulation—whether of toxic substances, defective consumer goods, or unsavory employment practices—can have effects throughout the population.

Together, the principal deficiencies identified in this chapter account for almost all the cases listed in Chapter 1 in which the government has failed to produce results equivalent to those achieved by some or all other leading democracies. If America could overcome these weaknesses, its relative standing would improve dramatically. Once these failings are explained, therefore, the reasons for the anemic performance of the United States should become much clearer.

5

WHY LEGISLATION IS OFTEN BADLY DESIGNED

IN THE STAID PAGES of a Brookings Institution monograph, Henry Aaron and Harvey Galper once described the federal tax laws as "a swamp of unfairness, complexity, and inefficiency."[1] As the authors went on to explain, "the accumulation of credits, deductions, and exclusions designed to help particular groups or advance special purposes conflict with one another, are poorly designed, and represent no consistent policy."[2] Unfortunately, critics could direct similar charges at many other laws that Congress enacts.

Much of the difficulty stems from the fact that laws in the United States do not come about through a unified, tightly organized deliberative process but emerge from what must surely be one of the most fragmented systems of government in any major democracy. Creating policies to address major domestic problems is a task in which the President, the two houses of Congress, the permanent bureaucracy, the courts, and the various state and local governments all play a role. Not only are these government entities relatively independent of one another; many are themselves highly fragmented, without strong central direction or control. All too often, instead of cooperating to arrive at well crafted solutions, the participants spar with one another to guard their prerogatives, promote their ideas, and expand their influence. Nowhere is there a unifying force powerful enough to take the proposals emerging from such a decentralized system and mold them into a coherent whole. Instead, the final result often reflects a desperate effort to cobble together a majority from a welter of differing interests and points of view.

The Executive Branch

The problem begins in the Executive Branch. Although the President has the authority to execute the laws and to propose new measures to Congress, there are serious limits to his ability to develop clear priorities and effective programs to submit to the legislature. With so many different programs to administer, the Executive Branch is hard put to coordinate its policies. In some cases, major programs and responsibilities are in the hands of independent regulatory agencies that are not even subject to direct White House control.

Equally inhibiting to the President is the fact that many fields of policy are not covered by a single statute but are the subject of many separate laws. Dozens of legislative programs exist for environmental protection, food inspection, urban development, and other policy areas. Coordinating the work of these overlapping initiatives is difficult because each has its own rules, procedures, and turf-guarding bureaucracies. Even if the President tried to consolidate or eliminate duplicate programs to achieve greater efficiency, he would have to gain congressional assent. Such approval is often impossible to obtain, because individual members or committee chairs have a personal interest in the programs in question and do not want their supervisory authority diminished.

In trying to pull together the separate fiefdoms in the Executive Branch to arrive at clear priorities and coherent proposals, the President must also contend with the wishes of administrators—who often have strong policy views of their own, not to mention ambitions to expand, or at least preserve, their current sphere of activity. In a formal sense, these bureaucracies are subject to the authority of the President. In reality, they frequently have legislative allies who will protect their interests regardless of the Chief Executive's priorities. Since Congress allocates the funds and writes the enabling legislation, career officials with powerful friends on Capitol Hill can often maintain their independence from the White House and undermine its efforts to achieve more coordinated policies.

Congress

The fragmentation of the Executive Branch is matched by a decentralization in Congress greater than that of any other legislature in an advanced industrial democracy. Individual members typically act like independent entrepreneurs to promote their own ideas and build support among their constituents. Many of them chair at least one subcommittee, which gives them a platform to hold hearings, introduce new bills, and bid for jurisdiction over proposed legislation that will enhance their visibility and influence.

Despite periodic attempts to reorganize Congress, authority over many important topics remains divided among a number of committees and subcommittees, both in the House and in the Senate. No less than eleven standing committees in the House, nine in the Senate, and literally scores of different subcommittees share jurisdiction over the Environmental Protection Agency alone. Increasingly, as in the healthcare debate of 1993–1994, two or more of these legislative units will consider a single piece of legislation in each of the two houses of Congress, creating added problems in trying to meld several separate bills into a single, internally consistent legislative result.

The process of securing workable compromises is especially difficult in the Senate, where members jealously guard their individual prerogatives. A single senator can filibuster a bill and thereby force the Majority Leader to obtain the approval of at least sixty members before voting on the measure. Individual senators can place a hold on legislation which can amount, in effect, to a veto if the leadership does not consider the bill important enough to press ahead and risk a filibuster. Unanimous consent is required to adopt a procedure limiting the amount of debate on a bill or the number of amendments that can be considered. As a result, resourceful senators have unusual power to delay or threaten to obstruct further proceedings when it serves their interests to do so.

Members are increasingly bold in exercising their power. Since 1980, the number of bills subjected to a filibuster has shot up.[3] Senators are more willing to place a hold on legislation, not only for their own purposes but as a favor to an influential interest group. According to one standard text, "The contemporary legislative process in the Senate is shaped by Senators' rampant individualism and their leaders' attempt to do their job within that context. Senators now routinely exploit the enormous prerogatives Senate rules give the individual to further their own agendas."[4]

The House of Representatives has not been as consistently anarchic through the years as its sister body. Indeed, at the beginning of the twentieth century, power over the House had become highly concentrated under autocratic leaders, such as Joe Cannon. But legislators chafed under such strong central discipline. In 1910, the members rebelled and stripped the Speaker of much of his authority. Power drifted increasingly into the hands of committee chairmen, who gained their position through seniority and ruled over their areas of jurisdiction with almost complete authority. As the Democrats achieved a seemingly permanent majority starting in the 1950s, more and more committees came under the control of long-serving Southerners, who often controlled the flow of legislation even though their views were much more conservative than those of other Democrats on their committees.

Eventually, resistance welled up again. In the early 1970s, a Democratic caucus reduced the power of chairmen and distributed authority more widely. Many new subcommittees were created, and placed in the hands of chairpersons with considerable independence. Before long, however, the pendulum swung back again. Members found it too difficult to operate in such a large body without stronger central leadership to manage the legislative process. Today, acting through committees they control, House leaders can decide when bills come before the full body and by what procedures they are considered. The Speaker and his team also wield considerable influence over individual members by virtue of their power to control appointments to committees.

Even with this added authority, speakers and their deputies are weaker than their counterparts in other leading democracies. Unlike legislators abroad, members of Congress do not owe a great deal to their party or its leaders. They have typically won their nomination and election to office by their personal appeal to voters after a campaign directed and financed by their own efforts. Once in office, they rely on their ample staffs to help them decide how to vote, instead of simply following the party line. Although House leaders can exert some leverage over individual members by their ability to influence committee assignments, they use such power sparingly.[5] Lawmakers may follow the party line out of loyalty or because they need the Speaker's help in getting some future piece of legislation passed, but individual members frequently vote against the wishes of the leadership. Moreover, to the extent that the Speaker uses his influence, his role is less to draft effective legislation than to attempt, insofar as possible, to accommodate and promote the separate concerns of as many party colleagues as he can.

In a legislature composed of such independent-minded lawmakers, finding common ground can be difficult—especially in the Senate, where super-majorities (sixty votes or more) are required to prevent even a single senator from blocking legislation. It is generally possible to come to an agreement when the differences are pragmatic in nature. If Congress must decide how much to spend on roads or how to apportion aid to schools, competing interests can usually find some formula that may waste money but will at least satisfy a majority. When the disagreements are ideological, however, compromise can be more difficult. Without some unifying force to impose a meeting of the minds, efforts to reach agreement can fail entirely or produce convoluted results that lack the virtues of any of the positions they are meant to reconcile.

The independence of legislators works in several other ways to impair the quality of legislation. If individual senators or key members of the House can block the passage of a law, they have great power to extract concessions in return for their cooperation. That is why congressional leaders and even the President will sometimes agree to help particular lawmakers by giving them special exceptions to benefit influential supporters, pork barrel projects to please constituents, or new programs that further their pet policy interest.

The need to assemble majorities from a body of legislators, all of whom depend on local support for reelection, also means that it is difficult to limit the scope of spending programs to the regions or localities where they are truly needed. No lawmaker wants to risk being accused by some future opponent of not doing enough to serve local interests. As a result, money for school aid, transportation, extra police officers, and many other purposes will often be distributed not to meet real needs but to serve the political ends of large numbers of legislators whose support is essential to secure passage.[6] That is why Grand Rapids, which has relatively modest uses for mass transit, can end up with a subsidy per passenger that is several times that of New York City, which lives or dies by its subway system.

Over the past twenty-five years, lawmakers in both houses have become more and more inclined to use their personal prerogatives in ways that make the process of drafting worthwhile legislation even more difficult.[7] In earlier times, individual members gave much greater deference to the work of committees, which were composed of colleagues specializing in particular fields of policy. Today, legislators who do not belong to the relevant committees are quicker to introduce amendments of their own, to filibuster (in the Senate) for policy changes in proposed laws, or to attach riders to appropriations bills or continuing resolutions. As late as the 91st Congress (1969–1971), individual members almost never proposed changes after committees submitted draft legislation. By the 1990s, amendments of this sort were being offered in more than one-third of all important bills. Although House and Senate leaders have developed ways of protecting committee drafts from irresponsible proposals, these defenses are not perfect. Growing numbers of floor amendments increase the risk of incoherence, since they can cause leaders to compromise in dubious ways, under pressure to attract enough votes to get legislation passed.

At times, entire committees will join enthusiastically in passing laws to lavish benefits on special constituencies. The explanation usually lies in the membership of the committees. Congressional leaders try to accommodate the wishes of party colleagues in making committee assignments. Members naturally tend to prefer appointments that help to assure their reelection. As a result, certain committees that serve particular groups, such as Agriculture or Veterans Affairs, come to be composed largely of lawmakers with strong constituent interests in the committee's work. Because of the influence committees have in writing legislation and negotiating its passage, the odds increase that Congress will eventually approve programs for farmers, veterans, and other interests that are larded with more benefits than a wholly disinterested body would allow.

Accountability

Greater unity and discipline might be forged even from such an unruly system if there were an independent force powerful enough to command the allegiance of the several parts and hold them accountable for the quality of legislation. In America, however, no such unifying force exists. The obvious person to play such a role is the President. As Chief Executive, he has formidable powers to command the attention of the people, to influence the agenda through his legislative program and budget proposals, to marshal public opinion behind his initiatives, and to use—or threaten to use—his veto power on laws he does not like. Yet for all the authority and prestige of his office, even a popular President cannot do much to ensure that bills emerging from the legislature are carefully written to create effective programs. Congress jealously guards its power to draft legislation and would resist pressure from the Executive Branch to tidy up inconsistencies, ambiguities, and extraneous provisions, most of which are put there for pressing political reasons. The President can veto a law he does not like, but that is too drastic a remedy to be employed often. As a practical matter, Presidents use this power only when Congress passes legislation that contradicts some cherished White House policy or includes provisions that are unacceptable to important constituencies.

Other possibilities for strong leadership seem even less promising. Majority parties in most parliamentary democracies have enough power to discipline their members and coordinate different parts of the government. America's parties are much weaker and cannot always command the allegiance of their members in a single house of Congress, let alone the different branches and parts of the government as a whole.

In countries such as France and Japan, the civil service has often helped add coherence and continuity to government programs by virtue of its prominent role in designing and executing policy and its ability, prestige, and permanence in office. Such influence, however, is hardly conceivable in the United States. Career civil servants in this country have rarely enjoyed substantial policymaking power and have never commanded the respect accorded to the French or Japanese bureaucracies. Because so many of the policymaking jobs are in the hands of political appointees, there is no way for career officials to acquire the stature needed to have a significant effect on the policymaking process.

Substantial pressure for coherent legislation might still materialize if public opinion were sufficiently strong and unified in support of congressional action. While pressure of this kind does arise now and then to force Congress to act on particular issues, there is rarely a consensus on what, exactly, should be done. Popular agreement of this kind is rare in any country, but it is especially unlikely in the United States. The population is too large and heterogeneous and includes too many varied interests to unite behind a specific policy, save in highly unusual circumstances.

Even without such pressure, some greater semblance of unity might occur if voters held members of Congress strictly accountable for the results of the legislation they produced. The pressure to create programs that work could force lawmakers to reconcile their differences more effectively. But accountability of this kind is hard to come by in a system such as ours. Too many citizens vote because of their feelings about individual incumbents rather than the record of the parties, and too much of the responsibility for results is divided among different units of government that are not even under the control of the same party.

Of course, when legislators vote for measures that have immediate visible consequences—either for a large segment of the public or for a powerful interest group—they will be held responsible. If their vote directly disadvantages important constituents, they can expect to have their action held against them and quite possibly suffer political damage as a result. That is why many lawmakers are reluctant to support legislation that raises gasoline taxes or prohibits handguns.

But what of a complicated job training bill or a law to reform welfare or a new measure to increase the supply of affordable housing? Here, the consequences may not become visible for several years. Moreover, the legislation may have been passed by a Republican Congress, signed into law by a Democratic President, implemented through regulations drafted by career civil servants, and administered in the field by officials of numerous state and local governments or even by members of private organizations. With so many separate participants, who is to blame when the program goes awry?

How can voters possibly know whether to hold such a failure against Republicans or Democrats in the next election?

Instead of being collectively responsible for the programs they enact, members of Congress are individually accountable to their constituents (and perhaps, in some degree, to their contributors). Most of the recent efforts to increase accountability have sought to emphasize personal responsibility toward the public by requiring lawmakers to disclose their votes and reveal their campaign contributions. As a result, if members of Congress vote for an unpopular measure or get caught in an embarrassing conflict of interest, they may be punished for their behavior at the polls. But accountability of this kind does nothing to make them collectively responsible for compiling a strong record of bills that successfully accomplish important public purposes. On the contrary, opening more of the work of individual lawmakers to public scrutiny often exposes them all the more to the centrifugal pressures of special interests and constituent groups that make it so difficult to agree on well-crafted, coherent legislation.

The lack of accountability does more than interfere with compromise; it undermines the quality and effectiveness of legislation. If no one can be held responsible for program failures, why should legislators considering a new policy care as much for its ultimate success as they do for its immediate popularity with the voting public and with powerful groups that have an interest in the issue? The consequences have been aptly described by one Republican lawmaker elected after years of managing a large business: "All my life I have been associated with people who worked primarily to achieve results. Now, I am working with a lot of people who are chiefly concerned with giving the appearance of being on the right side. There is a big difference."[8]

The emphasis on appearances rather than results affects the quality of legislation in a number of ways. It allows congressional leaders to make extravagant claims about their handiwork without much risk of being blamed if the programs do not work as advertised. When things go wrong, they can always point the finger at the White House or the bureaucracy. Thus, lawmakers can launch a new program with impressive goals that are well beyond the realm of possibility. Rather than reconcile conflicting approaches to a problem, party leaders can include them all in an effort to attract the votes required to get the legislation passed. Even contradictory views may end up in a final bill, either by including each in separate provisions of the law or by papering over the inconsistencies with vague and inconclusive language.

Such tactics may serve the political needs of Congress, but the long-term consequences for the body politic are usually harmful. Lawmakers who are rewarded more for appearances than for results face a constant temptation to please all important constituencies—or at least to avoid upsetting any of them seriously—even if such accommodation jeopardizes the ultimate success of the program involved. Many of the awkward compromises that appear in legislation come about in precisely this way. Congress will enact a seemingly bold new environmental program but create a very cumbersome, ungainly process of implementation replete with opportunities for reconsideration and review.[9] Alternatively, lawmakers will announce a new public-housing initiative with ambitious goals and timetables but appropriate far too little money to come close to meeting these objectives.

The problems just described throw further light on one of the paradoxes of contemporary American government. How is it that politicians have paid more and more attention to the wishes of their constituents while arousing greater and greater cynicism and distrust? The temptation to please everyone by emphasizing short-term appearances rather than long-term results suggests a reason. In the struggle to be reelected and retain support among the voters, lawmakers feel impelled to accommodate grassroots pressures that are often unrealistic, misinformed, or even contradictory. In seeking to respond to all significant interests—or at least *appear* to respond— legislators are tempted to pass laws that are badly designed or promise more than they can deliver. Later on, when the results prove disappointing, voters do not know whom to blame. They may continue to support their own representative in Congress, especially if he or she has brought tangible benefits to the district and labored to resolve constituents' problems. Over time, however, repeated disappointments with the effectiveness of government programs may leave people feeling frustrated, cheated, and cynical about the Congress as a whole.

Problems of Implementation

The fragmentation of authority that marks our system of government also complicates the task of implementing the laws. The proliferation of legislative committees and subcommittees frequently leads to the passage of many separate programs to deal with the same problem. For example, by 1995 Congress had enacted more than 160 separate programs for job training. Often, such programs are not all located within the same agency or Cabinet department; even if they are, bureaucrats in charge guard their turf and often have powerful allies in Congress to help protect their interests. This state of affairs creates unusual problems of coordination. Unfortunately, the needed cooperation is not always forthcoming. Thus, environmental policy has often been hindered by antipollution programs dealing with one medium (for example, water) that simply diverted the problem to another medium (for example, air). Even if program heads do their best to collaborate, the very existence of many separate programs often creates confusion and duplication.

The separation of executive and legislative authority can cause additional difficulties. When the two branches are divided, as in the United States, lawmakers rarely entrust the drafting of legislation to the administrators who have to carry it out; instead, they normally do the drafting themselves. They may consult informally with administrative officials, but they do not always do so or take the advice that is offered. The results of this process are often less than satisfactory, forcing those who execute the law to cope with language that is vague, incomplete, or even contradictory.

To choose but one example, when Congress acted in 1973 to make public transportation accessible to the handicapped, it never specified whether the law required "effective mobility" (that is, the provision of some reasonable method to ensure that the disabled can travel where they want to go) or whether the legislation demanded the more expensive "full accessibility" (that is, integrating the disabled into the regular community by making all vehicles of public transport handicapped-accessible).[10] Efforts to seek clarification from Congress proved unavailing. In the words of Joseph Califano, head of the Department of Health, Education, and Welfare (HEW), legislators found it "more fun to be Moses and deliver the commandments than to be the rabbis and priests who had to make them work."[11] Lacking authoritative direction from Congress, agency officials tended to vacillate between these two alternatives, depending on whether a liberal or a conservative administration was in power. The resulting uncertainty was especially hard on transportation companies and municipalities that needed definite answers before making costly long-term investments in transportation equipment.

To complicate matters further, power over national policy is not always in the hands of a single party. More often than not in the past fifty years, one or both houses of Congress have been controlled by a party other than the one occupying the White House. When this occurs, legislators may be especially suspicious of the Executive Branch and try to control its behavior by prescribing elaborate procedures, detailed mandates and prohibitions, and strict timetables. But this alternative works no better than leaving key provisions vague. Since lawmakers cannot possibly anticipate all of the practical problems that will arise under a new program, their rigid prescriptions often turn out to be difficult, if not impossible, to implement.

Added problems can result from the division of authority among federal, state, and local governments. In principle, federalism serves the interests of good administration by creating more opportunities for officials to innovate and adapt the law to local conditions. To achieve these benefits, accepted wisdom dictates that government should allocate functions to the lowest level capable of carrying them out effectively. In practice, however, matters are usually more complicated. Frequently, different aspects of a single program lend themselves to intervention by different levels of government. The federal government may be in the best position to provide funds or set minimum national standards, while local authorities will have a greater capacity to understand local conditions and adapt their services accordingly. Thus, Congress may respond not only by delegating implementation to the Executive Branch but by dividing responsibility among entirely different levels of government, each of which has its own popular mandates to fulfill.

However sound the reasons for sharing responsibility in this way, the result is often to dilute federal policy by entrusting the interpretation and implementation of programs to independent state and local administrations that have quite different agendas from those of the Washington officials who supply the funds.[12] For example, lower levels of government sometimes try to divert money that Congress has appropriated for the poor and use it for other governmental purposes.[13] When such cases arise, the federal government cannot fire the state and local officials and choose another set of agents to administer the program. Instead, the federal agencies involved will typically try to protect their interests by issuing guidelines and regulations. Gradually, uniform rules and procedures accumulate that do not always fit the local conditions to which they apply. Eventually, national programs can become rigid and uniform, threatening to destroy the very flexibility for which the federal system was created. Chains of command become excessively intricate. Delays grow longer as officials disagree over the proper course to pursue or allow requests to remain unanswered. In this way, dividing authority among separate units of government—for all its apparent advantages in promoting flexibility and limiting the risks of concentrated power—can vastly complicate efforts to implement laws effectively.

The Effects of Institutions and Culture

The special problems of policymaking in the United States are largely a product of our peculiar institutional structure, with its single-district elections, its weak political parties, and its divisions into separate branches and levels of government. Such a system is not easily changed. It is rooted not only in our Constitution but in long-standing cultural characteristics of the society from which it emerged. Americans have traditionally displayed a strong belief in personal liberty and initiative, a faith in competition as the best guarantee of good results in many areas of life, and a fear of concentrated authority in general and of official authority in particular. A highly fragmented government, with its separate levels, its several branches, and its multiple checks and balances, suits these tendencies very well.

The reverse is also true. Just as the surrounding culture helped to shape our institutions, so our institutions—with their divided powers, their guarantee of personal freedoms, and their strong safeguards against abuse—support and amplify the individualism, the reliance on competition, and the distrust of authority that characterize the larger society. Thus, the long-standing dispute about whether institutions or elements of our culture are chiefly responsible for our distinctive policies and procedures turns out to be fruitless in the end. Each is joined inextricably in support of the other, to the point that it is simply not possible to disentangle them and determine which is the fundamental cause.

Both system and culture contribute to the incoherence of much federal legislation. Single-district elections make members of Congress more intent on securing special benefits for their constituents, but so does the tendency of many Americans to support the individual candidate they prefer instead of voting by party affiliation. Similarly, although the overlapping committee jurisdictions and the prerogatives of members complicate the task of agreeing on coherent legislation, they survive because they further the ambitions of lawmakers competing to increase their personal influence, expand the jurisdiction of their committee, and ultimately make their own special mark on public policy. It is typical of our culture that American legislators should have the unique distinction among advanced democracies of being referred to by scholars as "policy entrepreneurs." Unfortunately, these traits of strong personal ambition, initiative, and competitiveness help to explain Speaker O'Neill's rueful conclusion that while the quality of individual legislators may be high, the quality of the results is not.

The Example of Superfund Legislation

A concrete example may help to illustrate more clearly the peculiar problems of drafting coherent laws in America. The case history that follows is not intended to be typical; no piece of legislation is. It is far from the best or the worst example of Congress' handiwork. Rather, it is a useful case to examine because it reveals the difficulties of policymaking and because reasonably detailed accounts of its progress through Congress are readily available.

The problem of toxic waste suddenly burst upon the public consciousness in the summer of 1978, when chemicals previously dumped in Love Canal, near Niagara Falls, began to seep into the basements of nearby homes and discolor their floors and walls. Angry residents protested loudly, but their complaints had little effect until the health commissioner of New York issued a report in September 1978. In it, the commissioner referred to Love Canal as "a public health time bomb" and described the situation as "profound and devastating, [a] modern-day disaster" constituting a "great and immediate peril."[14]

New York's governor, Hugh Carey, responded by offering to relocate all families living next to the canal. This gesture failed to mollify local residents, who were now fully organized. In the fall of 1979, a public-television documentary gave the situation more visibility. Soon afterward, activist Jane Fonda visited the site and declared publicly, with considerable emotion, that all local residents should be relocated. Further outcries ensued when a hastily done EPA report was leaked, disclosing a preliminary finding of abnormal chromosome damage to nearby residents.[15] At this point, the *McNeil-Lehrer News Hour, 60 Minutes, Good Morning America,* and other widely watched television shows weighed in to publicize the predicament of those living near the canal.

As it happens, no reliable study has ever shown that the chemicals in Love Canal had any adverse effects on human health. The EPA preliminary study was later discredited. A blue-ribbon taskforce of experts headed by the celebrated author-scientist Lewis Thomas found that "the design, implementation, and release of the EPA chromosome study has not only damaged the credibility of science, but exacerbated any future attempts to determine whether and to what degree the health of the Love Canal area residents has been affected."[16] These findings, however, did not appease many townspeople. On May 19, 1980, angry residents went so far as to hold two EPA officials hostage for several hours to dramatize their displeasure and frustration.[17]

Only two months after Love Canal first came to prominence, the EPA decided on its own initiative to send the White House a draft bill to extend its authority over hazardous substances, including chemical spills, which it had long wanted to regulate. To underscore the importance of the subject, the agency launched a nationwide effort to identify additional sites where toxic waste might pose a threat to neighboring residents. Word of new hazardous locations would subsequently be released at various points throughout the consideration of Superfund legislation, helping lawmakers to appreciate how many of them had a stake in the proceedings.

The bill that the EPA proposed was problematic in many respects. The agency took advantage of the prevailing fears about toxic substances, although it admitted when pressed that, "to date, EPA has not conducted any direct research on the health effects of hazardous waste."[18] No careful consideration was given to the possibility that the contaminated sites might be an appropriate subject for state rather than federal action. The practical difficulties of cleaning up the sites were greatly understated. Moreover, the EPA bill suggested no way to set priorities for remediating sites, nor did it specify how clean a site would have to be in order to be declared safe.

Agency officials sought to limit the use of general revenues to pay for the cleanup by proposing to rely on two other sources: a tax on chemical feedstocks, and the imposition of strict liability on the part of all who had contributed to polluting each contaminated site. The choice of chemical feedstocks was somewhat arbitrary, since the firms involved had rarely polluted the sites themselves. The choice seems to have been made largely for administrative convenience in order to restrict the levy to a limited number of large companies that had some connection to the problem and money enough to pay the tax. The imposition of strict liability on polluters was also questionable, since most of the latter had no way of knowing at the time they acted that they were doing anything wrong. In fact, subsequent studies showed that only 4 percent of the designated sites were contaminated as a result of illegal behavior.[19]* Worse yet, by making all polluters jointly and severally liable, the agency set the stage for a legal free-for-all, with everyone suing everyone else and some polluters having to pay amounts out of all proportion to any toxic waste they had contributed to the site.

As is normal in such cases, the Office of Management and Budget (OMB) received the EPA bill and solicited comments from several in-

---

* A *prospective* charge on all polluters might still be defensible as a way of making the cost of products reflect their full cost, including any charges for cleaning up pollution. A *retrospective* charge, such as that imposed by the Superfund law, would not have this justification.

terested agencies. In theory, this process was supposed to identify problems in the bill and correct them. In practice, the review disclosed very few of the proposal's deficiencies. The only substantial objection made involved the proposed tax on chemical feedstocks, and OMB quickly dropped this issue at the first indication that President Carter approved of "making industry pay."

Some of the troubling questions were eventually raised when the bill arrived in Congress. A group of conservative members, led by Republican David Stockman from Michigan, questioned the degree of risk actually posed by toxic-waste sites, criticized the lack of criteria for defining hazardous sites, and asked why local hazards of this kind could not properly be left to the states. These concerns fell on deaf ears, however, apparently because they were considered little more than ideological obstructionism by a right-wing minority.

Instead of looking at the facts and trying to educate the public about the lack of solid evidence of any threat to human health, members of Congress responded with extreme statements of their own. The representative from Niagara Falls declared: "I went into the basements of the people who lived on either side of the site. . . . I knew from what I saw and I knew from what I smelled that we had a serious problem there that was probably affecting the health of the people living in the nearby area."[20] Senator Stafford described the problem in even more lurid terms. "We are dealing with human lives that are devastated by the impacts of these chemicals; children born with permanent defects, adults stricken with crippling diseases, entire communities with their supplies of drinking water contaminated."[21] Strong words for a situation in which no adverse health effects have ever been proved.

After the Commerce Committee, the Merchant Marine Committee, the Public Works Committee, and the Ways and Means Committee had all considered the bill, a compromise emerged. Although the EPA originally asked for a $1.2 billion fund, the Senate Public Works Committee proposed the much larger sum of $4.1 billion, only to see this amount scaled back to $2.7 billion and then ·(to placate Senator Jesse Helms of North Carolina) to a more modest $1.6 billion. Agreeing with the EPA that it was best not to pay these amounts out of general tax revenues, legislators accepted the agency's proposal to hold polluters strictly and severally responsible for the cleanup costs of each site to the extent that fault could not be reliably apportioned among them. Congress also agreed to impose a tax on chemical feedstocks. Those who drafted the bill knew that the amounts provided by these sources were insufficient for the task. Even so, as the Senate committee report made clear, they were careful to limit the size of the tax on feedstocks to "that amount which economic analyses show not to stress the well-being of affected industries."[22]

In the course of hammering out the final legislation, backers of the bill felt constrained to make a number of special concessions to win the support—or at least quiet the opposition—of key lawmakers. To satisfy Ray Roberts, representative from Texas and chairman of the House Public Works Subcommittee on Water Resources, the scope of the EPA's authority over dredging inner waterways under the Clean Water Act was reduced. To help Senator Mike Gravel of Alaska, the bill was amended to allow compensation for fishermen harmed by toxic spills. Senator John Culver of Iowa obtained a similar benefit for growers of livestock and agricultural products. In deference to Senator Bob Dole of Kansas, the law made it clear that farmers would not be held responsible for pollution resulting from fertilizing the land. For Senator Al Gore of Tennessee, reductions were made in the copper industry's contributions to the cleanup fund. Finally, to spread the cleanup funds widely enough to attract broad legislative support, Congress added a provision "that among the one hundred worst facilities, to the extent practicable, one must be from each state."

The fruit of all this labor was a compromise artfully designed to satisfy the aggrieved while giving serious offense to no one (at least not immediately). Citizens worried by the threat of toxic waste received a new program to clean up polluted sites. The costs involved were paid for without visibly burdening the taxpayer. Environmentalists, along with other citizens, obtained not only the protection of the new program but assurance that polluters would have to pay for any damage caused. As for the feedstock companies, while they grumbled about a tax they considered unfair, they could still pass the burden along to their customers without suffering any appreciable economic injury.

Unfortunately, this seemingly attractive compromise concealed some serious flaws. As key members of Congress knew, the amount of money provided in the bill was far too small to take care of the underlying problem (which EPA officials had previously estimated with remarkable prescience to consist of some 1,200 to 2,000 sites, at a cleanup cost of $25.9 million per site).[23] While avoiding anything labeled as a tax on the public, Congress chose a levy on chemical feedstocks that would clearly be passed on to consumers and would probably be more regressive than a straightforward tax increase. Finally, the notion of making polluters strictly liable was bound to produce a swarm of lawsuits and to impose liabilities bearing little relation to any real wrongdoing by many of the defendants. No other industrialized nation has sought to finance similar cleanups by levying a specialized tax of this kind or by imposing strict liability, jointly and severally, on past polluters.[24]

As the new law moved into implementation, its latent defects became apparent. Those with high expectations for aggressive cleanup of contaminated sites were soon frustrated by the snail-like pace of the EPA, as the technical difficulties of the task (augmented by a singular lack of enthusiasm in the Reagan Administration) slowed progress almost to a halt. In the absence of any standard stipulating how clean a site had to be in order to be considered safe, officials argued over just how much progress had been made. Congressional critics charged that the EPA had managed to clean only six sites, whereas the agency replied that it had taken remedial action at 541 locations. With no criteria to guide the selection of sites, intense pressures arose to try to induce EPA officials to attend to particular locations and to spread their efforts (and the accompanying funds) to as many states as possible. Small businesses and other unsuspecting parties found themselves charged with contributing to the pollution of designated sites, and thus faced the daunting possibility of having to pay for the entire cost of cleanup. Litigation expenses began to consume large portions of the funds expended under the act, as the government sued likely suspects who then sued other possible polluters in an effort to spread the liability cost.

The only successful part of the law was the provision allowing the EPA to move quickly and spend up to $2 million per site to take care of emergencies. Under this provision, the agency was able to alleviate some genuine threats to drinking water and food supplies. Where such immediate dangers did not exist, however, more than eight years elapsed between the time the EPA first learned of a site and the date on which it was finally certified as safely cleaned.[25] In the first ten years, only sixty-three of 1,200 listed sites were fully cleaned, and only twenty-nine of these were delisted following verification that the cleanup was effective. The average cost per site proved to be approximately $30 million. Of this amount, some 36 percent of the private funds expended were devoted to "transaction" (mostly legal) costs—a much larger proportion than in other industrialized nations.[26] Fearing expensive lawsuits, many companies refused to build on potentially polluted, inner-city properties, frustrating the efforts of local officials to develop large tracts of urban land. As these problems emerged, rumblings continued to be heard from the academic and scientific community that the health risks of toxic sites had been grossly exaggerated and that the entire enterprise was diverting money and effort away from other, more productive uses, such as combating lead poisoning, radon, or addiction to nicotine.[27]

In short, what began as a compromise to satisfy all the interested parties ended by irritating everyone. Residents in affected areas were frustrated. The chemical industry felt ill-used. Polluters, especially the smaller ones, were dragged into expensive litigation and threatened with large liabilities whether or not they had engaged in any culpable behavior. Insurance companies were awash in lawsuits. Directly or indirectly, the public ended up footing most of the bill—which, of course, turned out to be far larger than initially advertised: $20 billion in the first twelve years, accounting for 25 percent of the total EPA budget.

This dolorous tale bears many traces of problems described in earlier chapters. The media did not help to educate the public, with their often overdramatized accounts of the events at Love Canal. Interest groups sought to encumber the law with self-serving exceptions and exemptions. Ideology played a role, as environmentalists pressed relentlessly to "make the polluters pay," and their liberal supporters in Congress dismissed the legitimate questions of David Stockman as conservative pettifogging. Beyond these contributing factors, however, two causes seem particularly important. One is the absence of any central force in Congress or the Executive Branch which could insist that legislators produce a well-crafted piece of legislation. The second is the lack of any serious accountability for results which could force the Congress not merely to reconcile the interests that were most vocal in the legislative process but to assume responsibility for drafting a law that would actually work fairly and effectively to achieve its intended goals.[28]

The Ultimate Dilemma

Notwithstanding repeated examples similar to Superfund, many scholars emphasize the virtues of our highly fragmented system. As they point out, a government divided into several branches and levels offers unusual opportunities for all voices to be heard, unusual room for experimentation and innovation, and unusual sensitivity to the local differences and needs of a large and diverse nation. Although its checks and balances will be frustrating at times, they offer protection against grandiose mistakes and allow a more cautious, incremental approach that may cope better with the baffling complexities of many issues governments face.[29]

These advantages are real enough. Yet the benefits are easily nullified by corresponding disadvantages. The experimentation and adaptability provided by our federal system are often diluted by bickering and red tape resulting from conflicts between Washington and the many state and local governments. The safeguards to protect citizens from error and abuse will frequently exact a heavy cost in terms of long delays that create injustices of their own. Most obvious of all, the divisions of authority that run throughout our government diminish coherence and accountability to the point of severely weakening many policies, especially in complex fields of endeavor such as health care, where planning and coordination are a prerequisite to success.

These problems leave evident traces on America's record in achieving the goals to which its citizens aspire. It is no accident that the United States enjoys its greatest successes in fields—such as the private economy, scientific research, and technological innovation—

where the government need only encourage individualism and creativity by limiting restrictions on competition or by subsidizing creative people, while we lag other major democracies whenever the government undertakes more complicated tasks such as devising a healthcare system or an effective urban policy. Nor is it surprising to find that America abounds in imaginative initiatives and experimental programs to attack the thorniest social problems but rarely manages to transform these successes into systems capable of flourishing on a large scale.

The much-touted virtues of incrementalism do not necessarily outweigh its drawbacks. Incrementalism might work well if policymakers were always free to learn from their mistakes and improve at will on existing policies. In practice, however, small step-by-step changes often create vested interests and changed conditions that limit the options available in future policymaking. This drawback may have been less serious in the days when the federal government was largely preoccupied with relatively simple tasks such as collecting customs and delivering mail. It is a much greater handicap now that Washington is responsible for addressing health care, poverty, environmental protection, and other complex issues with many interdependent parts. In approaching problems of this type, piecemeal reform can gradually result in a frozen mix of half-measures and partial programs that not only cause vast inefficiencies but dim the prospects for comprehensive reform.

The American healthcare system offers the most telling example of the drawbacks inherent in incremental reform. Repeatedly, piecemeal changes to solve particular problems have brought forth vested interests that have hampered later policymakers seeking to improve the system. The decision to encourage the spread of health insurance through collective bargaining helped to perpetuate a system of partial coverage while creating a network of insurance companies too powerful to be cast aside by subsequent policymakers. The decision to establish Medicare with fee-for-service pricing reimbursed by the government at prevailing rates led to inflated physician earnings that could not easily be scaled back once the system became too expensive. The expansion of malpractice litigation gave large victories to a few mistreated patients but resulted in no compensation, or delayed and inadequate recoveries, for the vast majority of those negligently injured. Only the trial lawyers emerged clear winners, causing them to fight tenaciously against any attempt to change the status quo.

The net result of this step-by-step process is a healthcare system that ranks poorly in comparison with those of most other advanced democracies. Despite its exceptionally heavy costs, it has failed to produce results that equal those of most other advanced democracies in terms of average life expectancy, infant mortality, or any other standard measure. Small wonder that Americans are more inclined than citizens of any other major country to regard their healthcare system as needing fundamental change. Yet when politicians such as President Clinton undertake basic reforms, they feel compelled to draft convoluted proposals to accommodate vested interests and still cannot make significant progress.

In the face of these frustrating results, it is easy to look longingly at more centralized systems of government where a single majority party formulates policy, gains the assent of a pliant legislature, and proceeds forthwith to implement the new law throughout the land. Intrigued by the prospects of such efficient policymaking, a series of scholars have studied these more unified regimes. Not all the observers have liked what they have seen. A central government that can frame large plans and have them enacted into law is also a government that can easily make big mistakes. A recent example is the decision by several European governments to attack unemployment by reducing the official retirement age, a policy that did little to reduce unemployment in the short run and placed intolerable long-term burdens on the viability of their public pension programs. A unified, centralized government can also ignore local conditions and stifle local initiative—weaknesses serious enough to have led many centralized governments (as in France) to try, with mixed results, to delegate more authority to regional officials.

The melancholy conclusion that emerges from this discussion is that there is no totally satisfactory institutional structure. Neither our own fragmented system nor the more unified parliamentary structure of a country such as Britain is ideal. Fortunately, however, the world is not limited to a choice between these two extremes. There are a host of intermediate steps that will not create a perfect result but may nonetheless produce a superior blend of the virtues and drawbacks of the two contrasting systems. For example, one can legitimately refuse to tamper with our basic institutional checks and balances but still seek ways to curb the excessive prerogatives of committee chairs and other influential members of Congress. Thus, there is good reason not to accept the status quo as immutable but to search for particular adjustments and reforms that may provide a bit more coherence and accountability without giving up the familiar advantages of our existing constitutional framework.

6

WHY REGULATION MAKES SO MANY PEOPLE ANGRY

IN 1994, PHILIP HOWARD found himself prominently placed on the *New York Times* bestseller list for his slim volume entitled *The Death of Common Sense*, cataloguing the follies of regulation in America.[1] The book presents a seemingly endless list of woeful tales. Mother Teresa's nuns had to abandon plans for a new home to help the poor in New York because of building codes that required installing a costly elevator the nuns did not want. Federal inspectors from the Occupational Safety and Health Administration (OSHA) cited a brick factory in Reading, Pennsylvania, for having railings forty inches high instead of the prescribed forty-two. A nursery school in Boston had to bolt a toy refrigerator to the wall to conform with federal safety standards. Such stories—half funny, half sad—make it abundantly clear why regulation in the United States is so irritating. To many Americans, the very word suggests laws that cost more than they are worth, intricate rules that no one can possibly read through (let alone understand), requirements that are sometimes ludicrously inappropriate for situations to which they apply, and costly lawsuits that drag their way through the courts year after year.

The popularity of Howard's book showed plainly that his account had touched a raw nerve, a festering sense of frustration common to the experiences and impressions of many readers. It is these perceptions that lead a majority of Americans to conclude that the government regulates too much and often makes matters worse when it intervenes. Available statistics seem to bear out these complaints. No other major industrial nation produces as many lawyers or spends as much on litigation as the United States.[2] No other government issues as many pages of new regulations every year. Few countries, if any, pay as much to improve the environment or to regulate relations between unions and employers. Yet comparative studies suggest that all this money, effort, and controversy does not yield impressive results. If anything, America's record in fields such as environmental regulation, highway safety, labor-management relations, and the prevention of work-related injuries is less successful than that of most other leading democracies.[3]

Excessive Cost

Not everyone who criticizes regulations is worried about the kind of vexations inflicted on the Boston nursery school and Mother Teresa's nuns. Many economists and large corporations have a more general complaint: that the regulatory system simply costs far more than it should for the results it achieves. Studies using the government's own figures claim that a majority of recent regulations involving health and safety and the environment impose greater burdens on business (and ultimately on consumers) than any benefits they promise through cleaner air and water or safer homes and workplaces. One investigator who looked at almost a hundred Superfund sites found that two-thirds of the cleanups cost more than $1 billion per life saved, far more than most people consider reasonable.[4] Policy analysts also assert that the government allocates money among its many regulatory programs in a manner that often bears little relation to the relative risks involved. As a result, they say, officials spend huge sums on expensive equipment and costly cleanups that may keep a few people from being killed or injured while devoting far fewer resources to other risks where modest amounts of money could preserve large numbers of lives.[5]

Many of these problems begin with a public that is often poorly informed about the relative risks of threats to human health and safety. Most people tend to exaggerate such hazards as toxic-waste sites or nuclear radiation while paying less attention to much greater risks such as indoor radon, not to mention familiar dangers such as riding bicycles or having X-rays.[6] These skewed perceptions are sometimes translated into law, especially when the public reacts strongly to some relatively minor hazard after reading accounts of a dramatic event such as the discovery of toxic waste at Love Canal.

For obvious commercial reasons, newspapers and television stations often make matters worse by emphasizing unusual accidents while ignoring more routine mishaps. Such publicity can reinforce the public's distorted sense of relative risks. It is surely one reason nuclear power construction virtually ceased after the Three Mile Island incident although nuclear plants had never caused a single death, while countless women continued to die each year of breast cancer because so few received regular mammograms.

In much the same way, enterprising reporters (along with opportunistic legislators) pay far greater attention to regulatory accidents and errors that threaten human lives than they do to dry accounts of the costs that regulations impose on the economy. As a result, mistakes that threaten lives can lead to embarrassing hearings, investigations, and public rebukes, while exaggerated estimates of risk that greatly inflate regulatory costs attract much less attention. The consequence may be a skewed culture of blame that encourages regulators to go to extreme lengths to minimize the possibility of injury or death, forcing companies to incur great expense to avoid dangers far smaller than those most humans willingly take every day of their lives.

Interest groups also help to cause misallocation of regulatory resources. Because some public-interest groups are better organized or more skillful than others, certain risks are regulated while other, greater risks go unnoticed or receive only cursory protection. Similarly, because some business groups are more powerful than others, certain industries manage to weaken the rules that apply to them, whereas other sectors labor under much more costly regulations.

For example, during deliberations over the Clean Air legislation of 1977, Eastern coal producers faced the threat that public utilities using their coal would have to install expensive scrubbers to minimize harmful emissions from the use of high-sulfur coal. Unable to block the rule outright, legislators from the Eastern states managed to extend the regulation to cover Western producers as well, even though

Western coal had low sulfur content and did not cause users to violate environmental standards.[7] In this way, Eastern lawmakers helped keep their coal mines from losing business, but only at the cost of burdening competitors with many millions of dollars in unnecessary scrubbers.

While the public, the media, and interest groups can all contribute to regulatory misallocation and excess, certain features of our system of government magnify the harmful effects. Under our highly fragmented legislative process, for example, Congress has enacted dozens of separate statutory programs to guard against carcinogens, regulate food and drugs, and achieve other health and safety goals. Multiple programs almost always lead to needless administrative costs and duplication of effort. In addition, different committees and subcommittees frequently have jurisdiction over different programs. Not only does this split authority make it hard to consolidate duplicate programs; it often stymies efforts to allocate resources to correspond with current knowledge about relative risks.

In addition, either to impress the public or to control what many lawmakers regard as an unresponsive, uncooperative bureaucracy, Congress sometimes imposes impossibly strict requirements in its environmental and safety legislation. The most famous example is the "Delaney clause," which ordered executive agencies to eliminate use of "all [food] additives that are carcinogens regardless how small the risk involved." Other statutes have explicitly forbidden regulatory officials from taking cost into account in considering new rules. Although regulators can sometimes find ways around such restrictive language, they frequently end by imposing more stringent rules than they might otherwise employ, while using the legislative language to justify rules that would otherwise seem extravagantly expensive.

The reasons just given may explain much of the inflation in regulatory costs and the distortion in allocating government resources. Still, they hardly seem adequate to account for regulations costing hundreds of millions, even billions, of dollars for each human life preserved or for thousand-fold differences among regulations in their estimated cost per-life-saved.[8] Nor do they explain the approval of numerous regulations that cost far more than any benefits they bring, based on calculations "using the agency's own estimates and figures."[9] Why would officials repeatedly authorize such bizarre results? The answer casts a revealing light on the controversy that has swirled around the regulatory process during the past thirty years.

Looking closely at the critiques of agency regulations, one soon finds that most of the regulations allegedly costing more than a defensible $3–7 million per-life-saved do so for one of two reasons.[10] While regulatory agencies often give equal value to lives saved today and lives saved in future years, critics typically discount the value of lives saved in the future, so that deaths avoided, say, ten years hence are considered to be worth only a small fraction of those prevented more or less immediately. In the case of cancer or other diseases with long latency periods, the use of discounting and the size of the discount make huge differences in the estimated benefits of a new regulation. As it happens, however, the question of whether or not to discount the value of human life turns out to be not a technical matter with a clear answer, but a deep philosophical issue over which scholars continue to differ sharply.

The second factor that often underlies the large cost estimates of regulation's critics has to do with differences over how to project the number of deaths avoided by various rules. Such estimates are extremely crude; they rely on the results of tests of dangerous substances on animals or humans, and extrapolate from these to try to predict the likely effects on people in real life, where exposure to the harmful agents is typically much lower. They also require combining risks from a number of factors into one overall probability of harm. Regulators tend to be more conservative than most of their critics in making these calculations, a difference that is, again, not a matter resolvable by logic or statistical technique but a question of how great a margin for error is prudent when dealing with human lives. Relatively small differences in these estimates can produce very large variations in the final calculation of cost per-life-saved.

Between them, these two methodological differences can cause estimates of cost per-life-saved to vary by a factor of ten, one hundred, or even one thousand. Further differences can sometimes result from the fact that critics often concentrate on the cost per-life-saved and do not try to take account of other, less quantifiable benefits of regulation such as preservation of environmental values, avoidance of illness, and the like.

The methodological differences just described are well known and much discussed. Nevertheless, critics attacking the cost of regulations have often failed to acknowledge clearly the effects of these underlying philosophical disagreements on the cost of the rules they condemn. At times, they present their cost estimates of agency regulations virtually as scientific facts "based on the agency's own figures," without making it clear that they have adjusted those figures by supplying their own discounts to the value of lives saved and their own "more realistic" estimates of risk. The clear implication is that government regulators are out of control, over the top, driven by some mad bureaucratic logic. In turn, defenders of the rules rarely acknowledge some of the weaknesses in the government's methods, such as the practice of combining a series of conservative risk estimates into an overall assessment that seems extraordinarily conservative.

Public discussion of these issues is mired in deep layers of distrust. Many regulatory defenders oppose the use of cost-benefit analysis; they consider it a tool used by free marketeers and business interests to minimize threats to health, safety, and the environment while tying up agency officials in endless disputes over methodology. Regulatory critics, on the other hand, are prone to dismiss their opponents as zealots who believe that environmental and other values are worth promoting at any cost to the economy.

The controversy is all too typical of the conflicts that surround most forms of government regulation practiced in the United States. Too often, partisan critics launch harsh attacks without doing enough to understand opposing points of view. Such tendencies go well beyond the disputes over risk assessment and cost-benefit analysis. Similar forms of argumentation are evident in almost every aspect of the regulatory process. As the following pages try to explain, the reasons lie embedded in the distinctive regulatory style common to the United States and, even beyond, in the culture of America itself.

Complexity

As Philip Howard points out in his book, many of the rules the government issues to guide economic behavior are not only costly but maddeningly intricate and hard to understand. The Code of Federal

Regulations currently exceeds 130,000 pages. The preamble alone to an OSHA rule about the use of formaldehyde runs to more than 500 pages. Why do regulations in America almost invariably become so complicated?

In part, the reasons reside in the nature of the job to be done. The subject matter itself often bristles with questions of a scientific and technical nature, such as the toxicity of chemicals or the cost and feasibility of new environmental technology. It is normally impossible to create rules that address such questions adequately without using language that is difficult for laypersons to understand. Moreover, in a country as large as the United States, regulations must be written to apply to tens of thousands—even millions—of firms, presenting an almost limitless variety of local circumstances and conditions that call for special treatment. Such diversity virtually compels a high degree of complexity and detail.

The resulting rules might fit better if the parties involved cooperated actively in drafting them. But close collaboration is rare. Public-interest groups, such as environmentalists or consumer advocates, find it hard to work with industry spokesmen they regard as adversaries. Industry in turn tends to be equally wary of public-interest groups and thoroughly suspicious of the government. Hence, the job of writing the rules is left to officials who often have no direct experience with the industries they regulate and do not always know how to communicate in language that company executives can understand.

Since regulated firms do not work closely with government officials to draft the rules, they have no stake in helping them succeed and thus are more likely to avoid complying if they can. As a result, the officials who do the drafting must strive to close every loophole and anticipate every evasive maneuver in advance. Rules written in this spirit are rarely brief, straightforward, or easy to comprehend.

Because of the strong possibility of legal challenge, government draftsmen must also try to write provisions that will stand up in court. The language used to achieve this result is chosen more to satisfy judges and withstand attacks from opposing counsel than to communicate clearly to the company executives who are supposed to obey the rules. Regulations written with such purposes in mind are bound to resemble an insurance policy more than a recipe for baking bread.

In principle, the passage of time should help to cure these defects. As companies complain to federal agencies or protest regulations in court, one might expect officials to clarify vague provisions through repeated application to specific sets of facts. In practice, however, though some clarification may occur, it is often swamped by other developments that add to the number and complexity of the rules. Regulated firms, anxious to avoid compliance costs and gain a competitive advantage, will often find ambiguities they can exploit to get around the new requirements. Other companies are then obliged to follow for competitive reasons. Before long, the government feels compelled to take action to close the loopholes, often by adding further prescriptions with accompanying qualifications and exceptions.

Meanwhile, other interested parties intervene from different parts of our fragmented system of government. Judges issue decrees invalidating certain rules, or calling for more elaboration of the regulations or greater flexibility to take account of special situations where the agency's requirements seem to impose unwarranted hardship. The Office of Management and Budget rejects proposed rules and asks that they be rewritten to minimize the burden on the economy. Congressional committees sometimes become advocates for special interests and may urge an agency to relax certain standards and tighten others, leading to further modifications.

Complication can even arise from within a regulatory agency. The constant coming and going of political appointees brings new top officials who are frequently quick to cast aside the policies of their predecessors and introduce new ones they consider improvements. In the case of traffic safety, for example, a major reason for the delays that caused the introduction of mandatory seatbelt regulations to lag by a decade or more behind those of most European nations was the constant shifting of policy resulting from changes in top officials.[11]

Over time, therefore, as agency officials lay a regulation on the anvil of experience, it is beaten into an intricate filigree of exceptions, qualifications, and refinements. Eventually, levels of detail and complexity are achieved that only experts can understand. In response, large companies hire more lawyers, while smaller firms simply go their way, often blissfully unaware of the rules until the arrival of government inspectors rudely awakens them to the restraints that govern their operations.

Incongruous Results

After all the effort that goes into creating federal rules, it may seem odd that so many regulations become incongruous when applied to actual companies and real-life situations. Why should Mother Teresa's nuns have to install an elevator they don't need, and why must factories rebuild their forty-inch railings to a height of exactly forty-two inches? Part of the answer is that regulators have to write rules for firms, situations, and problems of which they have no direct personal experience. More important is the fact that the government cannot possibly draft separate prescriptions for each of the innumerable firms under its jurisdiction. Instead, it must prepare one set of regulations to cover the entire economy, or at least single industries with a large and diverse assortment of separate enterprises. The resulting rules may fit a majority of the companies, or even 90 percent, reasonably well. Yet typically there will be a minority of firms with special characteristics for which the agency's requirements make little sense. In a country with 200,000 enterprises polluting the air and water and several million companies with employees who can be injured at work or discriminated against in their jobs, even a tiny minority of firms with unusual circumstances can mean a lot of angry employers struggling with rules that do not fit their particular situation.

To many people, the solution to this problem must seem obvious. Why not give regulators enough discretion to adapt their standards or simply waive them entirely when they do not make sense in a given situation? In fact, some informal give-and-take of this kind does go on. But flexibility is not as easy to achieve as one might think, especially in the atmosphere of distrust so common in regulatory settings. Environmental organizations, consumer advocates, and other public-interest groups often oppose efforts to grant inspectors greater discretion to vary the rules at the company level, fearing that clever executives will hoodwink officials into giving up more than they should.[12] Ralph Nader aptly reflected these suspicions in his reaction to reports that the Food and Drug Administration was talking with the food industry to find more cooperative ways of enforcing the law. "If the Justice Department held regular meetings with the Mafia suggesting that it knew of gambling . . . which if not stopped would lead to a raid of the premises, it would be following a procedure not unlike that used by the FDA to convince the food industry to obey the law."[13]

Agency heads, too, are often loath to allow inspectors in the field more discretion to adapt the rules to fit local conditions. Doing so will cause top officials to lose control and to run the risk of having subordinates make mistakes that could result in exposés by a daily paper or trigger a congressional investigation. Besides, if inspectors receive more discretion, the agency will have to invest more time and money to train them, and money and time are both scarce commodities in most regulatory agencies. Worse yet, exceptions granted to one firm are likely to provoke complaints from competitors demanding equal treatment. Since there are rarely bright lines to separate cases where flexibility is warranted from cases where it is not, relaxing the rules for a few firms may propel the agency into a never-ending effort to draw fine distinctions, creating more complexity, stimulating more litigation, and using more scarce resources. Rather than enter this thicket, agencies often prefer to stick with uniform rules.

Even the inspectors in the field may not relish greater discretion. In an environment of intrusive congressional committees, inquisitive newspaper reporters, and other outsiders who can embarrass a regulatory agency, the cost of making mistakes will often seem greater than any likely reward for resolving problems creatively. In these circumstances, the prudent inspector may well decide that the wisest course is to follow the written rules to the letter and not risk rebuke by searching for more flexible, commonsense solutions.

The Burden of Litigation

It is hardly surprising that so much litigation occurs in such an adversarial process.* Because the firms involved rarely play more than a formal role in preparing the rules, they have no stake in making the

---

* There is much dispute over how much litigation actually occurs under regulatory statutes. William Ruckelshaus, when he was head of the EPA, once made the oft-quoted statement that 80 percent of EPA regulations ended up being challenged in court. But after a more careful analysis, Cary Coglianese of Harvard University concluded that the true figure, even for important regulations, is closer to 30 percent. See Coglianese, "Assessing Consensus: The Promise and Performance of Negotiated Rulemaking," *Duke Law Journal,* 46 (1997): 1278.

process work. Instead, they often look upon regulations as an unreasonable interference to be resisted and contested wherever possible. Because the rules are typically complicated and filled with ambiguities, arguments frequently arise over their meaning. When companies are told to buy equipment costing millions of dollars or make major changes in their products or their marketing methods, even small ambiguities can be worth fighting about. Moreover, now that judges and lawmakers have extended the right to sue not only to regulated firms but to advocacy groups and others claiming an interest in effective regulation, the odds that someone will bring a legal action increase even further.

Another factor encouraging litigation is that at least one of the parties involved will often have something to gain by bringing suit, whether or not the ultimate decision turns out to be favorable. By going to court, environmental groups may be able to delay a controversial project. By suing in several different jurisdictions and filing claims under several different applicable laws, they may even succeed in blocking a corporation for years, by which time the undertaking may have to be modified or abandoned.[14] Less public-spirited parties sometimes file a complaint simply to harass a business rival or to extract a settlement from a company that cannot afford delay.

Regulated firms will often have reasons of their own to challenge regulatory rulings. They may genuinely feel that they have a valid objection. Even if they do not, litigation can work to their advantage, since they may be able to avoid having to obey the law until the case is completed, thus postponing the costs of compliance for many months or even years. For example, under the National Labor Relations Act, a company can often defeat a union organizing drive by issuing threats and firing a number of key union sympathizers. Months or even years later, the employer may be ordered to reinstate the fired employees with back pay (which may be small change, since the employees will have to deduct any wages they have received in the interim from other employers). Such penalties will often seem a modest price to pay for delaying an organizing drive and perhaps discouraging union supporters indefinitely.

In such a litigious atmosphere, with so many avenues for bringing suit or asking for review, a legal culture soon develops around a body of regulation. Attorneys come to specialize in the field involved. Accustomed to regulation and often cynical about agency officials and their excesses, they will not be deterred, as many laypersons might, by the fear of going to court. Instead, they will calculate the expected gains and losses from litigation and advise their clients accordingly. In the case of larger companies, the risk of adverse publicity will often cause executives to comply. With incentives as they are, however, the advice for many firms may be to go ahead and run the risk of being sued. That is one reason why so many employers continue to violate the National Labor Relations Act and why so many EPA regulations end in litigation.

Excessive Legal Burdens

By all accounts, the legal costs of regulation are much heavier in the United States than in other democracies.[15] In part, such expenditures are a natural outgrowth of the highly litigious, adversarial nature of the American system. But the reasons go beyond the sheer volume of lawsuits. Every stage in the regulatory process tends to result in greater legal expense than companies experience in other advanced countries. Firms in the United States face an unusually complex body of regulations resulting from intricate rules and duplicate, overlapping programs administered by multiple agencies and often by several different levels of government. Violating the rules, even inadvertently, will frequently bring fines and adverse publicity rather than a quiet talk with a government inspector leading to a verbal commitment to come into compliance. Under these conditions, it is only prudent to hire lawyers and seek a legal opinion before undertaking a new activity.

The cost of obtaining permits is likewise inflated in the United States because the regulatory system is so fragmented. Approvals that might come easily in a centralized, consolidated system take far longer and cost much more when authority over the activity involved is divided among several federal agencies, along with state and local offices. Once the necessary permits are in hand, firms must incur further trouble and expense submitting reports and documentation to ensure compliance. Because of the distrust that pervades our adversarial system, these reporting requirements tend to be more intricate and detailed than in many other industrialized nations.

Litigation is not only more frequent in the United States; it is also more expensive. Attorneys for large companies tend to charge more for their services than their counterparts in other industrial democracies. Proceedings on matters as complex as environmental regulations can drag on for several years and consume enormous chunks of their time. The technical nature of many regulatory hearings adds further expense by requiring the use of experts and scientific evidence. The skepticism that many lawmakers and judges display toward the government's work leads administrative agencies to rely far more than regulators abroad on specialists and scientific data in an effort to ward off attacks from Congress and the courts. As one comparative study of regulation points out, "Lacking sufficient stature to take a binding action that would be accepted by all interests, U.S. officials must seek another basis of action and defense. One of their few alternatives is to find refuge in objective scientific analysis and professional consensus."[16]

Litigating technical and scientific issues is particularly expensive under the adversary system in the United States. Experts must be countered with experts and scientific documents with scientific documents, else the opposing side may gain a critical advantage. When the subject matter is technical, the ultimate answer uncertain, and the stakes extremely high, no party will wish to take chances on being outgunned by scientists and data from the other side. Often, information and testimony pile up far beyond any real contribution they make to a better solution. Still, judges and regulators let the evidence in, rather than risk having the decision overturned on appeal.

Litigation also costs more in the United States because of the abundant opportunities our laws provide for interested parties to bring suit, intervene, and eventually appeal adverse rulings by regulatory agencies. These accommodating procedures exist to minimize the chances of error and unfair treatment. In this sense, our expensive regulatory process can be viewed as a monument to the pervasive distrust of official action and the desire to protect citizens in any possible way from the arbitrary use of power. Unfortunately, the costs of maintaining the monument are far greater than those of a more informal, cooperative system.

Ironically, all this expense and delay create substantial injustices of their own. Companies abandon worthy projects because they cannot afford to wait several years while litigation runs its course. Other firms agree to costly settlements rather than run the risk of spurious lawsuits brought by unscrupulous individuals. Litigants without resources cannot pursue their rights because of the heavy costs of litigation. Employees lose their jobs because it is worth firing union organizers to intimidate other workers (though doing so is in flagrant disregard of the law), in order to gain a year's reprieve while the case wends its way through all the available appeals. Pressing needs for regulatory action go unmet because government agencies have to spend so much of their time and money embroiled in litigation and multiple layers of review and appeal. Rules are made incomprehensible to ordinary people in an attempt to minimize the risk that decisions will be overturned by the courts. These are not the kinds of unfairness that the law seems able or willing to deal with effectively. Yet they exist, and as long as they exist, all the effort and expense of providing such extensive hearings and such abundant review will not come close to achieving perfect justice.[17]

Disappointing Results

After all the trouble, time, and expense consumed in implementing regulations, one might have hoped that the results would be superior to those of other countries with less costly and elaborate regulatory systems. Unfortunately, this is hardly the case. Rarely do the gains achieved in the United States exceed or even equal those of other countries that spend significantly less.

In part, our modest showing results from poorly designed legislation of the kind discussed in the preceding chapter. According to a detailed comparative study of regulation in industrialized countries, "much of the malaise of the U.S. regulatory agencies can be laid at the doors of Congress. Legislative goals show little regard for administrative and economic reality, and agencies have to thread their way through a minefield of ambiguous standards, unrealistic timetables, complicated analytical requirements, and tortuous rule-making procedures."[18] Faced with conflicting demands from public-interest groups and industry lobbyists, legislators seem unable to resolve the differences in a manner that will produce effective results. More often, they settle for labored compromises that try to give something to everyone.

For example, as previously noted, lawmakers often set ambitious goals and timetables to show their dedication to consumers and the environment, but appropriate far too little money for agencies to achieve the stated objectives. Thus, Congress gave OSHA a task of vast dimensions covering more than 6 million workplaces but provided an initial appropriation of only $35 million. The EPA has consistently failed to receive enough funds to achieve congressional timetables that have been said to "fall somewhere between the merely unrealistic and the wholly fanciful."[19] The Labor Department has far too few inspectors to detect all of the violations by employers seeking to avoid the minimum-wage and maximum-hours requirements of the Fair Labor Standards Act.[20]

At times, legislators also set ambitious goals while creating machinery to administer regulations that are too cumbersome to allow effective implementation. The complex structure Congress devised to implement the Occupational Safety and Health Act, with its several separate administrative bodies and its provisions for state participation, is a telling case in point. OSHA's unwieldy procedures have undoubtedly contributed to an exceptionally slow rate of producing health and safety rules that has left many occupational hazards effectively unregulated.

At a deeper level, our distinctive style of command-and-control regulation is fated by its very nature to have modest results. There are inherent limitations to relying on industry-wide or economy-wide rules rather than requirements tailored to the special circumstances of individual firms. In the field of workplace safety, for example, industry-wide rules tend prevent fewer accidents than do adjustments by individual firms to eliminate hazards unique to their operations. Moreover, experience suggests that the best rules for improving safety are often not ones that can be enforced successfully in an adversarial system. For example, Japan has had much greater success than America in reducing industrial accidents by emphasizing proper training rather than physical changes in plant and equipment.[21] For American officials, however, it is much harder to make certain that employers have instituted proper training than it is to ensure that they have installed appropriate guardrails or vents. In regulating millions of separate enterprises in an atmosphere of mistrust, officials must frequently make enforceability the decisive consideration.

When inspections occur, the abrasive interaction typical of business-government relations in America limits effectiveness even further. By concentrating on finding violations and levying fines, inspectors can easily provoke resentment and cause companies to do the minimum.[22] Officials look for violations instead of helping firms to solve problems. In response, companies withhold information to avoid the risk of being penalized. In such an atmosphere, regulation degenerates into a rigid, formalistic process that frequently obscures the most important opportunities for improvement.

The time and expense involved in developing and litigating rules have also taken a heavy toll on the effectiveness of regulation. In the course of prolonged legal and administrative battles, the government spends funds that could be better used to strengthen enforcement efforts. Promulgating a new standard has become so expensive for agencies such as the EPA or OSHA that officials have been able to attend to only a small fraction of the hazardous substances that fall within their jurisdiction. (In Sweden, for example, the counterpart of OSHA was able in three years to issue four times as many rules as OSHA managed to produce in the previous thirteen years.)[23] Agencies must frequently devote so much time and money to defending and enforcing their regulations against large companies that small and medium firms go relatively untouched. According to investigations by the General Accounting Office (GAO), many enterprises are not even aware of important rules that apply to them.[24]

In sum, the rule-based, adversarial style of regulation in the United States seems poorly designed to reach the goals that government intervention is meant to achieve. Too many opportunities for progress go unrealized, and too many firms go uninspected and unchallenged. Too much time and expense is required to formulate rules and see that they are obeyed. Unless Congress begins to allocate far more money to regulatory agencies than it has in the past, it will remain impossible for officials to achieve satisfactory results in an economy as large as ours by waging a rule-by-rule, firm-by-firm, lawsuit-by-lawsuit campaign to compel compliance.

The Root of the Problem

As noted earlier, the style of regulation in most other advanced democracies has taken a different form. Rules abound and constantly increase in number, just as in the United States. But they are more likely to develop through a collaborative process featuring close consultation with comprehensive organizations representing business and other interested groups (though not always with the full participation of newer advocacy groups representing environmentalists, consumers, and the like). Inspections rely more on adjustment and cooperative problem-solving than on citing violations and levying fines. Litigation is less common, in part because the law allows less scope for it but also because there are fewer disputes that are not resolved voluntarily.

The ultimate question, then, is why the United States has chosen its distinctive adversarial strategy rather than the more cooperative methods common to other highly industrialized countries. The answer is not that government officials have simply used poor judgment. Rather, there are special circumstances in the United States that make cooperative methods exceptionally difficult to use successfully.

America lacks the comprehensive business organizations commonly found abroad that include virtually all firms within their industries and command obedience from their members. In the United States, neither the Chamber of Commerce nor the National Association of Manufacturers has enrolled more than a small fraction of its potential members, and few industries have a highly organized, disciplined association with which the government can deal. Because American business is so fragmented and individual firms are so numerous and independent, government officials cannot easily negotiate agreement on a common set of rules but must typically impose them from above.

Even if business were organized, however, its leaders would find it difficult to bargain over rules because the government, like the economy, is more fragmented than its counterparts in most other advanced democracies. Individual agencies may find their decisions reviewed and overturned by the White House, or by Congress, or by the courts. As a result, it is hard for industry representatives to obtain authoritative answers on which they can rely. Moreover, the existence of so many agencies and avenues of review presents individual firms or employer factions with a constant temptation to break ranks and try to cut a better deal for themselves with friends in the White House or in Congress.

Efforts at collaboration and voluntary problem solving also suffer from the atmosphere of suspicion and resentment that hangs over business-government relations in this country. Industry representatives worry that concessions on their part will merely become a floor for further demands from government regulators. Individual firms hesitate to share information in a common search for workable solutions, fearing that their disclosures may eventually be used against them in an enforcement proceeding. On the other side, pushed by suspicious unions and public-interest advocates, government agencies are reluctant to take any step that might lead critics to accuse them of being coopted by business.

Under these conditions, a series of efforts in the twentieth century to introduce a more collaborative, corporatist style along European lines repeatedly failed. Franklin Roosevelt's ill-fated National Recovery Administration is the most spectacular example. Herbert Hoover's earlier efforts to launch cooperative schemes met a similar fate.

The inhospitable climate of the United States does not doom every effort at cooperation. In a few instances, such as the securities industry, a collaborative approach has proved quite successful. However, the circumstances there were peculiarly favorable to such an experiment. The companies involved were highly organized through the New York Stock Exchange, while the federal government could speak through a single independent regulatory agency. Moreover, the securities industry had special reasons for welcoming a cooperative approach. All of the firms involved had a stake in having effective rules to govern their operations and ensure the accuracy of the information they released to customers, since their welfare depended on developing high standards of truthfulness and integrity that would win the public's trust. Besides, the industry was always aware that the government stood ready to intervene with more coercive methods if cooperation failed.

The answer, then, is not that cooperative regulation is never possible in the United States—merely that the prevailing conditions are unfavorable. Cooperation is unlikely to succeed unless the circumstances in a particular industry are especially inviting or the government makes careful efforts to create incentives that will induce companies to overcome their suspicions and put aside their normal methods of adversarial competition.

Because the distinctive style of American regulation has such deep cultural roots, it is not surprising to encounter similar problems whenever rules are imposed, whether or not the government is involved. This fact is not always understood. Most critics blame our regulatory problems on bureaucrats. Others criticize judges. Still others point the finger at Congress, citing the problems of regulatory design discussed earlier in this study.

To test the conventional wisdom, it is useful to look for examples of regulation in America where there are rules but no government lawyers or bureaucrats involved. One place to begin is the system for compensating the victims of accidents, a system developed and operated principally by lawyers and judges. On examination, their handiwork turns out to suffer from the same shortcomings that vex participants in the regulatory arena. The body of rules is extremely intricate and often uncertain in its application to particular cases. Lawsuits occur with great frequency, and delays of two years or more are common before disputes are eventually resolved. When victims finally receive compensation, 40 percent or more of the money awarded goes to defray legal fees and expenses, and many negligently injured victims never receive any money at all. Even so, because of this cumbersome system, the United States manages to spend much more on resolving injury cases than any other advanced democracy.[25] Commenting on the results, Warren E. Burger, a former trial attorney and the Chief Justice of the U.S. Supreme Court, once observed: "Our system is too costly, too painful, too destructive, too inefficient for a truly civilized people."[26]

Even more telling are experiences drawn from regulatory practices quite outside the government where there are no public officials of any sort involved. One example is the Joint Commission for Accreditation of Healthcare Organizations (JCAHO), a private body designed to create and maintain high standards of quality in hospitals and other organizations responsible for giving care. The commission is privately staffed, without the direct participation of government officials (although JCAHO accreditation is a prerequisite for Medicare certification and state licensing).

Founded by organizations of surgeons and other physicians, the JCAHO has gradually assumed a more adversary stance toward the institutions it serves. Inspections resemble formal investigations more than collaborative efforts to solve problems. Rules have grown complex, inspections require costly preparations, and the standards used are often criticized for inhibiting newer, innovative methods to achieve greater quality. Following a series of interviews concerning these inspections at hospitals across the country, two experts in the field recently concluded: "We find that the producers of care almost never regard existing regulatory procedures as adding value. Time after time, our interviewees told us that outside regulators add only to costs."[27] Many universities would echo these comments in reflecting on the work of most of the privately administered accreditation bodies that periodically inspect their undergraduate programs and professional schools.

A final example comes from the colorful world of intercollegiate athletics. The National Collegiate Athletic Association (NCAA) is a private organization established to oversee the athletic practices of rival colleges and universities in order to promote fair competition. Years of exercising this responsibility have resulted in a 500-page rulebook of mind-boggling complexity. Looking further, one can readily find the same kinds of problems that make federal regulations so irritating: rigid requirements that do not always fit the circumstances of the schools to which they apply, annoying forms that member institutions must regularly fill out, investigations leading to punitive sanctions—and all this for only limited success in curbing the evils the association was meant to address.

The NCAA rules governing freshman eligibility for athletics offer a telling illustration of the problem. In the 1980s, the association passed a resolution (drafted by the author of this book) requiring students to pass a certain number of core secondary-school courses before they could participate as freshmen in varsity athletics. The rule was well intentioned: it sought to induce student athletes who were academically at risk to take a group of courses that would help them complete college successfully. But what would count as suitable academic courses among the bewildering variety of offerings available in American high schools? Beset with numerous inquiries and complaints about its rulings and definitions, the association eventually created an Initial Eligibility Clearing House. Soon, this new entity was overwhelmed by thousands of calls and letters asking questions and protesting NCAA rulings. The results were not to everyone's liking. By 1998, state attorneys general, legislators, and boards of education were complaining loudly and demanding an investigation.[28] Shortly thereafter, the NCAA had to change its tack abruptly and accept the high schools' own definition of what courses were college preparatory.

There is much grumbling among coaches and athletic directors about the proliferation of rules, and efforts are periodically made to deregulate. In the words of Dan Dutcher, the NCAA's director of Legislative Services, "Deregulation of NCAA legislation has been a topic of interest for many years."[29] Interest, yes; action, rarely. The association's effort to reduce the number of rules has been repeatedly undermined by an even stronger desire to curb some new stratagem, real or imagined, that rival coaches have adopted to gain a competitive edge. As Mr. Dutcher explains, describing a meeting convened to discuss simplifying the rules, "The results of that meeting were somewhat surprising. Rather than identifying regulations to be eliminated, football and basketball coaches suggested even more regulations. . . . Coaches in other sports were more supportive, but could identify few specifics."[30]

These examples suggest that the problems of regulation which seem so irritating to Americans have less to do with bumbling government officials than with the underlying conditions of our society. The immediate causes are often to be found in our institutional arrangements—the procedures that produce incoherent legislation, the laws discouraging many forms of industrial collaboration, the multiple opportunities for reviewing official action. But the deeper reasons for our regulatory problems and for the hostility they often provoke involve more pervasive tendencies in America toward personal freedom, fierce competition, and distrust of institutionalized power, governmental and otherwise.

The difficulties begin with the individualism and suspicion of authority so traditional in this country. These tendencies cause company officials to chafe at the government's efforts to limit their freedom of action. Facing keen competition, which is unleavened by strong trade associations and other intermediaries, many firms not only resent the government's interference but worry that official requirements or expensive legal proceedings will put them at a disadvantage vis-à-vis their rivals. As officials try to give authoritative answers to questions that do not have clear, demonstrable solutions, their rulings seem arbitrary and provoke continuing dispute. The periodic application of rigid rules to situations they do not fit gives rise to further resentment, while the delays and legal costs that the American regulatory system entails add to the aggravation. Under these conditions, it is hardly surprising that so many people feel aggrieved at the treatment they receive.

The deep cultural roots of these regulatory problems have important implications for those who seek to improve the current situation. Tinkering with the institutions and procedures of government may bring some relief. By themselves, however, such reforms are unlikely to do a great deal to curb the overgrowth of rules, the contentiousness of the process, or the complexity and cumbersomeness of the system. Any strategy that relies so heavily on forcing uniform rules on such a huge, diverse, competitive economy is likely to encounter many of the same problems. There is simply not enough money available to control the behavior of millions of separate enterprises using such expensive and cumbersome techniques.

Even in the larger enterprises that are inspected regularly, officials may not accomplish a great deal to improve the environment or increase workplace safety if they go on trying to impose a set of "correct" rules on a recalcitrant body of companies. The complexities of the task and the ongoing development of new knowledge and technology cause rules to be in constant need of adaptation and refinement. Public officials, regulated firms, and other interested parties will meet this challenge most successfully if they can find some way to work together to revise old formulas and search for better solutions. The adversary style of regulation common to the United States discourages such a process. To do a better job, reformers may need new strategies for influencing corporate behavior that do not provoke such resistance or require so much time and effort to implement successfully.

7

WHY WORKING PEOPLE AND THE POOR DO BADLY

"THE MORAL TEST OF GOVERNMENT," Senator Hubert Humphrey once said, "is how government treats those who are in the dawn of life—the children; those who are in the twilight of life—the elderly; and those who are in the shadows of life—the sick, the needy, and the handicapped."[1] By this standard, the United States does poorly. In comparison to other advanced democracies, America has few programs that protect all citizens from the elementary hazards of life. Instead, lawmakers have preferred to target most social programs to reach only the needy, leaving the rest to make their own arrangements or rely on working for an employer willing to offer them health insurance and other benefits. While the well-to-do under such a system can readily take care of themselves, those in more modest circumstances have a much harder time of it. As a result, far from protecting all Americans against the major hazards of life, government policies have contributed to many of the nation's greatest failures: limited access to health care, ineffective job training, persistent poverty, and shabby public housing, to mention but a few. Program after program has led to continued controversy, repeated tinkering, and results that fall conspicuously short of what most Americans profess to want and other industrial democracies long ago achieved.

The Limited Efforts to Protect Working People

A veritable mountain of scholarship has accumulated to explain why the United States did not follow the example of Western Europe by building a full-blown welfare state.[2] While the arguments are far too numerous to be recounted here, it is possible to touch upon the principal themes of the debate.

Some scholars have emphasized the effects of cultural forces that have long been prominent in America.[3] According to these writers, racial and ethnic divisions stunted the growth of strong unions. The individualism, self-reliance, and belief in unlimited opportunity characteristic of our culture made a strong labor party less attractive to many Americans and left them unimpressed by collective schemes to shelter citizens from the ordinary vicissitudes of life. Lacking either the strong support for economic equality and social solidarity so prevalent in Scandinavia, or the emphasis on social justice common to Catholic teachings in Germany and Italy, the United States never welcomed universal social-welfare provisions of the kind that grew up in Europe.

Other scholars have placed more emphasis on America's unique institutions.[4] Our peculiar constitutional structure, with its separation of powers and its doctrine of judicial review, allowed judges to restrict Congress' power to enact protective legislation; not until the 1930s did such laws meet with Supreme Court approval. Our system of federalism gave much responsibility to state governments, which often balked at costly social programs that might burden local businesses or cause them to move elsewhere. The early guarantee of white male suffrage meant that workers were never forced to join together politically, as they did in Europe, to fight for their most elementary political rights. Meanwhile, without proportional representation, labor parties found it hard to gain a foothold. Instead, unions had to choose between the Democrats and the Republicans, both of whom needed to appeal to a number of other constituencies with differing interests. Thus, when the prospects for social legislation brightened in the 1930s, labor leaders supported Franklin Roosevelt but soon found themselves at odds with Southern Democrats, who used the power they acquired through the seniority system to block any laws that threatened their supply of cheap labor.

All of the reasons just mentioned add something to a full explanation of America's limited welfare state. Nevertheless, most of them have chiefly to do with the early development of American social legislation. It is harder to find a convincing explanation of why so many of our social programs continue to have only partial coverage and modest benefits. However great the institutional obstacles may have been decades ago, more than sixty years have passed since the Supreme Court abandoned its earlier rulings and gave the federal government broad discretion to enact social legislation. Forty years have come and gone since Southern lawmakers cared deeply about preserving the supply of low-wage farm labor, and more than a quarter-century has elapsed since they could count on seniority and the control of key committees to have their way in Congress. Surely, something more is needed to explain why America's welfare state still lags far behind developments in other industrial democracies.

Some of the cultural explanations are also wearing a bit thin. Labor parties in Europe have remained strong even after an influx of foreign workers made the surrounding population much less homogeneous. On this side of the Atlantic, racial and ethnic hostilities have diminished greatly in the past fifty years, yet labor unions find it harder than ever to expand their membership. Individualism and self-reliance have not kept Social Security and Medicare from winning a secure place in the minds of Americans, but most forms of universal social legislation still cannot succeed in Congress.

In short, neither cultural nor institutional factors offer a complete explanation for the current condition of the American welfare state. An adequate theory must account not only for the limited progress of social legislation prior to 1960 but also for the sluggish pace thereafter. Furthermore, it must explain why certain social programs have been successful while others have lagged far behind their counterparts in other industrial nations.

Some scholars have argued that earlier social policies tend to shape subsequent legislation because it is only natural to pattern new laws after existing programs and to consider the experience and demonstrated capacity of government agencies in deciding what new duties to give them. According to this theory, one reason Congress has continued to balk at comprehensive social legislation is that earlier laws targeted aid to those in need and never created a strong federal bureaucracy similar to those common to most other industrial democracies.[5]

It is certainly reasonable to suppose that lawmakers take account of past experience and executive capabilities in planning new legislation. Nevertheless, legislators have often launched new national programs without a strong tradition of earlier involvement. Congress enacted a host of ambitious environmental laws beginning in the 1960s, although there was no experienced federal bureaucracy to carry them out and tradition favored leaving such issues to the states. Even in the field of social legislation, federal lawmakers have been willing to create new national programs and new bureaucracies to deal with affordable housing, workplace safety, employment discrimination, and a number of other issues.

Why has Congress been so unwilling to pass comprehensive social legislation? The Americans who could benefit from such protection number in the tens of millions. Most politicians seem very solicitous of their welfare; lawmakers from both major parties often argue for legislation on grounds that it will benefit America's "working families." Unlike the poor, who are often misperceived as mostly black and hence are liable to racial stereotyping, blue-collar workers continue to be symbolized in popular culture by Joe Sixpack.

On closer inspection, however, American workers, especially those with low or medium skills, turn out to be far weaker politically than their counterparts in other industrialized countries. In particular, they are much less inclined to vote. Throughout Europe and Japan, workers go to the polls with almost the same frequency as other segments of the population. In the United States, turnouts among those earning less than $25,000 per year hover around 40 percent or below, whereas they rise to 70 percent or more among those with incomes over $50,000 per year.[6] To a Congress sensitive to election returns, such differences handicap working people in securing laws to protect their vital interests.

Workers in the United States, compared to those in other advanced democracies, have also been singularly unsuccessful in developing strong organizations to represent their needs to the government. Hindered by the same institutional obstacles that have confronted all third parties in this country, working people have never succeeded in creating a viable labor party along European lines. Trade unions have failed to organize a large percentage of the workforce, and individual unions have often acted quite independently, sometimes disagreeing with one another openly on matters of policy. Neither the labor movement nor Congress has looked with favor on elected works councils of the kind that give European workers a means of negotiating with their employers at the plant level.

These weaknesses are not unique to labor; no large sector of the American economy has managed to create a strong, unified organization to promote its interests. Unlike most interest groups, however, the labor movement rarely has the good fortune of seeking to advance its interests at the expense of a diffuse, inattentive public. It must contend at almost every point with the determined opposition of employers. Facing such a powerful adversary, labor's failure to bring its supporters to the polls, coupled with a forty-year decline in membership, have gravely weakened its ability to advance the welfare of ordinary working people.

The fragmented state of the American economy has led the business community to resist unions tenaciously long after most European employers have come to terms with their labor movements. Neither employers nor unions in the United States were inclined to form strong comprehensive confederations. As a result, collective bargaining never followed the pattern in continental Europe, where negotiations normally take place on an industry-wide basis over minimum wages and other basic provisions, which are then automatically extended to all members of the industry. Under the continental system, the prospect of unionization is not especially threatening to individual firms, since all their competitors will be subject to the same negotiated terms. In the United States, on the other hand, where most bargaining occurs on a company-by-company basis, a firm that is organized risks finding itself at a serious competitive disadvantage with unorganized competitors. As a result, the decentralized system of negotiation in this country has led employers to continue resisting unions with a determination no longer evident in other advanced democracies.

In fighting with business over employment legislation and other benefits for workers, organized labor suffers from handicaps other than stunted membership. One disadvantage is financial. The escalating costs of political campaigns in the United States have undoubtedly caused both parties to become more sensitive to the concerns of those who supply them with funds. Under the American system of campaign finance, contributions come overwhelmingly from large organizations or from persons with incomes in the top 5 percent. Unions manage to contribute millions of dollars, but they are outspent more than 10 to 1 by corporations. Well-to-do individual contributors, who give far more money than corporations, are rarely committed to the job-related goals that most concern unions. Even Democratic donors tend to be wary of measures that might arguably hamper business or increase taxes to pay for the kind of employment benefits and safeguards common throughout Western Europe. As a result, in vying for the support of party leaders, labor unions often find their vital interests ignored and outweighed by the concerns of more important contributors.

Beyond their anemic membership and their comparative disadvantage in supporting political campaigns, unions are unusually isolated intellectually in the United States. They have no newspaper or magazine that reaches beyond their members and competes for the attention of opinionmakers. They lack strong allies in universities and think tanks to help promote their agenda. Within the Democratic Party, labor leaders no longer have to deal with Southern conservatives, but they are not much closer to the other factions that have come to prominence in Democratic circles. At best, these groups tolerate unions while preoccupying themselves with the rights of blacks, women, gays, and other special interests. Taken for granted by important elements in their own party and vulnerable to political raids on their constituency from the religious right and other social conservatives, the union movement is even weaker than its depleted numbers would suggest.

Obvious as they are, however, the organizational weaknesses of American workers do not provide a complete explanation for the halting development of social legislation. Most environmental regulation is likewise opposed by business interests, and costs corporations many billions of dollars each year. Yet in the late 1960s, Congress enacted sweeping environmental protection laws over business opposition even before large supportive grassroots organizations came into existence. These laws have persisted and have been strengthened even further, despite determined attacks by a conservative administration. Throughout this period, a highly supportive public opinion has succeeded in keeping environmental programs strong.

In the United States, working people can also count on popular opinion to support their interests. Large majorities of Americans favor the right to join a union, universal access to health care, more job training, and paid parental leave. Why isn't this public support enough to bring stronger protection for American workers?

There is at least one significant difference between laws that protect workers and measures that protect the environment or the consumer. Debates over employment legislation and social programs have provoked more heated ideological disagreement. Although ideology has never struck deep roots with the American population as a whole, and although the differences between left and right are narrower than they have tended to be in Europe, battles in this country between left and right have often seemed more intense. In the 1930s, for example, as Seymour Martin Lipset has observed, "many Republicans, especially Republican businessmen, [had] a far deeper sense of hatred toward Roosevelt and the New Deal than their British and Scandinavian counterparts [had] against their socialist opponents."[7]

Perhaps because so few Americans have been committed to any ideology and because so many have been independent of any strong party affiliation, they have inspired both the left and the right to battle for their affections with remarkable energy and sophistication. Each side has nurtured its own cadre of foundations, magazines, and think tanks with which to hone ideas and propagate them in policy circles throughout the country. Of late, each major political party has become more closely aligned with one of the mutually opposing philosophies—the Republicans with conservatism, and the Democrats with liberalism—thus enlivening and amplifying the debate even further.

The clash between rival ideologies has long been especially sharp in discussions of social and employment legislation. Conservatives are inclined to feel that individuals should provide for their own childcare, preschooling, healthcare services, and the like, and that the government's role should be limited to giving susidies to those who are demonstrably unable to help themselves. Liberals, on the other hand, are much more likely to support generous government programs to address these needs. As for protection from arbitrary firing, advance notice for layoffs, and parental leave, conservatives, strongly backed by business, generally favor leaving such questions to the marketplace, while liberals, with the enthusiastic support of unions, are again more inclined to impose appropriate legal safeguards. Ideological conflict over such issues tends to be much stronger than it is in the case of environmental legislation, where even staunch conservatives will admit that the market fails to afford adequate protection.[8]

Faced with this conflict, the American public has responded with much more ambivalence than it has in the case of environmental laws. Although large majorities believe that everyone should be entitled to health care, further probing reveals that the public is badly split on how much responsibility the government should take to bring about this result.[9] There are similar divisions on the issue of unemployment protection. Almost two-thirds of the respondents in a 1996 *New York Times–CBS* poll agreed that "the federal government should see to it that every person who wants to work has a job."[10] On the other hand, throughout the 1990s Americans were consistently more inclined to feel that "people are responsible for their own well-being and they have an obligation to take care of themselves when they are in trouble" than to place such a responsibility on the government.[11]

This ambivalence helps perpetuate an inconclusive struggle over employment laws. Working people have won some protection for their vital employment interests and gained at least limited parental leave and childcare subsidies for their offspring. But neither they nor their representatives manage to win many clear-cut victories. Instead, for reasons described in the previous chapter on the design of legislation, debates over blue-collar interests typically end in awkward compromise. Programs are enacted with only partial coverage, as in the case of parental leave, healthcare insurance, and protection from being fired unjustifiably from one's job. Other programs lack sufficient funds to accomplish their objectives, as has been true of such measures as the Occupational Safety and Health Act, relocation and retraining benefits, and Head Start. Still other initiatives, such as collective-bargaining laws, minimum-wage statutes, and prohibitions against discriminatory treatment in the workplace, have consistently suffered from inadequate enforcement, weak penalties, and crippling delays.

The experience of American workers over the past quarter-century raises serious questions about the mechanisms our democracy provides for protecting the interests of weaker segments of society. During this period, low-skilled and semiskilled male employees have seen their average wages fall dramatically. Their job security has eroded. The percentage of employers who provide them with health insurance and pension plans has declined. Many companies have preached the value of high-performance workplaces and then appropriated most of the benefits after their employees agreed to make the adjustments.[12]

Faced with these problems, employees can join a union and bargain for better pay and benefits, or they can organize politically or at least vote for candidates who are sympathetic to their interests. In principle, these opportunities seem adequate. In practice, however, unless matters become desperate, American workers have been slow to take advantage of the options available. In the past quarter-century, they have been less and less inclined either to vote or to join unions, even though their wages and benefits have been deteriorating. When they have voted, they have shown little willingness to follow their union leaders' bidding, while proving receptive to overtures from conservative groups (for example, the Christian Coalition) that appeal to them on social or religious grounds. Faced with such an irresolute response, Congress has felt little pressure to remedy the weaknesses in existing programs that protect working people.

These tendencies are troubling. Democracy assumes that individuals will take advantage of the opportunities the system provides to defend their interests. The experience of American workers shows that this assumption may be unwarranted. For many employees, the prospects for bettering their condition through joining a union seem too uncertain and too risky to warrant the effort to organize. The possibility that they could improve their condition through political action apparently seems even more remote, especially now that both parties often appear more intent on wooing other interests and other voting blocs. The net result is that the system is not working as planned to meet the needs of an important segment of the population, even though these needs enjoy wide support among the public as a whole.

The Weakness of the Poor

If there is anything on which Americans can agree, it is that no one should go hungry in the richest country on earth. As Bill Emerson, a Republican member of Congress, observed, "There's a feeling that in a nation of abundance, where there is surplus food, and, indeed, wasted food, no one should go hungry."[13] Ronald Reagan's Task Force on Food Assistance put it even more bluntly: "Hunger is simply not acceptable in our society."[14]

These words echo the feelings of almost all Americans. Over 90 percent of the public has affirmed that "it's not right to let people who need welfare go hungry."[15] Large majorities declare that they would be willing to pay higher taxes to increase spending for food assistance.[16] No organized opposition seems prepared to argue publicly against these sentiments. And Congress has responded. By 1997, the U.S. government was spending more than $39 billion in food assistance through a battery of different programs: food stamps, school breakfasts, school lunches, special supplemental food for women, infants, and children (WIC), nutrition for the elderly, and so on.

In that same year, 1997, the federal government announced the results of the most comprehensive survey ever undertaken to measure the extent of hunger in the United States.[17] According to this study, 4.16 million households totaling over 11 million people had experienced hunger during the preceding twelve months. Curiously, 53.5 percent of those with moderate hunger and 49 percent of those suffering severe hunger did not receive any federal aid at all. Despite insistence on all sides that hunger in America was unacceptable, and despite numerous programs to eliminate it, hunger in America continued.

Many analysts have explained why the government has failed to solve this problem. Even in good times, officials do not manage to publicize the availability of food assistance effectively enough that all potential recipients can apply. When budget cuts are needed, food programs are often a tempting target, and policymakers trot out a familiar series of reasons to support the reductions. Recipients are said to be abusing the system (although government estimates put the extent of recipient fraud at only 1–2 percent); congressional critics claim that the hunger statistics are exaggerated (although the government itself has now confirmed them); and conservatives argue that charitable organizations could do the job and do it better (a claim that the charities themselves have been consistently quick to deny). Meanwhile, hunger persists.

The saga of food assistance and the arguments it provokes are typical of many efforts to deal with poverty. Large majorities of the public want to do more to help the poor. No one disagrees, at least overtly. Periodically, political leaders call for more vigorous efforts. But when the dust clears, poverty rates and other indications of want continue well above the levels of other industrialized countries, especially among those who seem most deserving of help: small children. How can it be that our accomplishments so often fall short of what most people claim to desire?

Attempts to understand America's poverty programs must start with one elemental fact. Poor people in the United States have even less political power than low-skilled and semiskilled workers. They seldom take much interest in public affairs. They are less inclined to read daily papers or watch television news than Americans of greater wealth and education. They rarely vote. They contribute nothing to political campaigns. They are not likely to be union members. Apart from church, they seldom join organizations of any kind, at least the kinds of organizations that mobilize for political purposes. The more the government neglects their interests, the less interested in politics they become. As a result, they are increasingly marginalized and ignored by politicians and by the strategists who manage political campaigns.

Weak as they are, the poor are not without friends and allies. Churches lend support. Organized labor often lobbies for causes important to low-income families. Journalists regularly call attention to their plight. Advocacy groups, such as the Children's Defense Fund, fight on their behalf. Still, because these organizations cannot persuade the poor to vote, their efforts bring limited results.

Occasionally, needy families get added help from politically powerful allies when some organized interest group has a financial stake in government antipoverty programs. Farm organizations have pressed to enlarge the food stamp program, especially when their support can be traded in exchange for urban votes to maintain crop subsidies. Building contractors have sometimes fought to preserve federal subsidies for low-income housing construction. When all is said and done, however, people in poverty have no political power, and most of their potential allies have other priorities that render their support irregular and uncertain.

Would public policy change very much if more poor people flocked to the polls? Twenty years ago, Raymond Wolfinger and Steven Rosenstone found that voters and nonvoters had very similar views on policy questions—even social welfare issues.[18] These findings seemed to suggest that social policy in the United States would be much the same even if poor people voted with the same frequency as wealthier Americans. But later work has qualified the findings of Wolfinger and Rosenstone by showing that poor voters are somewhat more likely than affluent voters to support social-welfare programs. Moreover, even if the current views of poor people hew closely to those of mainstream America, it is not clear that they would continue to do so if more low-income citizens began to cast their ballots. Once poorer, less-educated Americans started voting as often as their more prosperous fellow citizens, politicians would work much harder to cultivate their support. Presumably, candidates would appeal to their special interests and promise to help secure more of the benefits given to lower-income groups in other advanced democracies. Elected officials would begin to find it advantageous to stand up for such legislation. Over time, therefore, the expectations and demands of these neglected citizens could well change, and as they went to the polls in greater numbers, their voice might become more powerful in the halls of Congress.[19]

Recent studies by Kim Hill and Jan Leighley seem to confirm this prognosis.[20] These investigators found that poor people vote at much higher rates in some states than in others. For example, in the mid-1980s, the difference in turnout among individuals with incomes over $50,000 and those with incomes under $12,500 was virtually nonexistent in New Jersey, while wealthier citizens in Kentucky voted at a rate almost two-and-a-half times that of their poorer fellow Kentuckians. Even in the same region, the differences varied considerably: in Louisiana, the ratio for rich and poor voters was 1.2 to 1, while in neighboring Texas, it was 2 to 1. Hill and Leighley then examined the levels of welfare payments in each of the states. What they found was a strong, consistent relationship between benefit levels and voter turnout among the poor: the higher the turnout, the higher the benefits. This pattern led them to conclude that "participation is critical in the formulation of social welfare policies."[21]

To illustrate the importance of political involvement, compare the way U.S. policy has developed for the poor with the way it has developed for the elderly, who are highly organized and vote heavily.[22] If one counts fixed assets, the average elderly American today has more wealth than the average citizen between the ages of eighteen and sixty-five. The pensions, medical coverage, and other benefits that retired persons receive are normally given in the form of entitlements paid in cash, indexed for inflation and determined nationally. In contrast, the benefits given to poor children are more likely to be means-tested, locally determined, paid in kind, and divided among a host of separate, often confusing programs. While the incidence of poverty among senior citizens has steadily declined over several decades, poverty rates for children have increased by 50 percent since 1970, and are now the highest of any age group in the population (as well as being far above the child-poverty rates of other advanced industrial democracies). When the interests of the poor and the elderly are pitted against each other, the outcome is rarely in doubt. In the words of a legislative leader from a large Eastern state, "If we have $20 million and the choice is between spending it for senior citizens or poor kids, it's no contest. The seniors get the money every time."[23]

This process was clearly evident in 1996, when Congress acted to reduce the deficit. According to the Washington-based Center for Budget and Policy Priorities, 93 percent of all the cuts in entitlements came from programs for low-income families, even though programs for the poor made up only 37 percent of total expenditures for entitlements other than Social Security and only 23 percent of all entitlement spending.[24] Similarly, 34 percent of the cuts in non-entitlement programs came from programs for the poor, although low-income programs accounted for only 21 percent of total funding for nonentitlement programs (excluding defense).[25]

With all their weaknesses, however, poor people do have one potential source of support. A majority of Americans say that they would like the government to do more to help the needy, and that has been true quite consistently since opinion polling began in earnest in the 1930s.[26] Even during the twelve-year period commencing in 1980, when voters repeatedly backed Republican candidates for President, 65 percent of Americans thought that the federal government should spend more for the poor; only 9 percent believed that spending should be cut.[27] In 1998, two-thirds of Americans felt that the government wasn't paying enough attention to the needs of poor people.[28] The same survey found that 65 percent of respondents thought that the government should give a high priority to reducing poverty, but that only 16 percent felt that Congress was actually doing so.[29] In a democracy, such clear preferences ought to count for something.

Besides enjoying wide public sympathy, poor people rarely have to contend with powerful enemies. Unlike the opposition that confronts the union movement when it seeks to amend labor legislation, to obtain universal health insurance, or to strengthen the hand of unions in organizing workers, no strong business or professional groups oppose giving more nutritional supplements to needy mothers or providing higher subsidies for Medicaid and childcare. Why is it, then, that public support has not succeeded in bringing forth programs for the poor that compare in generosity to those of other advanced democracies?

Examining popular opinion more closely, one soon finds that attitudes toward the poor are more ambiguous than they might seem initially. For one thing, feelings about antipoverty programs appear to be influenced by race. A recent analysis of opinion surveys in the mid-1990s revealed that the strongest predictor of negative attitudes toward the welfare program is a belief that blacks don't want to work.[30] Although racial prejudice has declined greatly since the 1930s, one thing that has not changed much is the belief that inequality among the races is chiefly caused by a lack of effort on the part of blacks. Almost half of all whites continue to view blacks as lazy, while only 17 percent regard them as hardworking.[31] Such sentiments are the more damaging because a majority of whites also believe that most welfare recipients are black. (The true proportion is below 40 percent.)[32] The negative effect of these beliefs on support for poverty programs has undoubtedly been magnified further by the public's misperception that welfare is one of the largest items in the federal budget.

The widespread cynicism toward government and politics also affects prevailing attitudes toward poverty programs. Curiously, neither distrust of government nor the belief that public officials don't care about people seems to have much effect on popular support for a wide range of programs, such as Social Security, environmental protection, or financial aid for college students. But cynicism and distrust do appear to have negative effects on attitudes toward welfare programs, aid to cities, unemployment benefits, and other government efforts to help the needy.[33] Thus, periods of high and rising distrust, such as America has experienced since the 1960s, are likely to be accompanied by diminished support for federal poverty programs.

The public also seems more conflicted about how best to help the poor than many opinion polls might suggest. Like citizens in other advanced democracies, Americans say they want the government to spend more to relieve poverty. At the same time, as shown in Table 4, they are far more reluctant than Europeans to endorse broad principles about the government's responsibilities toward the needy.[34]

Opinion surveys also show that Americans are much more inclined than citizens of other advanced democracies to feel that human beings are largely responsible for their own fate and that they have the ability to improve their lot by hard work. Conversely, they are less disposed than citizens abroad to believe that individuals are held back by bad luck, blighted neighborhoods, or other forces beyond their control. A clear majority—57 percent—*disagree* with the statement, "Success in life is pretty much determined by forces outside our control," compared with 42 percent of the British, 36 percent of the French, 33 percent of Germans, and only 31 percent of Italians.[35] Similarly, 63 percent of Americans reject the proposition that "hard work offers little guarantee of success," compared with 51 percent of Italians, 46 percent of the British, 46 percent of the French, and only 38 percent of Germans.[36]

Table 4. Percentages of respondents in five countries who agree with two statements about government responsibility.

	Respondents who agree (in percent)				
Statement	U.S.	U.K.	Italy	France	Germany
1. The government should provide a decent standard of living for the unemployed.	37	65	68	Not available	66
2. It is the responsibility of the state to take care of very poor people who can't take care of themselves. (Percent agreeing completely)	23	62	66	62	50

If Americans have any clear opinion about helping the poor, it is that government assistance should go only to people who cannot be expected to help themselves. But this is a shadowy line. How many of those receiving government aid are truly unable to help themselves, and how many are malingerers? How psychologically disturbed or physically handicapped or mentally deficient does a person have to be to qualify for help? And how can ordinary Americans know whether most or almost all recipients of public assistance are truly deserving and not abusing the system?

These uncertainties give rise to much ambivalence over government initiatives to aid the poor. Americans sympathize with the needy and feel that Congress should do more to help, but they are quick to grumble about waste and malingering and reluctant to acknowledge any broad obligation to assist the poor. They deplore the plight of the homeless but privately wonder why the panhandlers and the folks sleeping on park benches cannot pull themselves together and find a decent job.

Ambivalence offers fertile ground for perpetuating the ideological war between liberals and conservatives over the causes of poverty in America. Does the problem result from adverse social conditions and impersonal economic forces? Or is it primarily the result of a lack of initiative and effort on the part of the poor themselves? Are high school dropouts and teenage mothers in the ghetto largely victims of circumstances beyond their control? Or should one expect them to pull themselves out of the ghetto with a strong dose of initiative and hard work? Can private charity take care of those in genuine need? Or is the demand simply far too great for any agency other than the government to satisfy?

Committed liberals and conservatives divide sharply on these issues. Liberals have tended to back more generous benefits for the needy and to balk at requiring them to work unless the government provides ample training, childcare, and, above all, jobs paying decent wages. Conservatives are much more doubtful that the average poor person actually needs such assistance, unless he or she is too old or too sick to work. In their view, able-bodied individuals can almost always find a job if they really try; after all, countless other people do. Expensive childcare subventions and training programs are not truly necessary, and welfare allowances are doubly harmful, since they allow the government to extract money from taxpayers unnecessarily and then use it to discourage the poor from mustering the gumption to help themselves.*[37]

If the public were more united in its beliefs about the causes of poverty and the responsibilities of the State, these ideological battles might have little practical effect. But this is not the case. Against a background of public ambivalence, liberals can appeal to voters by stressing the plight of the homeless and the cheerless existence of disadvantaged children. Conservatives can make a persuasive case by pointing to malingering, promiscuity, and the dependence of single mothers on government handouts. As both sides strike a responsive chord, the controversy continues, with policy shifting back and forth in accordance with changes in the political complexion of Congress.

The Problems of Compromise

For years, the ideological disagreement of elites, nourished by deep-seated public ambivalence, has led Congress to cope with poverty

---

* In recent years, some conservatives have adopted a more extreme position based on deep moral disapproval of illegitimate births. According to this view, all welfare payments to single mothers should cease. Any illegitimate children born thereafter should be put up for adoption or, if no adoptive parents can be found, placed in amply funded orphanages. See, e.g., Charles Murray, "The Coming White Underclass," *Wall Street Journal* (October 29, 1993): A-14.

through a series of flawed compromises. These unseemly bargains include the initial exclusion of domestic servants and farm workers from labor and Social Security legislation; the willingness to let many states restrict medical and welfare assistance to only a fraction of the poor; the insufficient funding for programs such as Head Start, nutritional supplements for infants, and housing subsidies for the poor; and the imposition of elaborate, sometimes demeaning application procedures that discourage many eligible beneficiaries from applying.

In recent years, however, an opportunity for compromise has arisen. The government would provide more generous benefits to the elderly and disabled poor who cannot be expected to work. At the same time, lawmakers could insist that able-bodied mothers find employment, while making it easier for them to do so by guaranteeing adequate childcare, health benefits, job training, and, as a last resort, government-created jobs at pay rates sufficient to lift them out of poverty. In this way, the government could stop giving money to people who should be able to work, without denying adequate help to those who genuinely need it. This solution is close to the one adopted by countries (such as Sweden and France) that have been unusually successful in inducing single mothers to work.[38]

Such a compromise would appear to have broad public support. Since 1960, popular opinion has swung massively away from feeling that unmarried mothers who postpone employment should be at home with their children, and toward a belief that they should support themselves by taking a job.[39] Huge majorities favor appropriating funds for education, vocational training, and childcare to help unemployed mothers go to work.[40]

Despite this agreement on basic principles, elites are divided about how to put the principles into practice. Some favor having the government offer work, arguing that the economy does not always provide enough jobs and that many mothers in poverty lack the skills or the temperament to find employment in the private sector even in prosperous times. Others disagree, feeling that anyone who really wants to work can usually find it. Still others oppose a public jobs program because they feel that the government is incapable of operating such a program effectively, or because they fear that the effort will end by replacing private-sector jobs with lower-paying public positions for people moving off the welfare rolls. Finally, many leaders of the religious right resist on the ground that all welfare benefits are immoral because they reward women who have children out of wedlock.

These differences came to a head during debates over the Welfare Reform Act of 1996. The legislative struggle that ensued shows how differences can arise (even within the Republican Party) that make it difficult to agree on a workable result. By the mid-1990s, it was reasonably clear that public resentment against long-term payments to single mothers made some form of work requirement necessary, despite the continued uneasiness of liberals about forcing mothers to find a job. At this point, several contradictory approaches were proposed. Moderate Democrats and Republicans favored a work requirement coupled with ample funding for childcare, job training, health benefits, and the like. More conservative legislators, with support from the religious right, sought harsh provisions that would penalize welfare mothers giving birth to children out of wedlock. Republican governors, on the other hand, lobbied for a simple proposal to delegate power over welfare programs to the states, with minimal interference from Washington. Finally, budget cutters, who cared more about a balanced budget than they did about the problems of the poor, concentrated on seeking large cuts in federal appropriations for welfare, food stamps, and related programs.

The final result gave something to almost every faction, while failing to produce a coherent result.[41] Those concerned about putting welfare mothers to work obtained a strong work requirement with strict time limits. Those who condemned out-of-wedlock births received much rhetoric about the importance of reducing teen pregnancy and a battery of measures to tighten parental-support requirements, compel mothers under eighteen to live with their parents, and offer bonuses to states accomplishing the most to reduce the number of children born to single teenage mothers. Budget cutters won $55 billion in reduced appropriations over the next several years for related programs, such as food relief programs, assistance to legal immigrants, and payments for the elderly and disabled poor. When even these compromises failed to reconcile the ideological divisions among Republican lawmakers, the leadership eventually dodged the problem by delegating vast powers over welfare to the states.

Since the passage of the Welfare Reform Act, controversy has continued over the wisdom and humaneness of the new law. Supporters emphasize that welfare rolls have shrunk virtually by half, thanks to full employment coupled with vigorous efforts by many states to help the poor make the transition from welfare to work. Enthusiasts add that unforeseen surpluses have enabled many states to do even more than expected to supply training and childcare. On the other hand, detractors point out that many of those cut from the welfare rolls are still earning less than a poverty wage, and that the poorest 20 percent of single-mother families are now even worse off than before. They warn that the harshest effects of the reforms have failed to materialize only because of a booming economy, and that grave hardships await mothers whose benefits run out at a time when the country is in recession and jobs are not so easy to find. Meanwhile, they add, even prosperity and full employment have not cut the poverty rate substantially or brought it to a level close to that of other advanced democracies.

Beyond these differences of opinion lies another, more intractable problem that hinders attempts to find a fully satisfactory solution to the high rates of poverty. For reasons earlier described, wages for unskilled workers in the United States are unusually low in comparison to those of Western Europe: less than half the prevailing rate in Germany, and barely two-thirds of the level for all of Western Europe.[42] In fact, more than 25 percent of all American workers earn less than a poverty wage, and welfare mothers are often reluctant to work because they cannot find jobs that pay enough to lift them and their children out of poverty.[43] Yet conservatives (and most employers) would fiercely resist if the government tried to make work a more attractive alternative by boosting the minimum wage substantially. Even liberals might hesitate to lift the minimum wage enough to make work appealing to welfare mothers, for fear that too many jobs might disappear. As a result, unskilled wages continue to languish below the levels needed to allow a full-time worker to escape from poverty, and welfare mothers still lack sufficient economic incentives to seek work voluntarily.

The reasons for the persistence of so many working poor go far beyond the politics of the minimum wage. The American economy has come to rely on an army of low-wage service workers who are the product of substandard schools, ineffective job training programs, and a host of other social problems (including immigration policies).

The net result is a large body of employees who are not sufficiently prepared to hold a job that pays more than a poverty wage or even to find a steady job at all. Under these conditions, policymakers would find it very difficult to lower poverty rates to Western European levels without addressing not merely the low minimum wage but the inadequacies of public education and job training, which are in turn connected with the prevalence of crime, drugs, substandard housing, and all the other social ills that afflict the poor in America.

The sheer magnitude of these problems acts as the ultimate deterrent to creating programs that could reduce poverty to the levels achieved by other leading democratic nations. At a minimum, the government would have to provide massive retraining and improvements in urban education to give poor people the skills to be employable at pay levels substantially above the current minimum wage. Merely appropriating more funds for these purposes would probably not suffice, for finding ways to educate young people from broken families and urban ghettos has proved extremely difficult. Even if enough jobs miraculously materialized at wages sufficient to lift all able-bodied people out of poverty, a serious effort to induce welfare mothers to work would cost a lot of money in training, childcare, and health benefits. Against the huge demands of Medicare and Social Security, coupled with the strong resistance to any new taxes and the political weakness of low-income workers, reforms of this magnitude have hardly seemed possible. As a result, poverty rates in 1999 were still above 1973 levels even after years of growth and prosperity.

Social Security

One cannot fully explain our past failures to help poor and working people without accounting for the government's one great success in providing economic security and alleviating poverty. Social Security did not emerge all at once from Congress as a fully developed, universal system for giving pensions to elderly Americans. Like other pieces of social legislation, its benefits were originally meager and its coverage was far from comprehensive. In time, however, federal lawmakers kept raising benefits and making them available to more and more Americans—to the point that, today, the only working people not covered are employees belonging to other government retirement programs, such as those created for members of the armed services. As a result, Social Security, aided by Medicare, has cut the poverty rate among Americans over sixty-five from 35 percent in 1960 to only 9 percent in 1995.

The Social Security program was not originally meant to supply enough income to meet all retirement needs; it was intended only to provide a "basic floor of protection."[44] Even today, its benefits amount to a smaller share of previous earnings than the public pensions available in most other advanced democracies. Nevertheless, supplemented by private pensions and personal savings, Social Security has helped older Americans enjoy higher incomes relative to their pre-retirement earnings than the elderly of any other advanced democratic nation. Moreover, despite popular prejudices about government waste and inefficiency, the program uses a tiny portion of its revenues for administration—much less than most private pension funds.

Why has Social Security been so much more successful than health care, employment safeguards, or programs for the poor? Not for lack of ideological disagreement. As early as 1935, Kansas governor Alf Landon attacked the plan as "unjust, unworkable, stupidly drafted, and wastefully financed."[45] From the beginning, many Republicans resented the fiction that the program was a form of insurance in which beneficiaries "paid their own way." According to true conservatives, individuals should decide for themselves how to provide for their retirement, and federal subsidies should go only to those too poor to buy a pension on their own. A program of this kind would give more freedom of choice and encourage greater self-reliance. It would allow individuals added leeway to decide how to invest for their old age, making it possible to capitalize on the higher returns available in the private securities market.

In the eyes of conservative critics, the myths about the program have finally been exposed. Americans are coming to realize that the current Social Security system is seriously underfunded and threatens to place intolerable burdens on the active workers who will have to pay for the retirement benefits of the huge baby-boom generation.[46] Contributions earn less than the returns readily obtainable from gilt-edged bonds, let alone common stocks. The claim that everyone pays for their own benefits rings particularly false. As conservatives repeatedly point out, those currently retired have paid for only a small fraction of their Social Security pension, while younger workers are likely to put considerably more money into the system than their pension income will be worth in order to keep the program in balance during the next century.

Whether or not these arguments are correct, why have ideological disputes not led to the legislative fights and unsatisfactory compromises that have marked the evolution of so many other social programs? One reason, surely, is that no powerful interest groups in 1936 felt as strongly about keeping the government out of the pension field as the American Medical Association felt about blocking compulsory health insurance. The most likely heavyweight opponent, the life insurance industry, was divided about the effects of the program and decided not to take a position.

Political conditions in 1936, however, cannot explain the continued growth and popularity of Society Security in subsequent decades. Nor is the absence of powerful interest group opposition enough by itself to have assured the passage of effective, comprehensive social programs; the experience with poverty is proof of that. But old-age pensions differ from antipoverty measures in at least one important respect. Crucial to the success of Social Security is the fact that the public has never had the same ambivalence toward the program that it has displayed toward welfare, food stamps, or public housing. Even in 1935, over 90 percent of Americans believed that the federal government should provide pensions for the elderly.

The moral element has always been an important factor in the attitudes of Americans toward social legislation. All of the truly successful American social programs—the GI Bill, the first widely accessible public school system, the veterans' pensions after the Civil War—benefited groups with strong moral claims for State support.[47] In contrast, welfare legislation has met with disfavor because it benefits mothers who have children out of wedlock and do not work.* It was

---

* As the moral ground shifted after the late 1960s, and more and more Americans came to feel that single mothers should work rather than stay home with their children, popular support for Aid to Families with Dependent Children (AFDC) declined substantially. See Steven M. Teles, *Whose Welfare? AFDC and Elite Politics* (1996), pp. 41–59. At the same time, the public and Congress have been much more supportive of survivors' insurance for children whose parents have died or wives whose husbands have passed away than they have of efforts to assist single mothers under welfare.

primarily to preserve single mothers from idleness and dependency, not to save money, that Americans came to strongly favor welfare reform.[48] Unemployment insurance has likewise received only lukewarm support over the years, because of the feeling of many Americans that people out of work should be able to find a job on their own. In contrast, there are no moral qualms about Social Security. Whatever the truth of the matter, a large majority of Americans have continued to believe that individuals earn their old-age benefits by their previous contributions. And since all the beneficiaries have retired—and should not be expected to work—Americans have likewise had no worries about malingering and freeloading.

The last and equally important explanation for the continued success of Social Security is that it does not merely serve a politically weak minority, such as the poor, but benefits all elderly people. No one is likely to regard the program as a handout for "shiftless" minorities. Everyone either enjoys its benefits or looks forward to enjoying them someday. Even the young can thank the program for relieving them of the burden of having to take care of their parents. As a result, popular support for Social Security does not simply rest upon the charitable instincts of the public; it is firmly rooted in the self-interest of vast numbers of voters.

During the first decades of the program, when the cost of raising benefits was small and the needs of the elderly were great, the political advantages of expanding the program were irresistible. Now that the program has matured and Congress can no longer pay for benefit increases by expanding the number of covered workers, the burdens of financing Social Security and heavier. Unlike the poor and the unskilled, however, the elderly are now well organized politically. The American Association of Retired Persons (AARP) claims 33 million members, with a large budget and an ample staff. Americans over sixty-five also vote at a rate of 70 percent, well above the average turnout for the nation and far above the rate for poor people and low-skilled workers. Under these conditions, few politicians would suggest cutting old-age benefits to balance the budget.

In short, the Social Security program lacks most of the features that have hampered the growth of other social policies in America. Its constituency is not weak. It did not face determined opposition from powerful interest groups in its formative years. It does not awaken the fears of bureaucracy, waste, dependency, and freeloading that make so many Americans ambivalent about most social legislation. Thus, the program had none of the features that allowed ideological differences between liberal and conservative elites to divide the public and produce the compromises which mark our programs for health care, employment regulation, and poverty.

Conclusion

It is not hard to understand why the government has such a spotty record when it comes to meeting the needs of poor people. The problem starts with their extreme political weakness. Having largely withdrawn from the political process, those living in poverty have few assets besides the compassionate concern of most Americans and the absence of any strong interest groups specifically opposed to their welfare. Unfortunately, they face opposition of a subtler kind: ideological opposition from those who feel that the poor are largely responsible for their plight and that charities can better take care of any legitimate needs that remain; prejudice among those who feel that most of the poor are black and therefore too lazy to help themselves; and attacks from those who wish to cut the budget and who look upon poverty programs as a tempting, weakly defended target. Against such opponents, the poor have few weapons of their own, and their allies—the compassionate majority—turn out to be more ambivalent and more receptive to the complaints of ideological critics than opinion polls might lead one to believe.

In such an unequal contest, the poor rarely receive programs adequately funded to meet their needs. Even in good times, racial stereotypes and moral disapproval of "malingering" welfare moms and illegitimate babies undermine support for poverty programs such as welfare payments to single mothers. When budgets are tight, needy people quickly lose out to other interests with greater clout. According to John Deardourff, a Republican consultant, the point is not "that most governors and state legislators don't care about poor children and families in their states. But . . . politics is politics, and when the horse-trading starts in state capitals, poor children are often left behind. In state after state, children's advocates are outgunned by richer and more powerful interests, whether homebuilders, truckers, nursing home operators, trial lawyers, veterans, or the elderly."[49]

Working people fare better at the hands of Congress, since they are more numerous, suffer less from moral and racial disapproval, and have the benefit of unions to press their case. Even so, they are too poorly organized and vote too irregularly to win many decisive victories, especially against the resolute opposition of conservatives and employers. Faced with the public's uncertainty over the proper balance to strike between collective and individual responsibility, they must usually settle for compromise solutions that promise more than they deliver.

When beneficiaries of federal legislation are well organized and political leaders do not sense enough ambivalence within the public to sustain strong ideological differences, Congress is much more likely to enact successful, comprehensive programs. That has been the experience of Social Security in the United States, just as it has been in Western Europe for other forms of social legislation, such as unemployment insurance, programs for children, and health care. Under such conditions, it is much easier for lawmakers to provide sufficient funding and agree on a workable design. Indeed, in an effort to please constituents, politicians may actually grant too much in prosperous times—only to find that voters refuse to have their benefits reduced later on, even if it is evident that they cannot prudently be sustained.

Experience with social legislation, then, reveals a basic dilemma in trying to make democracy work in advanced industrial nations. If low-income citizens are politically weak and the public is ambivalent about their needs, as in the United States, government is likely to do a half-hearted job of protecting their basic interests, especially in periods of slow growth and fiscal austerity. When lower-income groups are well organized, however, and public opinion is favorable, as in most of Western Europe, the problem is no longer one of ignoring the needs of ordinary workers and people in poverty. Rather, the danger is that the government will offer ample protection to everyone but lose its capacity to adapt when changing circumstances so require. Politicians will agree to generous provisions in good times, only to find that in such a heavily organized society, it is extremely hard to trim benefits when the need arises, because of the universal reluctance to accept immediate losses in exchange for the shadowy prospect of eventual gains.

These differences are strikingly evident today in America and Europe. In comparison with countries such as France or Germany or Sweden, the United States has retained greater flexibility to cut budgets, trim benefits, adapt its economy, and reorganize and downsize its corporations. The problem is that this flexibility is maintained in large part at the expense of those segments of society that are the poorest, weakest, and least able to sustain further sacrifices. To its supporters, the American way is worth the hardships it entails because it has propelled the economy to levels of prosperity unequaled in the rest of the world. To families without health insurance, workers fired unjustly from their jobs, employees laid off from plants moving overseas, or single mothers trying to get by, the wisdom of it all may not be quite so clear.

III

REMEDIES

A VAST LITERATURE has accumulated proposing new programs and policies to aid the poor, protect the interests of working people, and improve various regulatory systems. Although some of the ideas are impractical and others inadequate, many would undoubtedly be helpful. Nevertheless, the lesson of the preceding chapters is that the most serious shortcomings of federal policy do not merely involve failures of judgment or imagination that can be put right by substituting better policies. Rather, they reflect larger problems stemming from causes deeply rooted in our institutions, our political system, and even our culture. With a little luck and much hard work it is always possible to change a particular law or reform a particular policy. To make a substantial improvement in the government's overall performance, however, one must address the underlying weaknesses through institutional or systemic reforms.

Fortunately, complaints about government have also produced a bumper crop of suggestions for changing our procedures and institutions. Journalists, politicians, and the general public have all made proposals of this kind. Since the three groups disagree on what is ailing Washington, one would expect them to differ in their choice of remedies. That is exactly what has happened. Chapters 8–10 discuss the best-known, most popular suggestions from each of the three groups.

Not surprisingly, the institutional reforms that command the greatest popular support are ones that put more control in the hands of the people. Among these are proposals to institute term limits, to make greater use of ballot initiatives and referenda, and to bring federal programs closer to home by placing them under the control of state and local officials. Each of these remedies receives the support of more than 70 percent of the public. That fact alone provides a sufficient reason for considering the proposals carefully.

Presidents and other high administrative officials have long favored remedies that seek to change the bureaucracy. Proposals of this kind range from steps to improve the training and recruitment of civil servants to attempts to substitute private entities for government agencies in carrying out public programs. Even more widely publicized is the recent campaign to "reinvent government," a series of measures organized by President Clinton and Vice President Gore to focus and motivate the work of public officials, while freeing them from the dense thicket of rules that hamper their creativity and cause much delay and needless paperwork. Governments around the world, including our own, undoubtedly suffer from administrative red tape, inflexibility, and inefficiency. If attempts at "reinvention" can attack these problems with even partial success, they will be more than worth the effort.

The remedies of choice for many editorial writers and public-interest activists are those that seek to change the way election campaigns are financed in order to reduce the impact of money on politics. There is much to say for such reforms. The campaign contributions of organized groups and wealthy individuals clearly feed the public's suspicion that policymakers in Washington are captives of special interests. It may be true that, in the past, journalists and other critics have exaggerated the effects of political donations on the work of Congress. In recent years, however, loopholes have emerged that permit special interests to direct so much private money to candidates, parties, and political campaigns that any thoughtful observer must worry about the effects on the policymaking process and on the confidence of the people in their government. As a result, proposals that seek to contain these risks merit the most thoughtful consideration.

Following a review of these familiar proposals, Chapters 11–13 take up a series of remedies aimed more specifically at the principal weaknesses of government described in the preceding chapters: the fragmentation and lack of accountability that lead to poorly designed, incoherent legislation; the command-and-control regulation that produces costly rules, lengthy delays, frequent litigation, and only modest results; and the political impotence of poor and working-class Americans that accounts for most of the deficiencies of America's social and employment legislation. These three weaknesses are largely responsible for the government's persistent failure to achieve the goals most Americans profess to favor. As a result, remedies that address these underlying problems deserve a prominent place in any comprehensive discussion of government reform.

In considering ways to improve our government, the following chapters share a difficulty common to all discussions of large-scale social reform. Big problems rarely have easy remedies. If they did, the necessary changes would have long since been made. Thus, any serious treatment will quickly encounter a dilemma. Simple measures will almost certainly prove to be trivial or ineffective, while remedies bold enough to promise major change are likely to seem utopian and unrealistic.

With this difficulty in mind, one can surely discard a host of changes that are simply too minor to warrant discussion. For example, there is little point in debating whether the President should be allowed to serve for only a single six-year term. Whatever the merits of such a proposal, it will hardly do much to overcome the kinds of difficulties recounted in this volume.

Conversely, there are other reforms that are too drastic to warrant consideration. Scholars can debate for hours whether our basic structure of government represents the ideal mechanism to cope with the current challenges facing a large nation-state. Certainly, a system of separated powers, elaborate checks and balances, extensive rights of review and appeal, and multiple layers of authority—federal, state, and local—takes a toll on the efficiency and effectiveness with which the federal government creates and executes its policies. No doubt these drawbacks have become more serious, now that Washington has taken on so many large and complicated responsibilities. But the basic features of our system have compensating virtues of their own: extensive safeguards against official error and abuse, abundant opportunities for experimentation, ample room for local adaptation. Moreover, these features are not only well established and enjoy extremely broad support; they are embedded in some of the most enduring characteristics of the American people—their distrust of power, their fear of injustice, their concern for individual liberty.

Under these circumstances, it would be unrealistic to spend time discussing reforms that would significantly alter the basic framework provided in the Constitution. Americans are not going to adopt a parliamentary system, or abolish state and local governments, or severely restrict judicial review of official actions. Nor should they; the consequences are too unpredictable and the reforms cut too deeply against the grain of our traditions. Fortunately, eliminating major constitutional changes from consideration, along with proposals for minor tinkering, still leaves a wide spectrum of remedies that are neither too trivial to discuss nor too drastic to take seriously.

8

BRINGING GOVERNMENT CLOSER TO THE PEOPLE

MOST AMERICANS HAVE a pretty clear idea of what ails the government. Politicians are the real culprits. They tell the voters what they want to hear in campaign speeches and then disappear to Washington, where they are quickly caught up in partisan squabbling or seduced by lobbyists to vote for special interests. In either case, they soon forget the voters they were elected to represent.

Those who share this view recommend various remedies to correct the problem. Although these proposals differ greatly, each seeks to diminish the role of professional politicians and give more control to the people. Limits on the length of time legislators can serve are meant to get rid of professional politicians and replace them with people a bit more like the folks who elect them. Ballot initiatives and referenda allow voters to express themselves directly on issues of policy and to enact measures that elected politicians refuse to pass. Devolving more authority from Washington to state and local governments would bring power down to levels that ordinary people can more easily understand and control. These, at least, are the benefits anticipated by legions of voters who enthusiastically favor such reforms.

Supporters seem to feel that ordinary Americans have a fairly accurate, down-to-earth idea of what the country needs and how to

solve its problems. The difficulty, they believe, is that special interests, political ambitions, and petty partisan disputes continually get
in the way. The question to consider is whether this diagnosis is
sound and whether remedies founded on such a premise can do
much to overcome the government's failings.

Term Limits: Getting Mr. Smith to Washington

Of all the popular remedies, term limits seem the least promising,
even though they are backed by more than 80 percent of the people.
By depriving candidates of the chance to stay in office for long periods of time, supporters mean to discourage professional politicians
from running and to replace them with ordinary citizens who will
never serve in Congress long enough to become beholden to lobbyists, blinded by power, or corrupted by the perversities of Washington. Despite these hopes, it is doubtful that term limits will either get
rid of professional politicians or remove the influence of special interests.

Even if lawmakers could serve in the House of Representatives for
only three terms, many professional politicians might continue to
seek office, hoping to run for the Senate or for some other elective
office after their six years came to an end. This is precisely what seems
to have occurred in California, where at least half of the first class of
term-limited legislators sought some other political office when their
terms ran out.[1] Legislators with such ambitions, of course, will be
just as "political," just as intent on reelection, and just as quick to
curry favor with interest groups to obtain financial support as current members of Congress. Indeed, such members might become
even *more* attentive to interest groups, hoping to keep their options
open for a good job as a lobbyist in the event that other political
openings were unavailable when their time in Congress ended.

At least some new legislators under term limits would presumably
be "amateurs" rather than professional politicians. If so, what kind
of "amateurs" would they be? As yet, no one knows for sure. But
few hardworking, successful people could afford to interrupt active
careers to spend six (or twelve) years in Washington. Instead, many
of those running would probably be somewhat atypical: persons of
wealth who could afford the time to have a fling at politics, or pro-

fessionals near the end of their working lives seeking a stint in Congress to cap their careers. Equally likely prospects would be candidates handpicked by a powerful interest group, which would help them raise the money to run for office and guarantee them a good job when their term in Washington ran out. A legislature made up of such people might not be any more representative of the voting population than the present Congress. Members picked to run by powerful interest groups could be even more beholden to their patrons than most of the lawmakers currently holding office.

One must also ask whether it is wise to replace seasoned politicians with "amateurs" restricted to limited periods of service. "What this means," concludes John Hibbing after examining the records of lawmakers over time, "is that requiring representatives to leave after a set number of years would likely result in a devastating loss of legislative acumen, expertise, and activity."[2] As in most demanding occupations, Hibbing adds, experience counts for a lot in politics. According to his calculations, members of Congress who have served longer are more effective in passing laws, even after allowing for their greater powers of seniority.[3] Time in office makes lawmakers more proficient at crafting legislation and steering it through the labyrinthine procedures of Congress. Years of service help members gain the knowledge needed to understand such complicated issues as health care or defense policy.

Lacking time to accumulate experience, lawmakers could become more dependent on their staffs or on experienced lobbyists for information and expertise, thus adding to the influence of groups that are neither representative of the people nor entitled in a democracy to have such an effect on the nation's policies. Although it is still too early to tell, analysts see indications in term-limit states such as Maine, Arizona, and Michigan that power is shifting away from legislators toward governors and civil servants.[4] In the end, according to Peter Schrag in his study of the California experience, "the winners from term limits will be, first, the lobbyists, who are never termed out; second, the governor and the executive branch, which still has the budgetary and policymaking expertise; and, third, the bureaucrats, who will stay on long after legislators go."[5]

These risks might be worth running if there were compelling evidence that long-serving members of Congress gradually become more remote or less attractive to their constituents. But the evidence on this point is not convincing. Senior lawmakers do not tend to lose voter support over time, nor are their approval ratings lower than those of their more junior colleagues.[6] Long-serving members are also less likely than they once were to become an entrenched oligarchy that controls the work of Congress without due regard for the will of the voters. Prior to the 1970s, when committee chairs wielded great power in Congress and seniority invariably governed advancement, Southern Democrats with safe seats and many years of service could have an enormous influence on legislation. Since the reforms of the early 1970s, however, seniority counts for less, and the power of committee chairs has diminished appreciably.

Term-limits advocates insist that Congress suffers from insufficient turnover, citing the extraordinarily high percentages of incumbent members who win reelection. Nevertheless, although incumbents rarely lose, they do retire at a sufficient rate that for the past several decades 15–20 percent of all House seats have changed hands every two years. More than half the members of Congress in 1996 had never served in that body prior to 1990. As a result, it is not at all clear that term limits are needed to bring new blood to the national legislature. True, current campaign finance rules make it possible for some incumbents to amass large "war chests" that can inhibit a worthy challenger from running and perpetuate their careers beyond their proper time. But surely the remedy for this problem is to change the campaign finance laws, not to expel all lawmakers after a few years, regardless of how good a job they are doing or how much their constituents want to keep them in office.

In sum, none of the arguments for term limits seems particularly strong. Legislators elected under limited terms could well turn out to be no more representative of the people than current lawmakers. Potential candidates of great ability might consider a legislative career less attractive and refuse to run for office. Term limits would certainly reduce the level of experience in Congress, especially if service were limited to six years. On balance, therefore, such a rule could well make matters worse rather than better. It is hard to perceive what benefits the reform could bring that would outweigh its considerable disadvantages and risks.

Direct Democracy

If term limits will not produce a crop of lawmakers who carry out the people's wishes more faithfully and effectively, perhaps the public can get what it wants by voting directly on important issues of policy. This is not a new idea. Many states, especially in the West, have allowed citizens to vote on initiatives and referenda ever since the Progressive era early in this century. But public support for this device seems to be growing. Since 1970, the number of proposals on the ballot has increased in states that already allowed initiatives, and additional states have adopted the procedure. Repeated polls show that Americans overwhelmingly approve of direct democracy and that comfortable majorities favor the use of national referenda.[7]

Some commentators welcome these developments. John Naisbitt, in his book *Megatrends,* has predicted a continuing rise in ballot initiatives and referenda because "we have outlived the historical usefulness of representative democracy, and we all sense intuitively that it is obsolete."[8] Several well-known scholars and political writers have endorsed the trend.[9] Technological advances have conjured up new visions of virtual town meetings and Internet voting on all manner of public questions.

Proponents have made two principal arguments for more direct popular participation. Most people who favor such proposals do so because they assume that voters will be free of pressure from interest groups and party bosses and hence able to make better decisions than legislators. At the very least, advocates insist, ballot initiatives will allow the public to get proposals passed which might otherwise be bottled up indefinitely in the legislature for political reasons. The second argument for direct democracy comes from political analysts who feel that voters will become less cynical about government and will take their responsibilities as citizens more seriously if they have greater opportunities to participate directly in the policymaking process. A recent article in *The Economist* goes even further. "By giving ordinary people responsibility, [direct democracy] encourages them to behave more responsibly; by giving them more power it teaches them how to exercise power. It makes them better citizens and to that extent better human beings."[10]

Direct democracy seems all the more natural, now that the average citizen is so much better educated and now that technology can bring so much more information about politics into the average household. Governing through elected representatives no longer seems as necessary as it did when most people never graduated from high school and attending college was a privilege reserved for very few. Some enthusiasts even look upon ballot initiatives as a natural step in the perfection of democracy. According to one journalist, "If democracy means rule by the people, democracy by referendum is a great deal closer to the original idea than the every-few-years voting which is all that most countries have."[11]

Despite these enthusiastic endorsements, direct democracy has some obvious limitations as a means of deciding policy questions. It is hard to put more than a few proposals on the ballot at one time without overloading voters with more issues than they can possibly evaluate thoughtfully. Moreover, of the scores of significant questions that require resolution every year, the only ones that lend themselves to the ballot are those that can be cast either in the form of a simple yes-or-no vote or as a choice among a limited number of options. A proposal to outlaw the sale of handguns may work well enough. But projects such as welfare legislation or healthcare reform, where the issues are typically complicated and multifaceted, are much harder to deal with.

For these reasons, it is unlikely that ballot initiatives could ever take care of more than a small fraction of the total business that comes before the legislature in a large, complex society. Any hope that direct democracy will replace the work of Congress seems quite out of the question. Still, it is worth asking whether direct democracy provides a superior way of resolving at least a limited number of important policy issues.

Ballot Initiatives

If voters come to impose their will more frequently on the legislature, how capable will they be of exercising their new powers responsibly? Several studies of the actual results of state ballot initiatives have reached quite favorable conclusions.[12] For example, Professor Max Radin ended his review of the history of initiatives in California by declaring: "One thing is clear. The vote of the people is eminently sane. The danger apprehended that quack nostrums in public policy can be forced on the voters by demagogues is demonstrably nonexistent. The representative legislature is much more susceptible to such influences."[13] More recently, as interest groups have perfected the art of rounding up petition signatures and growing numbers of their propositions have appeared on the ballot, observers have been more mixed in their appraisal. In his study of California politics, for example, Peter Schrag credits the growth of ballot initiatives with gravely weakening public schools, undermining public services, diminishing the legislature, and thwarting the interests of immigrants, blacks, and other minorities.[14]

Skeptics can support their view with many studies that show how ignorant and misinformed most citizens are about public affairs. Recent surveys reveal that the general public is no more knowledgeable about political and policy matters than it was decades ago, despite advances in educational levels and the spread of television.[15] Moreover, opinion surveys make clear how ignorant Americans are about many important issues of policy.[16] Apparently, the responsibility of having to vote on ballot issues does not lead them to inform themselves more adequately. On this score, investigations of voter behavior are sobering. Many citizens mark their ballots with very little understanding of the issues before them.[17] Most voters do not even read the pamphlets distributed by state officials to explain the pros and cons of each proposition. Up to one-third of all voters do not appear to use any source of information at all in marking their ballots.[18]

Other scholars are not troubled by such findings, insisting that voters can make sound judgments with surprisingly little information.[19] According to these authors, knowing what a trusted newspaper believes or how much money particular interest groups have spent for or against a ballot initiative may be enough to allow the average person to reach a reasonably shrewd decision on how to vote.

Cast in such general terms, arguments over voter competence are not likely to be resolved soon. Trying to judge how wise or unenlightened the electorate has been is bound to be a subjective task, and reasonable people will continue to reach conflicting conclusions. It is more fruitful, therefore, to change the question slightly and ask whether there are specific types of issues that are better suited to direct democracy than to the normal legislative process in arriving at decisions that serve the best interests of society.

The most compelling case for ballot initiatives involves proposals to improve the political process, such as efforts at campaign finance reform, where elected representatives are too self-interested to reach an unbiased decision. On matters of this kind, although the voters may occasionally support misguided reforms, they will at least be more objective and open-minded than their elected representatives. Another promising example involves questions in which legislative leaders and other key lawmakers are under heavy pressure from special interests armed with lavish campaign contributions.* Proposals to regulate handguns, insurance companies, or trial lawyers are all possible cases in point.

Aside from these examples, it is hard to imagine that voters can go to the polls every other year and consistently make wiser decisions than a full-time legislature. It is not even clear that they can reach conclusions that come closer to reflecting the true will of the people. Economist Kenneth Arrow and a number of other scholars have demonstrated the impossibility of obtaining a coherent set of public preferences in this way.[20] All that ballot initiatives can accomplish is to obtain the views of the electorate on a limited set of specific propositions or choices put before them. Much depends, therefore, on what procedure is used for deciding which choices will be presented for a vote and how the choices will be worded.

The process Congress follows, with all its faults, provides a way of deciding what comes to a vote through an orderly deliberation by representatives elected by the people. The propositions on a ballot, on the other hand, are not the product of a deliberative process carried out by elected representatives; they are drafted privately by self-appointed groups and placed on the ballot if their sponsors have the

---

* Some observers might include a third category of cases involving issues that turn primarily on basic questions of value, such as whether to restrict abortions or abolish the death penalty. There is no way to determine convincingly whether a legislature or the voters will arrive at more enlightened decisions on such questions. Nevertheless, some would argue that in a democracy issues of value are peculiarly appropriate matters for the people to decide. On the other hand, even questions involving basic values may be influenced by information and studies of a kind that most voters will not have considered.

money and organizational skills to obtain the requisite number of signatures on a petition.

Any careful look at the process of gathering signatures will reveal that money and organization are often more important than the significance of the issue to the public. Even proposals that attract large numbers of unpaid campaign workers need to have a costly support organization to train the volunteers and coordinate their efforts. Ironically, the organizations most capable of carrying out this task are often the same wealthy interest groups that citizens want to keep out of the legislative process. It is these groups that can afford to advertise widely and hire people to set up tables at shopping malls and other crowded locations to persuade the prescribed number of voters to sign a petition.

The propositions that emerge from this process are worded to achieve the result that their backers want, not to elicit a clear sense of what the voters believe. For example, a recent ballot proposal in California and Washington asked voters to approve or disapprove the use of race by public officials in university admissions, state employment, and awarding public contracts. In fact, each of these three situations involves very different considerations, and rational voters might legitimately feel differently about them. Nevertheless, the proposal, as written, demanded a single response covering all three cases.

Unlike legislation, moreover, most ballot propositions are put on the ballot without a serious attempt to compromise and adjust the language to take account of other legitimate interests. Granted, those who draft initiatives often try to anticipate objections and make appropriate modifications to minimize opposition to their proposal. But there is no assurance that the backers will engage in sustained discussions with other interested parties in an effort to satisfy their reasonable concerns. As a result, ballot initiatives are more likely to produce unanticipated problems and to ignore legitimate minority concerns than laws enacted by a well-functioning legislature.[21]

Once sponsors have gathered enough signatures to qualify an initiative for the ballot, they will usually need a lot of money to run a sophisticated media campaign that will reach enough voters to win the election. Fortunately, money does not always determine the final result; expensive campaigns by corporate and professional interests to promote self-serving proposals do not seem very effective. On the other hand, organized interests that spend a lot of money can usually defeat an unfriendly proposal. One large-scale study covering many different initiatives found that in elections where the opposition raised two-thirds or more of the total funds spent, the proposal lost 87 percent of the time.[22] Another large multistate study found that money, far from being neutralized by direct democracy, was the single most powerful predictor of whether a ballot initiative succeeded or failed, and that the side that spent the most prevailed 80 percent of the time.[23]

Money and organization would play a much greater role if America adopted a system of national referenda. The requisite number of names on a petition needed to qualify for the ballot would undoubtedly be several times the figure for a state referendum, requiring a far larger, more expensive signature-gathering effort. The cost of televising ads would be much higher. As a result, only the wealthiest, most powerful interest groups would normally be in a position to mount effective campaigns, and the process would become something far different from the spontaneous grassroots citizens' initiatives that most enthusiasts of direct democracy seem to envision.

Proponents of ballot initiatives have hoped that citizens would come to the polls in larger numbers if they were given an opportunity to determine policy directly. In practice, the opposite is more often true. Occasionally, highly publicized initiatives, such as California's Proposition 13 limiting property taxes, will lift turnouts above the normal levels. Studies of large samples of ballot proposals, however, reveal that on average 15 percent *fewer* voters mark their ballots for or against initiatives than they do in general elections for candidates running for statewide office.[24]

Not only are voter turnouts generally low; the citizens who do vote are not a true cross-section of the public. Lower-income, less-educated Americans go to the polls at rates far below the average, and when they go, they are less likely to vote for initiatives than for political candidates.[25] Thus, the results of ballot proposals are even less representative of public opinion as a whole than normal political elections.

All things considered, therefore, ballot initiatives appear to hold only limited promise for overcoming the ills of government. The number of initiatives that can be safely placed on a ballot without overburdening the voter is small, relative to the number of issues that most legislatures have to resolve. Those propositions that do qualify manage occasionally to break the hold of powerful interest groups or cause lawmakers to become more sensitive to public opinion on basic questions of value. Reformers can also use the initiative to good effect in forcing action on issues (such as campaign finance reform) where lawmakers are too self-interested to make reliable decisions. But there is no mechanism to ensure that only propositions of this kind will appear on the ballot, and the great majority of initiatives probably do not fit within any of these categories.

Whatever one may say about direct democracy, it is clear that ballot initiatives do not take special interests or their money out of policymaking. Nor should anyone suppose that interest groups will have less influence in determining which issues come to the voters for decision and which ones ultimately prevail than they do in the normal legislative process. No evidence exists that the opportunity to vote on more ballot initiatives will revitalize democracy. Residents of states with ballot initiatives do not seem less alienated and cynical than those in states that lack opportunities to vote directly on policy issues. Nor do they vote in larger numbers simply because there are policy proposals on the ballot.* Overall, therefore, direct democracy has a very limited potential for curing the ills of representative government.

Citizen Panels

Despite the limitations of ballot initiatives, there is often much to be said for finding a way to introduce a thoughtful and informed public opinion into the policymaking process. Political scientists James Fishkin and Robert Dahl have made intriguing proposals to do just that.[26] Both authors recognize the superficiality of polling results of the kind politicians often use. They also know how unrealistic it is to expect busy citizens to master the complexities of current policy

---

* In fact, voter turnouts have been slightly higher in states with ballot initiatives, but that difference seems to be accounted for almost entirely by the fact that the region of the country with the lowest turnout, the South, does not have states with initiatives. When states with and without ballot initiatives are compared, excluding the South, the difference in turnout is negligible.

questions. To overcome these weaknesses, they propose that representative samples of, say, one thousand citizens be assembled to consider a given issue, study the relevant facts, hear from all sides, deliberate, and eventually vote on the question. The outcome would not be binding on the government. But the results could at least let politicians know what ordinary citizens would think if given a chance to inform themselves and discuss the issues carefully. With enough publicity, a process like this might cause officials to take the conclusions seriously.

Such proposals are appealing. Citizens would have a chance not merely to react instantaneously to pollsters but to reach a considered judgment. In doing so, they could make up their minds without the prying journalists, lobbyists, campaign contributions, and other familiar pressures that can divert elected officials from serving the interests of the public. In this way, deliberative panels might help to discover the true voice of the people that many Americans feel has gotten lost in the maelstrom of contemporary politics.

For all their attractions, however, citizen panels have definite limitations. A few days will afford too little time for a group of laypersons to arrive at thoroughly informed, considered judgments on many of the most complicated issues confronting the nation. In considering a single subject in isolation, participants may not fully appreciate the budgetary limits under which the legislature must function and the tradeoffs that have to be made in deliberating over an entire legislative program. As a practical matter, moreover, once panels have completed their work, why should members of Congress prefer the panels' recommendations to the wishes of their own constituents? Presumably, what concerns practical politicians most is how the voters in their own district think, not what all American citizens might decide if they had a chance to study the issue in depth.

Citizen panels, then, could probably make a difference at the national level only in a few situations. There might be times, for example, when legislators want to do the right thing but need political cover. The conclusions reached by a citizen panel after a well-publicized deliberative process could accomplish this purpose. On other occasions, such a panel might conceivably reinforce public opinion in a particularly forceful way and give the extra push that a vacillating Congress needs to arrive at a sound conclusion.

Citizen panels could well prove much more helpful in resolving local or specialized disputes, such as siting controversial facilities, settling zoning disputes, or helping to build a consensus about priorities for health care or environmental protection. If necessary, panels assembled for these purposes could deliberate for more than two or three days. Their principal virtue would be to reconcile the values of the public with the technical knowledge of experts. And this is no small achievement. Already, well-organized citizen panels seem to have succeeded on questions of this kind in reaching workable, sensible solutions—perhaps more workable than either public opinion or expert calculations could have managed by themselves.[27]

Unlike term limits, then, citizen juries are not likely to do any harm. If they happen to make a poor decision, the legislature need not accept it. Their weakness lies in their limited utility for helping to resolve national issues. Citizen panels must be used sparingly or their impact will quickly diminish. Moreover, unless they meet for longer than a few days, they will be ill-suited to address more complicated policy questions, such as comprehensive healthcare legislation, tax reform, or balanced-budget proposals. Like ballot initiatives, then, citizen panels can help in certain situations, but they are unlikely to offer much relief for many of the most important problems hampering the work of government in America.

Devolution

Although Americans today deeply distrust politicians, they have greater confidence in state and local officials than in their representatives sitting in Washington. With these sentiments, it is not surprising that large majorities of the public favor devolving more power from the federal to the state and local level.[28] Presumably, they hope that such a shift will bring government more under their control and result in policies more responsive to their needs.

Until the 1930s, most of the important powers of government were lodged in the states. From Franklin Roosevelt's New Deal to Lyndon Johnson's Great Society, however, the federal government steadily increased its influence over domestic policy. In environmental regulation, labor relations, work safety, health care, old-age pensions, social services, and even such traditionally local tasks as law enforcement and education, federal dollars and federal policies came to assume far greater importance than ever before.

Beginning with President Nixon, and continuing after Republicans regained the White House in 1980, the pendulum started to swing the other way. President Reagan tried with partial success to return federal programs to the states, along with block grants to help pay for them. In 1988, Congress gave the states broad discretion to devise ways for encouraging single mothers to find jobs. In 1996, Republican majorities in the House and Senate backed a sweeping reform that delegated much more authority to state governments to move welfare recipients into the workforce.

Prominent figures from both political parties now agree that Washington should devolve more power to lower levels of government. Many lawmakers advocate moving entire programs and areas of responsibility out of the federal government, giving the states sole jurisdiction over functions such as housing, public education, and job training. Policy analysts—liberal as well as conservative—have also favored such a redistribution of power. In this way, they argue, Washington could clarify the roles of different levels of government while shedding a number of responsibilities that could be better administered by states and municipalities. For example, Alice Rivlin—later to become director of the Office of Management and Budget in the Clinton Administration—declared in 1992: "The proliferation of federal programs, projects, offices, and agencies in so many parts of the country [has] made the federal government increasingly unmanageable. It resemble[s] a giant conglomerate that has acquired too many different kinds of businesses and cannot coordinate its own activities or manage them all effectively from central headquarters."[29] Accordingly, Rivlin proposed that

> the states, not the federal government, take charge of accomplishing a "productivity agenda" of reforms designed to revitalize the economy and raise incomes. These reforms would address needs such as education and skills training, child care, housing, infrastructure, and economic development. . . . The following federal programs would be devolved or gradually wither away: elementary and secondary

education, job training, economic and community development, housing, most highways and other transportation, social services, and some pollution control programs.[30]

Rivlin is not the only Democrat to join the chorus for devolution.
The centrist Democratic Leadership Council has declared that successful government programs must "transfer more decisions and
control over public resources from Washington to citizens and local
institutions."[31] In the same vein, political scientist Paul Peterson also
favors efforts "to give back to states and localities custody over basic
public services and other programs that foster local development."[32]
When state and local authorities gain control over these programs,
Peterson adds, "the country enjoys a more efficient and productive
public sector."

What is the reason for this widespread support? In their enthusiasm, advocates sometimes imply that state and local officials will be
more effective than federal authorities. But such assertions seem
questionable at best. It is always possible to find outstanding state
agencies or municipal officials among the fifty states and more than
85,000 regional and local governmental units. Overall, however, the
lower levels of government have a mixed record of administration.
Most state governments were widely regarded as amateurish and
clumsy until about twenty-five years ago. Even now, levels of profes-
sionalism vary greatly from one capital to another, with some states
having done much less than others to modernize their operations.

Local governments have an even spottier record of accomplishment. Many large cities have notoriously bloated and inefficient bureaucracies. Few of them have done particularly well in fulfilling
their central responsibilities, such as providing public education, administering justice, enacting building codes, and maintaining infrastructure. In administering job training programs, they have long
been less successful than the federal government itself; too often,
they have used their authority over federal funds to indulge in patronage and cronyism. Granted, some mayors have had outstanding
records and have earned the enthusiastic support of their constituents. Comparing the work of local and federal governments as a
whole, however, no fair-minded person could say categorically that

the former have been more efficient, less corrupt, or more successful than the latter.[33]

A more plausible reason for devolution is that it would lighten Washington's heavy burden of responsibilities. With fewer programs to monitor and administer, federal officials could presumably do a better job with the tasks they retained, while Congress could provide more effective oversight. True as this may be, however, it is far from clear that overload is a major cause of Washington's problems or that federal agencies were more efficient before they assumed a host of new responsibilities in the 1960s. Governments in Europe have accomplished more in many fields than the United States, even though they have undertaken a more ambitious array of programs and usually delegate fewer of their responsibilities to local authorities or private organizations. In any case, if reducing the federal workload is a desirable goal, there are better ways of accomplishing it. A two-year budget cycle would be one alternative. Campaign finance reform that reduced the fundraising burdens of legislators would be another.

The strongest arguments for devolution have little to do with increasing efficiency or easing Washington's burdens. One good reason is that it will foster experimentation: fifty states (not to mention many thousand local governmental units) are likely to produce more promising innovations over time than a single federal bureaucracy.

Another important argument for devolution is that government programs will become more responsive to the wishes of the voters, since many separate programs for welfare, job training, and other public purposes will be better equipped than a single national policy to take account of local differences in values and priorities. Some observers press the point even further: they argue that vigorous competition among states and municipalities will make the public sector more responsive by driving each unit of government to devise the mix of taxes and services that best suits the preferences of its residents.[34]

At times, of course, almost everyone will agree that the benefits of experimentation and local competition are outweighed by other considerations that favor a uniform national approach. Allowing the states to impose fifty different social security systems or truck safety standards would cause needless burdens and inefficiencies, just as separate state regulations governing telecommunications and the information superhighway would hamper the process of technological change. Asking each state to create and equip its own army and navy would not only be inefficient but invite individual states to spend too little on defense in the hope that others would take up the slack. A great economic depression or some other national emergency might sometimes justify federal initiatives, such as a massive public-works program, that individual states were unable to afford. In still other instances, federal action may be needed to regulate hazards such as air and water pollution, where lax standards in one state could inflict damage on others. Beyond these examples, there is a widely shared moral sense that all areas of the country should maintain certain minimum levels of housing, food, and health care so that no Americans will go without the basic necessities of life simply because they happen to live in a state that cannot afford or will not provide what it takes to guarantee an adequate minimum standard for its citizens.

Most of the largest federal programs—defense, Social Security, and Medicare—can probably be justified on one or another of these grounds. However, a number of functions remain (many of them relating to economic development, such as job training, public education, and small-business assistance) that could properly be considered local in nature and left entirely to the states. Although state and local officials already have the power to implement most of these programs, shedding them completely from Washington's portfolio would lessen the overall burdens of the federal government and leave the states freer to create their own development programs in accordance with local needs and preferences. The problem is that many states would not wish to have the added programs if they had to pay for them. Moreover, the programs themselves are small enough, relative to the totality of federal responsibilities, that devolution would not significantly alter the overall distribution of state and federal functions.

Political analysts are much more inclined to argue about where to put control over redistributive efforts to aid the poor. For decades, Washington has supplied most of the funding for these purposes, but states have retained much power not only to administer the programs but—in matters such as welfare payments to single mothers and medical services to the poor—to decide how to set benefit levels and eligibility standards. Controversy has persisted over what part the federal government should play in determining the basic standards and requirements for these programs. Liberals have claimed a legitimate federal role in establishing minimum benefit levels and eligibility requirements. Conservatives have responded that such intervention often hobbles the states in finding innovative ways to save money, reduce fraud, and ensure that benefits are not spent on people who ought to get a job to support themselves and their families.

Critics of devolution contend that giving states responsibility over redistributive programs such as welfare and Medicaid will not lead to healthy competition but instead will produce "a race to the bottom" that could reduce many types of benefits below the levels that most citizens desire. According to this argument, states will hesitate to lift benefit levels above those of other states for fear that such generosity will attract more and more needy families while simultaneously pushing up taxes and driving away businesses and wealthier residents. Buffeted by such pressures, competition will force benefits and eligibility requirements to decline toward the levels of the least generous states, with unfortunate results for those in need.

On close analysis, it is far from clear whether such a race to the bottom is a likely possibility or only a figment of the academic imagination.[35] The debate has been lively and is unlikely to end any time soon.[36] While the arguments continue, however, there is a more compelling reason not to leave programs for the poor entirely to the states. As previously mentioned, poor people have very little political power. Their voting rates are low and declining steadily.[37] They are not organized to make their interests felt in state legislatures. For this reason, there is good reason to doubt the claim that devolution will create a competitive marketplace among the states that will automatically cause welfare and Medicaid to conform to the varying wishes of different state populations. It is more likely that benefit levels will reflect the distribution of political power in each state, with poor people in many states faring much worse than they would if they participated fully in the political process. If this is so, children who grow up in poor families may need the help of federal minimum standards so that they will not have to endure excessively low benefits for reasons beyond their control.

However this argument is resolved, there is a deeper flaw in the current policy debate over devolution. Too often, the discussion has focused on whether particular functions should be given *either* to the national government *or* to the states and municipalities. When analysts put the question this way, they misconceive the central issue. For many years, outside of a few fields such as military combat operations and diplomacy, the federal government has rarely assumed exclusive control over the functions it performs. Rather, Congress has provided federal funding and guidelines but left the implementation to the states. Sometimes, states administer programs themselves. Other congressional initiatives are administered by private companies, which perform an increasing variety of federally funded functions, not only supplying materials and constructing buildings but operating nursing homes, training welfare mothers to fill jobs, and providing a host of other services.

An even more striking development in delivering federal services is the growing use of private nonprofit organizations, a category that includes everything from universities and hospitals to job training organizations, charitable homes for the mentally ill, and community development corporations. Only 50,000 nonprofit organizations of all kinds existed in 1950. By 1975, the total had risen to 700,000. Fueled by massive new federal programs in the 1960s and 1970s, the number has continued to grow, to the point that there are now more than 1.5 million nonprofits, most of them receiving federal funding in return for helping to administer national programs.[38] By contracting with such entities, federal agencies can avoid civil-service rules and cut back and modify programs with far less difficulty than they could if they tried to use their own employees. In addition, a multiplicity of private organizations can offer more creativity and adaptability to local conditions than a large national bureaucracy. All in all, therefore, the growth of these new institutions represents an ingenious invention on the part of a society that wanted a wide range of social programs which only the State could afford yet distrusted government bureaucrats enough to prefer that private groups deliver the services.

Now that so many local entities are cooperating with federal officials to implement national policies, it is quite beside the point to argue over which level of government should be responsible for particular programs. In the vast majority of cases, responsibility must be shared among different levels and organizations, because all have distinctive contributions to make. The federal government is needed to set standards, provide sufficient funds, coordinate the work of many service agencies, and monitor the suppliers to ensure that services are adequate and that funds are properly spent. Local providers, on the other hand—be they county officials, private corporations, or nonprofit organizations—can supply creativity, flexibility, and familiarity with specific client populations.

Within these mixed systems, issues may arise now and then about which level of government should provide the funds, oversight, and coordination. But the truly important questions have to do with helping different entities work together more effectively and combine their special talents in order to operate a program successfully.[39] How can Congress resist the temptation to force expensive mandates on fiscally burdened cities without providing the money to pay for them? How can the federal government provide adequate coordination and impose proper accountability without subjecting local providers to a dense web of rules and procedural requirements that stifle their flexibility and blunt their capacity to innovate? How can a private organization depend on government funds without inhibiting its leaders from acting as independent advocates for their communities?[40]

Whatever the answers to these questions, the real problems of making federalism work are plainly different from those that dominate much of the recent debate. Any hope that Americans can change their government significantly by forcing Washington to turn over entire programs to the states is largely fanciful. Too much of what the federal government does has already been delegated. Too little of what remains can be spun off entirely to states and municipalities without putting important public ends at risk. The true challenge for the federal government lies not in deciding how to divide up its functions more neatly but in learning how to cooperate better with states, municipalities, and private providers to enhance the contributions of everyone involved.

A Flawed Premise

Despite the enthusiasm of the public for the reforms reviewed in this chapter, none of them promises to do a great deal to improve what ails our government. One problem is that the premise underlying all the remedies is badly flawed. Putting more power in the hands of the people is not a panacea for the nation's ills. It is a great delusion to suppose that, free of interference from lobbyists and politicians, Americans would easily agree on sensible solutions for the problems of the nation. On health care, welfare, gun control, and many other policy issues, popular opinion is confused or seriously divided. On the deeper questions of principle that divide liberals and conservatives, the public is often ambivalent.

More important, neither term limits, nor ballot initiatives, nor devolution promises to address the most important problems of American government: the incoherence of much legislation, the burdens and frustrations of regulation, and the inadequate protection given to working people and the poor. In some respects, these reforms could even make the problems worse. By turning experienced lawmakers out of office, term limits could undermine the capacities of the legislature and further impair its ability to produce coherent programs. Direct democracy would allow no opportunity for careful deliberation and compromise in developing well-constructed policies, but would leave this crucial task to whatever group happened to draft the propositions and amass the money needed to put them on the ballot. Devolution could further weaken the position of poor and working people by removing the federal floor beneath important benefits. In choosing their remedies, therefore, Americans have failed to make an accurate diagnosis of what ails our government and have seriously overestimated their own capacity to set matters right. It is hardly surprising, then, that the remedies they favor are unlikely to bring much relief to the patient.

9

REFORMING BUREAUCRACY

TALK OF TERM LIMITS and ballot initiatives to cure the ills of government calls to mind the Portuguese entrepreneur who tried to capitalize on the Lisbon earthquake of 1755 by selling anti-earthquake pills to survivors. When asked by the local magistrate to justify his actions, the accused replied: "Can you think of anything better to suggest?"[1] In the case of government, fortunately, there *are* other measures to suggest. One of the most widely discussed reforms, and a favorite of the Clinton Administration, is the effort to "reinvent" federal agencies in order to improve the performance of the bureaucracy.

Almost every President in recent times has launched some elaborate effort to make the Executive Branch work better. Franklin Roosevelt formed his Brownlow Commission to devise an extensive reorganization; Harry Truman and Dwight D. Eisenhower both created blue-ribbon commissions for the same purpose, each one headed by former President Herbert Hoover. Jimmy Carter tried to improve administrative management by introducing the Senior Executive Service. Ronald Reagan assembled a large committee of business leaders, chaired by Peter Grace, to identify waste. The most sustained undertaking of this kind, however, has been President Clinton's National Performance Review, headed by Vice President

Albert Gore. In 1993, the Vice President launched an elaborate study conducted not by an outside commission but by officials within the government itself. Their labors produced a comprehensive report with hundreds of recommendations, and a network of "reinvention laboratories" throughout executive departments and agencies to ensure continuing improvement and implementation.[2]

The governments of most other advanced democracies have also been engaged in heavy-duty reforms of their bureaucracies. From Ottawa to Paris to Wellington, New Zealand, the aims have been remarkably similar: to make government agencies and bureaucrats more focused on achieving results, more sensitive to the needs of the citizens they serve, more efficient in carrying out their work, and more innovative and flexible in responding to new circumstances and local conditions.[3] Some countries have moved quite boldly. For example, New Zealand has replaced permanent department heads with chief executives hired for prescribed terms under carefully drafted performance contracts that reward them handsomely if they succeed and remove them if they don't.[4] Britain (along with other countries) has privatized numerous government functions to make them compete in the commercial marketplace.

It is not surprising that similar complaints and similar reforms have emerged in so many different countries. All of the governments involved have been wrestling with a common set of problems since the 1980s: a sluggish economy, a more demanding citizenry, acute budgetary pressures, and a growing sense that all organizations must make full use of the new information technology. All have found that younger, more highly educated workers bridle at the close supervision and confining rules that have long been common to public bureaucracies. Faced with these pressures, political leaders everywhere have looked beyond government for inspiration. Paying greater attention to customers, delegating more to line officials, stressing initiative and creativity rather than obedience to clear rules and strict lines of authority are all part of a heavily publicized worldwide trend in corporate management. As huge, multinational companies have restructured, reengineered, and reinvented themselves, governments have turned to them for new ideas to solve their bureaucratic problems.

By all accounts, the United States has its full share of the difficulties that beset government bureaucracies worldwide. Surveys confirm what most Americans have long believed: that public officials are not motivated in the same way private-sector employees are.[5] Government workers are not as concerned with service, although the differences in this respect are less substantial than most critics suspect. More important, public-sector employees are less inclined than their private-sector counterparts to report that their superiors make goals and expectations clear or provide them with rewards and recognition for performing well. In addition, they are much more likely to feel that higher-ups are afraid to take risks or make changes, and are far less willing either to talk to superiors about their concerns or to make suggestions for improving the organization. In these attitudes, no doubt, lie the seeds of much of the rigidity and sluggishness for which government bureaucracies are famous.

The Clinton White House deserves credit for launching an ambitious effort to improve the quality of administration and for sustaining it over several years. Notwithstanding the hype and jargon that have accompanied the reforms, they represent an unusually determined attempt to overcome the inflexibility, waste, and red tape traditionally associated with official bureaucracies. But can these efforts create a more responsive, more adaptable, more efficient government? Or will the reformers rediscover what Machiavelli announced centuries ago: "There is nothing more difficult to carry out, nor more dangerous to handle, than to initiate a new order of things"?[6]

Improving the Civil Service

Vice President Gore and his team did not create their proposals out of whole cloth; they drew upon several strands of work from the long history of administrative reform. One of these is the tradition of civil-service reform exemplified most recently by the Volcker Commission, which reported in 1989 on ways to improve the recruitment, training, and deployment of the federal bureaucracy. The second strand, which has gained new prominence in recent years, is a tendency to look to the commercial marketplace and make more use of private providers to improve quality and lower costs. The third and final strand is an ambitious attempt to "reinvent" government by changing the incentives, the methods, and the overall strategy with which government agencies go about their work.

The Volcker Commission was a body of private citizens formed in the late 1980s amid concern that years of eroding salaries and declining respect for bureaucrats had created a "quiet crisis" in the federal Civil Service. Convened under the chairmanship of Paul Volcker, former head of the Federal Reserve Board, the commission made a number of recommendations.[7] It urged more vigorous recruiting and stressed the need to simplify a cumbersome hiring process that discouraged worthy candidates from applying. It called for better pay to offset a twenty-year decline of more than 25 percent in the real value of salaries paid to higher-level civil servants. It suggested more and better training, especially to prepare promising officials in mid-career for broader management responsibilities. It also recommended easing personnel rules and restrictions to make it simpler to fire and reassign poorly performing employees. Finally, the commission proposed that the number of political appointees in the federal government, then totaling some 3,000 people, be cut by at least one-third to halt the continuing decline in the number of challenging jobs open to promising career officials.

None of the changes the commission proposed was especially novel. Many had been urged repeatedly in the past. Yet few had ever been implemented permanently. In the end, most of the Volcker Commission's important proposals met a similar fate. Pay differentials between the government and comparable private-sector jobs have crept back above 20 percent, and most of the familiar weaknesses of the Civil Service are still in evidence. As one seasoned observer recently remarked:

> There can be little doubt that the quiet crisis continues. . . .
> [The] current hiring system for recruiting talent, top to bottom, underwhelms at almost every task it undertakes. It is slow in the hiring, almost useless in the firing, overly permissive in the promoting, out of touch with actual performance in the rewarding, penurious in the training, and utterly absent in the managing of a vast and hidden workforce of con-

tractors and consultants who work side by side, desk by desk with the civil service. Sad to say, when young Americans are asked to picture themselves in public service careers, particularly at the federal level, they picture themselves in deadend jobs where seniority, not performance rules.[8]

The key question, then, is not whether the Volcker Commission's recommendations were sound but why they have not long since been adopted.

Government officials offer various explanations. They insist that corrective changes are already under way; or they blame the neglect on a previous administration; or they plead the distractions of other pressing problems. But these are rationalizations. The fact is that reforming the Civil Service has rarely seemed important enough to merit high-level attention, and the changes that do get made often erode over time, leaving the original state of affairs more or less intact. Human nature has much to do with this inertia. When officials think about implementing civil-service reform, the benefits seem speculative and long-term whereas the costs are all too tangible and immediate.

Expanded training and larger recruiting budgets are attractive ideas in principle but easily discarded when it is clear that taking such steps would require cutting back other programs or jeopardizing other initiatives by which political appointees hope to make their mark. After all, what will better training actually accomplish? And when will the results begin to show? For a harried agency head, how can such intangible benefits outweigh the immediate cost and disruption of paying valued employees to leave work and study for a year in Harvard's mid-career program or Princeton's Woodrow Wilson School?

Top officials find reducing the number of political appointees an even less attractive prospect. American presidents relish the fact that they can place many more individuals of their choosing in high policymaking jobs than heads of government in other leading democracies. Such appointments offer opportunities to exercise control, award patronage, and gain the services of able people from the private sector. Why should a president trade these immediate advantages for the distant possibility that expanded opportunities for career officials will someday improve the quality of the Civil Service?

Politicians regard pay increases for top civil servants as almost equally unappetizing. Such raises are not popular with the public, which looks upon career bureaucrats as lazier and less competent than employees in the private sector. Closing the gap with private sector salaries costs a tidy sum, never a happy prospect during times when budget cutting is in favor. And what will the benefits be? Higher morale? Lower turnover? Better quality of new recruits? At best, these are all intangible gains that can usually be postponed for another year or two until the effects of further delay become obvious enough to force a major readjustment.

Lest one criticize political leaders too harshly for their shortsightedness, it is only fair to acknowledge that the benefits of civil-service reform *are* speculative. No conceivable pay increase will make top government posts financially competitive with the private-sector jobs open to graduates of leading schools of law and business. However aggressively federal agencies recruit, they must cope with a culture in America that has traditionally held government bureaucrats in low esteem. Even the one-third reduction in political appointments urged by the Volcker Commission would still leave all the truly attractive policymaking jobs in the hands of short-term recruits from outside the government. Besides, hasn't real success in attracting good people always depended on conditions beyond any reformer's control—notably, a widely shared enthusiasm for social reform, such as existed in the 1930s and early 1960s, in which public service is imbued with an excitement and meaning largely absent in these disillusioned times?

The cynical environment in which government must operate today also limits the prospects for instituting many of the familiar civil-service reforms. President Jimmy Carter tried unsuccessfully to introduce more flexibility and better training by creating a Senior Executive Service for the most promising civil servants. Those who were chosen could receive additional training and move to other departments in the Executive Branch to gain broader experience. In the end, however, skeptical career officials failed to take advantage of these innovations, fearing that Reagan's minions would use employees' requests to transfer as an opportunity to marginalize anyone suspected of being unsympathetic to the current administration.[9] In much the same way, suspicions of government hamper attempts to increase civil-service salaries, since many voters are convinced that higher pay will not bring better administration but will merely line the pockets of the same old bureaucrats who work in federal agencies today. Worst of all, the current climate of disapproval and distrust surrounding the government discourages many able college graduates from thinking seriously about careers in the Civil Service.[10]

Even the government's loyal supporters may harbor secret doubts about how much good will come from reforms such as those proposed by the Volcker Commission. Perhaps the use of so many political appointments does discourage talented young people from entering the career Civil Service. And it is certainly true that many political appointees have no direct experience with the posts they are called upon to fill, that they serve for barely two years on average, and that their rapid turnover leaves many important jobs unfilled for many months at a time. Even so, political appointees bring many advantages. They are unusually well educated, with 75 percent or more holding advanced degrees.[11] Many are outstandingly successful people who are willing to put their careers on hold for a few years to serve in Washington. Most of them have prior government experience. They work extremely hard; more than 80 percent devote at least sixty hours per week to their jobs, by their own calculation.[12] They bring fresh ideas to the government, while giving the White House more control over policy and greater leverage to overcome the traditional inertia of established bureaucracies.

It is also clear by now that most of the criticisms of the Civil Service that are commonplace in America are also evident in countries that have long had strong, respected bureaucracies. Even the most elite civil servants have problems. Outstanding academic records do not guarantee good judgment or great management skill. However smart they may be, permanent bureaucrats can easily become resistant to change and remote from the people they are supposed to serve. The fabled high civil servants of France are widely criticized for having a narrow, uniform perspective on their work.[13] As for Japan, one student of administration has remarked that "the Japanese administrative elite was more elitist than Whitehall, probably more closed, secretive, defensive, overconcerned with tradition and precedent than its British counterpart. It was also not as good as it should have been, given its talent, and it was a drag on the private sector with its excessive formalism and bureaucratisation."[14] If this is the verdict on an administrative corps chosen from the cream of Japanese youth, how much can one expect from the modest reforms proposed for our own bureaucracy?

In the end, therefore, the gains achievable through vigorous recruitment, proper training, good pay, and challenging careers continue to seem uncertain and long term, even though all of these measures are probably sensible steps that any well-run government should take. It is not altogether surprising, then, that civil-service reform has not enjoyed an especially high priority in Vice President Gore's campaign to reinvent government. Today, organizational changes are in vogue, not personnel reforms. As a prominent adviser to the Vice President declared: "The principal problem is not the people but the systems in which they have to work."[15]

Privatization

For those who look to the private sector for models, the chief deficiency of government is that it operates so often without the stimulus of competition. Private firms must pay constant attention to the quality of their product and the efficiency of their operations or face the loss of business to competitors. In contrast, federal officials have little reason to worry if their costs are inflated or their service is lackluster. They are rarely evaluated on such grounds, and there are often no suitable benchmarks with which to measure their efficiency or effectiveness.

Persuaded that markets are the best spur to efficiency and innovation, reformers have looked for ways to expose more government services to competition.[16] Such methods are not new; public agencies have long relied on competitive bids from the private sector for many goods and services. The Defense Department has contracted with industry for its weapons and supplies, just as many school systems have looked to private caterers to supply hot meals to their pupils. In the past twenty years, however, responding to budget cutbacks, officials at all levels of government have begun to make greater use of the private economy. Unlike most of the privatizing of the past, many of the newer efforts are not merely attempts to find lower-cost suppliers but a deliberate use of competition to motivate public-sector bureaucrats to improve the quality and efficiency of their services.

The most common form of privatization is simply to sell a government-owned enterprise to willing buyers who will run it as a private business. This strategy has been used heavily by former Communist nations and by governments in Western Europe and elsewhere that owned automobile companies, banks, and other ventures which could easily be put in private hands and forced to compete in the marketplace. Such transfers, however, are much rarer in the United States, because our government has nationalized fewer enterprises of the sort that can be readily sold to private owners.

A much more common form of privatization is to contract with private companies for particular services previously performed by the government. This practice works best when there are several competing firms that can do the work and when the service is of a kind that is readily specified in advance and easy to monitor for quality. Garbage removal and custodial services are prominent examples and have been contracted out by many cities and towns. By 1995, 50 percent of all municipal garbage collection, 70 percent of janitorial services, 37 percent of all street repairs, and 42 percent of all building maintenance for cities and towns were being performed by outside companies, and the percentages are continuing to grow.[17]

Contracting out has not been confined to simple activities of the kind just described. Officials at all levels of government have turned increasingly to private organizations, many of them nonprofit, to supply services for the poor, the sick, and the disabled. By 1995, government agencies had farmed out most of the publicly funded job training, nursing-home care, and counseling for welfare mothers. By 1980, more than 40 percent of the funds of private, nonprofit human-service organizations came from government contracts.[18] Overall, fewer than 50 percent of all social services in the United States were still being delivered directly by public agencies.[19]

Inviting outside companies to bid does not automatically keep the government from providing the services. Public employees often prevail in head-to-head competition with private suppliers. In Phoenix, for example, municipal agencies managed to win 60 percent of the contracts let by the city. This does not mean that privatization has failed. The real gains from contracting out do not come from using commercial firms, as such, but from the stimulus gained by introducing competition into the choice of public-service providers.

How much money has been saved by contracting out or using vouchers to shop for services? There is no definitive answer, but public officials consider the gains to be substantial. One recent survey found that 40 percent of local governments that contracted out reported cutting their costs by an average of more than 20 percent, with another 40 percent reporting savings of 10–19 percent.[20]

As privatization continues to spread, one is tempted to ask whether there are any government services that *cannot* be contracted out. On reflection, several functions seem too sensitive for such treatment: national defense, the intelligence services, key law enforcement activities, such as those of the FBI, and, quite possibly, certain elements of the administration of justice. Other government functions cannot be contracted out because they do not have the competing sources of supply required to make privatization work. Again, the armed services are the most obvious example: there are no competing private armies from which the Pentagon can choose. In other cases, government agencies have such specialized needs that no real competition is possible. Even for routine functions, such as garbage disposal, competing providers may not exist in thinly populated rural areas. Whenever competition is not feasible, of course, the benefits of contracting out will tend to disappear. Private monopolies can exhibit all the complacency and unresponsiveness that critics attribute to government agencies.

Competition in the ordinary sense is also hard to introduce into the provision of complex government services such as drug counseling, nursing-home care, or social work. Public officials find it difficult to specify in advance all the conditions that they want their providers to meet, and harder still to develop workable standards by which to judge the quality of service rendered. Imagine the problems that school board members face in trying to draft a contract specifying all of the standards for operating a school system, including a full set of performance criteria that reflect everything students are supposed to learn. Or imagine services such as nursing-home care, in which the clients the government serves are too sick or too vulnerable to assert their right to improved service and effective accountability. Under these circumstances, stiff competition to drive down prices may not be desirable, since it is likely to result in substandard quality of service and excessive corner-cutting to reduce costs.

In such cases, rather than resort to real competitive bidding, government agencies often concentrate on building close, continuing, trusting relationships with providers so that they can work together effectively. The suppliers do not really compete; their contracts will be regularly renewed unless budgets are slashed or a contractor behaves in a clearly unacceptable manner.* The challenge, then, is to build a satisfying cooperative relationship and still ensure that suppliers make a sufficient effort to improve services and eliminate unnecessary costs.

One way of avoiding these problems is not to contract out but instead to distribute vouchers that individuals who qualify for services can use to select their own provider. For example, rather than choose a private company to run the public schools, as some cities have done without success, officials can give vouchers to parents with which to send their child to the public or private school of their choice. In theory, efforts to attract students will bring some competition into a public school system and thereby foster innovation and improve student learning (although the latter point is still hotly disputed).

Vouchers offer an attractive way for the government to side-step the difficulties of setting performance standards and evaluating re-

---

* It is important to stress that privatization does not work automatically; it takes very careful government supervision to make sure that the public interest is properly served. Such oversight is easiest when the service provided is standardized and the government's objectives are simple and clear-cut. An apt example would be garbage removal. Even here, however, careful monitoring is needed to guard against corruption, since the award of valuable government contracts always creates risks of bribery and rigged bids. Further oversight is required to satisfy such other public goals as affirmative action (both by the government in awarding the contract and by the contractor in performing the public business) or environmental goals, such as recycling or the safe disposal of toxic waste. Even closer monitoring may be required whenever services are provided to individuals who are unable to evaluate the treatment they receive or are peculiarly vulnerable for other reasons. Nursing-home care and mental health clinics afford apt examples. Overall, experienced proponents of privatization such as David Osborn and Ted Gaebler estimate that proper oversight of government contracts can consume up to 20 percent of the total costs of performing the service. See Osborn and Gaebler, *Reinventing Government: How the Entrepreneurial Spirit Is Transforming the Public Sector* (1992), pp. 87–89.

sults without giving up the advantages of competition. In practice, however, it is no simple matter to make such a system work effectively. How can authorities help parents become sufficiently informed about alternative schools that they can make wise choices? What sort of transportation will be needed to make genuine choice possible? How can a school board ensure proper attention to goals that do not come automatically from parental choice, such as racial balance, adequate civic education, or extra services for handicapped children? Should authorities intervene to keep all the brightest children from flocking to a single school? And what will officials do with the failing schools populated by the listless students from apathetic families—those who remain behind after all the enterprising parents have moved their children elsewhere?

Once a voucher system is up and running, the government will have the added responsibility of making sure that public funds are not spent for frivolous or improper purposes. No school board will wish to subsidize schools with clearly unqualified teachers, even if these schools manage to induce some students to enroll. Nor should public officials force taxpayers to support a school that teaches anti-Semitism or white supremacy. As citizen complaints bring more and more of these problems to light, local authorities may face the difficult task of trying to prevent irresponsible practices without imposing so many restrictions and paperwork requirements that the innovation, energy, and diversity promised by a voucher system begin to disappear.

These problems suggest that privatization is not a panacea, nor will it do away with the need for competent government officials. Still, it has proved to be a valuable tool for increasing the quality and lowering the cost of many public services. The ingenuity displayed over the past few years in finding new ways to bring competition to government programs has been one of the brighter achievements in public administration.

At this late date, the prospects for further gains from privatization are limited. At the federal level, the government already spends less than 15 percent of the budget on services it administers itself. At state and local levels, public officials have now mined the possibilities of contracting out, to the point that most of the obvious potential gains have been realized. A few new areas, possibly public education, still remain to be exploited. In the future, however, government leaders are likely to find greater opportunities for improvement not in developing fresh candidates for privatization but in improving the quality of supervision for the vast array of services already performed by outside providers.[21] Even larger possibilities for reducing costs and improving performance may result from discovering imaginative ways to use the Internet to deliver a wide variety of traditional government services.

The "New" Public Management

Broader in scope than contracting out is an approach that government consultants like to call the "new" public management. Although its apostles describe its ingredients in different ways, four main principles crop up repeatedly in the burgeoning literature on the subject. The first precept is to define the purpose of each government program carefully and then to measure performance not by *inputs* (such as how much money was spent on training) or by *outputs* (how many unemployed workers underwent training) but by *outcomes* (how many of the trainees were actually employed six months after completing their training, and at what increase in pay over their prior wages). The second principle is that public officials should be especially responsive to their "customers"—the people or the organizations that use their services—rather than adhering rigidly to rules and procedures imposed from above. The third imperative, closely linked to the second, is that top executives should concentrate on establishing goals, articulating general norms, and monitoring results while giving line officials (or outside contractors) ample discretion to decide how the work should be carried out. The last precept counsels public officials not to spend all their time responding to problems after they occur but to pay more attention to identifying and removing the underlying causes.

Like other widely trumpeted management philosophies, the program just described does not represent as sharp a break with the past as some of its enthusiasts suggest. Yet much good can undoubtedly come from trying to implement the basic principles. Emphasizing results can channel more effort and energy toward activities that really matter. Although not every government program has clear objectives, many do, and it is important in such cases to keep the focus on outcomes. Otherwise, officials will simply keep track of less important inputs, such as the amounts of money an agency spends or the number of clients it serves, since these are much easier to calculate and much more under the government's control.*

Public officials would also do well to pay closer attention to "customers." It is true, as many critics have pointed out, that citizens are more than "customers" and that efforts to measure the government's success according to customer satisfaction can be misleading and superficial. Even so, much can be gained by asking officials to survey the people they serve or to use other means to discover what citizens think of the services they receive. Properly applied, such efforts can surely help to overcome some of the insensitivity and rigidity for which bureaucracies everywhere are famous.

Top officials may accomplish even more by giving greater discretion to their subordinate officers. Rarely can superiors draft rules that take account of every contingency or anticipate the best possible way of carrying out every task under every circumstance. As all large organizations are discovering, innovation lags if each new idea has to come from headquarters.

Similarly, because governments are prone to emphasize the pound of cure rather than the ounce of prevention, agencies can benefit from trying to concentrate more on underlying problems rather than merely treating the symptoms. When the Coast Guard reviewed its marine safety program from this perspective, it decided to pay less attention to enforcing rules and more to education and training, with the result that the accident rate in the towing industry fell from 91 per 100,000 employees to 27. Comparable gains could doubtless come from trying to encourage greater use of problem solving in many other kinds of government organizations.

The problem with the new public management is not that its basic principles are wrong but that its proponents, in their zeal, often paper over the problems and limitations of their approach. Consider

---

* In fact, it is often wise to keep track of *both* outputs and outcomes, since each has special virtues and limitations. Outcomes offer a better indication of the success and failure of government programs but may not provide a fair means of evaluating federal officials, since outcomes are often beyond their control. Conversely, outputs may allow a fairer evaluation of officials but a much less satisfactory measure of program effectiveness.

the emphasis on managing by results. This method may work well for many programs. In some agencies, however, such as the Justice Department or the State Department, the objectives that really count are so intangible as to defy any attempt at precise measurements of progress. In other cases, such as the public schools, serviceable measures are available for some but not for all important learning goals. One can test reasonably well for proficiency in spelling and mathematics but not for progress in civic responsibility, racial tolerance, ethical judgment, or even understanding literature. Emphasizing results under these conditions can easily cause teachers to put too much emphasis on training students to memorize facts that one can test and measure, at the expense of imparting more valuable material that cannot be assessed precisely. Teaching to make students genuinely excited about Shakespeare may give way to sterile drills to learn the titles of the major tragedies or to remember that Romeo and Juliet were children of rival families in Verona.

Efforts to measure results can also cause unfairness. For example, even if human beings could devise standardized tests to provide a perfect measure of student performance, the results would still give a distorted picture of a school's effectiveness, since teachers will not have as much effect on test scores as the innate ability of the students, their family influences, and the neighborhoods in which they live. Thus, in their desire to increase accountability and improve results, officials may hold teachers responsible for outcomes that are not truly within their control.

Reading the literature about empowering subordinates and holding them accountable for performance, one also wonders what will keep these officials from resorting to dubious methods to deliver the hoped-for results. Once agency heads begin to stress outcomes, and the results begin to affect the promotions and earnings of their subordinates, the temptation to cut corners is bound to increase. When the White House gave Oliver North broad discretion to act entrepreneurially to achieve a result his bosses wanted, the consequences were disastrous. When Internal Revenue agents heard that they would be measured by how much money they collected in unpaid taxes, some agents responded by tyrannizing poorer taxpayers who could be easily pressured into paying more. At the local level, teachers and principals in districts that offer bonuses for raising student test scores have been known to give copies of exams to their students in advance or to encourage slower pupils to stay at home on test days.

Anticipating such problems, the new management literature talks vaguely of enforcing "norms." And that is undoubtedly desirable. But one can hardly help noticing how much attention has been lavished on measuring results and how little to figuring out how agency heads can ensure proper adherence to norms without reinstating all those stifling rules that the reinvention movement is meant to abolish.

Enthusiasts of the new paradigm do not deny these difficulties. It is less clear that they appreciate the full extent of the problem. Amid all the talk of concentrating on outcomes and all the pressure to define objectives and measure results, one can predict that many government departments will overemphasize the goals amenable to precise measurement, use imperfect measures for other goals, and ignore still other aims that elude measurement of any kind. It is equally likely that subordinates will at times use dubious methods to achieve the objectives that affect their performance ratings. These pitfalls may account for the startling conclusion that one investigator drew after conducting a meta-analysis of more than 100 studies of agency performance: *the more agencies tried to measure outcomes, the less effective they became.*[22]

Other problems can arise in trying to decide just who the "customers" are that agencies are supposed to serve. Some agencies have no real clientele. Prisons are an obvious illustration. Even the Internal Revenue Service cannot be thought to serve the taxpayer in a truly meaningful way. Other public entities, such as schools, have multiple constituencies. Are a school's customers its students? Their parents? Prospective employers? The whole society? Clearly, all of the above could lay claim to the title, depending on whether one is talking about the athletic facilities, a vocational education program, or courses in civics. Moreover, these groups are not merely different sets of customers; their claims often conflict, as they do when schools have to decide how much class time to devote to civic education and how much to computer literacy.

As for granting more discretion to line officials, the rationale is clear enough. How else will large bureaucracies ever display greater creativity? How else can they adapt to the countless situations they face that their superiors cannot possibly anticipate? Still, as with management by objectives, administrative decentralization can entail subtle costs. To begin with, it may aggravate problems of coordination. After the British government had devolved much authority, it discovered that departments could no longer "speak to each other," since they had all purchased different computer systems. In a system as fragmented as the federal government, where many responsibilities are already divided among numerous separate agencies and programs, the conflict between coordination and decentralization could become very sharp indeed.

Thinking further about decentralization, one must also bear in mind why government agencies impose so many rules to control their subordinates. In place of the discipline of private markets, the federal government relies on congressional oversight to ensure accountability to the public. To fulfill this function, lawmakers hold top officials responsible for the conduct of their subordinates. The political process does not encourage legislators to tolerate agency mistakes in order to encourage line officials to display greater initiative in problem solving. Rather, the system rewards the enterprising member of Congress who ferrets out mistakes and publicizes them loudly. Newspaper reporters and television stations are all too willing to cooperate in this effort by publicizing bureaucratic follies and misadventures.

In this way, the current political environment creates a culture of blame. Because Americans distrust their public officials, because the media are attracted to stories of scandal and waste, and because politics are highly partisan, the costs of making a mistake in the public sector are typically far greater than the rewards for performing more imaginatively and efficiently. As long as this is so, high officials will feel pressure to minimize embarrassing errors by subjecting their subordinates to detailed rules and close supervision. Neither the National Performance Review nor other tracts on reorganizing government agencies come fully to grips with this problem. Nor is it apparent what these sources could recommend, since the forces giving rise to the culture of blame are largely beyond the reach of the Executive Branch.

Tight supervision is also a natural outgrowth of a system of shared authority in which the White House constantly struggles with Congress for control over the bureaucracy. To maintain control, a series of administrations have added more and more political appointees, so that multiple layers have come to separate even the highest bureaucrats from the cabinet secretaries they serve.[23] Organizational charts for federal agencies now include such exotic titles as "chief of staff to the assistant assistant secretary" and "principal assistant deputy undersecretary."[24] One reason for making all these outside appointments is to keep a tight rein on bureaucrats, and prevent them from serving the interests of the congressional committees that oversee their operations and approve their budgets. There is no reason to expect this practice to disappear, so long as the conditions that have caused it remain intact. Yet nowhere in the National Performance Review is the role of political appointees carefully discussed or the White House's continuing struggle to control the bureaucracy clearly recognized.

Even as straightforward a proposition as putting more emphasis on solving problems rather than treating symptoms can lead to greater difficulty than one might expect. In principle, the idea seems unassailable. In practice, however, it can conflict with putting customers first, because most people want symptoms attended to promptly and have little patience for long-term efforts to solve the underlying problems. Citizens who have been robbed or assaulted expect a police car at the scene within minutes, and will not be mollified by the news that patrols have been cut back to create a unit to study patterns of crime and their possible causes. One can always ask why the police should not attend properly to *both* prevention and cure. In the real world, however, limited budgets often force departments to make hard choices between the two.

The Problems of Implementing Administrative Reform

All efforts to reform and restructure large organizations are risky, trouble-filled affairs. This is just as true in the private sector as it is in the government. Attempts by CEOs to "reengineer" and reorganize their corporations attracted much publicity in the 1980s. Nevertheless, a Wyatt Associates survey of 531 restructuring programs found that "few companies achieved their profitability and performance goals through restructuring, and morale and motivation among the surviving employees suffered."[25] According to another retrospective study of efforts to reengineer private companies, up to 70 percent of the attempts simply failed.[26]

Large-scale programs to reform government bureaucracies are even more difficult to execute. To begin with, government leaders cannot conduct such campaigns in a quiet, unobtrusive manner. Reinventing the federal bureaucracy is a political event that Executive Branch officials must announce to Congress and promote in the media. Such a process typically leads to inflated rhetoric, extravagant claims, and formulas too simple to fit the complex operations of federal agencies. Even if such language impresses external audiences, public employees are likely to react with fear or cynicism or both.

The current attempt to reinvent government illustrates the problem all too clearly. The Administration credited reinvention with shedding more than 330,000 employees by April 1998, even though many of the jobs involved were civilian positions in the Defense Department which were cut as part of a post–Cold War reduction in the armed forces. Other reductions in the federal workforce were accomplished by merely contracting out work to the private sector. Thousands of pages of regulations were reportedly eliminated through reinvention, although many of them belonged to laws that had already been repealed. As exaggerations of this kind come to light, the credibility of the reforms is bound to diminish, not least in the eyes of the government officials charged with carrying them out.

Another problem with these massive campaigns is that the conditions that bring them into being tend to work against their ultimate success. One of two sets of circumstances typically persuades a President to undertake such wholesale reform. Some initiatives are launched during times of major legislative change, when existing administrative structures cannot cope with emerging problems and needs. The Brownlow Commission came into being in the 1930s under conditions of this kind. Unfortunately, in such periods high-level officials are often so preoccupied with the demands of creating and implementing new programs that they have little opportunity to give sustained, careful attention to the nagging details of administrative restructuring.

The other situation that provokes reform is a time like the early 1990s, when deficits and budget demands place great pressure on the government to function more efficiently. But periods of austerity are no more hospitable than moments of wholesale policy reform to making large administrative changes. Although serious reinvention and reorganization almost always require added funds for training, personnel budgets are often the first thing to go when money is tight. Thus, soon after the reinvention effort began, the Office of Personnel Management was cut especially severely and lost most of its training capability.

Administrative reformers also need stable, relatively calm conditions in order not to aggravate the tension and strain of making major changes in established procedures and routines. Large-scale reorganizations can go especially smoothly if the government is expanding, since employees who become redundant in one office have a chance at reassignment elsewhere. Budget deficits rarely allow such luxuries. Instead, they typically lead to personnel reductions which engender fear and defensiveness on the part of employees, making it harder for the government to gain the cooperation needed to make reorganization work.

Projects to improve the federal bureaucracy often run into further difficulties arising from the fragmented nature of the federal government. Corporations have a unitary structure in which ultimate authority is concentrated in the chief executive officer and the board of directors, who typically work in close cooperation. In the federal government, the executive and the legislative branches are independent of each other. White House efforts to reform the bureaucracy cannot include reinventing Congress, although the latter may be an important part of the problem. Even if the administrative weaknesses are wholly within the Civil Service, both branches will still claim authority over the bureaucracy, and each, at least to some extent, will compete with the other for power and influence. Under these conditions, efforts to reorganize almost always lead to conflict, since they are bound to be perceived (with some truth) as an attempt by one branch of government to enlarge its power at the expense of the other. Through the years, such tensions have repeatedly caused Congress to turn down some of the key White House proposals for reform, thus diluting the entire effort.[27]

A final difficulty in reforming the bureaucracy is that the political system works on a cycle more rapid than the time required to allow large administrative reforms to come to fruition. After four years of well-publicized effort, the National Performance Review had still not made much headway in most federal agencies; by 1996, only 37 percent of federal employees even believed their organization had made reinvention a top priority.[28] This slow pace is not simply a result of the cumbersome government bureaucracy; it is characteristic of attempts to make substantial changes in all large organizations. Most students of corporate restructuring have concluded that major efforts to change a company's culture and methods of operation require up to a decade to bear fruit.[29] It would be surprising if comparable efforts in the larger, more complicated world of the federal government could succeed in less time.

Unfortunately, few national administrations have as much as ten years to implement their plans. Over a decade, almost everything of significance changes. Key policymakers will be distracted by fresh crises that will divert their attention from the slow process of reorganization and change. Before the reforms are fully in place, the administration that initiated them will be replaced by a new one anxious to make its own mark rather than devote itself to the half-completed plans of its predecessor. In the end, many of the hoped-for reforms may never come to pass.

Administrative Reform in Perspective

For all the difficulties of improving the federal bureaucracy, periodic efforts at reform are well worth making. Every organization needs to be prodded at intervals to reconsider its purposes, review its procedures, and seek better ways of evaluating its performance. Along with the hyperbolic prose and condescending rhetoric about "finally bringing some common sense to government," several lasting benefits are likely to come from the reinvention efforts of the 1990s. By most accounts, the federal government is operating more efficiently and giving better service than it did before the current reforms began. The reinvention efforts have raised the status of public management while creating an ongoing process of administrative reform that has helped counteract the heavy priority customarily given to making new policy. Congress has also passed the Government Performance and Results Act, which should help institutionalize the practice of defining the mission of each government unit and evaluating its performance by measuring the progress made toward preestablished goals. In addition, the ingenuity displayed, especially by local governments, in exposing public functions to greater competition has already had many successes in reducing costs and increasing the quality of service.

While acknowledging these benefits, those who would improve the government need to recognize the limited gains from administrative reform. For all the criticisms aimed at federal bureaucrats, a recent survey conducted by the University of Michigan and the Arthur Anderson Company revealed that customer satisfaction is almost as high for government services as it is for private companies.[30] Probably, most allegations of bureaucratic waste are also overstated. No one knows exactly how much money the White House could save by reforming administrative practices. But the findings of a long series of high-level commissions suggest that the Executive Branch may waste considerably less than most critics of government have charged. Although these commissions have typically included members with extensive business or administrative experience, almost all of their investigations have resulted in recommendations yielding savings totaling but a tiny fraction of total federal expenditures. For example, the National Performance Review, for all its analysis and recommendations, envisaged annual savings amounting to less than 2 percent of federal expenditures. Only one commission—the Grace Commission—announced substantially higher prospective gains. On close examination, however, most of the savings turned out to depend on highly impractical suggestions or on changes in policy (such as welfare reforms) that required congressional action rather than administrative reform.[31]

In short, therefore, administrative inefficiency is a far less serious problem than the recurring deficiencies in legislative design. All of the waste produced by poor information systems, inadequate supervision of contractors, and insufficient competition cannot compare with the money lost through decisions of the kind that led to our badly constructed healthcare system, the jumble of separate programs to protect citizens from illness and injury, or a farm program that spent billions of dollars per year subsidizing those who least deserved help. All the frustration produced by insensitive government

employees and all the inconvenience caused by inefficient government services will not equal the harm done by failing to extend
health insurance to 44 million Americans. Nor will the efforts of
brighter, better-trained bureaucrats offset the costs of providing too
little money to adequately enforce a host of employment regulations,
or to give every eligible child a chance to attend a quality preschool
or have a college education. In short, if we truly want the government to do a better job of achieving the goals that Americans value
most, it is Congress, not the bureaucracy, that most urgently requires
our attention.

I O

CAMPAIGN FINANCE REFORM

EVEN A BRIEF GLANCE at the checkered history of campaign
finance regulation is enough to recall Lord Macaulay's words:
"Reform, reform, don't talk to me of reform. We have enough problems already."[1] In 1907, at the urging of President Theodore Roosevelt, Congress passed the first bill to regulate campaign finance—a
law barring campaign donations from corporations and national
banks. This prohibition, however, conveniently omitted contributions by corporate executives, so that Roosevelt himself managed to
finance his 1912 Bull Moose campaign with the help of a handful of
business allies. In subsequent decades, Congress enacted several laws
requiring disclosure of campaign contributions, but none of these
measures was vigorously enforced and all were easily circumvented.

In 1974, in the wake of the Watergate scandal, Congress passed a
more comprehensive campaign finance bill, which set strict limits on
the sums of money individuals and interest groups could give to candidates and placed a ceiling on the total amounts that candidates
could spend on their campaigns or contribute from their own personal funds. Two years later, the Supreme Court severely weakened
the new law in its 1976 *Buckley v. Valeo* decision.[2] Invoking the First
Amendment, the majority disallowed any legal limit on how much
candidates could spend from their own personal resources. This rul-

ing opened the door for wealthy challengers, such as Steve Forbes and Ross Perot, who could afford to spend millions of dollars of their own money in an effort to win public office. The *Buckley* case also struck down restrictions on how much candidates could spend on their campaigns (except in the case of presidential candidates who agreed to accept limits voluntarily in exchange for matching grants from the federal government). The court thereby allowed candidates to raise any amount they could for their campaigns. By 1998, many contenders for House seats were spending more than $1 million to get elected, while candidates for the Senate frequently spent more than $10 million. To amass these sums, sitting legislators had to spend more and more of their time soliciting donations, while able challengers were often forced to withdraw entirely because they could not raise enough money to compete effectively.

The Supreme Court did uphold the provisions in the 1974 law limiting contributions by individual donors ($2,000 per candidate per election cycle and $25,000 to all candidates, parties, and political action committees combined), and by PACs ($10,000 per candidate per election cycle). For fifteen years, these provisions succeeded fairly well in restraining individual and interest group donations. As the cost of campaigning grew, however, the pressure to find ways around the legal restrictions grew as well. By the end of the 1990s, huge loopholes had appeared which made a sham of most of what Congress had tried to accomplish. Lobbyists and political entrepreneurs learned to "bundle" together large numbers of small contributions from individuals, so that they could present substantial sums to candidates. Unions, corporations, interest groups, and even individuals began to purchase TV ads of their own to influence the outcome of elections. Although the law barred unions and corporations from running ads if they expressly advocated the victory or defeat of specific candidates, most judges construed the prohibition very narrowly. As a result, labor and corporate organizations had little difficulty devising unregulated "issue advocacy" TV ads that seemed clearly designed to affect the outcome of particular elections.

Individual donors were also successful in finding ways around the legal limits on campaign contributions. A series of rulings by the Federal Elections Commission opened up the possibility of unlimited gifts to political parties for registration and get-out-the-vote drives and other party-building activities. Gradually, both the Democratic and the Republican organizations began to spend this so-called soft money in ways that were linked more and more closely to specific campaigns. In 1996, the Supreme Court ruled that parties could spend as much as they wished on particular campaigns, so long as they did not work in direct collaboration with a candidate.[3] With these developments, wealthy donors were able, as a practical matter, to give large amounts of soft money for partisan election activities.

By the 1996 presidential election, the regulatory scheme enacted in 1974 had been altered beyond recognition. By one device or another, individuals, unions, and corporations could give virtually any amount to influence specific elections. Through the creative use of soft money, candidates could raise huge sums for their campaigns. Powerful lawmakers could even collect funds to distribute to other members of Congress, thereby increasing their own personal influence in future legislative battles.

On several counts, the system is now in urgent need of repair. Candidates depend more than ever on large contributions from wealthy individuals and groups. Increasingly, expensive campaigns fueled by donations from interested parties are spreading to elections for local office and judicial posts. According to a recent poll, three-fourths of the public believes that many public officials are making or changing policy decisions as a result of the money they receive from major contributors.[4] Legislators have to spend so much time raising campaign money that almost half of them feel they are hampered in carrying out their duties effectively.[5] Although many incumbent lawmakers dislike the burdens of fundraising, their superior ability to attract funds often discourages able challengers and thus deprives voters of a real choice at election time. Small wonder that by 1997, 89 percent of Americans had concluded that the campaign finance system required major changes or needed to be completely rebuilt.[6]

Like term limits and ballot initiatives, campaign finance reform gains its support from a strong popular desire to sweep away external influences that keep elected officials from single-mindedly pursuing the public interest. But campaign finance reform is different in one vital respect. Unlike the other remedies, measures that reduce the influence of money in politics hold real promise of improving the quality of American government, because they strike at all three of the principal weaknesses that have consistently dragged down the government's performance.

To begin with, soft money and other large campaign contributions intensify the pressures that produce incoherent legislation. Legislative leaders may see to it that large donors receive special subsidies or valuable exemptions from legal requirements. Committee chairs may withhold their support for constructive measures unless important backers get favored treatment. In these ways, laws are weakened by special provisions to please powerful interests.

Large corporate contributors are particularly likely to have a keen interest in regulatory programs. If business interests cannot block unwanted regulations entirely, they sometimes manage to extract concessions in the form of convoluted administrative machinery, inadequate appropriations for enforcement, light penalties, or overly elaborate opportunities to appeal and hence delay adverse rulings. All these compromises weaken implementation of the law. One may not be able to prove that political donations were responsible for such favors, but the fact that large contributors are so often the beneficiaries cannot help arousing suspicion.

Finally, money in politics accentuates the weakness of those who are not well organized. The problem is not merely that powerful interests sometimes use their financial clout to defeat policies and programs favoring the poor (although this may occur in some cases, such as debates over the minimum wage). Equally important are the efforts of powerful groups to defend their interests when they are threatened by Congress. If budgets are strained and serious cuts have to be made, those with money and power have the leverage to protect their positions successfully, leaving the weak and unorganized to bear the brunt of any sacrifices that must be made. This is precisely what occurred during the budget battles of 1981 and 1996, when Congress retained many pork barrel projects and dubious corporate subsidies while reserving the deepest cuts for programs such as welfare, Medicaid, and food stamps.

In sum, the dangers that campaign finance reform seeks to avoid are much more real and serious than those that have given rise to term limits, referenda, or devolution. Now that the law has been weakened to the point that special interests can give almost unlimited amounts, the risks are surely great enough to call for more effective safeguards to protect the integrity of the policymaking process.

Principles of Campaign Finance

Choosing the right set of rules to govern campaign contributions is a complex undertaking.[7] Part of the problem stems from the difficulty of predicting all the consequences of particular reform proposals. Congress may be able to prohibit specific kinds of campaign contributions, but it cannot keep powerful interests from wanting to have an influence on government. So long as that desire remains, added limits on political donations will simply cause interest groups to seek other ways of exerting leverage that are not prohibited and may even be immune from any restriction under the Constitution. It is always possible that the new ways will be even more dangerous than the old.

The other principal problem in drafting a sound program of campaign finance reform is that there are many separate objectives to consider, not all of which are fully compatible with the others. Among the most important aims are:

1. Insulating elected officials as much as possible from undue influence, either from particular companies and interest groups that give large sums to political campaigns or from the small affluent fraction of the population that accounts for the bulk of all campaign contributions.
2. Making sure that all serious candidates, challengers as well as incumbents, have enough campaign money to get their message across effectively, so that voters will have the information they need to make knowledgeable choices.
3. Avoiding rules that interfere unjustifiably with the opportunity for all interested parties to express their views on the issues and candidates involved in the election.
4. Freeing candidates from fundraising burdens so heavy that worthy challengers decide not to run and incumbents have to neglect their official duties.
5. Causing elections to turn as much as possible on the merits of the candidates rather than on the amounts of campaign money they can amass.

6. Creating rules that are not only ideal in principle but enforceable in practice.
7. Giving voters renewed faith in the integrity of government and the election process.

It is easy to fall into the trap of backing reforms to accomplish one or two of these purposes, while ignoring the effects on others. For example, it would be simple to prohibit all contributions from interest groups and to set very low limits on political donations from individuals. Such a reform might help to reduce the influence of wealth and power in election campaigns. By allowing only small individual donations, however, it would increase the burdens of fundraising and even prevent many candidates from acquiring the money to communicate enough information to enough people to allow voters to cast their ballots intelligently. Because of such conflicts, successful regulation requires the most careful effort to respect all the objectives of reform and to avoid side effects that could make the cure even worse than the disease.

Attacks upon the current system have provoked a wide variety of reform proposals. Conservatives who believe in markets and distrust regulation favor a completely open system that would remove every rule except a requirement to disclose all political contributions. Reformers who look more kindly on regulation would use public subsidies to induce candidates to agree to limits on campaign spending that cannot be imposed directly under *Buckley v. Valeo*. Those who are particularly anxious to give every serious contender a reasonable chance to compete would give an ample sum to all such candidates but place no restrictions on their ability to seek additional contributions. Still others would take private money completely out of political campaigns by making public funds the sole source of campaign expenditures. Because this proposal has the disadvantage of forcing taxpayers to support candidates they abhor, a few people have urged that all private contributions be banned but that the government give all eligible voters a voucher for a stipulated sum of money which they can contribute to the candidate or political organization of their choice.

These proposals represent radically different ways of combating the evils and excesses of campaign finance in its present form. The trick is to determine which approach comes closest to honoring all the objectives of an ideal system without causing harmful side effects.

Deregulation

Some critics doubt that anyone will ever construct a set of rules that can control campaign contributions effectively. As a result, they favor doing away with all regulation except a requirement of full and immediate disclosure of all donations.[8] In their view, this approach would maximize the freedom of individuals to express their political convictions by giving any sum they choose to the candidate or the party of their choice. It would allow new parties or worthy candidates with modest personal resources to run credible campaigns by gaining the support of rich patrons, just as Eugene McCarthy and Theodore Roosevelt did by turning to a few wealthy friends to finance their independent campaigns for the presidency. Deregulation would do away with laws that limit what challengers can raise and thereby keep them from acquiring all the money they need to defeat incumbents. By following this approach, Congress would avoid the many problems of enforcement that have dogged past reform efforts and led to all the loopholes, evasions, and hypocrisies that have discredited campaign finance regulation and increased public cynicism regarding the political process.

Proponents of deregulation are well aware of the objections critics will raise against their position. They understand that many people will be gravely concerned about the risk that lobbyists offering huge donations will influence policymakers. In response, they argue that money contributed by particular interest groups will usually be offset by like contributions from opposing interests. In addition, they claim, instant disclosure (by electronic posting) will disinfect the process of giving money by exposing it to the sunlight of publicity. Even if these safeguards prove insufficient, proponents deny that much harm will ensue, citing the series of studies by political scientists that have failed to detect any substantial effects from political donations on legislators' votes in Congress.[9]

Enthusiasts of deregulation have an answer for anyone who fears what wide-open campaigns could do to expand the influence of the powerful at the expense of the weak. As they view the situation, it is the present system that truly disadvantages the needy, since it forces candidates representing poor and disorganized constituents to finance themselves through the all but impossible task of attracting a mountain of small donations.[10] The only way the weak can ever hope to obtain enough money to elect their candidates is through the generosity of a few wealthy patrons. And that is precisely what the current law prohibits.

There is much ingenuity in these arguments. At the end of the day, however, proponents cannot dispel the fear that unregulated gifts will greatly enhance the influence of the rich and powerful. Perhaps careful research has not yet shown that political contributions have a significant effect on the way members of Congress vote. Nevertheless, these studies are almost all concerned with the effects of PAC contributions, which are limited to $10,000 per election cycle. The fact that gifts of such small size do not influence votes hardly proves that million-dollar donations will not affect the legislative priorities of party leaders or the wording of the bills they allow to reach the House or Senate floor.

Disclosure by itself scarcely provides an adequate deterrent to protect the public from these dangers. Granted, media stories about illegal donations from foreign sources may have slowed President Clinton's surge in 1996 and kept his party from winning back control of the House of Representatives. But even huge gifts rarely seem to create much political fallout, so long as they are not tainted by illegality or obvious impropriety. Few industries were less popular in 1996 than tobacco. Nevertheless, the large cigarette manufacturers gave millions of dollars in political contributions, which politicians and leaders from both parties eagerly accepted without apparent damage to their standing among constituents.

It is likewise true that large donations from one organization or sector are often countered by large donations from opposing forces. On particular issues, labor may help to offset business; truckers may oppose railroads. But powerful interests are often unopposed by organized groups in securing their objectives, especially when the goal is a tax concession here or a bit of regulatory relief there. Much waste and unfairness occur through the accumulation of these small favors. Moreover, public-interest groups representing environmentalists, consumers, or other constituencies cannot come close to matching the sums of money that industry can raise when the stakes are sufficiently high. In an unregulated environment where interest groups can spend whatever they can afford, resources are spread far too unequally to allow a fair fight on many important public issues.

Enthusiasts for deregulation make a valid point when they argue that campaign spending limits can prevent challengers from raising enough money to overcome the great intrinsic advantages of incumbency. If this is a problem, however, the best remedy is surely to raise the spending limits rather than eliminate all limits, which would tend to favor incumbents far more than their rivals. There are also plenty of other ways, such as public financing or free television and mailing privileges, that would do far more than deregulation to help most challengers.

A more intriguing argument from conservatives is that current laws disadvantage new voices and marginal groups that cannot raise enough money from small donors and need wealthy patrons to obtain the funds to participate in the political process. This argument reveals a genuine problem in our current political system. But it is highly doubtful that deregulation is the answer. Charitable motives will hardly be a match for self-interest in producing large amounts of money for political purposes. For every major gift to a worthy but untried candidate, for every large donation to a struggling political organization for the needy, there will be a flood of major gifts to friendly officials from corporate groups and other powerful organizations with important stakes in the policymaking process. If reformers wish to reduce the financial handicaps of poor people and other underrepresented groups, they would do well to choose some alternative means of solving the problem, such as public financing of campaigns, that will not open the door to unlimited donations by sources seeking to contribute for less savory purposes.

On balance, deregulation would serve primarily to enable powerful incumbent legislators to amass huge campaign war chests. There is hardly any limit to the funds potentially available to an influential member of the House Ways and Means Committee or the Energy and Commerce Committee. So long as such lawmakers remained free of scandal, the resources they could command in a deregulated system would keep almost any prospective challenger from venturing to run for office. As a result, while deregulation might help a few worthy candidates to stand for election, it would also threaten to make many incumbents even more invulnerable than they already are.

For all these reasons, deregulation promises not to diminish but to deepen the public's cynicism. If citizens are already alienated by the role of money in the political process, how much more disillusioned would they be if the media reported a stream of even larger donations from organized groups with important interests in the work of government. Enthusiasts of deregulation may reply that voters will rise up if they are truly upset and punish anyone accepting lavish gifts. But history offers few examples of grassroots revolts against political contributions legally given. Those who care about the integrity of the legislative process would be ill-advised to gamble on such an uncertain response to justify unlimited donations.

Partial Public Funding

Another group of reformers would impose stricter limits on private contributions, while offering subsidies to candidates who can demonstrate a threshold amount of voter support.[11] Such candidates would receive part of their campaign needs (perhaps one-third) from the government, either in the form of cash grants or discounted TV and postage rates. In return for this help, they would agree to abide by ceilings on their total campaign expenditures. In addition, as is true today, individuals would have to observe strict dollar limits on the amounts they could contribute; PAC donations would be barred completely, or severely restricted; and soft-money donations to political parties would be outlawed altogether.

Proposals of this kind do not entirely do away with the problems of private funding. Particular industries and interest groups could still contribute substantial amounts by spreading small contributions among many different lawmakers. Candidates would still have to spend time raising money. And the threat of independent expenditures and issue advocacy ads would remain. What partial public funding tries to do is to create limits that will keep these risks within reasonable bounds, recognizing that no conceivable scheme can do away with all of them. Thus, candidates would still have to raise money, but much less than before because of the spending limits and the federal subsidies. Private contributions would be held to levels low enough to avoid much risk of influence but ample enough to deter interest groups from resorting to independent campaigning. Public financing would be limited, but private supporters could contribute enough in addition to minimize the risk that candidates would lack the funds to get their message across. At the same time, government subsidies would be sufficiently large to persuade almost all candidates to accept the limits on total campaign spending.

These proposals do attempt to deal with most of the current problems of campaign financing. Nevertheless, even with fairly strict limits on the size of individual contributions, the great bulk of private campaign donations will continue to come from people in the top 2–5 percent of the income scale. Although such individuals are hardly monolithic in their political views, they are far from representative of the American people as a whole. They tend to be more opposed to progressive income tax rates, more favorable to business, and less supportive of labor unions or social legislation than the average citizen.[12] As Chapter 1 made clear, the United States already lags behind other advanced democracies in providing forms of social and employment legislation that majorities of Americans favor. Campaign finance laws that force elected officials to rely on the wealthiest 5 percent of the population for their campaign funds are likely to reinforce this pattern.

In trying to minimize several different risks simultaneously, partial funding schemes create additional problems. If everything went according to plan, such proposals might bring about substantial improvement. The problem is that the reforms try to strike a delicate balance among hazards that are all but impossible to weigh in advance. Will the limited contributions allowed suffice to deter powerful interests from resorting to independent campaigns? Will the public subsidies be large enough to induce candidates to accept limits on their spending? Will Congress keep the spending limits high enough to allow challengers to run an effective campaign? In the end, we do not know, and so the proposals must remain a gamble.

In theory, of course, Congress could enact such a scheme and then perfect it through a process of trial and error until it could substantially achieve all the goals of campaign finance reform. If it were easy to change the rules, such a process might provide the ideal answer. But few laws resist amendment more than campaign finance legislation, since those who must vote for changes often gain the most from the status quo. As a result, there is a premium on getting everything right the first time. Unfortunately, getting everything right the first time is a very tall order indeed—taller, one suspects, than ordinary mortals are able to manage.

Full Public Financing

More ambitious reformers would go further and offer enough public funding to candidates to pay the full cost of an effective campaign. Under such proposals, candidates could qualify for public funding only after proving that they were serious contenders by raising a prescribed sum of money in small contributions from residents of their state or congressional district. Those who qualified would then receive a large enough subsidy to make their case to the voters effectively (with the amounts being determined by past experience in funding similar campaigns). Candidates could raise additional sums if they wished, while lobbying groups and other interested parties could contribute as they chose (or pay for issue ads) with no restraint beyond a requirement for immediate disclosure.

Proponents of this reform believe that the greatest evil under current law is the tendency to exclude worthy challengers who cannot raise enough money to get their message across effectively to the voters. Public funding can remove this barrier, while allowing people to exercise their free-speech rights by contributing additional sums for television ads, mailings, and other forms of campaign communication. Underlying the proposal is a conviction that money in campaigns has sharply diminishing returns beyond a certain level. If this assumption is correct, public funding can give challengers an adequate chance to compete, without the need to curb private contributions or cope with all the problems of blocking evasive tactics and countering objections under the First Amendment.

If money were truly irrelevant to campaigns beyond a certain level, such a reform might hold real promise. But there is reason to question the premise. Certainly, politicians do not believe it, or they would not continue to intensify their fundraising election after election, spending amounts of money today that were hardly imaginable only a decade ago. For proof, one need only look at presidential candidates and observe how hard they work to raise vast sums of soft money for their campaigns, beyond the substantial amounts of public funding they receive under existing law. This experience suggests that public subsidies, by themselves, would simply encourage more challengers to run for office without overcoming the other defects in our current system. Interest groups would still make large contributions and thereby threaten to influence policy. Candidates would continue to spend excessive amounts of time raising money. And the public would remain just as cynical as before.

A bolder departure from the status quo would be to pay for the entire cost of campaigns in exchange for doing away with virtually all private campaign contributions, both from individuals and organizations.[13] Candidates who qualified and who chose to receive public funds would then be given a fixed amount for the primary campaign and, if they prevailed, a larger amount for the general election. Candidates receiving such support could not use any more private money, either from their own personal resources or from political parties, PACs, or individuals. If they decided not to take public money (thus freeing them to spend more than the prescribed limit), added public funds would be given to their opponents to the extent needed to equalize campaign spending by both sides. The same procedure would obtain if a candidate were attacked by advertisements, mailings, or other means of communication financed by private interests independent of the opposing party or candidate.

The scheme just outlined would accomplish several things. If all candidates accepted public funds, private money might cease to be a major factor in campaigns. Worthy candidates would no longer decline to enter a race because of the burdens of raising the money needed to challenge an incumbent. Sitting legislators would not be distracted by having to build a war chest to finance their next campaign. All candidates would vie with one another on an equal financial footing.

At one time, political veterans would have dismissed such a proposal out of hand as politically naive. According to the conventional wisdom, voters would never agree to subsidize politicians. In recent years, however, the public has seemingly had a change of heart—

inspired, no doubt, by a desire to get the taint of private money out of politics. Several polls have reported that substantial majorities favor some means of public financing.[14] In 1996, Maine voters actually approved a scheme of virtually full public financing for elections to state political offices. In 1998, majorities in Arizona and Massachusetts endorsed similar proposals.

Like all schemes to reform campaign financing, the "clean-money option" is not free of problems. Any proposal to pay for political campaigns with public funds must set some limit on the amount that candidates can receive and spend. In principle, such limits will help challengers by removing the natural advantage most incumbents typically enjoy in raising money. But there is an important qualification. Challengers will usually need to spend a tidy sum to convey their views to the voters and overcome the greater visibility and reputation of their incumbent opponents. As a result, spending limits must be set quite high or challengers may find themselves under an all but insuperable handicap in trying to become known and get their message across.

There is reason to worry about the prospects for setting ample enough spending limits. Most members of the public will probably underestimate the amounts needed to wage an effective campaign, and thus will be in favor of low limits. Budgetary pressures will afford another reason to keep the numbers low. Incumbents may agree not to raise the limits in order to preserve their natural advantage over potential rivals and keep the latter from mounting effective campaigns. Such reasons may explain why the amounts of public money distributed in Maine only succeeded in enticing less than one-third of all candidates to accept state funding in the first primary elections held under the new clean-election law.

Full public financing could also weaken political parties. If the Democratic and Republican organizations are forbidden to use private donations to support political campaigns, their usefulness will diminish and with it whatever influence they have in mobilizing voters and forging coherent legislative programs. One can, of course, counter this objection by allowing donors to give a limited amount to parties but restricting the use of such funds to general matters unrelated to specific political campaigns. Even this limited step, however, could go far toward reopening the loophole that eventually led to the flood of soft-money contributions in the 1990s.

The final risk in banning the use of private funds in elections is that interest groups might feel impelled to mount their own independent campaigns for or against particular candidates. In this event, private money could still have an influence on elections and, more generally, on the policymaking process. In setting legislative priorities, party leaders might be swayed in favor of any organization or group that regularly campaigned independently for their candidates. Individual lawmakers could be influenced in casting their votes by their desire not to antagonize interests capable of mounting strong independent campaigns against them in the next election.

There is no sure way of eliminating these risks. Under the First Amendment, lawmakers probably lack the power to prohibit issue advocacy and other forms of independent political expenditures. At most, Congress could try to reduce the scope of issue ads by barring such material if it mentioned candidates by name or exhibited their picture within a stipulated period (sixty or ninety days) prior to the election. Even this limited provision would withstand judicial scrutiny only if judges were persuaded that the restriction was truly necessary to avoid a substantial risk of allowing private interests to exert undue political influence.

Clean-money proposals seek to deter issue advocacy and other independent expenditures by giving extra public funds to candidates who are attacked by campaigns of this kind. Perhaps this strategy will succeed. As a practical matter, however, states may balk at matching such expenditures if they grow too large. Moreover, rival candidates will vigorously object if large sums of added funding go to their opponent simply because some independent group has chosen to spend substantial sums on advertisements that may not even be particularly effective. It is even possible that a well-heeled interest group would pay for political ads that clumsily attacked its favorite candidates so that these candidates would themselves qualify for added state funds.

In the last analysis, no one can be sure what effect full public financing will have on the use of issue advocacy ads to influence elections. Many corporations may not wish to use this tactic, fearing a public backlash if they engage so openly in partisan politics. But other organizations may willingly enter in, as the AFL-CIO did in 1996 by committing $35 million to defeat a designated list of incumbent Republican legislators. The tendency today is definitely toward more issue advocacy campaigns. In 1996, the Annenberg Center declared that interested groups spent $135–150 million for this purpose; in 1998, the same center estimated that issue advocacy expenditures had climbed to $275–$340 million.[15] Conceivably, public financing could accelerate the trend and lead to huge amounts of private money being spent on campaigns beyond the control of the public, the candidates, or the parties. Such a process could become so unruly and involve such vast amounts of special-interest money that the public would long for the good old days of the 1990s.

Campaign Vouchers

Yale Law School professor Bruce Ackerman has advanced a proposal that relies on full public financing but provides it in a novel way.[16] Instead of having the government give money directly to qualifying candidates, Ackerman suggests that each voter be given a voucher worth, say, $25 or $50, usable only as contributions to the candidates of the voter's choice. Candidates would receive an initial sum to communicate with voters and appeal for their support. Thereafter, the only money they could spend would be the money they raised by persuading voters to give them all or at least a portion of their voucher.

Arkansas recently passed legislation that roughly resembles a voucher system. Private-contribution limits were severely reduced: from $1,000 to $300 for statewide offices, and to $100 for other offices. At the same time, each individual received a 100 percent annual tax credit for political contributions up to $50 per individual and $100 per family. To encourage the collection of individual donations, new forms of political action committees were authorized which could receive no more than $25 from any individual but could then contribute up to $2,500 per candidate.*

---

* Tax credits will not produce the same result that vouchers will. Many voters will not wish to give up money in the present merely because the government promises to repay it many months in the future. Minnesota has overcome this problem by providing a simple refund plan. Individuals contributing up to $50 and families up to $100 can simply mail in a receipt and obtain a prompt refund from the state. Apparently, this provision has greatly increased the number of small donations.

Such proposals could have several advantages. They would reduce the power of wealthy people to dominate the financing of political campaigns. They would avoid the problem of using taxpayers' money to support weak or distasteful candidates; money would flow only in accordance with the express wishes of voters. They would relieve candidates of the burdens of fundraising by limiting the search for money to the period in which vouchers were distributed to voters. By giving each candidate an equal chance to compete for vouchers, such schemes might lower the financial barriers that currently put challengers at such a disadvantage. More important, vouchers or tax credits would give new power to voters of modest means and thus force candidates to pay attention to their needs instead of concerning themselves almost entirely with more affluent segments of the population. In this way, vouchers could create a potent counterforce against the many pressures tending to marginalize low-income citizens politically.

At first glance, voucher schemes seem almost too good to be true. Yet further inspection reveals a number of practical problems that accompany the imposing list of advantages. From the standpoint of practical politics, proposals of this kind would probably command less support than straightforward public financing, since legislators would worry about putting so much of the available campaign funding in new and unpredictable hands. Republicans would be especially likely to resist, fearing that lower-income voters would be more likely to favor liberals than conservatives.

A voucher plan could also leave challengers in almost as weak a position as they are today. Although in principle they would enjoy an equal opportunity to solicit vouchers, they could be gravely handicapped in their early appeals for support vis-à-vis their much better-known incumbent opponents. The latter could easily capitalize on their initial advantage by harvesting enough vouchers early in the campaign to create a strong bandwagon effect that would bury their opponents under a blizzard of advertising. Sitting legislators might even be tempted to increase their advantage by keeping the initial grant of money to all candidates at a low enough level that challengers would have difficulty mounting an effective early appeal for the vouchers they would need to sustain their campaigns.

Voucher systems also suffer from the fact that no one can be sure how much money citizens would contribute to the candidates. Clearly, the totals could not exceed the number of potential voters multiplied by the amount of the voucher. But some eligible citizens might refuse to use their vouchers, either out of apathy or as a protest in the spirit made famous by the well-known bumper sticker: "Don't Vote—It Only Encourages Them." Tax credits would yield even more unpredictable amounts, since it is so hard to know how many people will choose to give up money immediately that can be returned only many months later in the form of a tax refund. Quite possibly, then, a voucher scheme might yield too little funding for candidates to get their message across to the voters.

One piece of evidence gives special reason for concern on this score. Since 1972, taxpayers have been able to contribute a small part of their tax bill *at no added cost to themselves* to help pay for public subsidies for candidates campaigning for the presidency. Over time, the number choosing to allocate money for this purpose has declined steadily, from more than one-third of all taxpayers in 1973 to less than 20 percent at present. Sixty percent of taxpayers actually check "No" in response to the question whether they would like to make a payment for this purpose, even though their taxes would not go up one penny if they checked "Yes." Of course, the chance to help specific candidates might elicit more citizen participation than the option of merely supporting presidential candidates as a group. Higher percentages of citizens might decide to use their vouchers to keep voters with opposing views from wielding disproportionate influence. Still, experience with the tax return check-off offers a sobering reminder that voter reactions to voucher schemes are unpredictable and could conceivably produce too little money to permit an effective, informative campaign.

Professor Ackerman also suggested, and the Arkansas plan explicitly provides, that individuals be allowed to direct their campaign contributions to interest groups as well as candidates.[17] Such a policy would greatly increase the efforts made to solicit vouchers, but only at the risk of creating a much larger problem. PACs would have an even easier time collecting vouchers than they currently have raising money, since vouchers cost the contributors nothing. At first glance, contributing vouchers to PACs is simply another way by which individual citizens can promote their legitimate interests. But such practices create their own special problems. Wealthy PACs would gain an advantage, since they could presumably use regular dollars to mount high-powered campaigns aimed at persuading individuals to hand over their vouchers. Having collected ample supplies of vouchers, such organizations could then make even greater political contributions and exert even more influence than they do already. At the same time, incumbents would continue to benefit from all the advantages they currently enjoy from their superior ability to attract PAC support.*

Of course, one could always construct plans that would allow individuals to give vouchers only to candidates (or conceivably to political parties as well) and not to any other private organizations. But it is difficult to completely neutralize major differences in money and organization. If interest groups could not collect vouchers or make direct campaign donations of any kind, organizations with a strong grassroots network could continue to supply something essential to politicians running for office—namely, the ability to reach large numbers of citizens with requests to contribute their vouchers to specific candidates. Even organizations without large grassroots memberships could use green money to mount independent advertising campaigns for favored candidates or, in the case of unions and corporations, pay for issue advocacy ads.

In sum, voucher schemes could give added power to citizens of modest means and make them the object of political attention on an unprecedented scale. What such proposals would *not* do is remove the incumbents' advantage or take the influence of well-organized, well-financed interest groups out of politics.

There is one final problem with voucher systems (and with all of the other public funding schemes) that grows out of one of their great virtues. Each of these proposals tries to make it easier for prospective candidates to run for office. Full public financing, whether

---

* A related risk in any plan of this sort would be the creation of a black market for vouchers, whereby partisans would buy vouchers from individuals and funnel them to candidates. Of all the objections, this may be the least substantial. Buying vouchers would be akin to bribing voters; the appropriate remedy is to impose steep fines on anyone caught trying. Experience suggests that sanctions of this kind could keep such practices within tolerable limits.

through direct grants or voucher schemes, relieves candidates almost entirely of the burdens of raising campaign funds. Partial public financing simplifies the task considerably. Both reforms reduce substantially the huge financial barriers that currently discourage many prospective candidates from running.

By opening up elections in this way, such proposals fulfill a worthy democratic purpose. Suppose, however, that the reforms live up to expectations, and many more challengers come forward to vie for election. Presumably, turnouts for the primary will continue to be small (they currently average less than 20 percent), but the total vote will now be split among larger numbers of candidates. Under these conditions, very few votes will suffice to win the nomination (or at least to qualify for a runoff election where the applicable law so provides). Who will benefit from such a process? Not necessarily the best candidate, or even the most popular choice among all members of the party. Incumbents will continue to have a big advantage in most cases, not only because of their record and their visibility but also because of their existing political network. Where no incumbent is running, well-financed groups with strong grassroots organizations, such as the National Education Association and the Christian Coalition, will be able to have an influence on the outcome that is far out of proportion to their support in the electorate as a whole. In either case, the final result may be more the product of superior organization than an accurate expression of the popular will.

What Is To Be Done?

The history of past reforms makes clear how hard it is to know in advance what the consequences of campaign finance legislation will be. Certainly, those who passed the reforms of 1974 did not anticipate the rapid growth of PACs, the flood of soft money, or the emergence of issue advocacy ads. Similar surprises could await future reformers. Conceivably, public funding could push enough private money into independent issue advocacy to swamp any gains achieved by outlawing soft money and PAC contributions. On the other hand, it is also just possible that increased use of the Internet will lower the cost of communicating with voters and greatly reduce the dependence of candidates on large donors.

What conclusion emerges from these doubts and uncertainties? Clearly, no reform is without risks. Yet the way ahead may not be as murky as the preceding discussion might suggest. Granted, no one can yet be sure which of the various reforms will prove to be most suitable in the heat of a campaign. For that reason, since the stakes are so high and the task of achieving reform so difficult, it may be premature to commit the entire federal government to any one approach. Instead, the wiser course could be to allow some time for experience in the states to test the various proposals. Much experimentation is already under way. In addition to Maine's new scheme for total public financing, Arkansas has enacted a far-reaching tax credit plan.[18] Minnesota and Washington, among others, have begun using schemes with partial but generous amounts of public funding.[19] Other states may soon consider ambitious plans of their own. Within a decade, therefore, enough time should have elapsed to form a much better judgment about the various possibilities for comprehensive reform.

But what can be done in the interim to plug the gaping holes in federal campaign laws? There are at least three practical steps that would help counteract the worst problems under the current rules. First of all, Congress could close the soft-money loophole by forbidding parties from raising and spending any money that does not meet strict limits on the amounts that individuals and organizations can contribute. By this action, lawmakers would close a loophole that currently allows contributions of any size from individuals and groups with important interests in the public decisions of the federal government.

Second, Congress could tighten the definition of permissible independent expenditures to the extent the Constitution allows. Individuals and interest groups could be barred from spending large sums that appear to be independent of political campaigns but are actually used in coordination with the electioneering efforts of a candidate. Sponsors of issue ads could be required to disclose their identity and not hide behind sham front organizations. Congress could try to curb the use of issue advocacy ads by prohibiting those that plainly (even if not explicitly) urge the victory or defeat of specific candidates within a stipulated period prior to an election. Although such a rule would be subject to challenge under the Constitution, the government could make a strong argument that the risk of having outside groups exert an undue influence on elections and the policymaking process justifies this limited restriction.

Finally, to give all candidates a decent chance to convey their views, Congress could allow challengers as well as incumbents to send a limited number of free mailings to eligible voters in their district. To the same end, lawmakers could compel television producers to make a certain amount of free time available for candidates in federal elections. To improve the quality and substance of these communications, Congress might even add a requirement that candidates taking advantage of free TV time agree to deliver their message in person; this would inhibit the use of attack ads that convey little information about candidates but simply disparage opponents in order to discourage their supporters from voting.

The changes just described are only initial steps to take care of the most urgent needs for reform. No one would claim that they represent an ideal, permanent solution. Some may even be vulnerable to attack under the First Amendment. With all their limitations, however, these modest reforms could improve matters enough to keep the current system under control until experience in the states reveals how to construct a more comprehensive model that will do the best possible job of meeting the several objectives of a sound set of campaign finance rules.

Campaign Finance Reform in Perspective

Only the most starry-eyed utopians believe that America will ever succeed in insulating policymaking completely from the influence of money. Powerful interests will always seek ways to win a favored place in the minds of those with authority to affect their vital interests. Even if political campaigns are entirely financed with public funds and independent expenditures are somehow contained, lobbyists will find some means to give their sponsors an edge. They will arrange for their employers to make a handsome gift to the favorite charity of a key lawmaker. They will take pains to hire a close friend or a former staff member of an important committee chair. They will put more effort and resources into issue advocacy if they are blocked from giving money to candidates.

These facts of life, however, do not mean that all attempts at campaign finance reform are fruitless. The influence of money on policy was much less threatening when special-interest contributions were largely confined to $5,000 per election and wealthy contributors had not yet learned to use soft-money gifts or issue advocacy ads. Enlightened reforms can make things better, even if they cannot achieve perfection. They may work well only for a time, but they can be changed again. There is every reason, then, to press on in an effort to obtain the greatest improvements that human ingenuity will allow.

Experience with campaign finance reform, however, does expose one major problem. The normal processes of representative government simply do not work well when elected representatives are given the responsibility of developing laws that have such a vital bearing on their own political future. It is no accident, then, that the results have been so deplorable. Occasionally, when some scandal occurs and public feeling on the subject is intense, the government will respond, as it did in 1974. But lawmakers have too much at stake to act responsibly most of the time. Today, for example, even though almost 90 percent of Americans support campaign finance reform, Congress has refused to act. In many states, the people can protect themselves against such intransigence by seeking reform through a ballot initiative. At the federal level, even that option is unavailable.

The obvious way to overcome this problem would be to create a highly qualified neutral body that would meet at least every ten years to review the rules that govern elections and their funding. To be sure, experience shows that it is hard to guarantee the appointment of truly impartial, highly qualified people and equally hard to get their recommendations adopted. It would clearly not suffice to have Congress create a committee packed with partisan supporters; the unhappy history of the Federal Election Commission is proof of that. The job to be done demands individuals with the obvious capacity and reputation to speak authoritatively and to act without partisan or personal biases. Because of the subject matter involved, such a group would have to include members with impressive legal and political experience. To ensure that Congress would support its recommendations, the members would need to possess great stature. The importance of the task, however, could persuade the most eminent persons to serve. Federal appellate judges, or even Supreme Court justices, would combine the necessary impartiality with legal competence; former presidents could bring the needed political experience and stature, while remaining beyond the pull of narrow, partisan pressures.

Others may be able to find better solutions. The critical point is that sitting legislators are incapable of doing the job by themselves. No one would dream of allowing the winner of the World Series to decide the rules of the game for the ensuing season. Still less should we tolerate having Congress define the rules that will govern their own reelection. Rather, the creation of an impartial body with compelling qualifications seems essential if we are to ensure the integrity of a process that is central to our democratic form of government.

I I

TOWARD MORE COHERENT LEGISLATION

"THROUGH A COMPLEX MIXTURE of accident and intention," Morris Fiorina once observed, "we have constructed a system that articulates interests superbly but aggregates them poorly."[1] The federal government is unusually open to ideas from any quarter. But there is no internal mechanism powerful enough to resolve competing proposals into workable, internally consistent legislation. Nor does any outside force exist that holds lawmakers adequately responsible for the results of the programs they enact. Different branches of government, influential members of Congress, and assorted interest groups all compete to affect the shape of legislation. The laws that result are often a clumsy patchwork of compromises rather than well-crafted documents to achieve intended results.

There is no likely reform that by itself could induce Congress to enact more effective, internally consistent legislation. But critics have advanced several proposals of more modest scope that together might make a positive difference. Some of these changes involve intervention from outside—from political parties, the President, the courts—seeking to force Congress to write better laws or submit to corrective action. Others call for adjustments in Congress' internal procedures that could help it avoid some of the excesses, inconsistencies, and expedient compromises that often mar its handiwork.

Finally, there is one change that may lack adequate political support but could do much nonetheless to lend more coherence and accountability to the legislative process.

Strengthening Political Parties

Political scientists have long advocated strong political parties as a means to bring greater discipline to the work of Congress.[2] For these scholars, national parties that command the loyalty of their elected members offer the most promising mechanism for reaching across the divisions of government to forge greater unity and enact more coherent, more effective legislation.

How could parties gain the strength to play this role? Creating a parliamentary system is out of the question for the United States. A more realistic possibility is to make political parties the principal source of campaign funds for candidates running for office. Proponents of this strategy seek to undo the damage unwittingly inflicted by the reform legislation of 1974, which limited the size of donations parties could make to candidates and helped interest groups become the dominant force in campaign financing. If Congress restricted PAC contributions more severely, so that candidates had to rely more heavily on their parties for the "mother's milk of politics," legislators might have to pay greater heed to party leaders in deciding how to cast their votes in Congress.

As it happens, recent events have begun to make this strategy a reality. Both the Democratic and Republican parties have now become a more important source of campaign funds because of the rapid growth of soft money, which approached $500 million in the 2000 election alone. Lobbyists are also more inclined today to take their cue from party officials in deciding how to distribute their political donations. Some leaders in Congress have even developed PACs of their own so that they can distribute campaign funds to individual members in return for their loyalty in future legislative battles.

Legislative leaders have undoubtedly gained some influence over party colleagues by their increased power to dispense campaign funds. Nevertheless, this added leverage does not seem to have improved the quality of legislation in the way that political scientists hoped. The reasons are not hard to find. The power of money does not do away with the need for difficult compromises. Party leaders in the House do not always agree with their counterparts in the Senate on issues of policy, nor does either chamber necessarily agree with the President. Moreover, to the extent that the new money flowing to the parties comes in large chunks from powerful companies and interest groups, party leaders are under pressure to accommodate their donors in making policy. As a result, the legislation that emerges is still subject to the same centrifugal forces that have traditionally led to the special exceptions, windfalls, and other awkward compromises and distortions that have long marked congressional legislation.

There are also limits to what money can accomplish to control the votes of party members in the legislature. It undoubtedly helps to some degree. But some legislators are immune to the promise of campaign funds because they are strong enough politically and financially that they do not need party support. Even if lawmakers do accept help, party officials will hesitate to cut them off in the event that they refuse to toe the line in casting their votes. Political parties have a far greater interest in winning elections and gaining control of Congress than they do in influencing the votes of their members in the House and Senate. When push comes to shove, the parties would rather see their candidates elected, even if they are sometimes disloyal, than allow their opponents to win office. After all, it is the number of Democrats or Republicans, loyal or not, that determines which party will be in the majority, with all the power that majority status brings to chair committees and set the legislative agenda. As a result, a party will be reluctant to punish wayward members by withholding funds if doing so will jeopardize the reelection of its candidates.

There is one recent development, however, that seems to be accomplishing more than money could to make legislators follow the party line more faithfully than in the past. Both Democrats and Republicans are becoming more homogeneous ideologically. Conservative Democrats in the South are either changing their party allegiance or retiring and being replaced by Republican candidates. Conversely, moderate Republicans seem to be gradually leaving Congress and giving way either to Democrats or to more staunchly conservative members of their own party. As lawmakers on each side of the aisle become more similar in their views, party unity in congressional voting has increased. The vital question is how much this ideological solidarity will do to increase the quality and coherence of legislation by curbing the long-standing tendencies toward fragmentation, incoherence, and lack of accountability.

On the surface, the outlook seems hopeful. Lawmakers in a homogeneous party are generally more willing to subordinate their individual interests to the wishes of their leaders, because they realize that by doing so they can accomplish more to advance their ideological agenda.[3] They also see that they have less to fear from giving greater power to their leaders once their party is more united in its political views. Republican lawmakers from the South find it much easier politically to fall in line behind a Republican president than their Democratic forebears did when they were asked to follow the lead of Franklin Roosevelt.

It would be a mistake, however, to read too much into these tendencies. Members of Congress are cooperating more with their party leaders not because they have less power to vote as they choose but because they have fewer ideological disagreements with their party colleagues and share a common agenda that they hope to advance collectively. Under these conditions, there is still no reason to expect individual lawmakers to defer to their leaders when the interests of their constituents or their contributors are at odds with the party line. Members from both parties will keep trying to engineer the passage of special projects and benefits that save jobs and earn credit from voters in their own districts. Legislators from populous Northeastern states will continue to vote resolutely for generous urban assistance; Western Senators will go on resisting efforts to increase grazing fees or restrict water subsidies, regardless of how committed they are in principle to a free market and a limited government.

There are also limits to the degree of partisan unity that can emerge in a country as diverse as the United States. No two ideologies can possibly accommodate all of the strong convictions that animate Americans and the representatives they send to Congress. Libertarian conservatives will continue to have their disagreements with the religious right, just as trade union Democrats will periodically clash with liberal feminists and civil rights advocates. It is not clear that the compromises struck to paper over these conflicts will be much wiser or more coherent than those that Congress has reached in the past.

It is even conceivable that, in the long run, ideologically unified parties will help to weaken rather than strengthen the coherence of legislation and the accountability of Congress. Capitalizing on the apathy of so many voters, a minority of activists in each party have gained disproportionate power to draft sections of the platform and choose the candidates who run for office. Because these activists are more extreme in their views than the rank-and-file they represent, greater homogeneity can simply mean larger numbers of legislators who are more extreme than their rank-and-file supporters and poorly aligned with mainstream views across the nation. The distaste of many voters for both these alternatives may increase their inclination to split tickets to avoid having either side control both the Congress and the White House. This tendency would weaken accountability and produce greater conflict and more ungainly compromises between a president from one party and a Congress controlled by his ideological opponents. The end result could be a further loss of voter support for political parties, and even greater pressure on individual lawmakers to build their careers on their ability to win legislative concessions for the parochial needs of their constituents.

Intervention by Other Branches of Government

Political parties are not the only outside force capable of bringing greater order to the legislative process. For a time, many Republicans who wanted to impose greater discipline on government spending pinned their hopes on strengthening the President's hand by giving him a line-item veto.[4] The idea was that presidents, having more of a national perspective, might save the taxpayer money and neaten up legislation by striking many of the special appropriations for local interests that often clutter up bills.

In fact, the experience of many states that grant such power to their governors casts doubt on how well a line-item veto would serve these purposes.[5] Many governors hesitate to block projects that are dear to the hearts of fellow party members, or even to the hearts of opposing members whose support may be needed in future legislative battles. Certainly, President Clinton vetoed very few items. In the end, however, the experiment never received a full test. Not long after Congress voted in the line-item veto, the Supreme Court declared it unconstitutional, eliminating it as a potential device for improving the work of Congress.[6]

A few legal scholars have turned to another outside source to discipline Congress: they have proposed that the courts play a greater role in straightening out poorly crafted statutes. In an especially bold essay, Susan Rose-Ackerman has suggested that judges should refuse to uphold statutes such as public-housing laws, environmental measures, or preschool programs that clearly appropriate too little money to achieve their stated purposes.[7] In similar fashion, she adds, courts should invalidate extraneous provisions that have no reasonable connection with the principal aims of the legislation revealed in its preamble.[8] Following the same logic, judges could presumably go further and set aside unrealistic deadlines or inconsistent rules of the kind Congress has sometimes imposed on the Environmental Protection Agency.

While judges might occasionally improve the quality of legislation if they intervened in this fashion, there are limits to what even the most aggressive court could do to tidy up the compromises Congress often makes in cobbling together majorities to enact legislation. It is hard to imagine how judges could simplify the cumbersome administrative structure that Congress created to administer public television. Nor could they do much to overcome the proliferation of separate, overlapping programs that lawmakers have enacted in a variety of fields, such as job training, education, and consumer protection.

The principal problem with such aggressive judicial intervention, however, is that it oversteps the bounds envisaged for the judiciary under our constitutional system. American judges already play a greater policymaking role than the courts of any other industrial democracy. Because the language of the Constitution is frequently broad and general, Supreme Court justices have considerable discretion in reaching their decisions. Statutes too are often vaguely worded, offering federal judges substantial scope to resolve ambiguities by choosing the interpretation that best accords with common sense, basic fairness, and widely accepted principles of public policy.

But all these policy judgments are acts of interpretation. Judges do not explicitly override or invalidate the will of Congress, unless they find that it conflicts with the terms of the Constitution. What Professor Rose-Ackerman is suggesting would allow courts to strike down legislative provisions simply because they were inconsistent, unrealistic, or irrelevant to the statute's purpose. It would be very difficult in such cases to pretend that judges were interpreting Congress' statutory language. Rather, the federal courts would be taking it on themselves to decide whether Congress had done its work so sloppily, or been so devious or extravagant in what it claimed to have accomplished, that its provisions did not deserve to be enforced.

There are immense problems with interpreting the Constitution to grant judges such an extensive role. They are not elected by the people. They have no mandate to make policy explicitly (as opposed to taking well-established policies into account in order to make more sensible interpretations of ambiguous statutory or constitutional provisions). From a practical standpoint, judges may appear to be making policy, whether they do so explicitly or by, say, conjuring up a woman's right to an abortion from the murky language of the 14th Amendment. But there is a big difference in principle between interpreting a general constitutional provision to include a particular right and expressly claiming a broad power to overrule Congress on the grounds that it has failed to do its work properly.

Such an expanded role would expose the courts to much hostility from Congress, which would hardly take kindly to having its handiwork challenged for reasons such as internal inconsistency, inadequate funding, or unrealistic deadlines. Pressure would increase to treat appointments to the federal bench as political acts subject to ideological litmus tests. Nothing in the Constitution or the separation of powers envisaged by the founding fathers implies that judges should wield such vast supervisory authority. In a democracy, a judiciary of unelected arbiters, which already exercises policymaking powers unparalleled in the Western world, would be ill-advised to claim an even larger mandate to overrule the work of those chosen by the people to draft their laws.

Strengthening Congressional Leadership

If neither the political parties nor the courts nor the White House seems capable of remedying the weaknesses of Congress, the obvious alternative is to look for ways by which the House and Senate could reform themselves. One possibility would be to give majority leaders enough power to induce individual lawmakers to compromise their differences, to stop larding bills with self-serving extraneous provisions, and to cease using their prerogatives to block legislation or extract special concessions for constituents or financial supporters.

Empowering the leadership seems especially promising in the Senate, where the authority of the Majority Leader is notoriously weak. As George Mitchell once observed, "I don't have a large bag of goodies to hand out to senators, nor do I have any mechanism for disciplining senators."[9] By the rules of that body, assignments to committees, selection of the leadership team, and almost all other significant decisions are made by vote of the members. In addition, individual senators have important prerogatives unknown in the House of Representatives. They can hold up legislation by a filibuster, or even by the implicit threat of a filibuster. They can interfere with the orderly consideration of bills by refusing to go along with the unanimous consent required for proposed rules for structuring debate. As committee chairs, they have considerable ability to block consideration of bills they personally dislike. These prerogatives give unusual power to individual senators to stop progress, or threaten to do so, unless they obtain concessions to satisfy their policy views or constituency needs.

There are several ways to strengthen the Majority Leader's power. Senate presidents could have greater authority to strike extraneous provisions from bills, make assignments to committees, appoint and remove committee chairs, and order bills to be reported out of committee and brought before the full membership for debate. Such reforms would provide considerable leverage over individual members by making them dependent on their leader for valued committee assignments and for needed procedural rulings to help ensure a vote on bills of keen personal interest.

As it happens, members of the House of Representatives have already given their leaders extensive powers of this kind after living through the anarchic conditions of the 1970s. Having reduced the power of committee chairs, only to witness the rapid growth of floor amendments, delaying tactics, and other annoying behavior, most members came to the conclusion that everyone would gain by allowing the leadership to exercise more control. When Republicans achieved a majority in 1994, they gave their Speaker power to appoint committee chairs. In addition, the Speaker has acquired great influence over committee assignments by chairing the Steering and Policy Committee and appointing one-third of its members. He can likewise control the scheduling of legislation, the amount of time provided for debate, and the choice and sequence of amendments to be considered, through his power to appoint all the representatives of his party on the Rules Committee. In addition, because legislation is increasingly complex and because the practice of referring bills to several committees has become more common, committee chairs are more and more dependent on leadership intervention to gain final passage of their legislation.

These developments have given House Speakers more influence over individual members than they have had for decades. Nevertheless, there is little evidence that the laws emanating from the House are better drafted or more coherent than the bills being passed by the Senate.* The lack of demonstrable improvement calls into question whether strengthening the leadership is truly an effective way to bring about better-crafted legislation.

Why haven't the recent changes produced superior results? For one thing, legislative leaders do not necessarily use their added powers to produce well-constructed legislation. Their job is to do their best to promote the various interests and desires of their party colleagues in the legislature. If they fail in this, they risk provoking a serious challenge when the party caucus votes again to select its leaders at the be-

---

* House bills are admittedly freer from special items inserted at the insistence of powerful legislators to benefit particular groups, but this is not so much because leadership powers have become stronger as because the House has stricter rules than the Senate for preventing extraneous provisions.

ginning of the next legislative session. Thus, they are not likely to oppose pork barrel spending bills that benefit large numbers of their
members, or legislative formulas that spread money much more
widely than the purposes of a law actually require.

Legislative leaders will also be strongly moved to do what they can
to maintain their party majority in the legislature. They will be reluctant to insist on loyalty from legislative colleagues who make a credible claim that voting the party line will jeopardize their chances for
reelection. Leaders must likewise be sensitive to the needs of their
party for adequate campaign funds. Hence, in deciding what positions to take on proposed legislation, they will have to be mindful of
the concerns of important interest groups that provide vital support
for their party.

It is also far from certain that the interests of the majority party
will correspond to the interests of a majority of the American people.
Most members of Congress will have been chosen as candidates by a
small and not entirely representative fraction of eligible voters.
Many will be considerably to the left or to the right of most of the
citizens who are normally inclined to support their party. Hence, a
law that party leaders can get most of their members to support may
well displease a majority of the people.

In short, proposals to increase the powers of legislative leaders suffer from much the same weaknesses as suggestions for strengthening
the parties. Such measures will not necessarily result in more effective legislation, let alone legislation that satisfies most Americans.
Leaders respond to other imperatives that are often greater than the
desire for well-designed, coherent laws. Strengthening the hand of
Republican Senate president Trent Lott and House Speaker Dennis
Hastert (or their Democratic counterparts, Tom Daschle and Dick
Gephart) may help break a legislative logjam or quash an unreasonable demand, but it may also block desirable tobacco legislation or
keep Congress from voting a soft-money ban. It is true that strong
leaders will sometimes use their power to stop individual lawmakers
or small blocs from frustrating the desires of a majority of their party
colleagues. And that is not a trivial achievement. Even this step forward, however, could be accomplished without increasing the leadership's powers simply by changing the rules by which each house of
Congress carries out its business.

Changing Congressional Procedures

The Senate is in particular need of rules reform, since it is much more anarchic than its sister body. According to several careful students of Congress, "Senators now routinely exploit the enormous prerogatives Senate rules give the individual to further their own agendas."[10] These "enormous prerogatives" give a single member great leverage to insist on last-minute amendments and special concessions, in return for supporting a closely contested bill.

One procedural change—controlling the filibuster—would do a lot to curb such practices. Because filibusters no longer bring a halt to all business in the Senate, individual members feel much less inhibited from using, or threatening to use, this tactic. As a result, most important measures before the Senate now require a 60 percent "super-majority," and individual senators repeatedly use the threat of a filibuster to gain special favors.* To curb these practices, the Senate should require that some substantial number of members support a filibuster before allowing it to proceed. This change would curb the power of individual senators to delay legislation or block it entirely by the mere threat of a filibuster implicit in placing a "hold" on a proposed bill. It would also do away with the need to obtain unanimous consent to limit the time for debate on proposed legislation or to restrict the number of amendments to be considered. As a result, individual senators would find it more difficult to interfere with the orderly consideration of business and extract concessions in return for their cooperation. Instead, the Senate could follow the lead of the House and create a committee to decide how much time to allow for debate and how to structure the discussion.

The Senate would also benefit by adopting rules to place stricter limits on the practice of larding bills with special measures unrelated to the overall purpose of the legislation. At present, the House allows any member to move to strike provisions on the ground that they are not germane. The Senate would do well to follow suit. It is true that attaching an extraneous provision is sometimes the only way for in-

---

* In 1999, both parties agreed to end the unfortunate practice of anonymous holds. Senators wishing to place a hold on a particular bill must now disclose their names.

dividual lawmakers to force consideration of a worthy proposal that has been bottled up by the leadership or by a strong committee chair. The proper solution, however, is surely to provide other means for letting members bring such measures to the floor, rather than continue a practice that has allowed countless special benefits and other dubious provisions to become law without serious, specific consideration by the entire Senate.

Other changes in the rules would benefit the House of Representatives as well as the Senate. For example, congressional leaders could take greater pains to ensure that every important bill is taken up in an orderly and timely manner and published long enough before a vote to allow members to familiarize themselves with its contents. At present, bills pile up and are voted on in haste in the closing days of a session. Rules requiring that bills be published in advance are often suspended when time is short; members then complain that they are required to vote without knowing what it is they are deciding. Special concessions, ambiguous requirements, and extraneous provisions can all be rushed through without adequate consideration. Rather than continue this practice, lawmakers would do well to adopt a proposal made to the Joint Committee on the Organization of Congress: establish an agenda committee that will create clear legislative priorities, establish time limits for bringing bills to a vote, and monitor the progress of every bill with the backing of the leadership to ensure a more orderly consideration of important legislation.[11] Of course, no schedule can be inflexible; delays are bound to occur. But current procedures are more haphazard than they need to be, and careful scheduling and monitoring could bring greater order to the process.

Both houses of Congress could also benefit by reducing the size of committees and redrawing jurisdictional lines in order to minimize duplication and create committees more equal in workload and influence. Such a reform would be extremely difficult because it strikes directly at the power of individual lawmakers. Be that as it may, although no perfect solution is possible, reorganization of this kind would help reduce fragmentation, diminish conflict, and ensure that members would not have to divide their time and attention among too many separate committee assignments.

Still another corrective measure would bar multiple referrals—that is, the process by which two or more committees of the House or Senate can consider the same legislative item.* This practice increases the difficulty of hammering out clearly drafted, internally consistent legislation and thus contributes to the incoherence of many statutes emanating from Congress. Supporters will argue that multiple referrals bring more perspectives to bear on a single piece of legislation. But our fragmented system of government already produces an abundance of views. The very existence of two separate Houses of Congress ensures that at least two different committees will act on every bill. A more compelling reason for multiple referrals is to call upon various forms of legislative expertise that may be needed to consider a complex, multifaceted piece of legislation. In cases of this kind, however, other committees could be asked for advisory opinions without giving them the power to introduce a bill of their own. Where this seems impossible because several committees have major interests in a bill, the leadership could create a special taskforce drawn from several committees to consider the legislation, instead of allowing each of the interested committees to produce its own separate version.

Some committees of Congress—such as those dealing with agricultural affairs, banking, and education and labor—are consistently dominated by legislators with strong constituency interests in the subject matter that regularly comes before them. Such parochial memberships tend to produce legislation that unduly favors narrow interests. To avoid this result, greater efforts could be made in making assignments to ensure a more representative membership on all committees.

Changes of the kind just described would not work wonders. They would surely not resolve the more intractable differences of opinion that often make legislative compromise difficult. Nor would they provide the kind of accountability for results that could keep lawmakers from enacting clumsy, ineffective laws which offer something to please every interested group. Nevertheless, they would in-

---

* Republicans adopted rules to restrict the use of multiple referrals after they regained control of the House of Representatives following the 1994 elections.

hibit some of the least defensible practices in current use. At the same time, they would allow the leadership to husband its authority for use in forging more constructive, workable compromises to resolve larger differences of opinion.

Encouraging Deliberation

Opportunities for careful deliberation are surprisingly rare in Congress today. Half of the current members say that they have insufficient time to consider legislative matters.[12] Omnibus bills arrive, hundreds of pages long, giving many lawmakers no chance to familiarize themselves with the contents before they have to take a position. Members assemble on call to cast their vote, but there is little occasion for genuine debate, and speeches are often delivered after hours to an empty chamber, for consumption back home rather than the enlightenment of colleagues. Even committee work consists more and more of having lawmakers sit in a row facing cameras and public audiences, instead of convening around a table to engage in informal give-and-take with one another.

Meanwhile, the demands on each legislator's schedule have grown heavier. Members have to steal more and more time from legislative business to raise the necessary funds for the next election campaign. Now that voters are so disgruntled with Washington, many lawmakers feel that they need to spend more days in their districts talking with constituents. Some members even live with their families in their home state or district, traveling to Washington every week for the three or four days allotted for active legislative business.

As the pressures mount, lawmakers devote less effort to legislative matters, which they can delegate to staff, while spending more hours on tasks that cannot be delegated, such as fundraising and appearances before constituents back home. Of the time that remains for legislating, more is spent in open hearings and televised speeches to impress a distrustful cynical public, and less is available for speaking candidly to one another. Small wonder that one of the aspects of the job that most surprises new members is the limited opportunity to talk at length with colleagues.

Various changes could improve these conditions. Public financing of campaigns would free up substantial amounts of time currently spent attending fundraising events and telephoning donors. Moving to a two-year budget cycle, as many observers have suggested, would save countless hours that members could put to better use in legislative deliberation. Limiting the number of important committee assignments that members of Congress can hold simultaneously would allow lawmakers to give more attention to their most important responsibilities.

Freeing up time, of course, does not guarantee that members will use it effectively. To take advantage of the opportunity, congressional leaders would need to schedule more occasions for real debate within the House and Senate. Party caucuses would have to meet more often for substantive policy discussions. Committee chairs would also need to allow periods of serious deliberation among the members early in the legislative process, rather than continuing to hold hearings and present their own draft of a bill before having a full committee discussion and giving members a chance to make suggestions.

A useful though controversial step would be to conduct more committee hearings in closed session. In theory, opening meetings to the public builds trust and increases accountability. In practice, however, open meetings mean that organized interests watch every move that legislators make. On balance, the effect is probably to inhibit compromise and to encourage lawmakers to cater to special interests and influential groups at the expense of the larger public interest.

In the last analysis, no one can be sure that improving the opportunities to deliberate over legislation will produce a better product. But several things do seem clear. Congress is now operating in an environment that works in many ways to diminish the quality of its work. In addition to the pressures on legislators' time, trust within both of the Houses has declined (as it has in the country as a whole), making members more reluctant to cooperate with one another, abide by regular procedures, or defer appropriately to more experienced colleagues.[13] Lawmakers are more divided ideologically, which has further inhibited trust, cooperation, and the ability to compromise. Legislative work is constantly exposed to public view in an atmosphere filled with voter cynicism. Such an environment encourages members to use the public forum to attack Congress and criticize opponents rather than offer constructive ideas of their own.

All of these tendencies impede the legislative process, making constructive compromise, thoughtful deliberation, and careful drafting more difficult. The quality of legislation bears the imprint of these pressures. It is hard to imagine how the existing situation will improve without finding some way to reduce the time spent fundraising and appearing in public, while increasing opportunities for members to meet face to face to discuss their differences.

Increasing Accountability

Better legislative rules and procedures merely offer lawmakers opportunities to improve the quality of their work; they give no guarantee that the opportunities will be used wisely. To ensure better legislation, lawmakers need to be held accountable for results. Accountability, however, is precisely what is lacking in the American system of government. Because the system divides power among so many different units and levels of government, no one knows who is responsible when things go wrong. The challenge is to find a way of strengthening accountability that does not require impossibly drastic changes in our form of government.

Modest progress might occur by making more systematic efforts to acquaint Congress promptly with the problems that have resulted from its own faulty legislative design. For example, there is still no way of regularly informing Congress when federal courts encounter serious difficulty in construing a statute or understanding the lawmakers' intent.[14] Better communication between the judiciary and the legislature might lead Congress to clarify and improve its laws in cases where the ambiguity does not result from intractable political pressures.

Even more important is adequate communication between Congress and those who implement its laws. Fortunately, the National Performance and Results Act contains provisions designed to achieve regular interchange of this kind. Under this statute, each federal agency must specify its objectives for every program and develop ways of determining the progress made toward achieving its goals. Periodically, agency representatives are supposed to meet with the staffs of the relevant congressional committees to discuss whether problems in the wording and design of legislation interfere with defining clear objectives and measuring results. Many close observers feel that much of the difficulty in establishing clear goals stems from poorly worded legislation. Regular meetings of the kind now prescribed could provide an orderly way of bringing such defects to the attention of Congress, so that remedial action can be considered.

Such procedures may do something to tidy up poorly drafted laws. For most important legislation, however, efforts to fix responsibility after the fact will come too late to help much in calling the responsible officials to account. A more promising possibility, therefore, would be to find some way of pointing out the inconsistencies, unrealistic timetables, extraneous provisions, and clumsy administrative structures *before* Congress votes on a bill. If some objective, credible source could make more legislators aware of potential problems when they cast their votes, journalists might expose egregious provisions to public scrutiny while there is still time to correct them, and legislative leaders might be moved to use their power to create more workable laws.

How might such assessments be made? The work of the Congressional Budget Office (CBO) suggests one possibility. Congress could pass a rule that it will not debate or vote on an important piece of legislation without first referring it for analysis to some impartial body to analyze its feasibility, much as the CBO receives bills in advance and examines their effect on the federal budget. Either Congress could establish a new entity for this purpose or individuals could be assigned from existing offices such as the CBO and the General Accounting Office (GAO).

Such an entity would not attempt to judge the wisdom of the bill or try to take sides on questions of value and ideology. Rather, the point of the review would be to address more practical questions. Are the appropriations envisaged sufficient to achieve the prescribed goals? Is the administrative structure well designed to carry out the law's purposes effectively and without unnecessary confusion and delay? Are specific programs included that overlap or duplicate existing legislation in ways that promise to produce conflict, confusion, or unnecessary administrative costs? Are resources distributed (among programs, geographic regions, and so on) in a manner reasonably related to the needs being addressed? Are there specific requirements or deadlines in the bill that clearly seem unrealistic or incapable of being achieved without risking undesirable side effects? Are extraneous provisions included that confer benefits or seek to achieve purposes unrelated to the purposes of the legislation? To avoid the possibility of unwelcome surprises, congressional committees could, of course, consult informally with reviewing officials before completing work on their legislation.

Preparing such reports within exacting time limits would not be easy, especially in the late stages of the legislative process, when members make amendments on the floor and conference committees try to bargain out the differences between House and Senate. Often, the necessary work would have to proceed on a very tight schedule. Since the line between matters of implementation and questions of ideology is not always bright and clear, reviewing officials would also have to display great care and diplomacy in evaluating the handiwork of powerful congressional committees.

Although one should not minimize the difficulties, most of the judgments required are no more complicated or sensitive than the ones the GAO already makes in evaluating problems of implementation after programs have already been put into effect. Nor does the work involved appear to be more controversial or more beset by time pressure than that of the Congressional Budget Office when it estimates the budgetary impact of proposals such as the various competing plans put forward during the healthcare debates of 1993–1994. Since its welfare would depend on retaining the confidence of Congress, any reviewing agency would be highly motivated to go about its work in a responsible manner.

A more serious question is whether such official prior scrutiny would succeed in preventing Congress from making compromises and concessions that waste money and keep new programs from achieving their objectives. No one can be certain. But many lawmakers vote on bills they have not read, and most lack the time to ferret out all the inconsistencies and administrative pitfalls buried deep within scores of pages of dense, technically written prose. A lucid and concise exposition of problems could allow many conscientious legislators to pause and ask difficult questions. The risk of adverse media publicity would increase. The very prospect of having to answer to such scrutiny might cause committees to work harder to eliminate weaknesses before reporting out a bill. Although one cannot be entirely sure of the effects, the prospects for improving upon the current situation seem bright enough to warrant giving the procedure a try.

A More Drastic Alternative

Altering congressional procedures, giving more time for deliberation, and forcing lawmakers to consider the effects of their handiwork may all work to improve the quality of legislation. Campaign finance reform will also help by easing one source of pressure to weaken legislation and encumber it with special subsidies and benefits. But none of these changes will be easy to bring about, and the contributions that each will make to the coherence of the laws are limited.

Why is it that the list of reforms is not more potent? The most likely answer is that legislative incoherence is not merely the result of congressional rules and practices. The Congress we have is the product of our constitutional system of separated powers, our relatively weak political parties, and our highly individualistic society, in which many voters consider candidates separately on their individual merits instead of passing judgment on the record of an entire party. Such a system is hard to change even though it weakens accountability and encourages lawmakers to further their own personal agenda instead of working collaboratively to improve the record of their party.

If Americans were truly determined to do something about the excessive individualism in Congress, there is one reform that would do a lot to encourage greater unity and concern for the national welfare. Congress could pass a law requiring voters to choose between each party's slate of candidates for federal office, instead of allowing them to vote for a president from one party and a senator or member of Congress from the other.* This single step would radically alter the dynamics of policymaking in Washington. Divided government would occur much more rarely (never, if legislative terms were altered so that members of the House and Senate ran for office only in

---

* Third parties that could not nominate a full complement of candidates could create a full slate by endorsing nominees of other parties for the races in which they had no candidate of their own.

presidential election years). Legislators could still vote as they chose on individual measures, but their calculations would change significantly. Instead of thinking primarily of the effect of each vote on their own political standing, they would worry more about the success of their party, and (in the case of majority lawmakers) about the record of the President, since their electoral fortunes would now depend primarily on the voters' evaluation of the Chief Executive and the record of his administration.

Under such a system, the President would continue to listen carefully to his party colleagues in Congress. He would be interested in their appraisal of voter reactions to his policies, especially since individual members could still withhold their support if they felt that passage of an Administration bill would significantly threaten the party's prospects in their district. Nevertheless, the President's influence would grow substantially, because his personal popularity and the success of his Administration would be the most important factors determining the fate of party colleagues in Congress when they ran for reelection. Every member of the majority party would have a personal stake in trying to make the President and the party look as good as possible.

These changes would significantly alter the legislative process. The President would have greater leverage to reconcile differences and achieve more coherent, workable legislation. In addition, the majority party would become more accountable for its record. Without divided government, each party could no longer blame the other when things went wrong. With voters having to decide which party would do the best job, lawmakers would begin to worry more about the effectiveness of the legislation their party passed and less about how their personal positions might appear to their constituents.

Having citizens vote for an entire party slate would also require voters to make a choice they are much more qualified to make. At present, few people who go to the polls have a clear idea of how their representative has voted in the past, let alone how the opposing candidate will vote if elected. In contrast, most citizens are likely to have at least a general sense of the important policy differences separating the two major parties.

Could a requirement to vote for a single slate of candidates have harmful consequences? Perhaps. The current system may be untidy but it does leave room to take account of many local concerns and particular interests that might otherwise be overlooked by an all-powerful majority. Is this not a considerable virtue in a country as large and diverse as the United States?

Without question, our fragmented legislative process helps to protect some worthwhile local interests. But it is doubtful whether the overall result is ultimately for the good of the country. In a system in which some interests are far more alert and better organized than others, where lawmakers are constantly seeking more financial support, and where no one is accountable except for immediate, visible results, the cards are stacked in favor of questionable concessions and special benefits that do not serve the public interest. In such a world, there is no unseen hand that watches over the filibustering, foot dragging, tactical maneuvering, and horse trading to ensure that only worthy special provisions survive. Instead, disciplined, well-financed interests gain an unfair advantage over the unorganized, while Congress compiles a long list of dubious projects and special concessions that benefit particular groups and local interests at the cost of a gradually accumulating burden for the entire taxpaying public.

Of course, pork barrel measures would not cease if individual legislators felt collectively responsible for building a strong record of accomplishment. The party in power would still support special projects and other favors for key states and districts that would improve its chances in the next election. But there are important differences of degree. Many unnecessary projects and special benefits flow today to the states and districts of powerful lawmakers, not for reasons of election strategy but merely because the legislators in question enjoy bringing added benefits to their constituents. Much money is currently wasted by spreading appropriations for programs such as school aid or mass transit more widely than is actually needed. At least some of these dubious expenditures might be saved if presidents had more influence in shaping legislation and if lawmakers knew that they would be held accountable for their collective decisions.

A more plausible objection to slate voting is that it could succeed too well. By fostering party unity, it might open the door to grandiose mistakes that would have been watered down and modified under our current fragmented system. Those who count Mr. Clinton's healthcare plan as a disaster will think it a blessing that fellow Democrats were not pressured into voting for it to protect their leader from a damaging defeat. Dedicated liberals will likewise rejoice that President Reagan could not command a unified Republican majority to support the decimation of environmental programs and the dismantling of the welfare state.

It is doubtful, however, that presidents could simply push their proposals through if elections were altered in this manner. Under slate voting, Democratic lawmakers would have insisted that Mr. Clinton consult with them very closely about his healthcare plan, since they would have had a much greater stake in its success. The bill that eventually emerged from this process would probably have been substantially changed at the insistence of legislators who could sense its political vulnerability and warn of the subsequent backlash at the polls. (The same would undoubtedly have been true of many of President Reagan's proposals in the 1980s.)

There is one remaining objection to slate voting, however, that is both more practical and more potent. Put bluntly, Congress would be massively opposed to the idea. In keeping with America's faith in individualism, politicians would much prefer to sink or swim on their own record than tie their fortunes to those of the President and his party. Since control of the White House changes much more frequently than the typical seat in Congress, any requirement to vote for a slate is likely to diminish the power of incumbency and introduce more risk into the career prospects of sitting legislators. As a result, members of Congress are sure to resist such a reform as tenaciously as they can.

Of course, if a sufficiently powerful ground-swell of popular opinion arose in favor of such a reform, Congress might have no choice but to go along. At present, however, the public would almost certainly resist efforts to limit their freedom to pick and choose among the various candidates on the ballot. Because most voters seem to prefer divided government (perhaps as a way of neutralizing the more distasteful tendencies of both parties), they would not be swayed by talk of a need for greater unity and accountability.[15]

In the end, therefore, the problem of incoherent legislation—with the attendant waste, ineffectiveness, and concern for appearances rather than results—has its deepest roots in the desire of individual voters to make their own independent choice for each office on the ballot. Americans seem to cherish this right even though only a few are prepared to make the effort required to inform themselves on the merits of each candidate. So long as these sentiments persist, slate voting will remain merely a theoretical possibility. People will continue to grumble at the pork barrel projects, the poorly targeted spending, and the uncoordinated, overlapping programs that regularly emerge from Congress. Unfortunately, they seek relief in remedies, such as referenda and term limits, that have little prospect of improving matters and may actually make them worse. Until they come to grips with the true forces that make legislation incoherent, the most one can hope for is modest, incremental reform.

12

IMPROVING REGULATION

AMERICANS SUFFER THE FRUSTRATION of wanting many things for their society that only government can supply, while deeply distrusting the officials and institutions charged with bringing about the desired results. Nowhere is this pattern more apparent than in the field of regulation. With the approval of the public, Congress has enacted a long list of statutes to protect consumers, employees, minorities, women, and many other vulnerable groups. Administrative officials have taken great pains to translate this legislation into an intricate body of rules to govern the myriad conditions of a huge, diverse economy. Yet Americans complain loudly about the results.

Corporate executives and economists insist that many regulations cost much more than any benefits they provide. Public-interest groups reply that many of the rules do not go far enough. To allay the fears of everyone involved, rulemaking has been so encrusted with safeguards, appeals, and reviews of every kind that the regulatory process has grown ponderous, costly, and extremely complex. So much time and money are required to develop new rules and defend them in court, that officials can issue regulations for only a fraction of the hazards they are supposed to abate and cannot inspect most of the small and medium-sized firms within their jurisdiction.

Of the rules that do emerge, some turn out to have incongruous re-sults, many fail to achieve their goals, and most end up costing more than their proponents anticipated.

In light of all these problems, two aims are fundamental to reform. On the one hand, the government must make the regulatory process more efficient by avoiding unnecessary or needlessly burdensome rules and by reducing current levels of litigation and disputation. On the other hand, where intervention is needed, regulators must act with greater effect by making sure that more companies comply with the rules, treating more of the risks and problems within their scope of responsibility, and adapting their rules more adroitly to fit the spe-cial conditions of individual plants.

Avoiding Unnecessary Regulations

The easiest way to lighten the regulatory burden is simply to avoid imposing rules by relying wherever possible on the operation of the private marketplace. As late as the mid-1970s, critics could point to entire industries that labored under regulatory systems that were ei-ther ill-advised from their inception or had outlived any usefulness they once possessed. Starting in the Carter Administration, however, Congress removed much of this unnecessary regulation—in trucking, airline transportation, railroads, telephones, banking, and natural gas. Most of these reforms resulted in wholesale reductions in rules and red tape and large savings for consumers. More opportunities of this kind still remain in fields such as mass transit and telecommuni-cations. But Congress has already carried out enough of these re-forms that deregulation of entire industries no longer offers the dra-matic prospects for improvement that it once did.

Although few industries remain that are candidates for wholesale deregulation, many individual rules involving safety, environmental protection, and other social goals may impose greater costs than any benefit they bring to the public. Such regulations are hardly worth keeping. Ultimately, they place unnecessary burdens on consumers while diverting regulatory resources from other purposes where they could do greater good.

A useful first step to avoid such results would be for Congress to sweep away the arbitrary limits it has imposed through numerous statutes that keep agencies from weighing all the advantages and disadvantages of proposed rules before deciding whether to act. There is little point in ordering agencies to forbid all traces of carcinogens, however tiny, where the danger to humans is nonexistent or vanishingly small. Nor is it sensible to require officials to pay no attention at all to costs in developing rules to curb pollution.

The Executive Branch would also do well to continue and extend the current practice of subjecting each important new rule to a prior review to determine whether its anticipated costs promise to exceed its likely benefits. The government should conduct such reviews—as they are now being conducted—with the help of an independent body, such as the Office of Management and Budget, to avoid the risk that regulatory agencies will underestimate the costs or exaggerate the benefits of their own handiwork.

Applied with good judgment, a systematic look at benefits and burdens should help to minimize the imposition of rules that are demonstrably wasteful. In carrying out these reviews, however, a sensible analyst will need to be flexible enough to avoid spending millions of dollars and many months to do an exhaustive analysis of a minor rule or one whose benefits will obviously exceed the costs. Prudent officials must also refrain from trying to quantify the unquantifiable or from overemphasizing regulatory consequences that can be measured while taking little or no account of intangible effects that resist precise monetary estimates.

Even if every regulation had to undergo such a review, federal officials with limited funds could continue spending large sums to protect the public from small hazards at a cost of several millions of dollars per life saved, while failing to address other areas of risk where lives could be preserved at a bargain rate of only a few thousand dollars each. To address this problem, both Congress and federal agencies could benefit by making better use of comparative risk analysis. Granted, risk assessment is an imperfect art. Some hazards still defy careful analysis because of gaps in available knowledge, and some important values cannot be reduced to dollar amounts. Many existing studies need improvement and refinement, and much more work is required to standardize methods of analysis across different agencies and programs. Still, regulators already have much useful information on comparative risk that they can assemble and apply with prudence in many situations.[1] Armed with such data, officials will be able to point to at least some misallocations glaring enough to require adjustment.

With cost-benefit studies and risk analysis, the White House could discourage regulators from insisting that toxic sites be cleaned so completely that they cost exorbitant amounts for every added life saved. Officials could understand more clearly how to allocate funds, within the limits of their discretion, to increase their overall benefit to human health and safety. Better yet, if Congress were made aware of the relative costs of saving lives under various programs, lawmakers might even agree to use their budget authority to bring federal expenditures more in line with relative risk.

Encouraged by these possibilities, several enthusiasts have gone further to propose that Congress and the courts use their powers of review to make certain that federal agencies abide by the results of detailed cost-benefit estimates and refrain from issuing rules that cannot be justified by these methods.[2] Such proposals could do much mischief. Many of their supporters exaggerate the scientific precision of the analytic techniques involved and minimize the guesses and value judgments implicit in all such calculations.[3] Economists may be able to predict that the Family and Medical Leave Act of 1993 will cost employers close to $700 million dollars per year, but they cannot pretend to measure with objective precision the benefits that come from giving parents a chance to spend more time with a newborn child. Similar problems crop up repeatedly. How conservative should regulators be in estimating risk? Is it proper to discount the value of saving future lives and, if so, at what rate? Is avoiding death from a slow, debilitating disease worth the same as preventing sudden death from an automobile accident? Should the risks to humans from external, involuntary hazards, such as toxic emissions from a nearby factory, be treated the same as the risks people voluntarily assume every day by riding a bicycle or driving a car?

The answers analysts give to such questions can make substantial differences in their estimates concerning the benefits of specific regulations. The differences are not likely to disappear anytime soon by hiring better experts or by making further refinements in statistical technique. Rather, technical questions are mingled with value judgments to such an extent that any hope of consistently making comprehensive, objective calculations of costs and benefits seems unrealistic in the foreseeable future. What regulators need instead is a procedure that welcomes both quantitative and qualitative analysis without insisting that either is sufficient by itself or capable of yielding precise, objectively verifiable answers.

Because of the nature of the problem and the type of analysis required, it would be dangerous to have Congress review the costs and benefits of every major regulation before allowing it to go into effect, or to urge judges to subject an agency's cost-benefit calculations to close scrutiny in the course of reviewing its rules. In some instances, admittedly, interventions of this kind might improve the quality of regulations. But there are overriding disadvantages in having other branches of government undertake a close analysis of issues so inherently indeterminate and controversial.

Judges are not especially competent to pass judgment on such subjective, value-laden questions as whether it is proper to discount the future value of human lives or what price should be put on the life of a spotted owl or a snail darter. More rigorous judicial scrutiny might produce no improvement in results but merely lead agency officials to spend inordinate amounts of time and money assembling mounds of technical data in an effort to create unassailable decisions. For its part, Congress is notoriously vulnerable to special-interest pressures when it looks at issues that involve large costs for particular industries but are beyond the comprehension or concern of the general public. Rather than improve the quality of regulation, congressional hearings could merely substitute one set of opinions for another, while providing a further opportunity to delay unwelcome rules or overturn them entirely through the use of political influence.

A better alternative would be to have the White House encourage agencies to determine costs and benefits for matters that lend themselves to such calculations, while presenting their conclusions in qualitative terms for points that do not permit quantification. Final decisions would grow out of informal discussions within the Executive Branch, as they have in the past, and courts would confine themselves to deciding whether the government acted arbitrarily or capriciously. To help in evaluating the mix of quantitative and qualitative considerations, agencies might consider the use of citizen panels that would study the evidence, review the estimates of cost, benefit, and risk, and render advisory opinions on the proposed rule or the appropriate priority to give to the program involved. A few state and local governments have experimented with this approach in related situations, to their apparent satisfaction. Specialists in risk assessment who have worked with citizens' groups have also formed a good opinion of the judgments laypersons reach after being given a chance to consider the available evidence.[4]

Those who consider these methods too timid and who press for more exacting review by Congress and the courts make the same mistake they are seeking to correct. They concentrate on the benefits of adding one more safeguard to the process of developing new rules and ignore the added costs of attaching ever more elaborate reviews to an already lengthy, complicated task. Eventually, the procedures become so expensive and cumbersome that agencies cannot do their job effectively. Instead, they often adapt in dubious ways. For example, the National Highway Transportation Safety Agency shifted to a relatively ineffective policy of recalling defective automobiles because it allowed officials to avoid the obstacle course of trying to promulgate new safety regulations.[5] The Occupational Safety and Health Administration (OSHA) spends inordinate amounts of time and effort mulling over a few new regulations, while hundreds of toxic substances in American workplaces go unregulated and hundreds of thousands of enterprises go uninspected.[6] Outmoded regulations often remain on the books long after they have become technically obsolete, because agencies shrink from the arduous process of trying to promulgate a new rule.

By now, the regulatory process, like Gulliver in Lilliput, has been tied down with so many procedural requirements that agencies have difficulty attending to all the problems they are supposed to address. It would be a pity if controversy over the arcane techniques of risk evaluation and cost-benefit analysis set off a new round of expensive procedural tinkering. Prudently applied, these analytic methods can improve regulations and avoid excessively costly, onerous rules. But if the process is subjected to repeated challenges in Congress and the courts in a spurious attempt to guarantee the one "correct" result, the added burdens are bound to divert agencies from more important tasks while creating fresh tactical opportunities for obstruction and delay.

Making Regulation More Effective

There are three principal strategies for making regulations more effective. The simplest method is to increase compliance by making it easier for all companies covered by the laws to know what rules apply and, if need be, by teaching them how to comply. The second approach is more ambitious: it asks the government to arrive at a set of reasonable rules through negotiations with the interested parties, instead of having officials impose restraints after formal hearings. The hope is that discussion will bring the parties to accept the rules and cooperate in making them work, instead of resorting to evasion or litigation to escape the law's requirements. The third strategy would do away with rules by restructuring the market and adjusting its incentives in ways that will make companies choose to act in accordance with the public interest.

Improving Communication

General Accounting Office studies have found that more than half of the small businesses covered by safety or environmental regulations are not even aware of many important rules that apply to their operations.[7] Merely informing them, of course, will not ensure compliance. Nevertheless, despite the distrust and resistance to authority so common to this country, most people obey the law when they know what is expected. As a result, if regulatory agencies could do a better job of informing companies about the applicable rules, compliance should improve substantially.

Since the Code of Federal Regulations currently runs to more than 130,000 pages, letting companies know what rules apply presents a formidable challenge. Fortunately, technology now makes the task more feasible than it has been in the past. Officials can begin by translating the arcane language of existing regulations into terms that small-business owners can understand. Vice President Gore has already moved in this direction by initiating a massive rewriting and simplification of existing regulations as part of his National Performance Review.

The next step is to put all of the newly simplified regulations on the Internet, so as to bring them within easy reach of any business with a computer. This advance by itself may not improve matters much, since individual companies will still find it difficult to burrow through masses of requirements to winnow out the rules that apply to them. With the aid of an expert system, however—a program that asks questions and supplies information in response to the answers—the government can enable firms to feed basic facts about their business into their computer and instantly obtain printouts of the rules they need to know. Using the same techniques, government computers can provide immediate answers to any of the questions most frequently asked about the regulations in question. If companies have questions so specific that the expert system cannot respond, they can either consult their lawyers or call a phone number and receive an answer from a government representative.

After much delay, agency officials are experimenting with such procedures using a few sets of government rules.[8] Judging from the heavy use already being made of the website, there is an active market for information delivered in this way. Before too long, therefore, it is possible that the old adage—"Ignorance of the law is no excuse"—will no longer be a legal fiction but a realistic standard to expect of all small businesses in America. This advance by itself should cause a marked improvement in regulatory compliance throughout the economy.

There are many other ways in which more aggressive communication of relevant facts can change behavior for the better. For example, the EPA has attempted to persuade small businesses to shift from standard light bulbs to fluorescent lighting by informing them of the potential savings and agreeing to pay the companies if the savings do not materialize. At times, information will bring about constructive changes in behavior simply by alerting corporate executives to uncomfortable facts about their business. The best-known case is the program begun by the EPA in 1989 to publish the amounts of some 300 toxic materials emitted by 17,000 manufacturing facilities throughout the country. The mere disclosure of this information caused a number of companies to reduce emissions, either because they were previously unaware of what they were doing, or because of adverse public opinion, or even in some cases because their stock prices went down. Agency officials are trying to achieve similar results by offering inducements to firms to adopt environmental accounting and management systems that will provide regular information to executives about the environmental consequences of their operations. The hope is that merely bringing such information to the attention of top executives will lead to constructive changes in corporate practices.

Using information to influence behavior is the least intrusive instrument that government regulators can employ. That virtue alone commends its use whenever possible. Nevertheless, the value of information in changing behavior is limited. The shock effect of publicity often weakens over time. Moreover, not all offenders are likely to agree voluntarily to change their ways. For these reasons, information can supplement but rarely replace the more conventional forms of regulation.

Cooperation

Another alternative to command-and-control regulation is to invite interested parties to negotiate their own rules instead of having the government impose them unilaterally. Ideally, such a process can yield several benefits. If the principal parties agree, whether they be corporations and environmental groups or employers and employees, the rules they adopt are more likely to be workable. When the discussions are completed, companies should be more willing to comply with the regulations, both because the rules will seem more sensible and because the firms themselves will have had a part in creating them. If all goes according to plan, the experience of having negotiated successfully will leave most parties feeling better about the results, and also about the government that gave them the chance to participate in determining the restraints on their own behavior.

In the past twenty-five years, regulatory agencies have made a deliberate effort to bring interested parties together to produce new regulations through a process known as negotiated rulemaking.[9] Under this procedure, the various interested parties or their representatives must agree to collaborate in producing a rule. Representatives of the government participate along with individuals who speak for industry and public-interest groups. A facilitator is appointed to keep the discussion on track and to suggest useful ways of overcoming disagreement. Since public-interest groups rarely have much money, the government makes funds available to allow all sides to obtain needed information and expert advice.

Once negotiations start, they can continue for months or even years. Eventually, however, the discussions either break down or result in a proposed rule. In the latter event, negotiators submit the proposal to the government agency involved, which publishes it for comment in the usual way. If all goes well, since the major stakeholders have been represented in the discussion, the proposed rule will provoke little or no controversy and in due course will be approved by the agency.

This process has attracted much favorable comment. After a quarter of a century, however, only a few rules have been negotiated successfully: fewer than one-tenth of one percent of all federal rules promulgated during this period. Although more than three-fourths of the participants in successful negotiations feel positively about the experience, most of the hoped-for benefits have not materialized—at least, not yet. Negotiated rules have not been created any more rapidly than rules developed through the traditional procedure; a sample of ten rules developed collaboratively under the auspices of the EPA took an average of two and a half years to complete. Nor do negotiations seem to have been more successful than the traditional methods in keeping disgruntled parties from challenging the results in court.[10]

Why has cooperation failed to work as successfully as its supporters hoped? Normally, unless all parties believe that they can do better through negotiation than they will through traditional rulemaking, one or more will refuse to participate. Such consensus does not come easily. In contemplating a negotiation over new antipollution regulations, environmental organizations may feel that they lack the personnel to participate in long, time-consuming discussions, or perhaps they fear that they will be outmatched by the industry's superior command of expertise and information. Industry may overestimate its chances to prevail in court, or worry that government officials and environmentalists will gang up against them. Government officials accustomed to adversary rulemaking often suspect company motives and look askance at efforts to substitute a new, more cooperative procedure.

The fragmentation of the economy further complicates the process. In the absence of strong comprehensive private organizations representing industry and other interests, there are often too many parties involved to allow a manageable negotiation to take place. How can one gather all the dry-cleaning establishments in America to discuss appropriate limits on the use of chemicals? Representatives can be chosen, but who will select them and how can they claim the power to speak for all the other firms affected by the ensuing rule? Can anyone assemble, or even identify, all the environmental and neighborhood groups that could conceivably claim a stake in the outcome? If interested parties do not participate, however, they will feel no inhibitions about challenging any rule they consider unsatisfactory.

Where does this leave negotiated rulemaking? Conceivably, regulations agreed to by stakeholders will still prove fairer and more workable than requirements ordered by a government agency. Negotiated rules may eventually elicit better compliance and less controversy than standards imposed from above. If so, cooperation could increase as experience accumulates. Nevertheless, the American economy is so fragmented and the number of interested parties sufficiently large, that the prospects for assembling the stakeholders to search for a consensus on industry-wide rules seem remote except in a few highly organized pockets of the economy. For the foreseeable future, then, even enthusiasts doubt that negotiation will produce more than 5 percent of all the regulations that the government issues.

Although the outlook may be dim for negotiating rules on an industry- or economy-wide basis, government officials may have more success with a cooperative, consensus-based approach for individual companies. By adopting such a strategy, agencies will not only avoid the problem of how to include all the interested parties in the negotiation; they can also tailor their requirements to fit the circumstances of each company and thereby capitalize on opportunities unique to the individual firm when trying, say, to curb pollution or reduce workplace injuries.

With these advantages in mind, OSHA launched an interesting experiment to persuade individual companies to negotiate their own health and safety rules.[11] In the State of Maine, it selected the 200 companies that accounted for the greatest number of accidents and invited them to create their own safety plan, in cooperation with their employees or union representatives. Completed plans were then submitted to OSHA for review. If approved, the plans would immediately go into effect. OSHA would monitor the results and refrain from carrying out the normal inspections, with their typical complement of citations and fines. Unless accident rates increased, willful violations occurred, or other evidence came to light that the plan was breaking down, OSHA agreed to limit its involvement to routine oversight.

Soon, 196 of the 200 firms agreed to participate and began to work with their employees to produce suitable plans for OSHA review. Early indications looked highly promising. In fact, the plans the companies submitted contained *fourteen times* as many safety improvements as the number called for by existing regulations, apparently confirming the widespread impression that most hazards result from conditions specific to individual worksites that cannot be addressed by economy-wide or even industry-wide rules.

The bottom line, of course, is whether accident rates under the new plans decline. The first two years of operation seemed to indicate safety gains, but the improvements were modest at best. Perhaps greater progress will occur in time. A similar experiment several years earlier among unionized construction firms in California reportedly led to an impressive 40 percent reduction in the number of days lost from accidents.[12] For the moment, however, efforts by the Clinton Administration to expand this approach to other parts of the country have met with resistance by employers and even by the courts.[13]

Despite these obstacles, the OSHA experiments suggest larger possibilities for introducing cooperative regulation on a firm-by-firm basis. One of the most promising examples is the broad field of employment regulation, where the government could invite companies to sit down with their employees and negotiate rules and procedures to replace the entire panoply of federal workplace requirements.[14]

Such a process would work most easily in unionized firms. Employers and unions could simply agree to substitute their own agreement for government regulations, subject to ratification by secret vote of the employees and certification by the Department of Labor to ensure compliance with existing legal requirements. In this way, the parties could administer their own rules, using private arbitration to resolve disagreements. By doing so, both sides could escape the burdens of official inspections and lengthy administrative reviews.

In nonunion firms with more than a specified number of employees, companies and employees could agree to have workers elect a committee to represent them, in a manner similar to the selection of works councils in Europe. Management could then discuss a variety of subjects with the elected representatives, including productivity improvements, work rules, and training measures, as well as the establishment of appropriate grievance procedures to resolve disputes over disciplinary matters and complaints about racial discrimination, sexual harassment, and other conduct prohibited by law.*

Following the example of European works councils, employee representatives would not have legal authority to bargain over compensation or hours of work. More important, workers could not strike if an agreement did not materialize. Instead, some other method would have to be found to ensure that their interests were adequately protected. The most obvious step would be to require that all agreements be reviewed and certified by the government before acquiring any legal force.

To gain this approval, employers would need to accept certain minimum conditions. Their agreements would have to incorporate basic statutory requirements, such as prohibitions against discrimination, family leave laws, and advance notification in cases of layoffs. (Federal rules not covered by the agreement would continue to be enforceable through existing court and agency procedures.) Grievance procedures for complaints alleging wrongful dismissal, racial discrimination, or other violations of the agreement would have to include some form of independent arbitration as a final step. To help the parties conform with what federal law requires, the Labor

---

* Many practical details would need to be worked out to produce an effective system of workplace negotiations. For example, employers would have to agree not to discriminate against employee representatives for carrying out their official duties. Employees would have to agree to pay a small sum out of their paycheck to cover the expenses of obtaining technical assistance when needed. See Paul C. Weiler and Guy Mundlak, "New Directions for the Law of the Workplace," *Yale Law Journal,* 102 (1993): 1907.

Department could distribute model provisions for an agreement covering the safeguards mandated by statute or regulation. As further protection for employees, agreements would need to be ratified in a secret ballot by a majority of employees, and could last for only a specified term before having to be submitted again for employee approval.

Employers who negotiated a plan reviewed and approved by the government could rely on the agreement and its grievance procedures rather than on government regulations and other legal obligations covering the same subject matter. In this way, companies that agreed to establish review procedures with independent arbitration could avoid being sued in court for wrongful discharge or taken before the Equal Employment Opportunity Commission on charges of discrimination. Similarly, firms charged with sexual harassment or work-safety violations could insist that the allegations be considered under the grievance procedures stipulated in the agreement. Courts or government agencies would intervene only on a showing that the employer obtained the consent of the employees by fraud or misrepresentation, or that the company was deliberately refusing to abide by the terms of the contract, or that the agreement had somehow broken down and no longer adequately protected interests recognized by federal law.

By following this procedure, employers who reached a satisfactory agreement with their workers could gain the right to talk to their employees about ways to improve product quality and productivity, while escaping much of the burden and aggravation of government inspections and intrusive regulations. Federal officials in turn could gain the cooperation of the many employers wishing to obey the law, leaving them free to concentrate their efforts on companies presenting genuine compliance problems.

Critics will quickly retort that without a union to guide them and having no right to strike, employees will suffer, since they will lack the power or the knowledge to reach agreements and administer them in ways that protect their interests adequately. But workers who prefer the status quo can always reject an agreement. They should think carefully before doing so. Under current law, they are protected from discrimination on the basis of their race, gender, religion, or ethnic origin, but even if they are aware of their rights, they must often wait for more than a year before their complaints are heard by the Equal Employment Opportunity Commission. Employees can also go to court in some states if they have been wrongfully discharged, but they will again face long delays, and lawyers will often refuse to take their case, even for a contingent fee, unless they earn enough to ensure the attorneys a substantial monetary recovery. In theory, workers are covered by elaborate health and safety regulations, but many smaller plants are very rarely inspected, and their employers often do not know what rules apply to the enterprise.

Employees could always vote for a union if they felt that their interests would be better protected by doing so. As a practical matter, however, the overwhelming majority of workers are not organized now, and there is little prospect that they will become so in the foreseeable future. For them, the practical alternatives are either to settle for the status quo, with all its drawbacks, or to embrace the voluntary procedures just described.

Apparently, employees would like to have workplace committees. More than two-thirds favor *some* form of organized representation to discuss a wide range of issues with employers. Large majorities also feel that it would be a "good" or a "very good" idea to have arbitration to resolve individual grievances and a committee to discuss workplace standards with employers.[15] In fact, American workers, by a decisive majority, would rather have an independent employee committee than a labor union to discuss their interests with management in the workplace.[16] From the employees' standpoint, then, the path of cooperation and voluntary negotiation could seem far preferable to the current situation, with no effective representation in the vast majority of companies and with widespread noncompliance and long delays in pursuing legal remedies.

Employers also seem receptive to a legally authorized employee committee.[17] Most managers believe that jointly run labor-management committees can be mutually beneficial. Eighty percent of employers concede that employee members should volunteer or be elected by their fellow workers, with only 20 percent preferring that they be chosen by management.[18] Many employers even favor arbitration of disagreements that cannot be settled voluntarily.

The principal obstacle to adopting such a scheme is the formal opposition of employer groups and the AFL-CIO. Organized labor worries that joint committees would cause employees to feel less need to join a union, while many employers and their associations fear, to the contrary, that such committees would be a stepping-stone to forming unions. Thus far, such fears have blocked authorization for the kind of organization most favored by American workers and by a large number of employers as well.

Employment relations are only one of the areas that offer opportunities for persuading individual firms to adopt cooperative approaches to regulation. The Clinton Administration has strongly favored much wider use of mediation, arbitration, and other private forms of dispute resolution. Recent legislation and Supreme Court rulings have supported agreements to employ private procedures, including mediation and arbitration, to settle disputes involving the application of federal regulations. Such procedures, in turn, can substantially reduce the cost and delay of resolving disagreements through administrative and judicial proceedings.

In the environmental area, the EPA introduced a Common Sense Initiative several years ago to encourage companies and other stakeholders to sit down on an industry-by-industry basis and agree on better ways of limiting pollution. A similar initiative, Project XL, invites individual firms to submit proposals to show how they can lower their environmental pollution below the legal limits by ways other than complying strictly with existing regulatory requirements. If the EPA agrees, the companies can then enter into discussions with the agency, state officials, community organizations, and other stakeholders and negotiate a final agreement to replace existing statutory requirements. The incentive for companies to participate is the chance to agree on less costly methods than current laws allow to achieve better environmental results.

Opportunities for negotiated solutions arise in many different settings. Landowners, environmental groups, and interested citizens have joined together to develop local plans to address pollution around the Chesapeake Bay. Public-interest groups in Southern California have successfully negotiated agreements with developers and landowners to preserve wildlife under the Endangered Species Act.

Because these efforts are such a welcome change from the usual adversarial procedures, they have attracted much favorable attention. As with negotiated rulemaking, however, progress is agonizingly slow. By 1999, after several years of effort, only ten agreements had been negotiated successfully under Project XL.[19] Attempts to implement the Common Sense Initiative likewise produced meager results, so much so that the initiative was eventually abandoned.

Observing such modest gains from so many promising collaborative experiments, one must eventually ask why these methods are so slow to develop. Apparently, adversarial habits do not give way easily. Many union leaders, environmentalists, and public-interest advocates are instinctively suspicious of business and fearful that firms will take advantage of negotiations to gain relief from existing rules. Many lawyers thrive on the adversary system and resist attempts to substitute more cooperative methods of controlling behavior. Once negotiations have begun, long-standing habits of pressing one's interests as forcefully as possible do not give way easily to the give-and-take of a collaborative search for common ground. Strong value-differences over the relative importance of economic efficiency and environmental protection or job security often make agreement difficult to achieve.

Up to a point, government officials can encourage cooperation by creating stronger incentives to participate. The fear that the Endangered Species Act could put a stop to all development undoubtedly helped persuade Southern California landowners to enter into negotiations to preserve local wildlife. In similar fashion, higher Workman's Compensation awards for workplace accidents would undoubtedly increase a company's willingness to discuss better safety measures with its employees. So would a credible threat of vigorous enforcement of existing laws against employers that do not develop workplace agreements collaboratively. In the long run, then, opportunities for progress on a firm-by-firm basis seem brighter than the prospects for negotiating industry-wide rules, although the difficulties of introducing cooperation into a traditionally adversarial culture have clearly been more serious than early enthusiasts supposed.

Making Markets Work

The problems of obtaining effective collaboration and the waste and ineffectiveness of much traditional regulation have led many reformers to look for ways to protect the public without having to create rules at all. The most obvious possibility is to change the incentives of the market so as to preserve competition, while inducing firms to bring their behavior into closer alignment with the public interest.[20]

The simplest way of accomplishing this result is to impose a tax or charge on pollution or some other activity that the government wants to discourage. For example, if Congress wishes to reduce emissions of carbon dioxide to alleviate global warming, it can levy a carbon tax that will raise the price and hence inhibit use of the materials most responsible for producing the harmful emissions. Not only will such a tax lower the amount of CO_2 discharged; it will do so much more efficiently than a rule requiring that all firms cut emissions to a certain level or install a prescribed "cleaner" technology. Faced with the tax, firms that can reduce their use of carbon cheaply and efficiently will cut back more; companies that find it expensive to lower their use will cut back less. In this way, the overall reductions in CO_2 will be achieved at the lowest possible cost.

Monetary incentives can work in many other contexts to accomplish valid regulatory purposes. Several states have turned to tax incentives to reduce the use of fertilizers that contribute to toxic runoffs, and New York gives tax credits to truckers who convert to natural gas. Another measure that cities and towns now use increasingly is a charge to the public for picking up garbage. Disposing of refuse is a growing problem in many communities. Americans currently churn out more waste products per capita than the citizens of any other country. Part of the reason for so much garbage is that the cost of removal is hidden in municipal taxes, leaving consumers with little incentive to limit the volume. Charging each household for each garbage can emptied may help to cure this problem.

Offering rewards can also encourage consumers to act in ways that serve public ends. For example, a town may give citizens rebates on their waste-removal charges if they separate glass and metal objects from the rest of their trash, thus making recycling easier. Refunds for empty bottles may have a similar effect. Governments can levy a tax on products that damage the environment, such as used motor oil and batteries, with rebates given to any customer who returns them when their useful life has ended instead of dumping them where they can do harm.

Because monetary incentives accomplish their purpose efficiently and are relatively easy to administer, they would appear to be an ideal instrument of regulation—far preferable to the coercive rules that agencies normally impose. In practice, however, there are limits to their use. Taxes and rebates are not appropriate in cases where the government wishes to ban a substance entirely rather than simply diminish its use. Moreover, public officials are often unable to predict how much a given tax will lower the use of a harmful substance.* Once such a levy is imposed, agencies may find it hard to monitor companies to determine how much taxable waste they are actually discharging.

Political problems can also inhibit the use of taxes and rebates. For example, experts agree that the price of gasoline does not cover nearly all of the environmental and national-security costs resulting from its use. A substantial tax seems to offer an ideal remedy, at least for economists. As a practical matter, however, popular resistance to such a tax would be immense, despite the concerns most Americans claim to have about the environment. So great is the resistance, in fact, that Congress felt impelled in the 1970s to curb emissions not by placing a tax on gasoline but by requiring auto companies to install antipollution devices on cars—devices that actually cost consumers more than a gas tax, but did so in a form conveniently hidden from public view.

Companies also resist environmental taxes both because of the expense and because they suspect that once a tax is installed, Congress will raise it again in the future, not for environmental reasons but for revenue-raising purposes. In some cases, industries may actually prefer more intrusive command-and-control regulations, because their lobbyists have persuaded Congress to draft the rules so that they fall more heavily on new facilities and thus keep potential competitors from entering the market.

An alternative to taxes is the so-called tradeable permit, which is coming into growing use as a means of controlling emissions. To employ this technique, government officials first determine the overall

---

* Taxes may have other unpredictable consequences. For example, one city that introduced a charge for bags of refuse found that the number of bags declined but more garbage was crammed into each bag, with the result that handling costs increased.

limit on pollution required to meet environmental goals. They then distribute permits up to the desired limit, either by auctioning them off or by giving them to firms in accordance with the amounts of pollution they have historically produced. In order to cut emissions to the amount allowed by their permits, companies can either change their methods of production or, if this is too expensive, try to buy additional permits from firms that are willing to sell them. In this way, companies that can cut emissions cheaply will bring them below the legal limits, in order to have unused permits that they can sell to new enterprises entering the market or to existing firms that find it too costly to curb their own pollution. Once again, therefore, firms are rewarded if they lower their pollution below prescribed levels, and the total volume of emissions is reduced in the least expensive way. Better yet, the use of permits allows the government to avoid a major drawback of the pollution tax: regulators can set any limit they want on total emissions without having to guess at the results, as they must do when they use a tax.

Economists are almost unanimous in praising the superiority of market-based measures over conventional forms of regulation.[21] Congress and the EPA have responded by employing this method on several occasions in the past twenty years, most notably to curb sulfur dioxide emissions under the Clean Air Act of 1990. The total savings from these initiatives have been estimated at well over $1 billion per year.[22]

As yet, however, tradeable permits and related devices remain the exception rather than the rule in environmental regulation; they make up only a small fraction of all the government's efforts to curb pollution. Part of the explanation is straightforward and understandable. In their enthusiasm, supporters have frequently overestimated the cost savings and underestimated the practical problems of creating a suitable market for exchanging permits.[23] Before active trading can occur, someone must inform companies about the system and keep them apprised of current prices for permits. For markets with substantial numbers of firms, companies also need an intermediary to bring sellers and buyers together or even to buy permits and hold them until suitable purchasers appear.[24] In addition, officials have to monitor firms to make sure that their emissions do not exceed the amounts their permits allow.

Although creating a suitable market is more difficult and expensive than proponents originally acknowledged, experience confirms that it can be done. But there are further obstacles of a different sort. Together, they represent a cross-section of the problems that have historically bedeviled government regulation in the United States.

To begin with, business is often suspicious of efforts to introduce market-based initiatives. Corporations worry that once such a scheme is introduced, the government will use it to impose tougher limits and introduce further requirements. Once market-based systems are in place, firms are often reluctant to make long-term investments in cleaner technology on the strength of the initial price of permits, fearing that officials will change the rules in ways that affect the market in unpredictable ways.

Corporations often use their political influence to stop or dilute new market-based regulation. In order to satisfy opponents, lawmakers sometimes set the pollution limits so high that existing firms find little difficulty meeting them and hence have little need to buy permits. Companies have almost invariably blocked any attempt to make them pay for permits (for example, by having the government auction them off). As a result, existing firms have once again managed to gain an undeserved advantage over new competitors, who have to buy permits in order to enter the market.

Environmentalists, in turn, have resisted market-based methods, arguing that they are immoral "licenses to pollute." To win their support, officials have sometimes found it necessary to make damaging concessions. Thus, in devising permits to curb emissions in the smog-laden Los Angeles basin, environmentalists insisted on a provision whereby each subsequent sale of a permit would trigger an automatic 20 percent reduction in the amount of emissions it allowed. The result was to distort the market price and make the permits much less attractive than would otherwise have been the case.

Government agencies themselves are often none too enthusiastic about permits. After so many years of traditional regulation, agencies are heavily staffed with lawyers and technicians who are adept at defending rules in court but quite unversed in the economic and management skills required to create and operate an effective market for permits. To them, tradeable permits seem a threat to their careers, and they can be quick to seize on transient difficulties and minor problems to argue against such innovations.[25]

Despite these problems, tradeable permits do not face obstacles as formidable as those that have arisen in the effort to introduce cooperation into a highly fragmented, adversarial economy. Experience seems to have confirmed the value of market-based methods. Officials are becoming more adept at making them work and less resistant to their use. Environmentalists are increasingly recognizing the disadvantages of more traditional forms of regulation. As market instruments continue to spread and to demonstrate savings over formal rulemaking, they seem likely to take over a greater share of regulatory tasks, with a consequent reduction in many of the costs, delays, and other irritations associated with command-and-control methods.

Regulating Managed Health Care

The preceding problems, has examined three principal ways of regulating a huge economy filled with independent companies that are resistant to authority, suspicious of government, and struggling to succeed in a competitive marketplace. Officials can attack the problem frontally by enacting rules and imposing penalties, or they can try to persuade the interested parties to cooperate in drafting and enforcing appropriate rules, or they can avoid rules and penalties altogether by altering market incentives to induce competing firms to behave responsibly. These approaches are not mutually exclusive; they can be used in many different combinations, depending on the regulatory task at hand.

The problems of choosing a suitable strategy are all clearly evident in the recent debate over how to regulate the burgeoning managed-healthcare industry.[26] Managed care, which now covers more than 150 million Americans, tries to contain costs through the efforts of competing providers, such as Health Maintenance Organizations (HMOs). These entities typically assemble groups of physicians, enter into contracts for care with hospitals, and offer stipulated medical services to employers or individuals at prearranged prices. The HMOs use strong economic incentives and careful monitoring to avoid unnecessary care and thus keep rates low enough to attract subscribers and increase the rewards for owners.

The key problem presented by these plans is how to provide medical services at the lowest possible cost without eroding the quality of care.* Competition in search of profit can lower costs but will not necessarily ensure good care, since consumers rarely know enough about medicine to insist on proper treatment. Existing methods of regulation do not suffice either. Quality assurance programs and other forms of accreditation and review are helpful up to a point, but they merely set minimum standards and sometimes employ outmoded requirements that can actually impede the introduction of new and better methods of achieving quality.[27] The threat of malpractice litigation is ineffective, because only one in eight patients with legitimate grievances ever sues and because the risk of having to pay damages for improper care is diluted by the use of insurance to spread the losses among many physicians.[28] Besides, under federal law, most courts have refused to allow malpractice suits against HMOs, although they are often the organizations best situated to take effective preventive steps and most in need of incentives to force them to do so.[29]

After hearing many lurid tales in which patients were denied treatment or sent home too quickly from the hospital, a majority of the public now favors government regulation of HMOs.[30] Congress has already responded with a bill requiring managed-care plans to allow mothers to remain in the hospital for at least forty-eight hours following the birth of a child. Lawmakers have introduced dozens of other measures in state legislatures (as well as in Congress), proposing such rules as a ban on performing mastectomies on an outpatient basis, a requirement that women be allowed to visit their obstetrician-gynecologist without approval from a primary-care physician, and a prohibition on denying coverage for emergency room care if a "prudent layperson" would consider the situation an emergency.

---

* The discussion that follows does not try to judge whether managed competition among HMOs is the best way of organizing America's healthcare system. Moreover, the discussion considers only the problem of protecting the interests of the public and does not attempt to discuss other related issues, such as those arising between HMOs and the hospitals and other providers or between HMOs and employers.

Efforts to regulate the quality of care in this manner are bound to create numerous problems. There are so many ways to mistreat patients that Congress could eventually enact a staggering number of rules in response to repeated cries of protest over instances of shoddy care. States might do the same, producing even more requirements and more possibilities for overlap, inconsistency, and confusion. Because the needs of individual patients differ so markedly, most of these regulations are likely to make no sense in some of the cases to which they apply. Even rules that seemed reasonable when they were enacted may become outmoded and block creative new ways of lowering costs or improving care. Inspections to ensure compliance will be costly, and statutory terms such as "emergency," "medical necessity," and "appropriate treatment" are bound to give rise to disagreement and litigation. In short, relying on rules will almost certainly result in all the aggravations and deficiencies commonly associated with command-and-control regulation.

Rather than proceed down this well-worn path, Congress would do far better to look for other means of protecting the public. Instead of regulations, the first line of attack should be to strengthen market forces that will encourage each HMO to try to strike an appropriate balance between containing costs and maintaining quality.

One way to begin is to require reasonable disclosure by HMOs and continue current efforts to develop better ways of informing members and prospective members about how well different plans and HMOs are performing—what services they cover, how satisfied their members are, how they compensate their physicians, how their patient outcomes compare with those of similar plans. The more accurate and helpful the information, the more pressure the market will place on HMOs to emphasize quality as well as cost.

Better data, however, will not suffice to ensure proper care. Even if the relevant information were improved and presented in more understandable form, many of the insured today could not take advantage of it. At present, only 10–15 percent of consumers have access to any information about the quality of services.[31] More than 40 percent of Americans do not even have a choice of provider; they work for an employer who offers only a single plan, which is typically chosen on the basis of cost rather than quality.[32] A useful step, therefore, would be not only to encourage dissemination of information but also to ensure competition by making certain that all employees can choose among two or more health plans. Reasonably sized companies could be required to offer a choice among several plans. Smaller companies could join some sort of health mart or similar arrangement to give their employees the chance to shop among different providers.

Unfortunately, there are other limits to the value of information in improving care that are not so easy to resolve. Most people who choose their provider rely primarily on the advice of friends and relatives, and value such opinions more highly than what they read in published reports.[33] Those who do read the reports can absorb only so much data. No plan can anticipate every situation that will occur, or describe what treatments its members can expect under all conceivable circumstances. Outcome measures help to fill these gaps, but they cannot adequately reflect every procedure that a plan withholds or capture the long-term consequences of inadequate preventive care. They typically provide information on aggregate performance, not on the record of particular services or physicians. Because of these deficiencies, other measures are needed to make the market work sufficiently well.

The greatest flaw in the present healthcare market is that the incentives for providers to cut costs seem stronger than the incentives to offer excellent care, because consumers cannot know enough to generate effective pressure to ensure high-quality services.* The most important step toward correcting this situation is to place legal responsibility squarely on the provider best situated to affect the quality of care and hence most able to prevent illness or injury resulting from medical treatment.[34] This reform will force providers to balance their attempts to cut costs against their desire to avoid having to pay for any illness or injury caused by inadequate care.

By itself, however, placing liability on the proper party will not cure all the defects of malpractice litigation or encourage more than a small fraction of poorly treated patients to bring suit. Finding a

---

*In this discussion, "providers" is meant to include physicians, hospitals, and/or health maintenance organizations, depending on which is in a position to influence the nature and quality of health care provided.

better alternative is no easy matter and presents complications too intricate to allow suitable treatment in this text.[35] Suffice it to say that a fully adequate system of healthcare regulation should include some means of compensating a much larger proportion of injured patients, while reducing the uncertainties, the long delays, and the huge legal fees and related costs that are such a sorry feature of the current malpractice system.

Even the most artfully crafted compensation scheme cannot ensure a perfect balance between cost and quality of care or do away with all disagreements between patients and providers. Medical care requires innumerable judgments for which there is no one obvious answer. In any HMO, honest differences of opinion will constantly arise over what services are covered by the plan and whether referrals to specialists are warranted in specific situations. Regulators cannot resolve these problems satisfactorily either by imposing rules or by adjusting the incentives of HMO executives, hospitals, and physicians. Both patients and providers need procedures to resolve their disputes in a manner that is informed, inexpensive, and expeditious.

Lawmakers can solve this problem by requiring HMOs to guarantee patients a second opinion following decisions to deny treatment or referral to a specialist, with the right to appeal, if necessary, to a qualified, independent arbitrator for a final and prompt decision. Such procedures cost very little, and patients can be deterred from bringing frivolous complaints by being required to pay at least part of the expense of arbitration if their claim is not upheld. Several states have already mandated procedures of this sort, and there is no reason why all patients enrolled in a plan should not have the same protection.

A process of this kind, however, is still not sufficient. Many health plan members will not know that they have a right to appeal (or to sue if they have suffered from inadequate care). If they do know, they may lack the knowledge and skill to argue their case effectively. What members need, therefore, is some knowledgeable person who can advise them and, if necessary, assist them in having their complaint resolved.

One method of achieving this result would be to establish a system of ombudsmen to help individual members who need an adviser or an advocate.[36] This procedure has already been used successfully for nursing homes under an act of Congress. Fourteen states have established a similar system for Medicaid patients enrolled in HMOs, and several healthcare plans, including Kaiser, have embraced the concept as well.[37] Individuals who so desire could be permitted to choose other forms of representation. Union members could have their union represent them; employees with a works council could use a council member designated for the purpose; retired persons might receive such services from the American Association of Retired Persons (AARP). However chosen, the designated spokespersons would have considerable leverage in defending the interests of patients, since competing HMOs value the business of their members and will want to retain the good opinion of those who represent them.

This brief discussion cannot possibly attend to all of the innumerable details that will arise in devising a satisfactory system for resolving disputes under managed care. The essential point is this: competition among managed-care providers can accomplish a lot with the help of full disclosure, but it can never fully protect individual patients or eliminate all the differences of opinion that arise between members and HMOs. To counter these deficiencies, discussion among the interested parties will work much better than legislated standards of care, and private methods of resolving disputes are likely to prove less costly and more expeditious than formal legal remedies.

Managed care offers lessons that are widely applicable to other efforts to regulate business in America. Command-and-control techniques are often ill-suited to an economy composed of numerous independent businesses of varying sizes and descriptions that value their autonomy and compete vigorously with one another. Fortunately, viable alternatives are available.

In most cases, the first step should be to look for ways to solve the problem by making the market work better—through more information, taxes on effluents, tradeable permits, or whatever tool best suits the circumstances at hand. If measures of this kind are either unavailable or unworkable, cooperation will usually be the next best step to consider. But because cooperation often cuts against the grain of our fragmented, adversarial, competitive economy, it will normally succeed only with the stimulus of strong inducements, including the threat of heavier-handed intervention if the parties cannot collaborate effectively. In this sense, traditional rules and penalties can serve both as incentives to find a cooperative solution and as a last resort when no other method will work. By applying these principles, as agency officials are increasingly recognizing, the government can gradually limit the use of command-and-control techniques to a sufficiently small set of cases that it can enforce its rules without becoming mired in all of the controversies, costly delays, and petty irritations that have given traditional forms of regulation such a bad name.

I3

ENGAGING CITIZENS OF MODEST MEANS

"**F**ROM ANCIENT TIMES to the present day," writes political theorist Robert Dahl, "virtually all thoughtful advocates of democratic and republican government have strongly emphasized how democracy is threatened by inequalities in human resources."[1] Surely these "thoughtful advocates" would find much to worry about in the United States. Of all the major democracies, America is the one in which ordinary workers have the least protection against illness, unemployment, and other basic hazards of life, and in which government programs do least to assist the poor. The United States is also the only major democracy in which the voting rates of lower-income groups lag far behind those of more prosperous citizens. Americans earning more than $75,000 per year go to the polls at a rate virtually twice that of their fellow citizens earning less than $25,000, and the gap has been growing wider.[2] Few political observers doubt the connection between the meager legislative treatment of poor and working people and their limited political participation; in states where lower-income residents do vote more, social welfare benefits tend to be higher.[3]

It is tempting to plunge into a discussion of alternative programs to improve the lot of the poor and working classes. Policy analysts have written extensively on the pros and cons of many such proposals, and much can be learned from studying the debate. Poor and working people, however, suffer not from a dearth of policy measures to assist them but from their evident lack of political power to put such measures into effect. It is this fundamental weakness rather than another set of substantive remedies that most needs careful attention.

In considering this problem, there is little point in separating the poor from working Americans of modest means. Increasingly, poor people also work, at least part time, so that their interests in better employment legislation are identical to those of their fellow workers who do not happen to fall below the poverty line. In seeking the aid of the State, the poor are not numerous enough or powerful enough ever to receive the help they need through laws directed at them alone. Only insofar as they can join with other working people in a common quest for legislation can they hope to obtain effective programs to protect their vital interests. All Americans who happen to fall within the lower half of the income scale suffer from a common political weakness and consequently share an urgent need to join forces and participate more actively in the political process.

Who Is to Blame for the Neglect of Lower-Income Americans?

Before considering ways to strengthen the hand of lower-income Americans, however, one must first answer a threshold question. Who is at fault for the skimpy protection these citizens receive? In earlier times, sympathetic observers could attribute the political weakness of poor and working people to registration laws that inhibited them from voting and to politicians who tried to discourage them from going to the polls. Today, however, new "motor-voter" laws have brought registration well within reach of every American by allowing citizens to register when they renew their driver's license or collect their welfare check. If they still do not register, that is their right. If they suffer as a result, however, have they anyone but themselves to blame?

This is not a trivial question. Under current election laws, poor and working-class Americans who do not vote must surely share responsibility for low turnouts and their consequences. Still, the problem is not quite so simple.

Why does anyone bother to vote?[4] According to rational-choice theory, it makes no sense to do so, because—to borrow a rationale attributed to Edward Banfield—the chance that any single ballot will affect the outcome is smaller than the possibility of being run over by a truck on the way to the polls. Why, then, do so many citizens make the effort?

Some people vote because it is expected that they do so. They obey a norm, a widely recognized civic obligation they must respect in order to make democracy work.[5] Others cast a ballot out of enlightened self-interest. They have entered into a tacit bargain to vote with others of similar persuasion. By doing so, they stand to gain at the expense of others more casual about their civic responsibilities. If they did not vote, they could lose out to groups more disciplined in using their political prerogatives.

Whatever the motive, citizens do not act as isolated individuals when they cast their ballots. They have developed norms of citizenship instilled in them by others and reinforced by friends, party workers, family members, and editorial writers. Even those who vote out of enlightened self-interest are moved to do so by the contacts they have with like-minded friends and associates and by communications from political parties and interest groups.

For several reasons, Americans of modest means are less likely than their wealthier countrymen to develop civic norms or to receive encouragement to vote from friends and neighbors. In many lower-income communities, civic norms were stunted by decades of restrictive registration laws and intimidating practices in the South and in many big cities of the North.[6] Although the legal barriers to voting have eased greatly since 1960, officials in several states continue to resist requirements to simplify registration, and the legacy of exclusion inherited from earlier times may still contribute in some areas to the lack of a strong civic tradition among low-income Americans.[7]

Grassroots campaigning by candidates and party activists has also declined since World War II. Throughout the latter half of the nineteenth century, when voting rates in America reached a peak never again equaled, almost all eligible citizens cast their ballots according to their party preferences. Victory often went to the party that was most successful in getting its supporters to the polls, and Democrats and Republicans alike worked furiously to increase turnout. As partisan loyalties flagged, however, and local leaders could no longer reward faithful party workers with patronage jobs, grassroots efforts diminished.

In recent decades, political strategists have altered their campaign tactics to emphasize specially tailored appeals delivered to particular segments of the electorate by direct mailings and media ads. When choosing which voting blocs to target, political consultants rarely consider it wise to spend valuable campaign dollars appealing to poor and working-class communities.[8] As a result, whereas door-to-door canvassing, torchlight parades, and open-air rallies brought campaigning to working-class neighborhoods a century ago, lower-income citizens receive far less attention today and have fewer face-to-face contacts with politicians and their campaign operatives. According to the most sophisticated study of the falling turnout since 1960, *more than half* of the decline has resulted from the shift from grassroots mobilization to media ads and targeted mailings.[9]

Other trends in low-income urban communities have contributed to the declining turnout. Research shows that married people vote more frequently than single individuals, and that citizens are more likely to vote if they have friends and associates who would disapprove of them if they did not go to the polls.[10] In many inner-city neighborhoods, demographic changes such as the growth of single-parent families and the flight of middle-class households to the suburbs may have weakened the sources of social reinforcement that have traditionally strengthened feelings of civic responsibility.

As lower-income communities have reduced their participation, something of a vicious circle has developed. Less voting means less effort by campaign strategists to mobilize poor and working-class voters, and less inclination on the part of candidates to emphasize issues that appeal to these segments of the population. As campaign efforts diminish and candidates talk less about programs to help poorer neighborhoods, fewer Americans of modest means see much point in voting—which only leads politicians to ignore them even more.

The trends just described cast doubt on any simple notion that lower-income people are wholly responsible for their own failure to vote in larger numbers. Voting is not merely a matter of personal choice; it is just as much a product of the candidates who run, the programs they stand for, the campaign tactics they employ, and the prevailing social norms in the community. Although the apathy of lower-income groups may have led politicians to neglect their interests, political neglect has likewise helped to increase the apathy. As Steven Rosenstone and John Mark Hansen observed after their detailed study of nonvoting: "The actions of parties, campaigns, and social movements mobilize public involvement in American elections. The 'blame' for declining voter turnout, accordingly, rests as much on political leaders as on citizens themselves."[11]

Even if individual citizens *were* solely responsible for failing to go to the polls, the rest of society could not simply wash its hands of the matter and ignore the consequences. Failing to vote hurts others besides those who do not choose to cast a ballot. Poor children suffer when Congress fails to fully fund such programs as Head Start, housing assistance, and nutritional supplements for expectant mothers and their infant offspring, just as children share the hardships of reduced welfare payments, food stamp restrictions, and limits on healthcare benefits. It is not fair to ignore the plight of these young people simply because their parents will not vote.

Beyond the claims of lower-income Americans and their children, all citizens have an interest in the quality of our democracy. Thoughtful people at every income level would prefer to live in a just society in which all interests receive due consideration. Because most human beings are self-interested to some degree and cannot fully appreciate the needs and feelings of others, the surest way to make certain that all interests receive proper attention is to have every part of the adult population exercise its right to vote. For this reason, it is facile to dismiss depressed voting rates among poor and working-class Americans as a matter that concerns nonvoters alone. Every citizen who believes in a just and thriving democracy has a stake in achieving a high turnout at the polls.

Increasing Turnout among Lower-Income Groups

No law of human nature prescribes that Americans of modest means should vote at far lower rates than their more prosperous fellow citizens. Throughout Western Europe, poor and working-class citizens cast their ballots almost as frequently as more prosperous segments

of society; those with the least education vote at more than 90 percent of the rate of their well-educated fellow citizens.[12] In 1990, the
turnout of the least-educated voters in Finland and West Germany
actually exceeded that of their better-educated compatriots.

By now, analysts have discovered a lot about why voting rates are
high or low, and how they can be increased. What they have shown
is that the size of turnout is influenced as much by the rules that govern the political process as it is by larger social forces. For example,
comparative studies suggest that encouraging the creation of new
political parties by a system of proportional representation would
raise voting rates by more than 10 percent, because more citizens
would feel that their votes counted and that they had a chance to
elect candidates who truly reflected their views.[13] The surge in voting
in 1992 following the candidacy of Ross Perot demonstrates the way
new choices can boost turnout.

Other methods of pushing up voting rates are easier to implement.
Some of these measures would simply make voting more convenient.
For example, holding elections on Sundays or declaring election day
a holiday could raise turnouts by 5 or 6 percent, according to the
most careful comparative studies.[14] Conducting elections by mail
could yield almost as large an increase. Allowing voters to register
when they go to the polls or finding some other way to put them
automatically on the election rolls might lift turnout by as much as
5–10 percentage points.[15]

However meritorious such reforms may be, they would probably
not have much effect on the political influence of poor and working-
class Americans. The most important reason for the scanty voting record of lower-income citizens has less to do with registration requirements or convenience in getting to the polls than with their growing
isolation from political campaigns and their doubts that voting will
make a difference to their lives. By themselves, therefore, as experience under Motor-Voter laws confirms, efforts to simplify voting
tend to increase turnouts most not within poor and working-class
communities, but among more affluent young people and among
families that have recently moved from one area to another and have
not gotten around to registering.

A much more radical step to increase turnouts would be to make
voting compulsory, as it is in Australia, Belgium, Greece, and Italy,

among others.[16] Although such laws have rarely succeeded in lifting voting rates to levels close to 100 percent, turnouts of 85–90 percent or even more are common in several nations that require their citizens to vote.

Skeptics are bound to ask how the authorities enforce such an obligation, especially in poorer nations with high illiteracy rates, such as Venezuela and Brazil. The answer is that no country with compulsory voting makes a serious effort to apprehend and punish those who fail to cast a ballot. Apparently, the mere existence of an official requirement is enough to bring many more citizens to the polls. Thus, when Holland and Venezuela dropped their voting requirement (the only two countries to do so), turnouts immediately fell by more than 10 percentage points.[17]

As a practical matter, the chances are slim for introducing compulsory voting in the United States. Republicans would strongly oppose a reform of this kind, since experience around the world suggests that raising voting rates favors parties of the left. Business interests would resist out of concern that increasing the political power of ordinary working people might lead to a higher minimum wage, restrictions on layoffs, improvements in worker compensation, and other measures that could impose greater costs on employers. Even Democratic lawmakers might be wary of reforms to increase participation. Politicians of every persuasion who have managed to get themselves elected under the current rules will worry about the effects of a large infusion of new and unpredictable voters.

Even citizens with no special axe to grind may be troubled at the prospect of making people vote who have no wish to cast a ballot and show little interest in the issues involved in the election. Conceivably, compulsory voting by itself would cause politicians to pay more attention to less affluent citizens and thus increase their interest and political awareness. But that is a speculative possibility at best. The disengagement of many lower-income Americans has reached such a point that a compulsory-voting law might accomplish very little. Even if legal compulsion could somehow make them go to the polls, it could not force them to inform themselves or reflect with care on the choices they were making. Instead, higher turnouts manufactured by law could easily yield a bitter harvest of opportunistic candidates, broken promises, and frustrated hopes that would end in even greater cynicism.

Rather than advocate drastic new steps to increase voting, reformers might look for ways of encouraging low-income workers and community residents to join together to learn more and do more about the problems that concern them. Until people of modest means are engaged more actively in improving their working conditions and rebuilding their communities, requiring them to vote will not lead them to mark their ballots wisely. Nor is it clear that passing a law will even succeed in making alienated citizens go to the polls at all.

Organizing the Workplace

One obvious way to expand the influence of working people would be to strengthen unions. Unions can and regularly do gain important benefits for their members through collective bargaining: health insurance, decent wages, protection against arbitrary treatment, advance notice of layoffs, parental leave, even childcare. Unions are also the principal political force for educating workers about relevant policy issues and helping them obtain additional benefits through legislation. If organized labor could expand its membership two- or three-fold to match the levels achieved in Canada and Europe, much could be done to bring American workers the same safeguards and benefits normally given to employees in other advanced democracies.

But what are the prospects for major increases in union membership? Experience gives little reason for optimism. American workers have always been hard to organize, and most of the traditional reasons are still very much in evidence. Fearful that unionization will put them at a competitive disadvantage, employers continue to resist tenaciously. If anything, their efforts have become even more sophisticated and successful over the years. For their part, unions continue to be dogged by bad publicity and periodic exposés of corruption and mismanagement. The labor force is still crisscrossed by multiple racial, ethnic, and even language barriers. The sectors in which unions most need to expand are increasingly composed of technical and professional employees who have traditionally been hard to organize. This is a formidable list of problems.

The government could conceivably take steps to help labor organizers. There is no justification for the widespread use of illegal methods by employers to discourage unionization, methods that have produced a steadily rising percentage of campaigns marked by crude threats and firings of employees for exercising their right to organize. Such behavior persists because the legal remedies are so weak and so slow in coming that employers know they can gain more than they stand to lose by breaking the law.

Since these tactics are indefensible, Congress may agree at some point on ways to expedite union elections and stiffen the penalties to discourage threats and intimidation. Properly designed, measures of this kind could significantly improve the prospects for union organizers. Nevertheless, resourceful employers have plenty of defenses left that cannot be overcome by legal means, and workers have plenty of reasons for rejecting unions that have nothing to do with the fear of employer retaliation. Despite recent talk of a rejuvenated labor movement, unions have shown few signs as yet of developing new organizing strategies that can overcome these obstacles. As a result, no conceivable reform of existing labor laws promises to bring about a doubling or a trebling of union membership. Instead, the vast majority of American workers in the private sector seem destined to remain outside the labor movement.

The United States could encourage more employee organization if it followed the lead of Western Europe and authorized the election of works councils along the lines described in the preceding chapter. Unlike efforts to strengthen the hand of union organizers, authorizing works councils might not provoke all-out opposition by employers, since councils are only consultative bodies and cannot strike or bargain over wages.* Properly implemented methods of employee

---

* This is not to say that there would be no opposition if serious proposals were advanced to encourage works councils. Many employers feel that councils would prove to be a stepping-stone to unionization or the opening stage in a new wave of government regulation. Ironically, many labor leaders fear that works councils would make unions superfluous in the eyes of employees, thus placing further obstacles in the path of union organizing efforts. Such reactions illustrate the problems of trying to introduce substantial change in an atmosphere of widespread suspicion and skepticism not only toward government but between unions and employers as well.

consultation and participation have often improved productivity. For this reason, large majorities of employers state that they would like to have some means of discussing common problems with representatives of their employees.[18] As the National Labor Relations Act is presently construed, however, the law is not clear on whether employers are entitled to meet with any representative employee group other than a duly certified union to talk about subjects that could be considered working conditions or terms of employment. If Congress authorized works councils, this problem would disappear. In addition, as previously explained, employers could avoid periodic inspections, fines, and other regulatory burdens by agreeing to alternative safeguards negotiated with their works council, provided the agreement was approved by secret ballot of the employees and certified by the government. With these advantages, even employers who did not agree with all the features of a works council statute might still regard it as an improvement over the current set of laws and regulations governing the workplace.

Granted, works councils are not unions, nor is it likely that they could become an active force in politics to promote employee interests. But works council legislation could help in several ways to encourage greater organization and political participation on the part of lower-income Americans. By engaging in council activities, employees would become more aware of their needs for adequate healthcare, job training, childcare, and protection from arbitrary or unnecessary job loss. As experience brought out the limits achievable through negotiated agreements, participating workers might recognize their stake in adequate employment legislation.

Active involvement in employee committees could also be a stepping-stone to other kinds of political and community involvement. Those who participate actively in organizations of this kind are more likely to be recruited to work in political campaigns and to join community groups. Council members could acquire greater confidence in working together and thus seek out opportunities to serve in civic and neighborhood organizations. Experience gained from exercising responsibility in council activity could develop valuable leadership skills for other kinds of cooperative endeavors. These possibilities are more than pipe dreams. Most empirical studies on the subject have found that active participation in employee organizations does increase the likelihood of voting in elections, working in political campaigns, and engaging in civic activities.[19]

In short, participation begets more participation. As scholars are increasingly finding, joining organizations builds social capital and mutual trust that make it easier to work together to solve other common problems. Working together leads in turn to political participation. At present, lower-income Americans are not much involved in organizations, apart from churches. Works councils could be a way of reversing this tendency. Properly designed and encouraged, they might not only contribute to greater productivity, better working conditions, and less onerous, inappropriate regulation; they could help overcome the political apathy that contributes to the persistent failure to provide many of the legislative benefits and safeguards for working people that most Americans claim to favor.

The Challenge of Organizing Poor Communities

Residential neighborhoods and communities are another locus for mobilizing poor and working-class Americans to take a greater interest in politics and civic affairs. Idealists and social reformers have long attempted to do just that. Since the first settlement houses sprang up more than a century ago, churches, social workers, radical organizers, and (more recently) charitable foundations have reached out to assist the residents of poor and immigrant neighborhoods. For generations, however, two problems have repeatedly hampered these efforts. Either reformers tried to offer services to the poor, in which case they risked becoming paternalistic outsiders who did things *for* but not *with* the communities they tried to serve; or, if they did succeed in organizing poor people to help themselves, they soon aroused the ire of local political leaders, who were generally adept at destroying or coopting every independent power base that could pose a threat to their own continued control.

The War on Poverty and the activism of the 1960s helped to revive community organizing. Out of the ferment of that tumultuous decade emerged two separate strands of grassroots activism that persist to this day. The first is the community organizing movement, which owes its origins to the late Saul Alinsky, a pioneer in mobilizing low-income neighborhoods. Attracting former campus activists and civil rights workers, the movement gave rise to several new organizations—Citizen Action, ACORN (Association of Community Organizations for Reform Now), and the IAF (Industrial Areas Foundation)—which mobilized residents of poor communities and confronted business leaders and public officials to demand fair treatment and better services. The second form of grassroots activism owed more to the old settlement-house tradition and sought to reach out to neighborhood residents by helping to plan and coordinate social services. The most visible fruits of this effort were the Community Development Corporations (CDCs), which sprang up by the hundreds to build housing and bring economic development to inner-city neighborhoods.

During the 1980s, both forms of community activism developed new vigor in low-income areas threatened with federal cutbacks in urban programs. Aided by foundations, state and local governments, and federal money, CDCs multiplied. They succeeded in renovating or constructing several hundred thousand new units of affordable housing and more than two million square feet of commercial space.[20] The community organizing movement had a more mixed record, and some of its offshoots, such as ACORN, found it difficult to expand their membership or sustain much real momentum. But the IAF did achieve noteworthy successes in the Bronx and in several Texas cities, while gradually expanding its operations to new locations. By the mid-1990s, it was active in more than forty cities throughout the nation.

The future of these initiatives is hard to predict. Attempts to strengthen poor and blue-collar communities have often experienced a brief initial success followed by eventual failure and disappointment. Time and again, reformers have had to grapple with a series of daunting problems. How to find a permanent source of funding? How to sustain the interest of local residents during a long, often frustrating process of trying to overcome extremely difficult community problems? How to develop indigenous leadership instead of relying on outsiders who come and go, often with an agenda more radical than that of the neighborhoods they serve? How to work closely enough with the city government to obtain needed help for local residents, without being coopted by the political establishment or riven by internal partisan disagreements?

Through decades of effort to help hard-pressed communities, activists have been repeatedly stymied by these problems. In recent years, however, a few grassroots organizations have shown signs of discovering effective solutions.

The IAF—Saul Alinsky's legacy to community mobilization—has made slow but steady progress in a growing number of cities with the aid of an unusual strategy.[21] Unlike other militant community organizations, it has financed its operations through agreements with local churches that have promised to contribute just what community organizers have long lacked: a steady, long-term source of funding. The commitment to social justice shared by participating ministers and priests has also lent a much-needed moral fervor to sustain and inspirit the work of rank-and-file activists and supporters. Although the IAF supplies well-paid organizers to assist its members, the organization makes every effort to develop leadership from the ranks of community residents themselves and to rely on them to develop their own policies and priorities. The "Iron Rule" that IAF leaders impress on all their organizers is "Never do anything for people that they can do for themselves."

Programs vary from one city to another, depending on the needs and desires of the local membership. In San Antonio, where the IAF has been active since 1972, the organization began by pressuring city leaders to give a fair share of municipal funds to pave the streets, improve storm drainage, and carry out other programs to upgrade the infrastructure in Mexican-American neighborhoods. Since that time, officials have channeled more than $1 billion to these communities for such projects.

In recent years, as the IAF has gradually won greater acceptance from the power structure, it has moderated its confrontational stance. Its leaders have launched programs to cooperate with teachers and principals in improving public schools, to join with local businesses to organize job training programs, and to work with government agencies in building affordable housing. To increase its influence, organizers have increasingly reached beyond low-income neighborhoods to involve suburban churches in creating multiracial, metropolitan-wide alliances. The IAF does not formally endorse candidates or engage in partisan politics. But it does ask local politicians to support its projects and rewards them at the polls if they fulfill their promises.

The IAF has not yet managed to solve all of the dilemmas confronting community organizers. While it has proved adept at mobilizing lower-middle-class residents, it has had a much harder time involving the genuinely poor or even persuading them to vote. IAF leaders have also failed thus far to develop a clear strategy for influencing policy at the state and national levels. Without some means of doing so, the organization can carry out successful local projects but still fail to bring about the larger changes needed to make a major difference in the lives of lower-income Americans. These are substantial challenges. After more than twenty years of effort, however, with signs of progress visible in neighborhoods across the country, the IAF seems closer than any other movement to developing a viable model of sustainable community organization and revitalization.[22]

Local initiatives to improve human services in poor communities have followed a different path. Community Development Corporations have continued to grow, expanding their activities beyond housing to include more emphasis on job training and commercial development. In the early 1990s, local activists gained a further boost when several major foundations agreed to fund multi-year programs in several cities. The aim of the foundation efforts in each location was the traditional goal of developing and coordinating an array of interrelated services with the help of local leadership and resident participation.[23]

Both the new foundation initiatives and many CDCs seem to be moving away from direct service delivery. The emerging model is one of a facilitating agency that does not render services itself but offers coordination and technical assistance while acting as a catalyst to initiate and nurture new programs that fill gaps in the existing array of local services. For example, the most successful CDCs seldom provide job training themselves, but try to bring community colleges together with networks of companies to create training programs tailored to employers' needs.

Because these initiatives are newer than many of the IAF efforts, more questions remain unanswered. Can community service organizations develop enough grassroots participation to be authentic representatives of community needs instead of merely the latest model in a long series of social agencies controlled by well-meaning, outside professionals? Will the government funds on which these ventures depend continue to be forthcoming? Most important of all, will the new grassroots organizations content themselves with simply improving local services or will they undertake the more arduous task of building strong communities led by residents who can articulate their needs and display enough ingenuity and initiative to persuade government agencies, area businesses, and other influential groups to help them find solutions? The long-term significance of these community initiatives will depend on the answers to these questions.

Prospects for Organizing Communities

Vast problems still stand in the way of revitalizing poor and working-class communities. Over the past several decades, notwithstanding the efforts of grassroots groups to organize residents, rebuild housing, and improve local services, larger social forces have helped to worsen conditions in many lower-income neighborhoods. Concentrations of poverty have increased in many urban areas as manufacturing jobs disappeared and middle-class blacks and whites departed for the suburbs. Drug use has spread like an epidemic through many inner cities. Single-parent families have proliferated. Random acts of violence have terrorized entire neighborhoods.

In the face of such problems, can CDCs, human-service networks, community organizing, and other grassroots initiatives reconnect poor communities with the rest of society and engage residents in the political and civic life of the nation? Or are their efforts merely transient episodes in the life of inner-city neighborhoods, like the first ebullient stages of the settlement-house movement or the early days of Community Action programs in the War on Poverty? No one yet knows. But one subtle change seems to be occurring in the larger society's stance toward poor communities that offers grounds for guarded optimism.

What public officials, bank presidents, developers, and other influential figures are beginning to realize is that they need viable inner-city organizations to achieve their own objectives. More school systems are coming to accept the growing consensus among researchers that active parental involvement in the education of their children helps to improve performance. Housing developers and managers are learning that strong tenant organizations can prevent deterioration and decay. Banks are finding that they need strong neighborhood groups to assist them in evaluating lending risks to comply with the Community Reinvestment Act. Local employers seeking skilled workers are discovering that resourceful community organizations can help screen applicants for job training programs and lend needed support to enable trainees to finish the course successfully.

Interest in encouraging grassroots mobilization could conceivably increase as more becomes known about the impact of community mobilization on a growing range of social problems. Investigators have already claimed to have found that the extent of neighborhood organization and social interaction is linked to levels of crime, health, and educational achievement.[24] If experience confirms that organizing residents and involving them actively in community affairs can actually help overcome such important problems, the rest of society will undoubtedly become more supportive.

Even now, as more and more influential people perceive the value of strong community-based organizations, the hostility of the local establishment toward the Community Action agencies of the 1960s has given way to more positive attitudes. To be sure, not everyone shares these feelings. Mayors are still skittish about independent sources of power, especially if the new community organizations seek to mobilize large numbers of voters. Whether city officials are now prepared to accept such organizations is still open to question. Some undoubtedly are not. But other, younger politicians are more inclined to see advantages in neighborhood organizations that will cooperate in improving policing and improving the schools. As former Baltimore mayor Kurt Schmoke observed, reflecting on his experience with the IAF, "It's a gamble because if you have powerful organizations out there, when it comes to disagreements, they have influence. They can battle you. But the benefits outweigh the risks."[25]

The organizing work of groups such as the IAF could eventually do a lot to increase political participation. As neighborhood residents organize to solve community problems, they may come to recognize the importance of political involvement while developing leadership skills and communications networks that will make their participation more effective. In time, active grassroots organizations are bound to demand that politicians pay greater attention to the problems of lower-income communities. Even the most nonpartisan neighborhood groups will see an advantage in registering people and encouraging them to vote in order to support candidates who take an interest in their needs. In turn, as political leaders perceive these tendencies and try to take advantage of them, parties will begin to pay more attention. Eventually, a mutually reinforcing process could emerge whereby successful grassroots organization causes officials to respond, which in turn encourages more local residents to become politically involved.

Could governments do more to nurture this process of grassroots renewal and help it to succeed? The answer is not as clear as one might think. Even with the best of intentions, officials who try to help can actually undermine community organizations and weaken their ability to accomplish their objectives. Nonprofit service organizations that depend on government funds find that public officials often impose requirements and demand large amounts of paperwork to ensure that taxpayers' money is not allocated foolishly or spent improperly. If neighborhood service agencies are to function at all, therefore, they must abide by external guidelines that define whom they can help and how the help should be delivered. The complicated forms and procedures that the government requires can force neighborhood activists to hire outside managers, who gradually acquire influence over the affairs of the organization at the expense of local residents. Slowly but surely, neighborhood organizations can lose their autonomy, along with the flexibility, informality, and entrepreneurial vigor that made them successful in the first place.[26]

At the same time, enlightened government can do a lot to bring people of modest means back into the political life of the country. Local authorities can take the initiative to reach out and encourage neighborhood groups to help in organizing community policing, managing a housing project, or giving advice and cooperation for improving local schools. Of course, such requests must be sincere. Formal mandates that require citizen participation will often breed one-sided, ineffectual relationships; the long series of failed community advisory groups is proof enough of that.[27] The key to success is a genuine desire on the part of city officials to receive aid and advice from neighborhood residents, and to allow them real opportunities to collaborate in making policies for law enforcement officers, housing projects, and schools. Often, busy officials will not want to share power or risk the contentiousness and delays that community participation can bring. Nevertheless, as evidence accumulates that strong community partners can help the city solve some of its problems, the incentives for genuine collaboration should increase.

Where suitable, policymakers can also supply social services through vouchers rather than outright grants, so that community organizations are freer to compete for clients instead of having to conform to all the guidelines and directives that often accompany direct government funding. Governments at every level can help local groups achieve greater financial independence by offering limited tax credits to those wishing to contribute. Public officials and foundations can create a more favorable climate for developing grassroots organizations by establishing agencies to offer legal services, training, or technical advice on how to find project funding, renovate dilapidated housing, or develop a neighborhood health clinic.

Whatever the government does, mobilizing residents and nurturing leadership and organization in poor and working-class communities will continue to be difficult, frustrating work. In many cities, the goal is still far out of reach. In some urban areas, however, the building blocks for successful mobilization and self-help are coming into being: the community-based social services, the local leadership, and the grassroots organizations capable of articulating local needs, launching community programs, and acting as a viable partner for interested organizations in the outside world. Beyond these struggling neighborhoods, banks, businesses, local governments, and other powerful institutions are starting to perceive an interest in helping urban residents organize to improve their institutions and rebuild their economic base. New financial institutions are finding ways to gather outside resources and invest effectively in inner-city neighborhoods. Whether these ingredients will be enough to produce more active, successful lower-income communities and whether such involvement will lead to increased political engagement are still anyone's guess. But one can begin to imagine how this *might* happen, and that is itself a significant change over the situation only a few short years ago.

Political Parties

Political parties offer another vehicle for mobilizing lower-income citizens and involving them in politics and public affairs. Indeed, this is one of their traditional, even essential, missions. As Walter Dean Burnham has observed, "Political parties, with all their well-known human and structural shortcomings, are the only devices thus far invented by the wit of Western man which with some effectiveness can generate countervailing collective power on behalf of the many individually powerless against the relatively few who are individually—or organizationally—powerful."[28]

At one time, political parties in the United States succeeded very well in encouraging citizen participation in all segments of society. By the late nineteenth century, they were better organized and more successful at turning out the vote than their counterparts in Europe.[29] Aided by newspapers that openly advocated the party line and buoyed by parades, rallies, marching bands, and other public celebrations, Democrats and Republicans managed from 1870 to 1890 to bring the turnout of eligible voters to more than 75 percent, a level never again equaled in the United States.

In many larger cities, parties developed political machines to organize the residents of working-class neighborhoods and bring them to the polls on election day. Under the leadership of the local political boss, a machine would divide cities into precincts of approximately 1,000 residents, each with its own captain. Captains usually held a government post of some sort, but their real job was finding ways to help local residents and seeing to it that they voted on election day. The services were varied, ranging from helping men find work and solving their problems with the local bureaucracy to distributing turkeys at Thanksgiving and Christmas. Here and there, such activities could still be found even in the 1970s, as revealed by the testimony of a Polish precinct captain in Chicago:

The very first thing I do each morning, I get my car out of the garage and I take a ride through the alleys. Many of the people . . . have a piece of furniture to throw out in the alley, or a mattress, and I'm afraid that punks will set a match to it and set a garage on fire. I stop at the [streets and Sanitation] ward yard . . . and give a list to the superintendent. . . . And they'll pick it up. I also see when a man needs a garbage can. . . . If a fella really needs one, I'll tell him "Look, when you get home from work, come over and pick one up." They're happy to get them. Also, the Latinos ask questions or explanations of some of the papers they get. Many times, if they have a traffic violation, we have a lawyer in the organization who goes and represents these lads in court for no fee to them. That's a free service that the organization provides if a fella gets a ticket.[30]

With all the faults of the big-city machines, precinct captains and ward leaders did help many immigrants and poor working people to survive in a harsh economic environment. Yet theirs was not a politics based on issues or political convictions, nor were their bosses particularly interested in encouraging citizens to become better informed about policy issues. The methods they used were much more practical. Machine leaders offered patronage to recruit precinct captains, who then rendered services to residents in return for their votes.

Tainted as they often were by corruption, city machines became the favorite target of reformers. Eventually, Progressive forces managed to weaken the bosses' grip on the political process. The growth of a merit-based civil service and the consequent decline of patronage gradually reduced the power of machines to reward their loyal precinct workers. The growth of government social programs during the New Deal undercut many of the services by which precinct captains gained the support of local residents. The final blow came with the advent of media-dominated campaigns, which minimized the role of party workers and made the support of the bosses less important to politicians. By the 1990s, even the Chicago machine was only a shadow of what it had been throughout the first two-thirds of the century.

In recent decades, local party organizations appear to have revived somewhat.[31] Most county headquarters have a full-time staff person, and more party volunteers are making efforts to canvass door to door, conduct registration drives, and call up voters on election day to get them to the polls. Unlike the old-time precinct captains, many of today's activists become involved through interest in the issues rather than a desire for a government job. Still, party activity in most areas tends to quicken only at election time; there is little evidence yet of any year-round effort to educate citizens and involve them in politics and civic affairs.[32]

Will political parties make greater efforts in the future to reach out to lower-income Americans? Quite possibly. The alternative is to continue spending more and more money in an attempt to appeal to a dwindling number of better-educated, more affluent swing-voters who still go regularly to the polls. Eventually, the law of diminishing returns may force political strategists to reconsider this policy.

Continued efforts to simplify voting and registration procedures could hasten this process. In the past, campaign strategists have often hesitated to invest resources in registration drives, knowing that citizens registered after costly, time-consuming efforts may never bother to vote on election day. Same-day registration and other similar reforms could overcome these inhibitions by lowering the costs of bringing new voters to the polls. Full public financing of election campaigns could limit total spending and cause parties to put more emphasis on enlisting volunteers to get out the vote. Most of all, effective community organization could awaken lower-income neighborhoods to the need for greater political participation and make mobilization efforts easier and more attractive. In time, these forces could lead campaign strategists to alter their priorities and direct more money and effort to bringing lower-income citizens into the political process.

Will Organizing Low-Income Americans Truly Help the Country?

Not everyone will welcome efforts to organize poor and working people and engage them more actively in the political life of the country. After all, lower-income groups are typically less educated and less informed than their fellow citizens. Will it truly help society if more of these people flock to the polls? Not according to Charley Reese of the *Orlando Sentinel*: "The idea that there is some benefit in ignoramuses and morons pulling levers next to names on a ballot is one of the evil myths of post-modern America."[33] At least a few political scientists agree. As Thomas Dye and Harmon Ziegler have observed: "If the survival of the American system depended upon an active, informed, and enlightened citizenry, then democracy would have disappeared long ago; for the masses of Americans . . . have a surprisingly weak commitment to democratic values. . . . But fortunately for these values and for American democracy, the American masses do not lead, they follow."[34]

John Stuart Mill is perhaps the best-known political philosopher who dealt explicitly with the pros and cons of encouraging voting by the less-educated, less-knowledgeable members of the community.[35] Mill was not prepared to advocate depriving such citizens of their franchise. Still, he worried about the consequences of allowing the ignorant masses to vote. His solution was ingenious: give everyone a vote, he argued, but give two votes to graduates of Cambridge and Oxford.

Today, Mill's proposal seems more notable for its pluck than for its practicality. Ironically, however, voting patterns in the United States have gradually come to bear an eerie resemblance to what he recommended. Whereas every adult American citizen has an opportunity to cast a ballot, the highly educated now vote at roughly twice the rate of the least educated. The result is that in America, as in Mill's proposal, knowledge and education are privileged, although no particular segment of the adult population is formally disenfranchised. In the United States, moreover, this result has come about without the awkwardness in Mill's solution of explicitly giving one class of people more votes than another.

There is something seductive about a system that works so quietly to ensure that the ballots of the best-educated, most accomplished members of society count more heavily. Researchers have confirmed that nonvoters are much less informed about public affairs than those who go to the polls.[36] With civic knowledge already at a low ebb in America, a pattern of voting that heavily favors college graduates could strike the casual observer as a providential way of ensuring a reasonably enlightened electorate.

The flaw in the argument is that better-educated, more affluent citizens may not take sufficient account of the legitimate needs and claims of those who are not so fortunate. Will voters who have never lacked decent medical care, adequate food for their children, and affordable housing for their families fully comprehend the predicament of those who often go without these necessities? Will they insist that their needier fellow citizens receive adequate protection against suffering and privation?

There is reason to be skeptical. Mill himself considered it a "universal truth . . . that the rights and interests of every or any person are only secure from being disregarded when the person interested is himself able, and generally disposed to stand up for them."[37] The record of the United States amply confirms this proposition. Although a majority of Americans have consistently agreed in principle that the government should do more for the poor, ensure equal opportunities for everyone, and provide universal access to quality health care, the comparisons made in Chapter 1 show all too clearly how far the practice has fallen short of these ideals.

Even when the government has intervened, and even when it has intervened at the instigation of those most inclined to be of help, the resulting policies have often failed to meet the real needs of those they meant to benefit. For example, surveys show that welfare recipients in the 1990s were as opposed to the system as other Americans, not just because the benefits were meager but because they felt that welfare encouraged "people to be lazy" and made it "financially better for people to stay on welfare than to get a job."[38] Thus, the long-standing opposition of many Democrats to work requirements turned out to be more a reflection of elite liberal sentiment than a valid expression of the needs and values of poor Americans. Much the same may be true of the current opposition to experiments with school vouchers, which often provoke vigorous attacks from liberal elites while attracting wide support among low-income families.

Deciding how much protection to allow for the major hazards of life or what programs to enact to increase opportunities for the young is as much a matter of values as of education and expertise. No group of citizens can be counted upon to have the wisdom or the objectivity to decide what is best for others. Rather, a healthy democracy permits all segments of society to participate in resolving such questions so that they can determine for themselves where their own best interests lie.[39]

Business interests, however, have another concern more concrete and more specific than the fear of seeing greater numbers of poorly educated citizens marching to the polls. If workers and other low-income groups succeed in organizing themselves politically, what will keep them from using their power to push through social policies and employment laws so generous and far-reaching as to hinder the growth and dynamism of the American economy?

Many influential people probably fear such a result. Their worries may help explain the lack of interest in making greater efforts to encourage full political participation by the poor and working classes. Such concerns are not groundless. In most of Western Europe, where much higher percentages of lower-income citizens vote and have powerful political parties and labor organizations to represent them, governments have responded by creating an overextended welfare state that apparently cannot be sustained. Growth rates in the 1990s were lower than they should have been and unemployment rates were considerably higher, yet some of the governments involved found it hard to adjust their protective work rules and welfare benefits to conform to the dictates of the world economy. Organizations representing the working classes were the principal obstacle blocking these reforms.

Would a similar fate befall the United States if poor and working people managed to vote and organize themselves into a more potent political force? Not necessarily. Some of the programs that lower-income Americans should presumably favor would build human capital, improve the quality of the workforce, and encourage faster economic growth. Better schools, improved job training, broader access to college, fully funded child nutrition programs, and higher-quality, universal preschool are all prominent examples. Other reforms, such as universal access to health care, would have no obvious effect on the economy one way or the other.

Where problems could arise would be in the field of employment rules, where political representatives of working people might follow the lead of their counterparts in Europe and press for severe restrictions on layoffs, a much higher minimum wage, a shorter work week, and more inclusive, longer-lasting unemployment benefits.

Not every reform of this kind would be unwise or unjustified; American employment laws are deficient in various respects. Still, worker demands could conceivably push safeguards and benefits to a point that would interfere with productivity and growth.

Does this possibility justify resisting efforts to lift voting rates and increase community organization among the poor and working classes? Hardly. There is much experience in the fifty states from which to judge whether strengthening the political muscle of lower-income Americans would, on balance, do more harm than good. This record gives scant support for the dire predictions that political Cassandras have uttered through the ages about the dangers of encouraging the masses to vote.

As it happens, some states have much higher voting turnouts than others among poor and working-class voters. When the states are compared, far from collapsing into economic stagnation, intolerance, or civic strife, those in which lower-income citizens vote more heavily tend to have a substantially larger per capita Gross State Product and much higher ratings on an overall livability index (a composite rating based on forty-three separate rankings covering a wide variety of items, including economic prosperity, health, education, crime, and environmental conditions).[40] On both measures, the average rank of these states fits comfortably into the top half of the fifty states. It is the states where lower-income residents are least inclined to vote that tend to lag behind, falling into the bottom half, on average, in both overall livability and per capita Gross State Product.*

If doubts remain about the wisdom of greater political mobilization, the best answer rests not on pragmatic grounds but on democratic principles. Even if the vote of lower-income Americans posed a threat to economic growth and prosperity, their political weakness would still be unfortunate. Although farm subsidies have been

---

* The nine states with the least class bias in voting (under 30 percent) had an average rank for overall livability of 18 among the fifty states (where 1 is highest). Their average rank for per capital Gross State Product was 14. The nine states with the greatest class bias in voting (over 80 percent) had an average livability ranking of 33 and a ranking of 26 for Gross State Product. These comparisons may not show that higher voting *causes* better performance by states, but they do cast doubt on claims that encouraging voting by less-affluent, less-educated citizens threatens the welfare and prosperity of society.

wasteful and a drag on the economy by most informed accounts, no one wants fewer farmers to vote or favors the disbanding of their political organizations. No reasonable person wants the elderly to go to the polls less frequently because their political power makes it hard to cut back Social Security or restrict Medicare. Mill's observation still stands. Since no group can claim to know what is best for others or care deeply enough about their welfare, the ends of democracy are best served when all citizens and groups have equivalent power to influence the policies of their government.

It is especially unfair that the most fortunate segments of society should be so powerfully organized while the least-skilled, least-educated citizens remain so politically weak. The record of the United States bears witness to the consequences. As experience in the states suggests, greater political participation by lower-income groups will help mitigate these results and bring society closer to the goals that large majorities of Americans support. There is much to be said, therefore, for vigorous efforts to organize poor and working-class Americans and to encourage them to vote and engage more actively in the civic life of the country.

IV

THE ROLE OF THE PEOPLE

NOW THAT THE PROBLEMS of government have been analyzed and the principal remedies explored, can we point to some primal cause that sits at the root of all the government's difficulties and offers clues to further reforms that will result in genuine, lasting improvement? It is tempting to respond by blaming our elected leaders and by seeking salvation in some bold measure, such as term limits, that promises to bring a new breed of politician to Washington. As we have seen, however, there is no convincing evidence that the quality of our political leaders has declined, let alone any reason to believe that term limits or any similar reforms would improve matters significantly. Should we therefore look to our institutions, shaped as they are by a Constitution designed more to guard against tyranny and abuse than to produce effective solutions for today's complicated problems? If not, does the chief reason for our frustrations lie with the powerful interest groups that contribute such large sums to our officials and use such sophisticated methods to lobby politicians and influence the public debate? Or might the principal cause of the government's travails rest instead with Americans themselves through their ultimate power to guide their political leaders by the votes they cast at election time?

Much has already been said about the way in which our institutions contribute to the most serious failings of government. With our separation of powers and our federal structure, there are so many different power centers that it is hard to enact coherent legislation or implement carefully planned programs to cope with the complicated problems that so often confront public officials today. Weak political parties undermine the one obvious source of discipline that might allow sufficient coordination to mesh the different parts of government into a more harmonious whole. Meanwhile, single-district voting under a winner-take-all system has seriously hindered the development of a labor party along European lines—the type of party that could effectively represent the interests of poor and working people.

Regardless of the influence one ascribes to our institutions, there is scant prospect of changing them in any substantial way to try to make our government work better. However much Americans may complain, they do not wish to run the risk of altering the fundamental structure of government set forth in the Constitution. They like the safeguards that the separation of powers provides, regardless of the system's effects on clear legislation and efficient administration. They relish the chance to put different parties in the White House and the Congress so that each can counter the excesses of the other. To alter the constitutional framework is to tamper with the sacred text that defines what seems most essential to our liberties and our distinctiveness as a nation.

Rather than criticize the basic institutional structure, most people prefer to point the finger at powerful interest groups that strive to promote their private ends at the public's expense. Such accusations are understandable. Influential lobbyists undoubtedly win many concessions and special favors that weaken legislation and make it less coherent. Through their efforts, Congress often alters regulatory laws in ways that diminish their effectiveness. Adept at defending their turf, well-financed interest groups frequently leave the poor and unorganized to bear the brunt of the cutbacks that lean times periodically require.

As has been mentioned earlier, however, almost every serious study of American interest groups has found that private-sector lobbies are not as influential as most people seem to believe. They frequently give way before a sustained demand by voters, as business groups discovered in the 1970s when they were faced with strong popular pressure for consumer and environmental protection. Because America's major power blocs—notably business, labor, and farm interests—are so fragmented, they have tended to be less successful than corresponding organizations in Europe and Japan in securing subsidies and protective legislation to promote their interests. If American interest groups are not as powerful as their counterparts abroad, it is difficult to hold them primarily responsible for the many areas in which the United States has fallen behind other advanced democracies in fulfilling goals that large majorities of Americans support.

However strong or weak they actually are, interest groups in the United States are a perennial target for reformers seeking to improve the government. Over the years, legislatures have passed a long series of rules to keep such activities as lobbying and campaign donations within tolerable bounds. But there are limits to what such reforms can accomplish. Although Congress has the power to limit campaign contributions, the First Amendment hinders attempts to prevent organizations from spending liberally to promote their policy aims. Because many lobbyists can command large sums of money to publicize their views on policy issues and because such issues are inextricably bound up with legislation and election campaigns, it is impossible to curb the power of wealthy groups completely. Under the best of circumstances, private interests are likely to continue to wield more influence than one would prefer in an ideal world.

What of the third major force affecting our government—the public itself? It is unfashionable in many circles to suggest that the American people might be responsible for many of the government's shortcomings. Nevertheless, the role of citizens in any true democracy is so important that one can hardly discuss the performance of the nation's political leaders without considering the possibility that Americans, as the saying goes, are simply getting the quality of government they deserve.

Intimations of the people's influence have already cropped up at various points in the preceding chapters. The public has a lot to do with the way in which the media cover public affairs. Popular opinion is important enough to elicit costly grassroots lobbying efforts mounted by powerful interest groups in Washington. Americans, as it happens, even bear much of the responsibility for divided government, gridlock, and partisan conflict between Congress and the President, not to mention the negative campaigning people criticize so roundly at election time.

Much more important than these scattered examples is the role the public plays in helping to create the problems of government particularly emphasized in this volume. As earlier chapters pointed out, the unwillingness of poor and working Americans to organize and engage in the political process does much to account for the notable inadequacies of the government programs enacted to address their needs. At the same time, the ambivalence of so many people about where to place the blame for poverty and other social ills helps perpetuate the long-running dispute between liberal and conservative elites over how the government should respond.

Public sentiment also helps to explain the government's tendency to spend large sums on certain health and safety risks while devoting much less attention to minimizing other hazards in ways that could save lives at far less cost. More generally, the widespread popular belief in competition, the fear of concentrated power, and the insistence on elaborate safeguards against abuses of authority by the State have all contributed to the peculiarly abrasive, rule-ridden, litigious form of regulation characteristic of the United States. In fact, it is because these features of our regulatory system have such deep cultural roots that similar problems arise when rules are made and enforced not by Congress and the bureaucracy but by judges or even by wholly private entities.

The behavior of the public likewise contributes to poorly designed legislation. In particular, the widespread tendency to choose among electoral candidates on their individual merits rather than the record of their party makes it difficult to hold the government accountable and encourages lawmakers to cater to local needs rather than subordinate them to their party's national program. In an earlier time, the suspicions Americans have traditionally harbored toward the State helped bring about the highly fragmented institutional structure that complicates efforts to enact coherent legislation or to hold elected officials responsible for their policies. Through the years, similar attitudes have continued to affirm this basic system and preserve it from substantial change.

Not only is the public implicated in the most important weaknesses of America's government; its role promises to be critical to any serious effort to improve upon the current situation. As the preceding chapter has argued, reformers will never remedy the plight of poor and working-class people merely by thinking up new programs to address their needs. Real progress must await a willingness on the part of lower-income Americans to make their voices heard by participating more actively in the political process. Campaign finance reform may help prevent wasteful subsidies, avoid damaging concessions to special interests, and thereby increase the coherence of legislation, but effective campaign finance reform is highly unlikely without the insistence of large numbers of citizens. Strong public pressure seems equally necessary to gain new regulatory safeguards, just as it was vital in securing the environmental and consumer legislation of the late 1960s and early 1970s. Meanwhile, public participation is proving increasingly important to the success of new initiatives in collaborative regulation, as it has been in implementing other programs to improve schools, maintain housing projects, and reduce crime.

In the end, interest groups, institutional structure, and citizen influence may be so intertwined that one can never disentangle them and prove convincingly which has the greatest impact on our government. Surely, however, the public is among the most important forces, if not *the* most important. It is surprising, therefore, that commentators have devoted so little attention to the people as a potential source of improvement in the performance of our government. At least until recently, most political scientists have treated the citizenry as a given—a phenomenon to be studied, surveyed, and measured rather than a resource to be nurtured and developed. Perhaps they have considered the public too vast and too immutable to be a plausible object of reform. If so, their response is hardly justified. Scholars who have written about Americans as workers have lavished much attention on the effects of education and training in improving productivity and earnings. Since citizens are so central to a true democracy, why shouldn't reformers pay as much attention to nurturing civic capacities as labor economists, employers, and government officials give to the development of vocational skills?

In light of these questions, the concluding portion of this book will explore a series of issues about the part the public plays in civic affairs. Chapter 14 takes up the threshold question of how much influence people actually have over the policies of their government. Most Americans today are convinced that they have very little say in Washington and that politicians pay virtually no attention to their views. Clearly, this impression needs to be carefully evaluated. If it is correct, there is little point in delving further into the public's role.

A second subject that has long provoked spirited debate is how capable citizens are of exerting a constructive influence on the policy decisions of their government. Public servants, scholars, and political analysts have been divided on this question ever since the Founders met in 1789 to draft the American Constitution. Chapter 15 takes up that issue in detail.

Chapter 16 considers how actively engaged Americans are as citizens and how their civic behavior affects the performance of the government. These, too, are controversial questions. Scholars differ on how well Americans are fulfilling their civic responsibilities and disagree even more about whether current levels of civic engagement represent a significant problem for our democracy. A careful look at the evidence, however, will reveal several worrisome trends that have already had unfortunate effects on American politics and government and threaten to have even more serious consequences in the future.

The final chapter explores what can be done to encourage citizens to play a more active and effective part in public affairs. This is a large subject, covering topics ranging from teaching children American history to easing registration laws. In recent years, it has ceased to preoccupy educators, philosophers, and public leaders and has become a peripheral topic of interest only to civics teachers and a few foundations. If civic behavior is already damaging the effectiveness of our government, however, and if it promises to have even worse effects in the future, no review of possible reforms would be complete without considering the prospects for doing a better job of preparing citizens for the challenging task of making democracy work.

14

HOW MUCH INFLUENCE DO CITIZENS HAVE?

IN 1991, THE KETTERING FOUNDATION asked the Harwood consulting firm to conduct a study of why Americans were so cynical and disapproving of their government.[1] Through a series of focus groups, the consultants found that the participants were not at all apathetic or uninterested in public affairs. Instead, they felt shut out, marginalized, unable to have a say in how to put things right. As the president of the Kettering Foundation observed, "This sense of being pushed out of the political process cuts to the core of how Americans view politics."[2]

Opinion polls seem to confirm the Harwood findings. Most people are convinced that members of Congress pay little attention to ordinary citizens except at election time. Toward the end of 1997, 76 percent of Americans agreed (as have similar majorities for many years) that "generally speaking, elected officials in Washington lose touch with the people pretty quickly."[3] Only 29 percent believed that "most elected officials care what people like me think."[4]

These are serious charges; democratic government cannot work well if lawmakers do not care about the views of their constituents. But is the verdict correct? Most Americans plainly think so. But it is hard to square this view with the strong approval they express about the job their own representative is doing. If clear majorities feel that their member of Congress is performing well, can the Congress as a whole be unresponsive to the wishes of the people?

How Responsive Is the Government?

Fortunately, a number of researchers have tried in various ways to answer this question. A few scholars have attempted to gauge the responsiveness of the federal government as a whole by measuring how frequently policies change in accordance with public opinion. The most widely cited of these studies was conducted by Alan Monroe, who sought to discover how often the government acted in accordance with policies that a majority of the public favored. According to Monroe, between 1960 and 1979 the government took positive steps in 63 percent of the cases in which the public favored action, responding much more frequently (72 percent) to problems that the public rated as the most important and somewhat more frequently (67 percent) to problems ranked among the top five.[5] More recently, during the period 1980–1993, Monroe found that the government became somewhat less sensitive to public opinion, responding appropriately in only 55 percent of his sample of cases.[6]

A slightly different study was conducted by Benjamin Page and Robert Shapiro.[7] These authors sought to discover how often the federal government responded in accordance with *changes* in public opinion. Their findings showed that the government acted appropriately in approximately two-thirds of the cases. On occasions in which popular sentiment moved more decisively, appropriate action was even more likely. When opinion shifted by as much as 10 percent, the government acted accordingly in 87 percent of the cases. When changes of 20 percent or more occurred, the response rate rose to 90 percent.

Do such studies prove that American lawmakers are *sufficiently* responsive to the public will? If legislators were supposed to follow the wishes of the people on every vote, the answer would clearly be no. But few people have ever wanted Congress to be *that* responsive. As James Madison remarked in Federalist Paper 63, "There are particular moments in public affairs when the people, stimulated by some irregular passion, or some illicit advantage, or misled by the artful misrepresentations of interested men, may call for measures which they themselves will afterwards be the most ready to lament and condemn."[8] Hence, according to Alexander Hamilton in Federalist Paper 71, "The republican principle . . . does not require an unqualified complaisance to every sudden breeze of passion or to every transient impulse."[9]

When might one wish legislators *not* to vote according to the wishes of their constituents? Presumably, no one should expect lawmakers to take account of popular sentiment if most voters have not even thought about the subject. When the issue at hand involves accelerated depreciation of machinery for tax purposes, or new methods of regulating interstate banking, or some other technical question remote from the interests of ordinary people, there is rarely a considered popular opinion for members of Congress to follow.

In other instances, the public will have views about an issue but be misinformed about the facts. For example, most citizens are in favor of cutting foreign aid, but large majorities believe incorrectly that the government spends more on humanitarian foreign assistance than it does on health care. One can readily understand why legislators would not feel obliged to follow public opinion in such a case (although a conscientious lawmaker might try to inform constituents of the facts).

Citizens have stronger grounds for asking legislators to be responsive when the issues have to do with matters that touch the lives and vital concerns of ordinary people. Even here, however, there may be exceptions. For example, should lawmakers respond to Americans' deep concern over drugs by appropriating billions of additional dollars to try to keep cocaine and heroin from entering the United States if they are convinced that such a policy is futile? However urgent the problem, voting for remedies that legislators do not believe will bring results may simply increase the public's distrust while lowering its confidence in government even further.

Most people will at least expect their representatives to respect values that matter a lot to large majorities of constituents. Residents of Montana will feel strongly that their representative should vote against gun control measures that interfere with their hunting, just as Cuban-Americans in Florida will believe that their congressman should never vote to give legitimacy to Fidel Castro. Yet even the case for respecting widely shared values is not compelling in every instance. Should a conscientious lawmaker respect the strong feelings of her constituents if they conflict with her own firmly held moral principles? Looking back on Southern legislators who refused to honor the segregationist beliefs of their constituents, most Americans would applaud them for their courage rather than condemn them for disregarding voter opinion.

The most widely discussed dilemma for elected representatives occurs when they honestly disagree on policy grounds with the considered view of their constituents. Most Americans believe that conscientious lawmakers should defer in such circumstances to the wishes of the majority.[10] But some thoughtful critics, echoing Edmund Burke, believe just as firmly that voters have no right to expect anything but the honest judgment of their representative.[11] This difference of opinion is no closer to resolution now than it was when Burke first pronounced on the subject. The only point that commands general agreement is that lawmakers who take an independent stand should genuinely differ with their constituents on the merits, and not ignore them merely to please campaign contributors or other special interests.

The point of these examples is that "responsiveness" is a much more elusive concept than many citizens seem to believe. Because of the complexities, no one can be sure how often a legislature *ought* to follow the views of the citizenry. The appropriate figure is certainly less than 100 percent, but it is impossible to say how much less. As a result, one cannot look at the legislative voting record, match it against trends in public opinion, and decide whether Congress has been suitably responsive.

Other findings suggest that legislators do pay a lot of attention to what their constituents think. For example, a number of researchers have looked at how members of Congress go about making up their minds on policy questions. Despite the suspicions of many Americans, these investigators regularly find that lawmakers regard constituent opinion as an important consideration in reaching their decisions.[12] As one would expect, moreover, the studies uniformly show that the more an issue matters to constituents, the more influence their views tend to have on the legislator's final decision.[13]

In a particularly interesting inquiry, investigators sought to determine the extent to which differences in the social and economic policies of the various states could be explained by differences in public opinion. The study concluded that the relationship between the values of the people and the policies of their state legislatures was very strong.[14] In fact, differences in the liberal-conservative orientation of the public turned out to have a much greater impact on policy than differences in education, income, and other socioeconomic variables. As the authors point out:

> Ultimately our message about representation in the states is a simple one. At the ballot box, electorates hold a strong control over the ideological direction of policies in their states. In anticipation of this electoral monitoring, state legislators and other policy makers take public opinion into account when enacting state policy. These means of control are uncertain in any particular application but accumulate to create a striking correlation between the mean ideological preference of state electorates and the mean ideological tendency of state policy.[15]

A comparison study makes much the same point: "When the public asks for a more activist or more conservative government, politicians oblige. . . . [They] constantly and immediately process public opinion changes in order to stay ahead of the political wave."[16]

Some skeptics may dismiss these findings on the ground that politicians can manipulate public opinion by distorting the facts so that citizens accept whatever their leaders do. But this is far too harsh a verdict. Officials may sometimes succeed for a time in hiding or distorting information on matters of foreign policy (such as the Gulf of Tonkin attack or the Iran-Contra cover-up) where immediate, accurate reports are hard to come by. When important domestic issues are involved, however, the government can rarely control all the sources of information. Instead, investigative reporters, opposing politicians, and a variety of independent groups can usually ferret out the facts and interpret them as they choose, making it all but impossible for public officials to manipulate popular opinion for their own purposes.

There are strong a priori reasons for suspecting not only that members of Congress are genuinely responsive but that they are *more* responsive to the views of their constituents than their counterparts in other legislatures around the world. Members of the House of Representatives must compete for the vote of their constituents more frequently than lawmakers in other democracies. In order to win, candidates for Congress and for most other elective offices in the United States must gain voter approval not merely in a general election but in a primary as well. Since Americans tend to support individual candidates more than political parties, legislators need to pay close heed to opinion back home when casting a vote. Observing these pressures, a longtime British student of American politics has concluded: "The simplest, most central consequence of American politicians' electoral vulnerability—obvious, but requiring to be stated explicitly—is that most officeholders in the United States are extraordinarily sensitive to the opinions and demands of the men and women upon whom their political future depend; the voters in their state or district or in the nation at large."[17]

Politicians themselves show increasing signs of *thinking* that the views of the people matter. Members of Congress are allocating more of their personal staff to service in their district and spending more time themselves with voters.[18] Legislative leaders pay increasing attention to polls and focus groups. The President worries constantly about his popularity rating, apparently because his standing with the voters has an effect on his influence with Congress. As one well-known political consultant and presidential adviser has put it: "Today, a politician does not just need public support to win elections; he needs it to govern. . . . When a president's popularity dips below 50 percent, he is functionally out of office.[19]

Equally revealing is the behavior of major corporate lobbies and other interest groups in trying to influence the legislature. Many of these organizations are spending more and more money on grassroots campaigns to mobilize local support for positions on bills before Congress. During the great healthcare debate of 1993–1994, for example, special interests spent an estimated $100 million or more to influence public opinion through TV ads, mailings, and telethons.[20] It is hard to believe that experienced lobbyists would invest such large sums for this purpose if they did not believe that lawmakers were highly responsive to public opinion and the views of their constituents.

There is also much evidence to show that citizens have been gaining rather than losing influence in recent decades. Since 1960, primary elections have almost completely supplanted party conventions and backroom deals as the official method of selecting candidates for office. Ballot initiatives and referenda have come into greater use in a larger number of states. Federal programs have increasingly provided for citizen participation, and judges have granted the right to sue and intervene to more and more groups of interested representatives of the public. Even recent changes in public administration—total quality management, vouchers, community policing, and other participatory methods—are primarily ways of making public officials more responsive to the wishes of the citizens they serve.

Several highly experienced journalists have remarked on how exceptionally sensitive American politicians have become to grassroots sentiment. According to David Broder, one of America's most respected political commentators, "public opinion, as reported and magnified by the press, has grown so powerful in the United States that it has become the near preoccupation of government."[21] George Will makes much the same point, asserting that "government today involves minute measurement of public appetites by servile politicians worshipful of those measurements."[22]

It is only fair to add that not all reporters agree with this conclusion. For example, William Greider complains that Congress pays little attention to the many millions of ordinary people who work in factories, clean office buildings, and hold other kinds of menial jobs that offer very modest wages and little or no influence or power.[23] He marshals an impressive list of examples to buttress his position. But it is important to ask why such legislative indifference exists. The most obvious reason is that relatively few of these lower-income Americans vote in the United States, and even fewer pay much attention to the legislative record of their representative or to the issues raised in congressional campaigns. It would be unfair to blame lawmakers for this result or to condemn them as unresponsive. Democratic theory does not claim that elected representatives will reflect the opinions of all the people. It merely holds that they will respond to the views of those who take the trouble to go to the polls and elect them to office.

Another prominent journalist, E. J. Dionne, finds Congress unresponsive in quite a different way.[24] As he sees it, lawmakers have come increasingly to favor extreme positions on the right or on the left. As a result, they are constantly embroiled in debates in which neither side reflects the views of the mainstream of America.

Dionne is surely correct in pointing to the increased polarization of Congress. Over the past half-century, the political arena in the United States has become much more ideological: environmentalists, feminists, ethnic minorities and other groups have been pressing insistently on the left, while libertarians, business organizations, fundamentalist Christians, and neoconservatives are increasingly organized and vocal on the right. These movements have often led to ideological divisions in Congress that seem unusually sharp and out of step with the views of most Americans.

Once again, however, the reasons for this polarization contradict any simple claim that legislators are unresponsive to their constituents. With fewer and fewer people bothering to go to the polls in primary elections (the average turnout among eligible voters is now less than 20 percent), candidates are often chosen by a minority of voters who are more extreme in their views than their nonvoting party members, let alone the citizenry as a whole.[25] The same is true in selecting the convention delegates who draft the Republican and Democratic platforms.[26] It is hardly surprising, then, that both parties sometimes advocate policies that are further to the left or to the right than most people would prefer. If only a small percentage of eligible voters choose to go to the polls, Americans can hardly complain if their representatives pay special heed to the views of the minority who put them in office.

It is false, therefore, to claim that politicians do not care what people think. Legislators undoubtedly vote against public opinion periodically for a variety of reasons: personal conviction, interest group pressure, or fear of antagonizing a highly organized, deeply concerned minority, such as those who fight against gun control. But lawmakers are often influenced by popular opinion and rarely vote against a sentiment that is clearly and strongly felt by voters in their districts. When public opinion loses out, it is usually mistaken, faint, ambiguous, or felt most strongly by people who do not bother to go to the polls. Interest groups may dilute legislative action or delay it entirely for a time. But if citizens care enough about a policy question to inform themselves and make their wishes known, they will usually have their way in the end.

Why Do Americans Feel So Powerless?

If there is so much evidence to demonstrate the influence of popular opinion, why are so many Americans convinced that they are powerless and that their needs and their views do not count in Washington? While no one can answer this question with certainty, there are several reasons voters might mistakenly conclude that their representatives are not listening. Some of those who feel strongly about certain issues may assume that most people agree with them, forgetting that in a large and diverse society there will be many citizens who harbor contrary views. Others may overestimate the capacity of the government to solve important problems. Convinced that there are simple solutions to difficult issues, they quickly conclude that politicians must be perverse for not adopting them. Still others may confuse a popular consensus on ends with an agreement on means. More than 80 percent of Americans believe in universal healthcare insurance, but disagree sharply over the methods to bring about this result. In these circumstances, citizens may wrongly jump to the conclusion that Congress must be ignoring public opinion if it cannot agree on legislation to extend coverage to everyone.

Current practices of campaign finance also add to the public's sense that citizens have lost control over their government. Newspapers regularly report the large sums that important interest groups contribute to members of Congress and other candidates for election. Observing this behavior, one could easily get the impression that only those who pay can have an influence on politicians. As Democratic fundraiser Johnny Chung reportedly said, "I see the White House is like a subway—you have to put in coins to open the gates."[27] If an experienced party fundraiser has this impression, no one should be surprised if most citizens agree, even though careful studies have concluded that the impact of special interests on policy, especially important national policy, is far from clear.

At the same time, even as they read about lobbyists and their donations, Americans must also be aware of the interest politicians take in opinion surveys and focus groups. If there is any part of the political process that attracts more attention than lobbyists and their campaign gifts, it is the growing role of political consultants, with their battery of polls and other elaborate indicators of public sentiment. Is this not convincing evidence of the importance attached to popular opinion in the councils of state?

Apparently not; Americans seem distinctly unimpressed by the increased attention paid to polls and focus groups. To most citizens, politicians only *appear* to be interested in what the public thinks. In reality, when they commission surveys, they are simply trying to figure out how they can package their proposals in a way that will be most appealing. Far from being responsive, they merely want to manipulate people for their own purposes. Or so many Americans seem to think.

Although the public's suspicions are understandable, they are almost certainly exaggerated. When politicians use polls and focus groups to shape their agenda and refine their message, they are doing more than trying to manipulate the electorate for their own ends. Survey data give them a framework of values, priorities, and prevailing opinions which they normally try to respect in order not to lose public support. At the same time, because popular opinion almost always contains ambiguity, doubt, inconsistency, and division, there will usually be a variety of positions open to politicians which do not clash with voter sentiment as they perceive it. Within this range, they choose according to their own values and beliefs, using such support as they can find within their survey data to justify their positions to the people. At times, their explanations help to clarify and even modify people's opinions on the issue. At times, public reactions cause their own views to change. Thus, an interplay occurs between elected representatives and their constituents in which each responds to the other in a search for a mutually acceptable solution.

Whatever else they may be doing, politicians engaged in this process are surely paying attention to what their constituency thinks and reacting to what they learn. Granted, people have many facets to their personality, and politicians do not necessarily appeal to the best and most enlightened side of their nature. In a highly competitive system that attracts candidates of great ambition, officeholders crafting their message will normally choose the approach best calculated to move their audience rather than the position that is most high-minded and highly principled. Reflecting on this process, voters may disapprove of these appeals to their baser instincts. They may come away from the experience disillusioned with politics and politicians, just as many people come away from their television sets disillusioned with the media.* But it is hardly justifiable to react by simply blaming politicians and accusing them of being unresponsive. If citizens do not like the way their elected representatives are responding, they should try to work harder and inform themselves about the issues so that those they put in office cannot persuade the public to their point of view by exploiting popular ignorance and prejudice.

In sum, whether or not Americans approve, there is little reason to believe that politicians have lost touch with the constituents who elected them or have ceased to care what voters think. On the contrary, the evidence summarized in this chapter reveals the strong and constant influence that public opinion has come to exert on politicians in Washington. As one well-known political consultant recently declared: "Once upon a time, elections settled things for the term of office. Now, they are mere punctuation marks in an ongoing search for public support and a functioning majority. Each day is election day in America."[28]

---

* Both politicians and the media are driven by the forces of competition to pay close attention to the public and to shape their message to attract the widest possible following. To this end, both make ample use of polling and focus groups. And yet, although the messages that result may accurately gauge the feelings and desires of the audience to which they are directed, they are not the messages people feel that they should be receiving. Americans may react as expected when they mark their ballots and choose their TV programs. But they emerge from the experience with precious little confidence or trust in the politicians and media moguls who appeal to them in this fashion.

15

HOW CAPABLE ARE AMERICANS OF SELF-GOVERNMENT?

IF AMERICANS TAKE A DIM VIEW of federal officials, most officials are inclined to return the compliment. According to a survey in 1998, 77 percent of presidential appointees and 81 percent of senior civil servants do not believe that "Americans know enough about issues to form wise opinions about what should be done."[1] By a margin of 47 to 31, members of Congress agree.[2]

Such doubts are not new. From the debates of the founding fathers to the present day, murmurings of concern have been heard in high places that ordinary people may be incapable of making democracy work. "The evils we experience flow from an excess of democracy," declared Elbridge Gerry, adding that in his own state, Massachusetts, voters had a dangerous habit of electing "the worst men" to the legislature—"men of indigence, ignorance, and baseness."[3]

In the years that followed, public schooling helped increase the people's knowledge of public affairs and enlarge their understanding of American institutions. Yet doubts about their capacities persisted. Walter Lippmann wrestled with the problem of how to inform the public adequately on the great issues facing the country, and ultimately concluded that the job simply couldn't be done.[4] Instead, he came to believe that the average citizen "lives in a world which he cannot see, does not understand and is unable to direct."[5] The economist Joseph Schumpeter, author of *Capitalism, Socialism, and Democracy,* was even more blunt: "The typical citizen drops down to a lower level of mental performance as soon as he enters the political field. He argues in a way which he would readily recognize as infantile within the sphere of his real interests."[6]

Since Schumpeter and Lippmann rendered their gloomy verdicts, the work of citizenship has grown more arduous and difficult. Public issues have increased in number as the government has taken on added tasks of great complexity—organizing health care, providing world leadership, protecting the environment, repairing urban blight. New knowledge has made old problems more complicated. Vast quantities of information and opinion tumble forth from television networks, cable, the Internet. Citizens could spend all of their waking hours trying to keep abreast of this material. Yet the competition for their time is increasingly intense as demands at work grow more exacting, the lure of the shops more enticing, the opportunities for continuous entertainment more numerous and seductive.

Under these conditions, how qualified *are* the people to make sound judgments on candidates and policy? One reason learned observers have long disagreed so profoundly on this issue is that the question is too multifaceted to permit a clear answer. One must break it down into more manageable pieces. Can citizens convey a set of *basic values* and general principles for a legislature to bear in mind in reaching its decisions? Do they have reasonable *expectations* about what government can and should deliver? Can they convey a useful set of *priorities* for elected officials to follow in setting the policy agenda? Do they learn enough from the media and their own informal discussions to arrive at *informed opinions* on how to resolve the more important issues on Washington's agenda? Only after considering these questions separately can one hazard a response to Lippmann, Schumpeter, and all who join them in doubting the capacity of Americans for effective self-government.

Basic Values

Over the years, Americans have communicated something of inestimable worth to their elected representatives. In pondering legislation, members of Congress can be sure that most citizens agree on certain fundamental ideas about their government. These beliefs form a common creed that offers lawmakers a firm foundation for their deliberations, while contributing much to the unity and stability of the Republic. The most essential of these beliefs is an all but unshakable faith in the Constitution and the system of government that it provides. In 1996, after decades of casting aside old verities and traditions, 83 percent of Americans continued to believe that "whatever its faults, the United States still has the best system of government in the world."[7] The strong support for the Constitution and for the values it embodies (the rule of law, government by the people, individual liberty, equality under the law, due process) gives Congress a set of basic precepts about what is fair and proper for the government to do—precepts that lawmakers must heed, or risk the loss of public approval.

During the past half-century, Americans have also agreed on several basic goals for the society. By very large majorities, they affirm the importance of prosperity and full employment; equality of opportunity; reasonable security against illness, violent attack, unsafe products, and other familiar hazards of life; and a commitment to certain intangible values, such as maximizing individual freedom, observing basic standards of personal responsibility, and helping people in need who cannot help themselves.[8] Sharing common objectives, like sharing basic values, has great advantages for a society. Although it does not guarantee agreement on specific questions of policy, it does provide an accepted framework within which competing proposals can be compared and evaluated.

Expectations

Ideally, if the public is to give useful guidance and render sound collective judgments at the polls, it should have a reasonable set of expectations for what its government can accomplish. Citizens should not ask their political leaders to do more than human beings are capable of achieving or expect them to behave in ways that are contrary to human nature. Otherwise, the public is bound to be frustrated and disappointed, and eventually lose confidence in politics and public affairs.

Since most people have such a low opinion of politicians and bureaucrats, one might suppose that they would have modest hopes for what the government can accomplish. Not necessarily. Amid the hoopla surrounding presidential campaigns and the constant glare of publicity on the Oval Office, the public often seems to have an exaggerated view of what a president can achieve.[9] Because Americans take such pride in their country and have such confidence in its *system* of government, they may likewise come to believe that Congress should be able to do more than is humanly possible to resolve the nation's problems. Thus, in 1997, when Americans were asked whether the government's seeming inability to solve the nation's problems was due primarily to the difficulty of the issues or to the incompetence of public officials, only 17 percent thought the issues were too difficult.[10] In 1993, 71 percent of respondents affirmed that "as Americans, we can always find a way to solve our problems and get what we want."[11]

While remarkably optimistic in general, Americans are more cautious in their expectations of what the government can do about specific issues. Asked in 1998 about a list of major problems, two-thirds or more of the public rated the government's performance as only fair or poor. Yet when pollsters inquired whether this record was the fault of the government or a result of the complexity of the issues, large numbers of those who expressed dissatisfaction pointed to the difficulty of the problem as the chief contributing cause.[12] On some issues, such as reducing juvenile delinquency and overcoming poverty, very large majorities stressed the difficulty of the task rather than the ineptitude of the government. Even in the case of such seemingly manageable tasks as providing for the elderly and setting academic standards for children, almost as many dissatisfied respondents blamed the complexity of the problem as put the blame on the government.[13] In short, although Americans may overestimate the government's capacity to deal with certain questions, such as drugs, they do not appear to have unrealistic expectations about its ability to address many of the other items on its agenda.

Contrary to the view of some political scientists, Americans also show little sign of having such relentlessly rising expectations that they demand more than any government can deliver. It is true that in the past hundred years, Americans have come to recognize a growing list of problems, such as racial discrimination, pollution, and the needs of the handicapped, that they would like the government to address. But expectations do not seem to have risen markedly in the past twenty years, nor do the public's demands seem unreasonable by the prevailing standards of advanced democratic nations. If anything, citizens in other advanced nations want their government to do more than most people in the United States are inclined to favor.[14] Since many of these countries have made greater progress than the United States in pursuing a number of common goals, the problems with our government's performance cannot easily be ascribed to excessive expectations.

Americans seem much more unrealistic in their sense of *how* legislators and other elected officials ought to go about their work. In a large and diverse country such as the United States, filled with competing interests and ideologies, people are bound to differ sharply about many policy issues, and Congress will normally reflect these differences of opinion. Nevertheless, what citizens seem to want and expect from their elected representatives is a legislative process that is harmonious, constructive, and largely free of partisan disagreement and bickering. As John Hibbing and Elizabeth Theiss-Morse discovered after a series of focus-group discussions, "People do not wish to see uncertainty, conflicting options, long debate, competing interests, confusion, bargaining, and compromised imperfect solutions. They want government to do its job quietly and efficiently, sans conflict and sans fuss. In short, we submit, they often seek a patently unrealistic form of democracy."[15]

Underlying this desire for harmony is a highly optimistic sense of how much agreement exists in the United States on major issues of public policy. Because Americans are so united on the general purposes of the society, they seem to assume that a similar consensus exists on the proper means to achieve these goals. Persuaded that ordinary people agree on such questions, they cannot understand why lawmakers are unable to produce legislation without constant bickering and dissension.

The public also has distorted expectations about the kinds of people who run for political office. Their model of a public official is Jimmy Stewart in *Mr. Smith Goes to Washington,* a man without personal ambition who travels reluctantly to Congress out of a sense of duty, does the right and sensible thing, and eventually returns home to the cheers of grateful friends and neighbors. Unfortunately, nothing in our political system suggests that candidates like Mr. Smith will appear in substantial numbers. In choosing people to fill high government office, Americans have traditionally favored a system of elections that forces candidates to raise large amounts of money and participate in long, drawn-out campaigns. Those who step forward must be prepared to sacrifice a lot in exchange for a chance to help govern the most powerful nation on earth. These conditions virtually guarantee that most candidates will be unusually ambitious for office and, once elected, exceptionally anxious to stay in power, preferably with the least possible opposition. As a result, Americans are bound to be disappointed with politicians because the system they have embraced is calculated to produce the very opposite of the reluctant amateur immortalized by Jimmy Stewart.[16]

Americans are equally unrealistic in their sense of how politicians should behave before and after winning office. They would like their candidates to avoid speaking in generalities and to refrain from endlessly attacking their opponents. They believe that elected officials should stay away from lobbyists and well-to-do donors and courageously do battle with well-heeled selfish interests. They want their representatives in the legislature to stand up resolutely for their principles, while simultaneously paying close heed to the wishes of their constituents.

Under current conditions of American politics, it is almost impossible for politicians to live up to these expectations. Even if they want to explain their policies in detail, the dictates of television prevent them from speaking at any length on substantive issues. Moreover, in today's political environment, candidates are often reluctant to be too specific about their own views, realizing that in discussing controversial issues with a cynical, suspicious audience, it is far easier to offend some of the voters with detailed, concrete proposals than it is to impress the others with bold, imaginative ideas. Forced to raise large sums to finance their campaigns, politicians are bound to spend much of their time courting large donors and trying to avoid making enemies of powerful interests whose support they may need in future elections. Once in office, expected simultaneously to show the courage of their convictions and to obey the wishes of their constituents, they cannot fail to be criticized at times for either pandering to public opinion or being indifferent to the views of the people who elected them.*

If the public's unrealistic and often contradictory demands merely left politicians unappreciated and misunderstood, one could shrug the matter off as the inevitable price of a career in public life. But frustrated expectations have more serious consequences. They are an important cause of the cynicism and distrust of politics and politicians that have soured many Americans on government. Left to fester, such feelings could discourage talented young people from seeking careers in government and infect the larger public with a deeper alienation from public life.

Priorities

In addition to conveying a set of values and expectations to guide their elected representatives, citizens also help to set the agenda by indicating the problems which they want their government to resolve. Pollsters regularly report on the public's priorities. Apparently, these preferences matter. Investigators have consistently shown that federal lawmakers respond more readily to issues about which the electorate feels particularly strongly.[17]

How sound are the public's priorities? Such a question is impossible to answer, since the relative importance of different issues is a matter of opinion rather than logic. Still, there are a few generalizations one can safely make that throw some light on the issue.

---

* Americans are also inconsistent in their demands for how Executive Branch officials should go about their work. The public wants an effective, efficient bureaucracy, but it also wants a bureaucracy that is meticulous in respecting individual rights while providing abundant opportunities for people to challenge and appeal official actions. Moreover, as James Q. Wilson has observed, "Americans want a lean, efficient government, but they also want a carefully restricted government, one that will not only educate children or build highways, but will do so in ways that appear to broaden civil rights, improve the environment, subsidize minority-owned businesses, buy American-made products, hire employees on the basis of objective criteria, and empower legislators to address our grievances." Thus, "we often get a fat government even when we say we want a lean one." James Q. Wilson, "Can the Bureaucracy Be Deregulated? Lessons from Government Agencies," in John DiIulio (ed.), *Deregulating the Public Service* (1994), pp. 37, 59.

Anthony Downs once observed that "American public attention rarely remains sharply focused upon any one domestic issue for very long—even if it involves a continuing problem of crucial importance to society."[18] Health care offers an apt example. The United States has long stood out among leading democracies for failing to provide health insurance for all of its citizens. Through most of the 1990s, more than 40 million Americans lacked such coverage even though large majorities of the public had long supported universal access to quality care. The priority attached to this issue, however, moved up and down dramatically during this period.[19] In June 1993, 29 percent of Americans considered health care one of the two most important problems for the government to address. By August 1994, toward the end of the national debate over the Clinton healthcare plan, the proportion rose to 55 percent. By September 1995, however, the percentage had slipped to 25 although the problems of our healthcare system remained essentially unchanged. By June 1997, only 9 percent of the public placed universal access among the two most important issues.

Such fluctuations have an effect on the development of policy. For the public to educate itself and arrive at a reasoned, informed judgment on complicated issues such as health care or crime, several years of discussion may be needed. If people's priorities shift rapidly, politicians may be tempted to delay in the hope that the public's attention will turn to other things. Even the media may not be willing to sustain the public debate long enough to allow an enlightened consensus to form.

Occasionally, ignorance and misinformation can also distort the public's priorities. For example, the sudden urgency about crime that Americans conveyed to Congress in the mid-1990s seems to have resulted in part from the mistaken impression that crime rates were rising, perhaps because of the growing emphasis on violence in the media. Momentary waves of unwarranted anxiety over toxic wastes at Love Canal and other supposed threats to human health have likewise put strong pressure on legislators to act in ways that seem exaggerated and unnecessary to many knowledgeable experts.[20]

Certain other common human tendencies can also influence the public's priorities. A familiar example is the inclination to value short-term concerns more than long-term interests to a degree that cannot be justified on rational grounds. Almost everyone shares this tendency, at least to some degree, but it is exacerbated in times of widespread suspicion toward government. As trust declines, many citizens cease to believe that long-term benefits will ever materialize, and their willingness to make immediate sacrifices declines accordingly. Thus, throughout the 1990s, policymakers found it difficult to gain support for raising payroll taxes or postponing the retirement age in order to ensure the long-term solvency of the Social Security system, even though prompt action would have made the remedy easier to bear.

Another trait that most people share is that they care more about the prospect of losing a benefit they already have than about the possibility of receiving an equivalent advantage they do not currently possess. This sentiment also grows more pronounced when distrust is acute, since people become more inclined to discount promises of benefits. Left unchecked, such tendencies lead to a set of priorities that powerfully favor the status quo at the expense of policy changes that could be beneficial for the country.

The fluctuations and distortions just described ought not to obscure the contribution that public opinion makes to democratic government by communicating the people's priorities to their elected representatives. No group of experts or experienced statesmen is equal to the task of deciding which of the innumerable possibilities for legislative action most need attention. Specialists and other knowledgeable persons can supplement popular opinion and correct some of its errors and exaggerations. But fixing priorities in a democracy involves making value judgments about what matters most to people, and this is a task that plainly requires hearing the views of the people themselves. Despite occasional distortions, Americans seem to perform this function adequately most of the time.

Opinions about Policy

The discussion thus far has described what the public can offer to help the government choose its priorities and guiding principles; it has not said much about the quality of the judgments citizens make when legislators look to popular opinion to help them decide how to vote on specific issues. In this regard, the usefulness of the public's views depends a lot on the kind of policy question that lawmakers are addressing.

Value Judgments

The public is most likely to offer helpful guidance to lawmakers in resolving long-standing issues that turn primarily on considerations of value. To be sure, Americans are sometimes ambivalent; their conflicted feelings about individual responsibility and the obligations of society have helped perpetuate the bitter, inconclusive debate between liberals and conservatives on a long series of social-welfare issues. But the public has succeeded in arriving at a reasonably clear consensus on a number of controversial value-laden questions, such as those involving abortion, legalization of marijuana, school busing, capital punishment, and the need for welfare mothers to work. In today's world, where so many special interests and advocacy groups hold rigid positions and make exaggerated claims, the people frequently have a more balanced judgment on controversial issues of this kind than the lobbyists and public-interest groups that flock to congressional offices to press their case.

Americans also have more stable views about such questions than they have about national priorities. One exhaustive study showed that public opinion on more than half of a long list of policy issues varied no more than 5 percent over a period of several decades.[21] Most of the big changes, such as attitudes toward desegregation of housing and schools, civil liberties, and the appropriateness of women working, took place gradually over many years. When sudden movements did occur, most of them were in response to crises or important new developments that made the changes quite sensible.

Shifts in public opinion on underlying questions of value have often had important effects on national policy. Mounting support for extending the concept of Social Security to cover medical costs for the elderly helped persuade President Johnson and Congress to enact Medicare.[22] The growing sense that racial discrimination in the workplace was wrong led to the enactment of Title VII of the Civil Rights Act.[23] A massive shift in opinion in favor of having single mothers find jobs played a critical role in producing congressional support for work requirements under federal welfare programs.[24]

Complex Policy Issues

What about more complicated questions, such as healthcare reform or improving education, where policymakers must consider many policy alternatives and take account of masses of relevant information? Here, it is useful to begin by asking how knowledgeable Americans are about the kinds of facts that bear on significant policy issues of this kind. On this score, the evidence is not encouraging. Repeated surveys have shown that most Americans do not know such basic facts as the approximate level of unemployment, or the number of Americans lacking health insurance, or the current poverty rate.

Will Rogers is said to have remarked that the big problem was not just that people didn't know enough but that so many people knew so many things that weren't so. This is certainly true in matters of government policy, even in the case of subjects of great relevance to the public. In 1996, almost half of Americans believed, contrary to fact, that the number of jobs in the economy had fallen over the preceding five years, and 70 percent answered incorrectly that the number had not increased.[25] Eighty percent mistakenly felt that inflation had not dropped in the preceding five years.[26] More than 60 percent responded incorrectly that unemployment had either risen or stayed the same.[27]

The public is equally misinformed about what national policies have accomplished. In 1995, for example, 69 percent of Americans expressed the view that the annual federal budget deficit had grown worse in the preceding three years, although it had actually decreased by almost half.[28] Substantial majorities agreed that in the past twenty years the quality of the air we breathe had deteriorated and that the proportion of elderly people living in poverty had increased, whereas in both cases the opposite happened to be true.[29] Approximately 60 percent of Americans in 1998 did not believe that the Clinton Administration had reduced the total number of federal government employees or that the government was functioning more efficiently than it was a few years earlier, even though there was good evidence to support both assertions.[30]

The mistaken impressions just listed, however, did not arise in the course of a national debate over specific policy issues facing the government. Americans could conceivably be uninformed or even misinformed about many matters but still be capable of enlightened judgments on important policy questions after learning from a lively public discussion of the subject. In principle, such a debate will create a "marketplace of ideas" from which the public will gradually gain a grasp of the relevant facts and eventually arrive at an informed consensus. But how do such debates work in practice and how much help do they give the public in arriving at considered judgments? These are questions of vital importance to the functioning of democracy—especially today, when politicians seem more inclined than ever to consult opinion polls in making legislative decisions.

A national debate should have several characteristics. It ought to provide abundant opportunities for all points of view to be heard. No interested group should be too weak to present its ideas effectively or so powerful as to dominate the discussion through superior organization and resources. In addition, for the marketplace of ideas to operate effectively, the competing arguments need to undergo a process of analysis and critique that will winnow out misinformation, faulty reasoning, and irrelevant arguments. Throughout, the issues must be explained in terms that the public can understand, with the help of enough reliable information to enable citizens to follow the debate and arrive at reasoned conclusions.

In the United States, national debates plainly do not lack for ideas and competing points of view. On subjects of importance to voters, interest groups and advocacy organizations abound, ensuring that a wide variety of opinions will come to the attention of Congress and the public. With many leading universities, large cohorts of trained professionals, and an ample supply of newspapers, magazines, and learned journals, America boasts a greater number of experts, a wider range of critiques and reports, and a more impressive volume of research and analysis on issues of policy than any other country in the world.

Greater difficulties arise when the public has to respond to this flood of ideas and arguments to try to arrive at some sort of consensus on whether and how the government should act. An initial problem with the debate is that money gives some participants an advantage over others for reasons having nothing to do with the merits of their case. On certain issues, powerful corporate interests can produce more studies, present them more persuasively, and disseminate them more widely than the advocacy groups that oppose them. This imbalance has become more obvious in recent years, as important legislative proposals are increasingly fought out through something akin to political campaigns, replete with mass mailings, television ads, and other elaborate publicity techniques.

Another problem with public debates is that the number of participants is often so great, the issues so complex, and the channels of communication so numerous that ordinary people cannot possibly keep abreast of the discussion. This is especially likely in a government as fragmented as that of the United States. During the healthcare debates of 1993–1994, for example, members of Congress introduced twenty-seven different proposals which the media then referred to by 110 different names. Each plan came with its own rationale backed by elaborate reasons and supporting data. Only specialists could have had the time and knowledge to make their way through this welter of competing proposals. Even the most attentive citizens were likely to remain in a state of considerable confusion.

Ideally, the media should sift through mounds of claims and counter-claims and present the relevant arguments in a form readily understood by the average voter. But newspapers and television reporters do not always perform this function as well as one might like. Helping readers understand complex debates and recognize key issues requires journalists to supply much repetition of important facts and arguments and much analysis of background information. These are tasks that many reporters neither enjoy nor do especially well. Their forte lies in covering new stories and late-breaking developments. Many years ago, Walter Lippmann pointed out that the press "is like the beam of a searchlight that moves restlessly about, bringing one episode and then another out of darkness into vision."[31] As Lippmann added, however, "men cannot do the work of the world by this light alone. They cannot govern society by episodes, incidents, and interruptions."[32]

Some editors are wary of efforts to go beyond the reporting of events and explain the complexities of policy proposals. Such stories are much harder to write than accounts of the political infighting and tactical maneuvering of well-known figures in Washington. Making sense of complicated policy discussions often requires levels of technical understanding that few reporters possess. Unless the experts agree, journalists will find it hard to do more than appear impartial by quoting specialists on both sides of the issue. Such exchanges are often tedious and unenlightening. Many people quickly tire of them and will not make the effort required to follow the arguments closely. Even careful readers will often come away from statements by opposing experts no wiser than when they began.

Once again, the healthcare bill provides a particularly apt illustration. During the early stages of the debate, newspapers did make valiant efforts to inform the public, sometimes devoting several pages to a detailed explanation of the Clinton plan. Before long, however, reporters began to turn from the substance of the debate to the conflicts and maneuverings of different congressional factions and lobbying groups that vied with one another to gain the upper hand. Meanwhile, well-heeled interest groups pumped out a steady stream of facts and arguments to attack the Clinton plan and discredit the claims made in its behalf.

Under these conditions, the debate left the public in a state of high confusion. Three months after President Clinton's initial speech, following countless media stories and public pronouncements, 56 percent of the people were still uncertain about the vital question of whether the President's plan guaranteed that workers would retain their healthcare coverage if they changed jobs.[33] A large majority continued to believe that the government spent less on health care than on humanitarian foreign aid.[34] Most people thought that children had better access to care than the elderly, despite the existence of Medicare and the more than 10 million children who lacked any insurance at all.[35] Only 25 percent of Americans said they knew what a health alliance was, although such entities were a critical part of Mr. Clinton's plan.[36]

By the end of the debate, reputable survey analysts offered the ultimate indictment. One week after President Clinton's initial speech describing his proposal, 21 percent of the public believed that they knew a lot about the plan. By October, the proportion that felt this way had dropped to 15 percent; in November, it fell further to 13 percent. By August of the following year, when the proposal finally died, the number of citizens who considered themselves well informed about the plan remained at 13 percent.[37] By these calculations, the public felt that it knew *less* about the issues after they were fully debated than it did in the early months after Mr. Clinton first unveiled his plan.

Does Confusion Matter?

The preceding account seems disheartening indeed. How can anyone observe the frequent misapprehensions of the voters and the confusions that befog many public debates without doubting the capacity of Americans to arrive at sound conclusions about complex policy issues? Surely, public opinion cannot lead to good results if so many people are muddled and mistaken about even the most elementary facts.

Oddly enough, many scholars take the opposite view. They insist that Americans somehow manage to overcome the misperceptions and ignorance of individual members and make remarkably sound collective judgments about policy questions. According to Benjamin Page and Robert Shapiro, after a detailed analysis of opinion surveys over five decades, "The public as a collective body is capable of holding sensible opinions and processing the information made available to it. . . . It is simply not the case that the collective policy preferences of the U.S. public are nonexistent, unknowable, capricious, inconsistent, or ignorant. Instead, they are real, meaningful, well measured by polls, differentiated, coherent, and stable. They react understandably and predictably to events and new information."[38] Buttressed by these findings, Professor Page concludes in a later work: "So long as useful information is available and is publicized by at least some highly visible cue-givers and opinion leaders, ordinary citizens have the skills and motivation to sort through contending views and pick (or reshape) those that make sense and are helpful. . . . The marketplace of ideas actually works reasonably well, most of the time, so long as there is reasonable competition and diversity in the information system."[39] This verdict is affirmed and amplified by a number of other students of public opinion.[40]

How can experts possibly maintain such a view amid all the evidence of voter ignorance, confusion, and misinformation? Scholars such as Page and Shapiro do not deny how ignorant many Americans are about the most basic information relating to public affairs. But it is wrong, they say, to assume that voters need to know a host of facts about American government or current policy issues in order to go to the polls and choose intelligently among rival candidates. Despite being ignorant of many things, people can make shrewd guesses based on relevant scraps of information. Most voters are reasonably aware of how Republicans and Democrats differ on basic issues. Simply learning the party affiliations of the candidates, therefore, gives voters a useful clue about which candidates to support. Television debates, editorial comment, and the views of trusted friends yield other valuable hints.

Page and Shapiro would concede that citizens often make errors of fact and judgment about issues of immediate political importance. But they point out that such mistakes are likely to be random. As a result, the errant votes of uninformed people tend to cancel themselves out so that more knowledgeable citizens have a decisive effect on the outcome. In this way, collective decisions come to embody greater wisdom and understanding than the opinions of the average voter might suggest.

Although this analysis seems plausible, it is not entirely convincing. If better-informed citizens exert a disproportionate influence (assuming that the errant votes of ignorant and confused individuals cancel out), are the more enlightened voters reasonably representative of the electorate as a whole? Probably not. Knowledgeable voters are likely to be more affluent and better educated, and on many important issues may have interests and opinions that are very different from those of poorer citizens with less schooling. As a result, it is not entirely reassuring from the standpoint of democracy to find that the votes of poorly informed citizens tend to nullify each other.

Moreover, both in referenda and in election campaigns, there are many important questions on which Americans display misunderstandings that are decidedly *not* random and hence are not likely simply to cancel each other out. If a substantial fraction of the public believes that welfare is the largest item in the federal budget, opinion polls will produce a view of welfare reform that is very different from the one they will convey if everyone is aware that the true level of spending is less than 2 percent of the total budget. If 40 percent of the people do not know that America imports most of its oil from abroad, they will presumably be less inclined than those who do know the facts to support conservation measures or programs to find alternative energy sources.

It is difficult to test these suppositions empirically, since opinion polls rarely include both questions to test the respondents' knowledge of relevant facts and questions that solicit views about related matters of policy. But a few surveys of this kind exist. What they seem to show is that widespread misunderstandings about facts directly related to government programs often have significant effects on people's policy views even after one controls for other influences.[41] Thus, in a 1996 opinion poll, people who incorrectly believed that the standard of living of blacks was equal to or higher than that of whites were 14 percent more likely to oppose affirmative action. Those who wrongly believed that foreign aid cost more than Medicare were 12 percent more likely to favor cutting aid and 7 percent less likely to support cuts in Medicare. Respondents who erroneously felt that crime had increased in the past few years were 15 percent more likely to support cuts in welfare, while those who were under the false impression that air quality had worsened were 5 percent more inclined to resist any cuts in environmental spending.

Despite these biases, several studies assert that Americans have performed quite well in voting on policy issues in states with initiatives on the ballot.[42] The authors of these reports have examined long lists of initiatives in various states and have concluded that few of the results were manifestly unwise and that the overall record compared quite well with that of the average state legislature. To explain these results, other analysts have pointed out how much voters can deduce about an initiative from a few stray facts, such as who is backing the proposal and how much they have spent to have it enacted.[43]

Such findings are reassuring. Still, the conclusions are open to question. Knowing that insurance companies have gone to considerable lengths to promote an initiative on the ballot may help many voters make up their minds, but it is scarcely an infallible guide to wise judgment. Researchers have found that even though cues of this kind are helpful, they are far from a perfect substitute for adequate knowledge.[44] Besides, what can one really make of the conclusions scholars reach about the soundness of referendum results? In the past twenty years, California voters have approved initiatives severely limiting property taxes, establishing a state lottery, imposing term limits, extending the death penalty, authorizing marijuana use by doctor's prescription, limiting immigration, and dismantling affirmative action. What such actions reveal about the wisdom of voters is plainly a matter of opinion, not a subject for authoritative expert judgment. Not surprisingly, then, while some writers who have studied the results of ballot initiatives praise the judgment of the voters, others have arrived at the opposite conclusion.[45]

People who are poorly informed may be even less capable of giving enlightened answers to callers conducting opinion surveys of the kind politicians increasingly consult in deciding how to vote on policy questions. When pollsters call, there are no party labels to help individuals decide. Friends and associates are not likely to have talked about the issue. Newspapers may not have editorialized on the subject. Thus, citizens have many fewer clues to rely on than they do when they go to the polls to cast their ballot on election day.

In the end, this much seems plausible. Ignorance and misinformation are likely to do least harm in helping voters choose among candidates. Even here, however, choices may become more erratic as increasing cynicism leaves voters with fewer cues and sources of opinion they are willing to trust. The effects of ignorance are likely to be greater in voting on ballot initiatives, since there are no party labels to serve as cues. They will be greater still in surveys by political pollsters, when citizens often respond with little or no opportunity for prior discussion.[46] Thus, as the public presses for more referenda and congressional leaders turn increasingly to opinion polls to help them decide how to vote on a pending bill, misinformation and ignorance promise to have more harmful effects on the policymaking process than they have had in the past.

Summing Up

What conclusions can one reach on whether Americans have the interest and capacity to exert a constructive influence on their elected representatives? On this score, there are considerable grounds for optimism. Although many citizens have only a limited, imperfect knowledge of public affairs, they do seem able to offer useful guidance to policymakers in a number of ways. Most important, Americans agree to a remarkable extent about their system of government, its basic institutions and safeguards, its fundamental precepts of fair play, and the principal goals of the society. Such a consensus may not yield exact answers for how the government should deal with complex policy problems. Nevertheless, it does give a valuable framework within which policy deliberations can proceed—one that politicians ignore at their peril.

The public is also able to direct the attention of elected representatives to the problems and concerns that it most wants the government to address. These priorities are sometimes distorted by misinformation, exaggerated views of what the government can accomplish, or a persistent unwillingness to give adequate weight to future needs. The popular agenda may also shift too rapidly to sustain a prolonged debate on complicated issues. Still, the public's priorities are often useful and influential. By all accounts, Congress is especially likely to respond to issues that concern people deeply, and in most cases that is all to the good. After all, who is better qualified than the public to judge what subjects matter most and what problems most need attention?

The public can likewise give helpful guidance on reasonably clearcut issues that are heavily value-laden, such as abortion or the death penalty. Popular opinion on such questions seems to be reasonably stable, much more so than it is in assigning priorities. Since information and expert analysis alone will not resolve issues of this kind, the public's value judgments provide a particularly appropriate basis for decision in a democracy.

The uses of popular opinion just described are easily substantial enough to counter the pessimists who imply that citizens in the modern world are incapable of giving useful guidance to lawmakers. Nevertheless, the public is not always able to arrive at enlightened judgments. It is especially likely to lose its way when it encounters issues that have a number of possible solutions and involve a lot of complicated information—issues such as reforming health care, regulating telecommunications, or providing for the national defense. Even in complicated cases of this kind, the public can often communicate certain preferences that are helpful to legislators in deciding how to proceed. In the debates over President Clinton's healthcare bill, for example, public opinion polls suggested that most Americans wanted to ensure access for everyone but not if such a step saddled them with substantially higher taxes, or limited their right to choose a doctor, or required a large new government bureaucracy. These preferences hardly specified a concrete plan for Congress to adopt, but they did provide useful guidelines for lawmakers in evaluating competing proposals.

Beyond this limited guidance, however, public opinion offers little help in determining specific policy solutions for complex problems. Most people are too ignorant of essential facts, too susceptible to widespread misunderstandings, and at times too vulnerable to prejudice to serve as reliable guides. They engage too rarely in discussions of the issues to arrive at thoughtful conclusions. As President Clinton's healthcare proposals revealed, even a prolonged national debate may not always enlighten them. Public knowledge of the facts can actually diminish in the wake of a torrent of claims and counterclaims fueled by elaborate media campaigns by well-heeled interest groups. With multiple solutions to choose from, poorly informed citizens will not necessarily cancel out one another's opinions. Although a few scholars still insist that the public is capable of consistently sound policy judgments, they do not appear to take sufficient account of the fact that ignorance is not randomly distributed and that widespread misunderstandings and prejudices can often skew the results.

Finally, Americans have expectations for politics and the political process that are often unrealistic. Convinced that presidents can often accomplish more than is humanly possible, that legislators should be able to arrive at sensible decisions without prolonged disagreement or controversy, and that politicians should refrain from pandering to the voters yet still reflect the views of their constituents, the public seems fated to endure repeated disappointment over the government and those who run it. The result of these vexations is a greater dissatisfaction with politics and politicians than the facts truly warrant.

In sum, the public's capacity to guide our democratic government appears to rest somewhere between the pessimism of a Walter Lippmann and the optimism of those who set great store by the wisdom of collective public judgments. From this mixed verdict, one conclusion more emerges. No collective magic, no unseen hand, no ultimate store of folk wisdom exists to guide the public to reasonable conclusions. Rather, there is every reason to believe that popular opinion tends to improve not only with better information but also with greater attention and effort on the part of the people and more opportunities for deliberation to test ideas and hear new facts and arguments. Now that politicians pay so much attention to the public's views, the quality of our government depends more than ever on active citizenship. A critical question for our democracy, then, is how much effort citizens are prepared to make to help their government function effectively.

16

THE AMBITIONS AND REALITIES OF CIVIC PARTICIPATION

THERE IS NOTHING ODD about the fact that Americans have an influence on their government. In a democracy, citizen opinion is supposed to influence the choices of public officials and the shape of legislation. What is remarkable about American democracy is the wealth of opportunities citizens have to make an impact. The United States has an unusually large number of elections and elective offices. Voters can express their will not only in general elections but in a wide array of primary contests, initiatives, referenda, and opinion polls. Because Americans play such a prominent part in the political process, the effort they devote to their civic responsibilities has an importance greater than it might possess in a country where the citizens' role is largely limited to voting every few years for the party of their choice.

The Growing Gap Between Citizens' Powers and Civic Participation

The abundant opportunities for influence that Americans possess are the product of a long series of citizen efforts to assume greater responsibility under our system of government. Against the intentions of the Founding Fathers, Americans gained the power to elect their president and senators directly. The franchise gradually expanded to include women, blacks, and eighteen-year-olds. Primary elections have supplanted party conventions in most states. Voter independence has grown substantially since the twentieth century began, when only 3 percent of the voters split their ticket. Ballot initiatives and referenda have substantially increased in number.

Not only have citizens in the United States succeeded in gaining greater influence; they would like to expand their role even further. Huge majorities favor wider use of ballot initiatives to allow citizens to vote on more policy issues. Equally large numbers support term limits in the hope that citizens can elect a new breed of politician who will be more like themselves and more attentive to constituents. In a 1999 opinion poll, when asked how much influence the public's views should have on government decisions on a scale of 1 to 10, the median respondent answered 9.[1]

Recent advances in technology promise to create even more opportunities for citizen participation. With the aid of the computer, some cities have allowed citizens to use the Internet to ask questions of local officials and submit suggestions for improvement. Other municipalities have experimented with electronic town meetings, featuring interactive discussions followed by votes on various propositions. One prominent political consultant foresees the further step of using the Internet to conduct national town meetings where important public issues will be discussed, participants can ask questions and receive answers, and millions of citizens will eventually "vote" on particular questions.[2] Such debates will arguably count more heavily than opinion polls, because everyone will know how the people voted and will hold their representatives accountable if the legislature disregards the popular verdict.

In light of the growing power of the people and their apparent desire for even more political influence, one might expect that they would be paying closer attention to public affairs and working harder than ever to fulfill their responsibilities as citizens. Yet just the opposite is true. Although Americans are the most patriotic people of any major democracy, their pride in the United States is not matched by an equivalent effort to carry out even their most basic civic duties.

The primary measure of civic responsibility in democratic societies is the proportion of citizens who vote. By this criterion, Americans do especially poorly. Throughout most of the twentieth century, voting rates in the United States were much lower than in almost all other advanced democracies. From 1960 to 1995, the average election turnout in thirty-seven other countries almost invariably exceeded 70 or 80 percent of the eligible citizens, with only a modest decline in recent years.[3] During the same period, turnout in American presidential elections was 20–40 percent lower than the average for most of these nations, and declined much more sharply. From the early 1960s to 1996, voting in presidential elections fell by 25 percent, from well over 60 percent to slightly less than 50 percent. In off-year elections for Congress and for governorships, turnouts dropped from 48 percent in the mid-1960s to 36 percent in 1998. Over the same period, voting rates in midterm primary elections plummeted from approximately 30 percent to barely more than 17 percent. These trends are all the more remarkable since they occurred in a period when registration barriers were falling and education levels were increasing throughout the population.

Citizens have not only become less interested in voting over the past thirty years. According to the monthly Roper surveys, they have participated less in all forms of political activity, as Table 5 makes clear.[4] These trends differ markedly from the postwar patterns in Western Europe. There, although party activity seems to be declining and voting rates have dropped slightly, almost every other form of political participation has risen substantially over the past few decades.[5]

Curiously, Americans *claim* to be as interested as they have ever been in politics and public affairs. Yet various scraps of evidence cast doubt on how genuine these professions of interest really are. Televised presidential addresses attract smaller audiences than they did in the 1960s, newspaper readership has declined, and media coverage of politics and government is shrinking for want of interest. According to one study using seventeen separate indicators of popular participation, citizen deliberation over political and civic issues declined by 25 percent from the early 1970s to the early 1990s (although Americans seem to have reversed this decline to some extent since 1992).[6]

Table 5. Trends in political participation in the United States, 1973 to 1994.

Type of participation	Relative change 1973–74 to 1993–94 (in percent)
1. Worked for a political party	−42
2. Served on a committee for some local organization	−39
3. Attended a public meeting on town or school affairs	−35
4. Attended a political rally or speech	−34
5. Wrote to a congressman or senator	−23
6. Signed a petition	−22
7. Was a member of a "better-government group"	−19
8. Held or ran for political office	−16
9. Wrote a letter to the newspaper	−14

Source: *Roper Report Surveys,* 1973–1994, as reported by Robert Putnam, *Bowling Alone: The Challenge and Revival of American Community* (2000), p. 45.

What accounts for this growing political apathy? In large part, the withdrawal from politics is part of a much larger trend encompassing sharp declines in many forms of social interaction ranging from dinner parties and bowling leagues to fraternal organizations and neighborhood associations.[7] Probably, the causes are multiple, including the rise of television, suburbanization and urban sprawl, and the growing pressures of work.[8]

Political apathy is especially marked among lower-income Americans whose voting rates have declined much more rapidly than those of other segments of the population. The special reasons for their civic disengagement have already been discussed in earlier chapters. But dwindling political participation is not confined to the poor and working classes; younger generations at all income levels have exhibited the same tendencies. Even among college freshmen, the percentages reporting that they frequently discuss politics or that they attach some importance to keeping up with public affairs have dropped by half, reaching their lowest level in more than thirty years of polling.[9]

The political withdrawal of the young is only the latest step in a process of steadily declining civic interest from one generation to the next. Over the past two decades, the proportion of people over sixty who profess to be "interested in politics" has remained fairly stable at 57–58 percent. But the level of interest among those aged thirty to fifty-nine has fallen from 55 to 40 percent, with a further drop from 45 to 35 percent among Americans in their twenties.[10] In contrast to the pattern in earlier generations, young people today have less knowledge of public affairs than their parents or grandparents had at the same age.[11] According to a 1990 survey by the (then) Times Mirror Center for the People and the Press, the generation of Americans aged eighteen to twenty-nine "knows less, cares less, votes less and is less critical of its leaders and institutions than young people in the past."[12] In 1996, fewer than one-third of American citizens under thirty bothered to vote in the presidential election, and fewer than one-quarter of the potential voters in this age group went to the polls in the 1998 congressional elections.

The point is not that young people have become selfish and uninterested in working for good causes; they participate more in community service activities than their parents did at a comparable age. Many of them have simply come to feel that government does not offer an effective way of accomplishing something worthwhile for other people.[13] To their generation, community service is no longer a stepping stone but an alternative to being involved in politics.

Just why younger, highly educated Americans care so little about public affairs is not entirely clear. A steady diet of television since early childhood may have contributed, along with a growing concern with making money.[14] But the government younger Americans have experienced in their lifetimes must also seem very different from the government their grandparents grew up with. To those who began paying attention to the world in the 1930s and 1940s, Washington was associated with the efforts of a charismatic president to rally the nation against the ravages of a great depression; with the passage of Social Security and later, Medicare; with the success of the Marshall Plan; and most of all, with the triumph of the United States over totalitarian aggressors in the last great war, in which the forces of good seemed unambiguously aligned against the forces of evil. Younger Americans have had a vastly different experience. They grew up hearing about Watergate and Vietnam and went on to experience oil embargoes, massive deficits, the Iran Contra scandal, and controversial interventions in Central America and other foreign countries. The government they observed in their formative years was described to them by highly critical reporters and seemed, in any event, a more contentious, partisan, unpleasant affair than anything their grandparents knew. Although younger Americans have lived through unprecedented prosperity, these good times have been linked much more closely in their minds with the workings of the free market than with the policies of enlightened political leaders. To them, the government must seem ponderous, ineffectual, and often irrelevant.

There is every reason to believe that levels of political participation will sink still lower in the future. Older generations will gradually be replaced by younger cohorts with much weaker tendencies to vote or become involved in other ways with government. More and more, children will reach their majority without having had parents who bothered to instill in them a sense of civic responsibility. All Americans will increasingly have the benefit of customized information that will allow them to choose what they read and thus more easily avoid the evening news or the front page of the local newspaper.

Dismal as they seem, current levels of political apathy are not unprecedented in the United States. Voting rates were as low as they are today in 1920 and 1924, before commencing their gradual rise through the 1930s, '40s and '50s. Earlier still, more than a century and a half ago, Tocqueville declared that Americans "find it a tiresome inconvenience to exercise political rights which distract them from industry. When required to elect representatives to support authority by public service, or to discuss public business together, they find they have no time."[15]

What is unique about our current situation is the wide and growing divergence between the meager effort citizens devote to politics and public affairs and the pervasive influence that government policies have on their lives and that they in turn have on their government. Never has there been such a gap between the attention officials pay to public opinion and the care with which the public makes up its mind. Never has government mattered so much to the lives of Americans, yet never has citizen involvement been so anemic. And the differences are gradually growing wider.

Some observers insist that Americans do wish to take a greater part in politics and government; they simply feel neglected and shut out of the system.[16] The evidence belies this explanation. No doubt people *believe* that they are ignored and pushed aside by uncaring politicians and powerful special interests. But actions speak louder than words. When citizens are given a chance to participate directly by voting on important issues in ballot initiatives and referenda, they fail to take advantage of the opportunity; if anything, they tend to vote even less for ballot propositions than they do for candidates seeking statewide political office.[17] The same tends to be true of local elections, where individual citizens have much more direct opportunities to influence choices that affect their lives, such as zoning proposals or membership on school boards. What people seem to want, therefore, is the power to participate, not the hard work of actually doing so.

Is the Problem Real?

Not everyone is troubled by the evidence of a growing indifference toward politics and public affairs. Some people do not believe that the problem even exists. According to the late Everett Ladd, president of the Roper Center for Public Opinion Research at the University of Connecticut, "If the public now showed signs of abandoning its historic inclination to join with others to meet common needs; if positive energy applied to social improvement were dissipating, . . . we would in fact be facing a crisis of American citizenship."[18] According to Ladd, however, no such signs exist. In his view, there is little reason to question the vigor of citizenship in America if one looks carefully at the data on "the levels of engagement of individual citizens documented here—involving millions of kids in the physical training, competition and friendships of soccer leagues; enhancing and enjoying our natural environment; supporting school programs in almost every city and town; helping the elderly and the infirm; sustaining vigorous community religious life, etc."[19]

Even if this optimistic account were factually correct (which is far from clear), it assumes that community service and participation in democratic self-government are similar enough that spending more time volunteering or joining soccer leagues and church groups can somehow make up for paying less attention to politics and public affairs. This is simply not true. However admirable community service may be, it can never take the place of government or achieve the common goals that large majorities of citizens embrace for their society. Charitable organizations have repeatedly made this point in response to proposals to move government out of programs to alleviate poverty, homelessness, and a host of other social ills. Their arguments need no repetition here. It is sufficient to point out that the United States ranks behind most advanced democracies in addressing a long list of familiar social problems, despite having one of the highest levels of volunteer effort in the world. That fact speaks eloquently to the need for effective democratic government if we are ever to achieve our common goals.

Through the years, other commentators have actually welcomed citizen apathy, arguing that a declining interest in government may be a sign of good health for the society. One political scientist, Heinz Eulau, even claimed that apathy signals contentment with the status quo and thus represents a "politics of happiness."[20]

It is true that most Americans seem quite happy with their own lives. This personal satisfaction may help explain why chronic dissatisfaction with government does not lead people to react more vehemently. Even so, Eulau's reference to a politics of happiness scarcely fits the current situation in America. The poor, who vote the least, are hardly the most pleased with the way the government has treated them. Nor can declining turnouts at the polls over the past thirty-five years be said to reflect a rising tide of satisfaction with Washington. On the contrary, they have been accompanied by a severe and growing disenchantment with politics and government.

Still other observers acknowledge the anemic political participation and do not celebrate its existence, but remain unconvinced that the problem is serious. Michael Schudson, for example, in his interesting history of civic life in the United States, considers it unrealistic and unnecessary to expect citizens to give much time to politics and public affairs.[21] Rather, it is enough that citizens keep a watchful eye on events and mobilize for action only when some threat arises that warrants their attention. As he puts it: "Picture parents watching small children at the community pool. They are not gathering information; they are keeping an eye on the scene. They look inactive but they are poised for action if action is required."[22]

There are several problems with Schudson's argument, quite apart from his intriguing analogy between policymakers at work and small children splashing in a pool. Surely, citizens should be more than monitors keeping an eye out for signs of trouble. They must act periodically by voting in primaries and general elections. They need to form opinions on policy questions, especially now that their views seem to be of such interest to policymakers. One would hope, moreover, that they could occasionally discuss important issues with friends and associates and not merely sit as observers while chatting about other things.

The principal flaw with Schudson's view of citizenship, however, is not in the concept itself. He is surely correct in pointing out that ordinary people cannot be expected to master the details of every significant government initiative, let alone arrive at carefully reasoned opinions on all policy issues. Rather, the weakness in Schudson's argument is his assumption that Americans are currently keeping sufficiently involved and informed to carry out their monitoring function adequately—that they are truly "poised for action if action is required." While this may be true of some interest groups and some segments of the population, it is hardly an accurate description of many other parts of American society. Lower-income Americans, in particular, seem to react to unfavorable policies and official neglect not by leaping into action but by retreating further into sullen indifference.

More generally, sagging election turnouts, declining participation in political activities of every kind, and public ignorance about important policy issues indicate that most Americans pay far too little attention to the work of government at all levels to serve as effective monitors. The signs of indifference are everywhere. Many parents are even uninformed about the quality of the schools their children attend—oblivious to mediocre teaching, unaware of shoddy educational practices, and infrequent in their attendance at parents' meetings.[23]

Most Americans, however, remain unconvinced that citizen apathy really matters. Yes, they say, it would be better if more Americans voted. But almost half of all eligible citizens still cast their ballots in presidential elections. A substantial minority—apparently at

393

least as large as in other leading democracies—continues to play an active part in political campaigns and other civic affairs. If this many people still participate, isn't there enough involvement to allow our democracy to function adequately? Can't elections still keep politicians suitably responsive to the will of the public? Unfortunately, the answer is almost certainly no. The growing disengagement of Americans from politics and public affairs has a disturbing number of adverse effects on the quality of government.

To begin with, now that so few people turn out to select party delegates to state conventions, both Democrats and Republicans are vulnerable to determined interest groups that can mobilize large numbers of supporters when the occasion requires. Already, activists in such organizations as the National Education Association, the Christian Coalition, and the National Federation of Independent Business populate party conventions far more than their actual numbers in the population should allow, with the result that they can often insert policies into the platform that do not command broad rank-and-file support.

With only 15–20 percent of potential voters bothering to vote in primary elections, well-organized groups that can get their supporters to the polls can also affect the selection of candidates to a degree out of proportion to the strength of their membership in the electorate. Moreover, because individuals with strong ideological convictions are more inclined to vote than moderate middle-of-the-road Americans, candidates can often be nominated despite having more extreme liberal or conservative views than the rank-and-file of their party.

In the general election, candidates cannot take the more extreme elements in their party for granted and move unequivocally to the center, as they could if almost everyone voted. While bidding for the median voter, candidates on both sides must also "mobilize their base" by continuing to appeal to more ideologically committed elements in the party, where many of its most active supporters can be found. As mainstream Americans vote less, therefore, their influence wanes, and they increasingly come to believe that neither party adequately represents their interests. Ideological divisions emerge within the legislature that are deeper and more intractable than the differences felt by a majority of Americans. The ensuing partisan bickering inhibits negotiation and compromise, while further alienating the public from politics and public life.

Another consequence of citizen apathy is its effect on the tactics of conducting election campaigns. When only one-half of eligible voters participate in presidential elections and only one-third cast a ballot in off-year congressional races, elections begin to turn not only on the views of the citizenry but on which party organization is more effective and spends more money in getting its supporters to the polls. Skillful candidates also design their campaigns to exploit public indifference and alienation. They craft their messages not merely to attract sympathetic voters but to arouse hostile feelings among the supporters of rival candidates so as to discourage them from casting a ballot. The ensuing campaigns are more negative and help to increase voter cynicism even more.[24]

Once elections are over and winning candidates take office, apathy enhances the power of lobbyists and their clients. As fewer people pay attention, interest groups have an easier time affecting legislative deliberations. Carefully orchestrated, well-financed grassroots campaigns have greater influence on policy than they should. With few people voting, lawmakers must be more careful not to offend organizations that are capable of mobilizing their membership to vote against unfriendly legislators and defeat them in future campaigns.

To be sure, in the best of circumstances, there are limits to what an alert electorate can do to contain the influence of lobbyists. The most involved citizens cannot be expected to keep up with every piece of legislation and every attempt by interest groups to gain a regulatory concession. Yet the fact remains that lobbyists seeking special favors thrive on ignorance and inattention. The less informed and less involved citizens become, the more difficult it is for citizen advocacy groups to rally opposition and the easier it becomes for special interests to get their way. The less people participate actively in the work of public-interest organizations, the more likely it is that these groups will take extreme positions or fall into the hands of leaders whose personal agenda does not accurately reflect the desires of those they claim to represent.

Civic indifference also makes it easier for Congress to succumb to gridlock and political self-interest. With control of the White House and Congress often divided between Republicans and Democrats, the government may fail to act at all if public opinion is not strong enough, informed enough, and insistent enough to demand attention. Without intense citizen pressure, lawmakers are unlikely to place the interests of democracy and good government above their own careers. Campaign finance reform and other proposals to improve the election process will languish forever in House and Senate committees, and lawmakers will resist efforts to curb the use of pork barrel projects, patronage, and other questionable methods of rewarding supporters and currying favor with constituents.

Now that politicians pay so much attention to surveys and polls, it is more important than ever that citizens be reasonably informed about the policy questions being debated in Washington. Citizen indifference not only increases ignorance but breeds misinformation and prejudice, which carry added risks of distorting decisions in Washington. One reason the United States allocates less of its GDP to foreign aid than any other major country is that Americans vastly overestimate the amounts being spent for this purpose and hence oppose any attempt to appropriate more. Asked how much the government *should* spend, most people favor a figure far *above* what Congress actually provides. Much the same is true of congressional appropriations for the arts. Race affords still another illustration of the mischief ignorance can cause. Most Americans believe that blacks are lazier than whites, that most people on welfare are black, that blacks are as well off economically as whites, and that welfare payments make up a much higher fraction of the federal budget than is actually the case. Such mistaken beliefs have significant effects on public opinion toward welfare policies and other programs for the poor. Only an attentive electorate can avoid repeated distortions of this kind.

As previous chapters have made clear, one of the worst features of citizen apathy is that it is spread so unequally throughout the population. In contrast to low-income people in Western Europe, poor and working-class Americans vote much less and care much less about public affairs than their better-educated, more affluent compatriots. It is no accident, then, that lower-income groups have received so little protection in the United States and lack basic safeguards and benefits, such as guaranteed access to health care and paid parental leave, that other advanced democracies granted long ago to all their citizens.

Once Congress has acted, alienation and apathy inhibit citizens from actively participating in efforts to implement new programs, especially in lower-income neighborhoods. School reform languishes in the absence of strong parent groups that help teachers improve student learning. Public housing projects decay more rapidly when authorities cannot call on tenants organizations to help keep buildings from deteriorating or from becoming overrun by drugs and vandalism. Now that one government agency after another has discovered what it can gain from active cooperation with the community, an uninvolved, indifferent citizenry has come to be a greater liability than earlier generations may have suspected.

Ironically, then, most of the things that Americans dislike about politics are aggravated by disinterest and disengagement. Apathy leads to greater partisanship in government, to less responsiveness to public opinion, to more demagoguery and negative campaigning. It strengthens the influence of well-organized interest groups. It causes the media to put more emphasis on scandal, sensationalism, and "infotainment" in order to attract the attention of the public. It even hampers the efforts of officials to carry out government programs.

One final danger arising from civic apathy could eventually prove even more important than the rest. Participation in government is more than a way of helping democracy work well. It is the common bond that holds together an extraordinarily diverse society. More than any other leading democracy, America is a country that preserves its unity through a shared belief in its Constitution, its institutions of government, and its democratic principles. Today, the forces of unity are under strain from a variety of sources: the growing diversity brought on by an influx of immigrants from many lands speaking many languages; the escape into private walled communities by thousands of affluent citizens; the increased segmentation of television audiences, the emergence of multinational corporations with allegiances to many countries; the explosive growth in the number of special-interest groups, each intent upon its own particular policy objectives.

In the face of these fragmenting pressures, Americans surely need to strengthen the forces that unite them. First among these forces is the common set of responsibilities (as well as rights) that citizenship in the United States entails. Any trend toward loosening these commitments through the slow spread of civic indifference and disengagement weakens the bonds that hold Americans together as a nation.

Restoring the Balance

What can the country do to restore a proper balance between citizen influence and civic responsibility? Two possibilities come to mind. The first is to cut back the obligations of citizenship so that they are more closely aligned with the modest effort Americans seem willing to devote to public affairs. The second is to find ways to increase active and informed citizen participation.

There is much to be said for the first approach. Americans are currently asked to go to the polls more often and make up their minds about a greater number of candidates and elections than any other citizenry in the world. Through ballot initiatives and private polls, their opinions are solicited, recorded, and publicized on more issues than in other major democracies. This multitude of choices and opportunities would be fine if Americans also led the world in their zeal to participate in the democratic process. Yet they show no sign of taking a greater interest in politics or devoting more time than citizens of other democracies to inform themselves about candidates and current issues. If anything, they seem less engaged and less informed. Under these conditions, rather than deplore the apathy and indifference of so many Americans, why not fall in line with other major democracies by pruning our civic responsibilities to bring them into better balance with the limited effort citizens are willing to devote to public affairs?

One way of compensating for the lack of civic participation would be to encourage the continued growth of lobbying groups and advocacy organizations so that they will represent as many interests and segments of the population as possible. Through this process, citizens can delegate most of their civic duties to representatives who are willing to work hard at promoting their interests in Washington and advising them on how to vote and communicate with public officials on matters important to their welfare.

Americans are far along this road already. The innumerable groups and organizations that currently exist in Washington play a useful role in helping to ensure that more and more interests are represented in the policymaking process. Through the efforts of the Concord Coalition to combat huge federal deficits, even the voice of unborn generations has resonated loudly through the corridors of power.

At the same time, interest groups cannot do everything. The most completely organized society will not fully compensate for an apathetic citizenry. However hard they try, lobbyists are unlikely to have much influence if their members do not vote. With all the will in the world, they cannot overcome the adverse results of declining turnouts on the quality of elections or remedy the vast inequalities of wealth and political influence among different interests and segments of the population.

A dense network of advocacy groups will also fail in several ways to serve the national interest. A society so organized will teem with vested interests struggling to preserve the status quo and keep policymakers from terminating outmoded programs or unnecessary benefits and subsidies. A cacophony of appeals from different lobbying groups will not help citizens form a balanced judgment on which candidates to choose or what policies to support to further the general welfare. Nor will a host of contending organizations representing particular interests do much to preserve our democracy as a unifying force for America's diverse society. If anything, relying more on interest groups to make democracy work will deepen the divisions separating different elements of the population.

Commentators have suggested a number of other ways by which to lighten the load of civic responsibilities. Some political scientists would limit the use of primary elections, arguing that media-dominated campaigns coupled with low turnouts lead to the selection of photogenic candidates who can raise a lot of money but often lack the skills to govern.[25] Other groups are trying to curb the growth of direct democracy by restricting the use of ballot initiatives. George Will even favors term limits—not for the reasons that animate most supporters but in the hope that such a reform will blunt the impact of popular opinion by bringing candidates to power who are not professional politicians pandering to the public and guided by poll results but private citizens willing to exercise their independent judgment.[26]

Whatever one may think of these proposals, they are likely to encounter strong popular resistance. Why would angry, frustrated voters agree to limit their own powers and grant more discretion to the very politicians they distrust? Americans may be less and less active politically, but opinion surveys suggest that they want more power, not less. They will certainly not agree to do away with primary elections and go back to political conventions dominated by party regulars. Nor will they favor limitations on the number of ballot initiatives; in fact, large majorities favor greater use of this device. Term limits have a brighter future—but not for the reasons that persuade George Will. Moreover, they are unlikely to work as Will anticipates. Instead of producing a body of strong, independent-minded legislators, they may simply give rise to a crop of inexperienced lawmakers who rely too much on staff members, lobbyists, or executive branch officials for information and advice. Few knowledgeable observers believe that the country will be better served as a result.

A different strategy for limiting the citizens' role is to give more policymaking authority to entities made up of experienced people who are neither elected nor subject to strong grassroots pressures. One way of achieving this result would be to expand the role of the judiciary. Another would be to create new independent agencies, such as the Securities and Exchange Commission. Still another would be to utilize expert bodies, such as the commission of elder statesmen proposed by George Kennan to give advisory opinions for the Congress and the President on long-term problems facing the country.[27]

The United States has already gone further than any other country in allowing the courts to make decisions that are the prerogative of elected officials in other democratic nations. More remarkable still, judges have wielded these powers and retained greater respect from the people than any other branch of government. But the power of the judiciary may have already reached its limit. At the zenith of judicial activism in the 1970s, courts were presiding over entire school districts, prison systems, and mental health facilities in response to recalcitrant or incompetent government officials. By all accounts, this experience was neither attractive to the judges involved nor especially effective as a permanent method of administering public services. The courts have since retreated from this high-water mark of judicial activism and show little sign of wanting to return.

Commissions made up of eminent figures have long been used to address specific problems, such as housing policy and race relations.[28] At times, their work has educated the public, stimulated debate, and collected much useful data on important subjects. Occasionally, they have helped to resolve difficult issues, as in the case of the bipartisan commission appointed to reform Social Security in the early 1980s. More often, however, they have simply been a convenient device for presidents to build support for political decisions already made or to satisfy the public that something is being done about problems that have aroused widespread concern. More ambitious efforts to use such bodies for policymaking purposes can easily come to naught. The saga of Hillary Clinton's commission to reform the healthcare system is the most spectacular recent example.

Much the same is true of efforts to create permanent institutions led by experts that operate without interference from politicians. Starting with the Progressives in the early twentieth century, reformers have tried this technique on many occasions with only intermittent success. The Federal Reserve Board has performed reasonably well. But on the whole, independent administrative agencies are not noted for the superior quality of their decisions, nor have they been free of the political influences and interest group pressures they were created to avoid.

Despite the reservations just expressed, there are a few measures to limit the citizens' role which could bring about positive results. The most promising example, described in Chapter 11, would be to require voters to choose among party slates rather than making separate choices among the candidates for a long list of offices. This change would give citizens a task that is much more within their powers while providing some sorely needed accountability for the work of Congress. These advantages, however, will almost certainly fail to persuade politicians and will probably not even convince the citizenry. Americans may not wish to spend much time preparing to vote, but they resist any effort to limit their range of election choices.

Even if citizens were more accommodating, no effort to shrink their responsibilities can repair all of the damage done by apathy and disengagement. Americans could agree to limit the choices they make in the voting booths, eliminate primaries, and give more responsibility to expert commissions, but they would still have to know enough to vote intelligently in presidential and congressional elections. As long as politicians keep paying attention to opinion polls, the public will need to inform itself sufficiently to reach a reasoned judgment. If programs of school reform, public housing, and law enforcement are to work properly, local communities must continue to organize and participate to help the effort succeed. If our society is to protect itself from dividing along ethnic or economic or ideological lines, Americans will still need to strengthen the common bonds of civic commitment.

In sum, if we are to keep our democracy strong and narrow the gap between the influence citizens possess and the effort they devote to public affairs, we are unlikely to succeed by trying to curtail the powers of the people. Americans would not agree to such proposals, nor would our democracy necessarily be improved as a result. The obvious alternative is to look for ways of encouraging citizens to give more time and energy to their civic responsibilities. But what would such an effort entail and could it possibly hold any realistic chance of success?

17

BUILDING CITIZENSHIP

As the twenty-first century begins, a vast competition is in
progress to capture the time and attention of the American people. Employers are asking more of their employees. Women are being
drawn in increasing numbers into the workforce, willingly or not.
Advertisers use their wit and wile to persuade consumers to buy new
products, take up new hobbies, travel to new places. Entertainers of
all kinds—television personalities, athletes, impresarios, and actors—produce ever more lavish and enticing diversions to occupy as
many leisure hours as they can persuade the great American audience to spend.

In contrast to these efforts, it is striking how little energy is devoted to trying to engage citizens more actively in the affairs of their
government. Civic education in the public schools has been almost
totally eclipsed by a preoccupation with preparing the workforce for
a global economy. Most universities no longer treat the preparation
of citizens as an explicit goal of their curriculum. Newspaper editors
and TV producers give diminishing amounts of space and time to reporting on politics and policy issues. Congress appropriates far less
money to public-affairs broadcasting than do the governments of
other leading democracies.

The civic health of the nation has not always suffered from such neglect. For almost 150 years—from Madison and Jefferson to Woodrow Wilson, Theodore Roosevelt, and Louis Brandeis—prominent Americans gave much thought to how the nation's policies could foster the qualities of citizenship essential to effective self-government. University presidents considered ways in which the college experience could train students as civic leaders. School authorities worked to assimilate immigrant children and instill in them a belief in American democracy and a sense of civic responsibility. As Theodore Roosevelt once remarked, "The prime problem of our nation is to get the right type of good citizenship. . . . In a democracy like ours, we cannot expect the stream to rise higher than its source. If the average man and the average woman are not of the right type, your public men will not be of the right type."[1]

Michael Sandel has described in vivid detail how this civic preoccupation was gradually overtaken by other concerns and priorities.[2] As the twentieth century wore on, more and more public debate came to focus on material goals, notably economic growth and the equitable distribution of resources. Excluded groups, notably black Americans, did struggle for full political rights. But the idea of purposefully encouraging Americans to be active citizens came increasingly in question. Efforts at civic education began to raise the specter of indoctrination and to rub uneasily against a sense that individuals should decide for themselves how to live their lives without having the government promote any particular set of values, even the basic democratic values of civic participation. School authorities grew increasingly preoccupied with other matters, first with managing the tensions of racial integration and then with raising student test scores. University leaders spoke less and less about citizenship and civic responsibility. Grassroots efforts to mobilize the people and get them to register and vote gradually diminished. By the 1980s, the subject of citizenship had all but disappeared from view.

Within the past few years, people from various walks of life have begun to express concern about the decline of civic participation. Editorial writers have devoted columns to the dwindling turnouts at the polls and the signs of political apathy among the young. Foundations have announced an interest in supporting initiatives to revive civic interest. A few newspapers have launched experimental campaigns to encourage readers to become more active in solving local problems. Several university presidents have declared a responsibility and a commitment on the part of higher education to do more to help their students become better citizens. What program of action might develop from these fresh stirrings of interest? What sort of a program needs to emerge in order to make a substantial difference?

Toward a More Active Citizenry

Any serious attempt to strengthen citizenship must start in the schools.[3] Taking civic obligations seriously does not come naturally. As rational-choice theorists point out, citizens acting purely in their own self-interest may not even bother to vote, since their single ballot will have too little chance of affecting the outcome to justify the time and effort required to inform themselves adequately and go to the polls.

Both Washington and Jefferson understood this clearly.[4] So did Horace Mann, father of public education in America, who declared: "One of highest and most valuable objects to which the influence of a school can be made conducive consists of training our children in self-government."[5] The early years are crucial for imparting a basic understanding of democracy and a strong sense of civic responsibility. If the schools fail in this task, it will be hard to make up the deficit in later life.

Interestingly, a 1996 survey found that 86 percent of Americans regarded civic education as a "very important" aim of education—a higher percentage than that recorded for any other educational goal.[6] Nevertheless, fewer than half of all states require high school students to complete even a one-semester course in government or civics. The task of preparing citizens earned barely a mention by the nation's governors in their 1990 statement of educational goals, and the Department of Education waited until 1998 to measure civic competence (in contrast, competence in math and science is tested every year).[7] The department's 1998 survey showed that roughly 75 percent of high school seniors were "not proficient in civics; one-third lacked even a basic comprehension of how the government operates, while only 9 percent could give two reasons why citizens should participate in the democratic process."[8] These results could not be compared with the last previous assessment, in 1988, since the questions asked had changed. But the 1988 results revealed that the performance of 17-year-olds had declined significantly since 1976 and that students even then had only a superficial understanding of the subject.[9] Earlier comparisons had likewise found that civic competence diminished markedly from 1969 to 1976.[10]

At present, civic education is in considerable disarray. There is much confusion over its purposes, with writers on the subject emphasizing a welter of objectives ranging from a knowledge of American history to the development of analytic skills, moral sensitivity, and even a global perspective. The teaching tends to be didactic and dull. Most of the standard texts describe political processes and institutions without doing much to show how policy issues will affect students' lives or how the legislative process actually works in practice.[11] Rights are emphasized far more than civic responsibilities. Students frequently have little opportunity to practice democracy through participating in a student government. Not surprisingly, most investigators have found that civic education in its current form has little or no subsequent effect on voting or other forms of democratic participation.[12]

Amid these dispiriting conditions, there are a few hopeful signs. Some studies have found that civics courses taught by the discussion method which feature material on current policy issues can have a lasting effect on the civic knowledge of students and their interest in keeping up with public affairs.[13] The same is true of a project—called Kids Voting, U.S.A.—in which students discuss elections in school and at home and go with their parents to vote.[14] Researchers evaluating community service programs in high school have found that participants show increased levels of interest in helping others and volunteering for civic activities.[15] These findings give grounds for hope that civic education could enjoy greater success if it received additional effort and resources.[16]

An effective civics program would begin in the early grades and last through high school. It would embody clear priorities: all students should understand the essential values and principles of democracy, recognize the basic obligations of citizenship, and appreciate the importance of these obligations to a healthy democracy. It would convey an accurate sense of how the institutions and processes of government and politics actually work, in order to help overcome the unrealistic expectations that many Americans have about politicians and their legislative efforts. In conveying this message, civics teachers would rely as much as possible on active class discussion, using cases and problems to encourage critical thinking and to demonstrate the link between government policies and the welfare of students and their families.

To the greatest possible extent, schools should try to help their students experience the values of democracy by encouraging participation in student government and community service. As in Kids Voting (and in Costa Rica, for that matter), students could be asked to participate in elections—although the votes of anyone under eighteen would not count. Conceivably, high school students could debate the use of available community funds for youth programs, such as athletics, after-school programs, and community service initiatives, and local officials could consider their recommendations seriously in deciding how to allocate the money. Whatever the methods, the essential point would be to restore civics education to its place as one of the principal functions of public schooling. To permit continuing improvement, government officials should provide ample funds to assess different models of instruction and determine their long-run effects on voting and other forms of civic participation.

It is characteristic of Americans to place great faith in education's ability to resolve all manner of social problems. This would undoubtedly be a mistake in seeking ways to develop more active citizens. Important as schools are, there is little evidence that the higher voting rates commonly found abroad are due to better civic education. Indeed, comparative studies suggest that teenagers in several other advanced democracies have even less interest in politics and voting than their counterparts in the United States.[17] Clearly, then, there is much to be done after students leave school to ensure high levels of civic participation.

Students who go on to college enter institutions that were originally founded to give students the breadth of knowledge and the habits of critical thinking that would enable them to become active citizens and leaders in democratic communities. Today, most colleges offer a wide assortment of classes and extracurricular pursuits that help fulfill this purpose. Typically, there are courses on government, history, economics, and sociology; an active student government; Democratic and Republican clubs; community service programs; and a host of student activities in which to learn the skills of leadership and effective collaboration. By all accounts, these opportunities yield results. Studies on the effects of undergraduate education "almost invariably indicate changes during the college years toward . . . greater interest in social and political issues, and greater interest and involvement in the political process."[18]

Despite these positive findings, there are warning signs that more is needed to strengthen civic education on the nation's campuses. Freshmen who enroll today have less interest in public affairs than at any time since polling began thirty years ago. Participation among college graduates in political affairs has been dropping, even more so in absolute terms than among Americans with only a high school education. In fact, college students today are less inclined than the adult population as a whole to feel that politics is relevant to their lives.[19]

Meanwhile, the traditional liberal arts curriculum has ceded much ground to more practical forms of instruction. A majority of American undergraduates today are enrolled in vocational majors using curricula that restrict the liberal arts to a small fraction of total classroom hours. Where vocationalism has not prevailed, undergraduate education has changed profoundly, with far fewer requirements and a much larger menu of courses than the traditional liberal arts curriculum contained. While these changes have broadened student choice, they have also made it possible for students to select a course of study that has little civic relevance and bears scant resemblance to the earlier conception of a liberal education. When citizenship does gain official recognition, it is frequently used as a rationale for courses on cultural diversity or international understanding that have no explicit relation to government or informed participation in the political process.

Recently, several colleges have proclaimed their intent to undertake a serious examination of the role of undergraduate education in preparing citizens. That is welcome news. Among the colleges that have completed major curricular reviews in the past twenty years, few have given any conscious thought to their civic purposes. Most do not even take responsibility for encouraging their students to register and vote. Seldom have universities tried to define the goals of civic education or to consider what courses and forms of instruction might best fulfill them. Seldom have they tried to figure out how to integrate different aspects of civic education to enhance their overall effectiveness. For example, polls reveal that many students consider community service important but regard the government as irrelevant. Small wonder; faculties rarely make any substantial effort to link community service to coursework so that students can understand how the conditions they observe in homeless shelters and housing projects connect with larger questions of public policy, which must ultimately be addressed in order to solve the underlying problems. Worse yet, although almost all courses and activities directly related to civic education are voluntary, few college faculties have thought about how to reach those students who do not choose to participate. Apparently, like so much else on campus, citizenship is looked upon as merely an option along with choral singing and participation in intramural sports.

Beyond schools and colleges, national service of some sort could provide another means of developing greater civic interest. This idea has attracted attention ever since William James delivered his famous speech calling for a program of peacetime service that would provide a "moral equivalent of war" by fostering solidarity and civic spirit.[20] Today, James's suggestion seems all the more compelling now that the disappearance of the draft has removed one of the few opportunities to gather Americans from all walks of life in a common civic undertaking.

Proposals for national service have provoked strong opposition, ranging from union worries that such programs would take away jobs to libertarian fears that young Americans would have to serve against their will to fulfill some hare-brained liberal vision.[21] Aside from these concerns, there are plenty of practical problems to worry about. What sort of work will participants do? How large a program can the government administer effectively? What effects will such service have on the long-term civic behavior of those who participate? Such questions make any proposal for compulsory national service seem premature at best and possibly unwise even in the long run. Still, the promise of voluntary service seems great enough to merit renewed efforts to expand existing programs and to experiment with others. Meanwhile, researchers should monitor the results to discover what long-term effects the programs have on the willingness of participants to vote and participate in the work of citizenship.

Civic education and community service will have little lasting effect unless their lessons receive encouragement and support in later life. An obvious way to provide such reinforcement would be to create more opportunities and inducements for people to engage in all sorts of organizations and activities devoted to self-government and mutual advancement. Undertakings of this kind already exist in every community and neighborhood throughout the country. Still, participation rates in organizations other than churches are modest among lower-income groups, and some scholars claim that they have dropped sharply in the past two decades even among college-educated Americans.[22]

Previous chapters have pointed to many possibilities for new and expanded forms of self-government: works councils, community organizations, parent involvement in public schools, and patient groups to negotiate over healthcare plans. Government agencies and foundations could encourage these ventures by supplying seed money and establishing intermediary organizations to offer training and technical assistance. Recent research suggests that participation in such grassroots organizations can build trust, civic competence, and political involvement while helping officials carry out their policies more effectively.[23] In fact, increased involvement in civic activities seems to be linked with all manner of desirable outcomes: lower crime rates, better schools, healthier children, even greater happiness.[24] If these findings are only partially correct, taking steps to boost citizen participation must be one of the most fruitful investments an enlightened government can make.

However active and involved they may be, citizens can fulfill their democratic responsibilities only to the extent that they are informed. Americans already have a vast profusion of sources—newspapers, magazines, television, radio, and most recently the Internet. As Chapter 3 pointed out, however, all is not well amid this torrent of news and information. Media coverage of politics and public affairs is shrinking. Faced with dwindling audiences for their product, newspaper publishers and television producers place increasing emphasis on entertaining readers and viewers and grabbing their attention with sensational stories. Many editors feature conflict, scandal, and political maneuvering at the expense of more substantive coverage, often to the point of distorting reality.

Against this tide, a few newspapers and television stations are experimenting with a new effort called "civic journalism" to involve citizens more actively in the problems of their community. Newspapers engaged in this endeavor first ascertain what issue concerns local communities the most, and then combine intensive coverage of the subject with specific efforts to organize meetings, encourage citizen involvement, and inform people of what they can do, and what other communities have done, to address the problem.[25]

In some instances, these campaigns have substantially increased public awareness and citizen involvement. Nevertheless, the movement is currently under fire from many editors and journalists for diverting resources from other news-gathering activities and jeopardizing journalistic objectivity. Worse yet, civic journalism has not yet shown that it can increase media audiences. Without some positive effect on the bottom line, the movement will be hard pressed to grow or even survive. Still, there is much to be said for continuing the effort to find new ways of interesting citizens in government and convincing them that grassroots participation can make a difference. If newspapers cannot persuade their readers that government is relevant to their lives and that informed participation can change it for the better, they will have a difficult time halting the slow erosion of credibility and circulation that has plagued them for the past several decades.

The precarious state of civic journalism offers a pointed reminder of the impact of market forces on media behavior. As many analysts have observed, newspapers and TV stations in a competitive market have a chronic tendency to underemphasize public affairs, since they cannot reap a return on the value of developing a more informed citizenry. To counteract this deficiency, private foundations could try to experiment with imaginative public-affairs programs that might attract more than a tiny share of the television audience. But private foundations are unlikely to suffice; governments will have to share in funding public-interest programming if the needs of citizen education are to be fully met. At present, Congress appropriates only a tiny sum each year to help support public affairs programs.[26] This is far less than what is needed to provide the public with interesting, informative programs on major current issues such as health care, Social Security, and campaign finance reform.

To be sure, such added support could merely provide greater quantities of information in more attractive packages to a tiny fraction of interested Americans. If so, Congress would succeed only in widening the growing gap between knowledgeable citizens and those who are scantily informed, leaving the public as a whole no better off than before. Hence, lawmakers would need to increase funding gradually and accompany it with careful monitoring and research, in order to learn by trial and error how to expand the size of the audience and improve the effectiveness of the programs. The sums required for such a venture are so small relative to the importance of the task and the size of the federal budget that the attempt seems well worth making. Congress could easily fund such an initiative in its entirety simply by using the receipts from anticipated sales of the public spectrum.

Governments at all levels can take other steps to help citizens gain the information they need to fulfill their civic duties. Congress can continue to encourage the development of the Internet in ways that ensure access to everyone, so that all citizens can inform themselves about public affairs and participate more actively in government. Already, several cities have experimented with new technology to do a better job of informing residents about local issues while enabling them to convey their views to city officials. Freedom Channel.com allows users to watch brief speeches by candidates outlining their position on any of a number of public issues.

Beyond these efforts, the United States needs many more opportunities for public deliberation about policy issues of importance to the lives of citizens. Americans have traditionally relied on the hope that a lively marketplace of ideas will eventually cause the "truth" to emerge. If the public seems confused, the remedy must be to supply more information, more analysis, more debates. The healthcare discussions of 1993–1994 have revealed the limitations of this approach. President Clinton's proposal elicited one of the most vigorous public debates within memory, yet when the hubbub had subsided, the public felt less informed than it claimed to have been at the outset. With interest groups issuing highly partisan messages, rival politicians weighing in with inflated rhetoric, experts offering conflicting judgments, and reporters turning their attention increasingly to political infighting and intrigue, the process seemed to mislead and confuse as much as to enlighten.

In criminal trials, where lay juries receive information and arguments in an adversary setting under close judicial supervision, jurors deliberate at length among themselves before making up their minds. The chance to try out ideas, test hypotheses, and listen to the reactions of others is crucial to arriving at a sound collective judgment. In the public arena, such discussions seem no less important. Yet they occur far too infrequently to fill the need, and by some calculations public deliberation about civic concerns has dropped substantially in the past thirty years.[27]

The problem is not merely a lack of opportunity for deliberation. As Nina Eliasoph records in her fascinating book on citizen behavior, different types of people have their own special ways of avoiding serious discussion of political issues.[28] Cynics escape by dwelling upon the foibles and machinations of powerful officials and institutions, while convincing themselves that they have somehow made themselves immune from these malign forces. Community volunteers immerse themselves in practical helping tasks but dismiss as a waste of time any effort to discuss the larger social and political forces that contribute to the human problems they confront. Apathetic citizens feel powerless to affect political outcomes and persuade themselves that social problems are simply individual tales of poverty, unemployment, or homelessness. In their effort to achieve greater harmony and consensus, communitarians often shun discussions about current issues that could be divisive and unpleasant.

How can we break through these tactics of avoidance to engage more Americans in serious public deliberation? Holding meetings will not be enough. Discussions must lead to some tangible action—voting, calling on officials, forming groups to work in schools and neighborhoods—to have enough meaning to bring busy people to participate. Local initiatives need to be clearly related to government policies and then to political involvement in order to convert passive individuals into engaged citizens.

Fortunately, organizations such as the Public Agenda Foundation, America Speaks, and the League of Women Voters are creating new opportunities for deliberation. The Kettering Foundation has set about organizing National Issues Forums to talk about questions of public policy in many locations throughout the country. The Industrial Areas Foundation involves residents of working-class communities in continuing conversations about how to act on local issues that affect their lives. Discussion groups on public affairs have begun to develop on the Internet. There is every reason to encourage all such forms of deliberation to help citizens acquire a deeper understanding of the complexity of policy issues, so that politicians, when they seek constituent opinion, will hear something more than impressions gleaned from casual exposure to a barrage of messages, many of them from biased sources.

Beyond fostering deliberation, the government can work in a variety of ways to induce more citizens to vote and to engage in the political process. Amending campaign finance laws would be one important step toward this objective. By reducing the influence of money on government, such a reform could diminish the cynicism and sense of powerlessness that many Americans feel today. At the same time, as better ways of funding campaigns make it easier for good candidates to run, there should be fewer of the lopsided or uncontested elections that rob citizens of a meaningful choice and diminish their incentive to vote.

Governments could take other important steps to increase voter turnout. Either they could assume responsibility for registering voters, as other advanced democracies do, or they could follow Minnesota's lead by providing for same-day registration. Similarly, officials at all levels could find ways to make it simpler for citizens to vote, either by mail or electronically. Through such steps, parties and candidates might find it profitable to invest more money encouraging people to go to the polls, instead of continuing to concentrate their resources on persuading small groups of likely voters who are undecided.

In order to develop a more informed, deliberative, active citizenry, it will not suffice to adopt only one or two of the measures just described. In isolation, none of these steps has much chance of making a lasting difference. Emphasizing civic education in the schools will accomplish little if it receives no reinforcement in college and in adult life, just as attempts to attract larger audiences to public-affairs programming may come to naught without making greater efforts to prepare active citizens in our schools and colleges. Each of the measures fortifies the rest and gains strength from the others in turn. Thus, success ultimately depends on a recognition by Americans everywhere that civic engagement in the United States is weak and growing weaker, and that our government and our democracy cannot prosper without a comprehensive effort to build a stronger sense of citizenship throughout the population.

Prospects for Renewal

Since the need is urgent and the remedies so obvious, one would suppose that the prospects for a rebirth of civic engagement would be bright indeed. After all, building citizenship has been the principal aim of education and the chief preoccupation of democratic communities since the days of ancient Athens. As Pericles declared in his celebrated funeral oration, "We do not say that a man who takes no interest in politics is a man who minds his own business; we say that he has no business here at all."[29]

Today, the importance of government is greater than ever, and the challenge of keeping abreast of public affairs has become exceptionally difficult and demanding. Surely, then, there should be wide support for efforts to reengage Americans in the work of citizenship. Curiously, however, this is not the case. On the contrary, the reaction is often markedly unenthusiastic.

One reason for this tepid response is that important groups in the population stand to gain from widespread public apathy. As conservative activist Paul Weyrich once declared, "I don't want everyone to vote. Our leverage in the election quite candidly goes up as the voting population goes down."[30] Successful politicians of both parties who have prospered under the status quo may see danger in encouraging new groups of citizens with uncertain views to vote and be more active in local politics. Corporate lobbyists may well conclude that they can accomplish more for their clients if citizens are not especially alert and involved in public affairs. Grassroots organizations can expect to wield greater influence if they can rouse their followers to action while the rest of the citizenry stays uninvolved.

In addition to those who oppose greater civic engagement, there are many more who simply feel that low voting rates and declining political participation do not matter very much. The citizens who suffer most from apathy—lower-income Americans, in particular—seem to have given up on politics. Those who are best equipped by education and experience to appreciate the problem tend to be doing quite well under the status quo and seldom feel a vital personal stake in increasing citizen participation. To them, other problems in the world seem much more urgent and important.

Finally, many people who would prefer to have a more active, informed citizenry believe that the goal is simply impossible to achieve. As they see it, Americans are too numerous and diverse, their indifference too great, and the competition for their time and attention too intense to give such a project any realistic chance of success.

The idea that nothing can be done is only the last in a long series of rationalizations put forth over the years to allay concern over the low level of civic involvement in America. As mentioned in earlier chapters, some prominent scholars have asserted that apathy is really a form of contentment; others claim that those who fail to participate are too ignorant or too dangerous to be safely trusted with the vote; still others allege that even citizens who seem apathetic and uninformed are actually keeping watch on elected officials and are managing to use the few scraps of information they possess to arrive at sound collective judgments on public issues.

Of all the rationalizations used, the claim that nothing can be done is the hardest to disprove, since no comprehensive, coordinated effort to develop active citizens has ever been tried. But several items of evidence counsel against dismissing the enterprise out of hand. Low and declining voting rates are not inevitable. Turnout among the working classes and the poor is very high in most advanced democracies and was once very high in the United States, averaging over 70 percent of eligible voters from 1864 to 1900. Even in the years from 1922 to 1942, poor people in several Northern cities voted more heavily than affluent residents.[31]

In the 1990s, citizens with less than a high school education who first went to the polls during the New Deal continued to vote for president at levels in excess of 60 percent. In a few states, such as Minnesota and Montana, voting rates still run above 70 percent in national elections. Even today, one can find low-income communities in major cities that respond to grassroots canvassing and attractive candidates with turnouts well above the national average.

Much survey evidence also exists suggesting that the potential for civic engagement is still robust in the United States. More than 80 percent of young Americans respond affirmatively to the statement, "I want to do something to serve my country," a figure far higher than in other advanced democracies."[32] Participation rates in voluntary associations and volunteer work remain above those of other leading nations, despite the recent fall-off in political involvement.[33] Efforts to encourage community service have had a strongly positive response in many colleges. In the country as a whole, according to a 1997 poll by the Roper Center, 47 percent of Americans assert that they would be more satisfied with their lives "if I felt like I was doing more to make a difference in my community."[34]

At present, the trend toward declining citizenship is self-reinforcing. Cynicism and apathy cause the behavior of government and politicians to deteriorate, leading to further cynicism and apathy. With sufficient effort, however, the process might be reversed. Greater participation in public affairs could help the government function better and thus diminish the hopelessness and alienation that drive so many Americans to shun elections and withdraw from civic life.

One reason for such pessimism about the outlook for civic renewal is the tendency to pose the challenge by asking whether Americans can attain some predetermined level of responsible citizenship.[35] As political theorists describe it, a healthy democracy requires that citizens be conscientious about voting and willing to make at least a reasonable, continuing effort to inform themselves about candidates and issues and to discuss these matters with their family, friends, and co-workers. With these prerequisites defined, the question becomes whether it is realistic to imagine an America in which all or even a large majority of citizens would behave in such a fashion.

Viewed in this way, the prospects for achieving a healthier democracy seem bleak. Fortunately, however, we need not achieve total success in order to make the enterprise worthwhile. Even modest gains would make a significant difference. If voter turnout in primary elections doubled from 20 to 40 percent, highly organized special-interest groups would find it much harder to nominate candidates who are not genuinely representative of party members as a whole. If a larger percentage of voters joined public-interest groups and began paying closer attention to issues before the Congress, powerful lobbyists would have a more difficult time obtaining special favors. If the poor could vote at rates approximating the national average, as they do in other advanced democracies, they could make their voices heard much more clearly by lawmakers at all levels of government. If fewer Americans were so misinformed as to believe that more than half of all welfare recipients are black, or that foreign aid is one of the largest items in the federal budget, or that toxic wastes are our greatest environmental threat, the odds of enacting more enlightened legislation would improve. Moreover, as several scholars have pointed out, the votes of the ignorant and uninformed often cancel out, leaving a decisive role to the minority of voters who take the trouble to educate themselves about the issues. If larger numbers of poor and working-class citizens paid closer attention to ballot initiatives and election campaigns, the critical group of knowledgeable voters might be more representative of the entire society, making the results less dependent on the views of a highly educated, rather atypical minority.

The ultimate reason for seeking to encourage citizens to become more interested and involved is simply that their role is too important to let the current apathy continue to spread without a determined effort to overcome it. To be sure, an active citizenry cannot do everything needed to overcome the most important weaknesses of American government. Citizen involvement will not do away with the difficulty Congress has in reconciling conflicting interests and combining them into well-designed legislation (although it can help prevent some of the concessions to powerful lobbying groups, the excessive partisanship, and the neglect of important interests that mar so much current legislation). Grassroots organization will likewise not eliminate the contentiousness that so often accompanies federal regulation (although it may facilitate collaborative efforts with industry to replace the traditional command-and-control methods that cause so much friction, delay, and ineffectiveness). Even granting that greater citizen participation is not a panacea, however, it does appear to be essential for addressing a surprising number of the problems that trouble Americans most about government and politics.

Until the public is more active in behalf of campaign finance reform, Congress is unlikely to make any substantial change. If the poorest and weakest segments of the population do not trouble to inform themselves and participate in the political process, lawmakers will rarely make adequate provision for their vital interests. Unless middle-of-the-road Americans vote in greater numbers, they will perpetuate the partisanship and polarization that have come to hamper so much of the government's work. Until readers and viewers become more interested in substance and less attracted to conflict, personality, scandal, and human folly, no amount of exhortation by intellectuals, public figures, or even journalists themselves will move the quality of reporting to a higher level or shift political campaigning from attack ads to discussions of substance. As long as citizens are uninvolved in their schools and neighborhoods, even the most skillfully devised reforms will often yield disappointing results in improving student performance, lowering crime rates, or stemming the deterioration of public housing projects.

Today, democracy in America finds itself at a critical juncture. Voters are acquiring more and more influence while paying less and less attention to public affairs. This is a trend that bodes no good for the country. Most of the things Americans like least about politics and government are linked to current patterns of public apathy and alienation. Conversely, few of the reforms that would help make government function better will come about without more active and informed citizen participation. In the end, therefore, people do get the quality of government they deserve. No easy remedies or institutional fixes will cure our discontents as long as so many citizens look upon the State merely as an entity to supply them with services in return for paying taxes. Democracy is a collective venture which falters or flourishes depending on the efforts citizens invest in its behalf. Until Americans acknowledge this fact and act accordingly, they are unlikely to get the kind of government they want or see their country achieve many of the goals to which they claim to aspire.

NOTES

INDEX

NOTES

Introduction

1 "American Public Opinion in the 1990s," *Public Perspective,* 9 (February–March 1998): 84.
2 Pew Research Center for the People and the Press, *Deconstructing Distrust: How Americans View Government* (1998), p. 115.
3 William G. Mayer, *The Changing American Mind: How and Why American Public Opinion Changed between 1960 and 1988* (1992), p. 343.
4 John R. Hibbing and Elizabeth Theiss-Morss, *Congress as Public Enemy: Public Attitudes toward American Public Institutions* (1995), p. 45.
5 "Confidence in Institutions," *Gallup Poll Monthly* (April 1994): 5–6.
6 Pew Research Center, *Deconstructing Distrust,* p. 31; Paul Light, *The True Size of Government* (1999), p. 49.
7 Derek Bok, *The State of the Nation: Government and the Quest for a Better Society* (1996), p. 6.
8 Thomas E. Mann and Norman J. Ornstein (eds.), *Congress, the Press, and the Public* (1994), p. 50.
9 Hibbing and Theiss-Morss, *Congress as Public Enemy,* p. 63.
10 Pew Research Center, *Deconstructing Distrust,* p. 100.
11 Ibid., p. 123.
12 Karl Zinmeister, "Indicators," *American Enterprise* (March–April 1995), p. 16.

13 Everett C. Ladd and Karlyn H. Bowman, *What's Wrong: A Survey of American Satisfaction and Complaint* (1998), p. 103; Seymour Martin Lipset and William Schneider, *The Confidence Gap: Business, Labor and Government in the Public Mind* (1983), p. 304.

14 Adam Clymer, "The Body Politic: Nonvoting Americans and Calls for Reform Are Drawn into Sharp Focus in 2000 Races," *New York Times* (January 2, 2000): 1, 20.

15 Mann and Ornstein, *Congress, the Press and the Public*, p. 159.

16 William Greider, *Who Will Tell the People? The Betrayal of American Democracy* (1992).

17 E. J. Dionne, Jr., *Why Americans Hate Politics* (1991).

18 George F. Will, *Restoration: Congress, Term Limits, and the Recovery of Deliberative Democracy* (1992); Alan Ehrenhalt, *The United States of Ambition: Politicians, Power, and the Pursuit of Office* (1991).

19 Jonathan Rauch, *Demosclerosis: The Silent Killer of American Government* (1994).

20 David S. Broder, *The Party's Over: The Failure of Politics in America* (1972).

21 Hedrick Smith, *The Power Game: How Washington Works* (1988).

22 Pew Research Center for the People and the Press, "Washington Leaders Wary of Public Opinion" (April 17, 1998), p. 16.

23 The opinions of legislators here and in the following paragraph are based on interviews by the author with a number of members of the House and Senate, conducted in the fall of 1995.

24 Alan D. Monroe, "Consistency between Policy Preferences and National Policy Decisions," *American Politics Quarterly,* 7 (1989): 3; idem, "Public Opinion and Public Policy, 1980–1993," *Public Opinion Quarterly,* 62 (1998): 6.

25 See, e.g., Janet M. Grenzky, "Shopping in the Congressional Supermarket: The Currency Is Complex," *American Journal of Political Science,* 33 (1989): 1.

26 David R. Mayhew, *Divided We Govern: Party Control, Lawmaking, and Investigations, 1946–1990* (1991).

27 Hans-Dieter Klingemann, Richard L. Hofferbert, and Ian Budge, *Parties, Policies, and Democracy* (1994), p. 153.

28 "The Text of President Clinton's State of the Union Address to Congress," *New York Times* (January 28, 2000): A16.

29 For a valuable and more extended treatment of this theme, see Christopher Beem, *The Necessity of Politics: Reclaiming American Public Life* (1999).

30 The quote from Justice Brandeis appears in *Olmstead v. United States,* 277 U.S. 438, 485 (1928).

1. Is America on the Wrong Track?

1 Everett C. Ladd and Karlyn H. Bowman, *What's Wrong: A Survey of American Satisfaction and Complaint* (1998), p. 19.

2 "American Public Opinion in the 1990s," *Public Perspective* (February–March 1997): 32.

3 *Public Perspective* (February–March 1998): 12.

4 Derek Bok, *The State of the Nation: Government and the Quest for a Better Society* (1996).

5 Mark Miringoff and Marque-Luisa Miringoff, *The Social Health of the Nation: How America Is Really Doing* (1999), pp. 82, 93, 99.

6 "Text of the President's State of the Union Address to Congress," *New York Times* (January 28, 2000): A16.

7 Lawrence Mishel, Jared Bernstein, and John Schmitt, *The State of Working America, 1998–99* (1999), pp. 11, 355. There appears to be a difference of opinion on how America's productivity stands *vis-à-vis* that of other nations. Mishel, Bernstein, and Schmitt claim that America has been overtaken by France and Germany (p. 359). But the McKinsey Global Institute, in *Manufacturing Productivity* (1993) and *Service Sector Productivity* (1994), has concluded that America still retains a substantial lead.

8 Mishel et al., *The State of Working America*, p. 380.

9 Sue Schellenbarger, "Work and Family," *Wall Street Journal* (June 26, 1996): B1.

10 Times-Mirror Center for the People and the Press, *The New Political Landscape* (1994), p. 52.

11 See, e.g., Robert Erikson and John H. Goldthorpe, "Are American Rates of Social Mobility Exceptionally High? New Evidence on an Old Issue," *European Sociological Review*, 1 (1985): 1.

12 See Mishel, et al., *The State of Working America*, p. 309.

13 Bok, *The State of the Nation*, ch. 8.

14 Ibid., ch. 3.

15 Ibid., ch. 4.

16 Ibid., ch. 11.

17 Ibid., ch. 12.

18 Ibid., ch. 13.

19 Ibid., ch. 14.

20 Ibid., ch. 17.

21 Miringoff and Miringoff, *The Social Health of the Nation,* p. 139.

22 Commonwealth Fund, *Can't Afford to Get Sick: A Reality for Millions of Working Americans* (1999), p. 6.

23 U.S. Department of Agriculture, *Household Food Security in the United States in 1995: Summary Report of the Food Security and Measurement Project* (1997), ch. 5.

24 Quoted in Bob Herbert, "Senior Citizens on the Bread Line," *New York Times, Week in Review* (April 11, 1999): 17.

25 Bok, *The State of the Nation,* ch. 6, p. 122. See also, e.g., Detlef John, "Environmental Performance and Policy Regimes: Explaining Variations in Eighteen OECD Countries," *Policy Sciences,* 31 (1998): 107.

26 Quoted in Neil R. Pierce, *Citistates: How Urban America Can Prosper in a Competitive World* (1993), p. 300.

27 The counterarguments are discussed in greater detail in Bok, *The State of the Nation,* ch. 19.

28 A. B. Atkinson, *The Economic Consequences of Rolling Back the Welfare State* (1999), p. 184. See also Robert E. Goodin, Brude Headey, Ruud Muffels, and Henk-Jan Dirven, *The Real Worlds of Welfare Capitalism* (1999); and Robert M. Solow, "Welfare: The Cheapest Country," *New York Review of Books* (March 23, 2000): 20, 22.

29 McKinsey Global Institute, *Manufacturing Productivity* (1993), Executive Summary; McKinsey Global Institute, *Service Sector Productivity,* Introduction and Summary, p. 3, ch. 4, p. 7 (1992).

30 See, e.g., Atkinson, *The Economic Consequences of Rolling Back the Welfare State*; Paul Pierson, "Irresistible Forces, Immovable Objects: Post-Industrial Welfare States Confront Permanent Austerity," *Journal of European Public Policy,* 5 (1998): 539.

31 Pew Research Center for the People and the Press, *Deconstructing Distrust: How Americans View Government* (1998), pp. 95–96.

2. The Role of Government

1 Everett C. Ladd and Karlyn H. Bowman, *What's Wrong: A Survey of American Satisfaction and Complaint* (1998), p. 76.

2 Ibid., p. 43.

3 Hart-Teeter, "Findings from a Research Project about Attitudes toward Government," survey conducted for the Council for Excellence in Government (Washington, D.C., March 1997), available on the World-Wide Web at [http://www.excel.gov].

4 David Broder, "Amid Economic Gains, a Fear of Lost Values," *International Herald Tribune* (July 1, 1999): 7.

5 See, generally, Derek Bok, *The State of the Nation: Government and the Quest for a Better Society* (1996).

6 McKinsey Global Institute, *Manufacturing Productivity* (1993), Executive Summary; McKinsey Global Institute, *Service Sector Productivity*, Introduction and Summary (1992), p. 3, ch. 4, p. 7.

7 Printed in Jean-Jacques Rousseau, *Politics and the Arts: Letter to d'Alembert on the Theatre*, ed. Allan Bloom (1960), p. 148.

8 There are other ways of assessing a government's performance. Some scholars have proceeded by asking how well the government is living up to the various criteria that are said to define a healthy democracy. For example, Nelson Polsby speaks of "seven institutional characteristics, which can be used as a baseline for gauging contemporary American governmental performance." (Alan Brinkley, Nelson W. Polsby, and Kathleen Sullivan, *New Federalist Papers: Essays in Defense of the Constitution* [1997], p. 161.) These characteristics include keeping policymaking in the hands of popularly elected officials; maintaining universal suffrage; avoiding arbitrary restrictions on the right of citizens to run for office; conducting free and fair elections; upholding freedom of speech, especially in matters of politics and public affairs; maintaining a variety of channels of communication; and preserving the freedom of citizens to associate as they choose.

By these standards, government in the United States is functioning very well, and that is no small achievement. But the standards Polsby uses measure how closely the institutions of government conform to democratic criteria, not how well they are succeeding in moving the country toward the goals most cherished by its people. A government can live up to all of Polsby's criteria but still not perform effectively in meeting the needs of its people. Elected officials may control policy but not be especially competent or enlightened. Everyone may be free to vote, but large numbers may refrain from doing so, with the result that their interests are not well represented. Citizens may speak and associate freely, but even if they have something important to say, they may lack the resources to make their voices heard. Such qualifications could be multiplied. What they suggest is not that the basic criteria of democracy are unimportant or poorly conceived—only that they are not sufficient to ensure that the government is doing an effective job of helping the people fulfill their aspirations.

Another way to judge a government, suggested by Kent Weaver and Bert Rockman (*Do Institutions Matter?* [1993]), is to consider how well it compares with other countries in its capacity to deal with fundamental challenges, such as setting priorities, targeting resources, making innovations, managing social and political cleavages, and implementing the laws. The assumption is that governments that compare well in carrying out all or most of these tasks must be performing effectively.

Such an analysis comes closer to measuring effectiveness, but it too has limitations. The effectiveness of a government is influenced by a host of forces and circumstances peculiar to each situation it faces. As a result, one cannot generalize about a nation's capabilities without considering many different cases, each requiring analysis of a large body of facts. Even after conducting such an elaborate inquiry, one may still arrive at inconclusive results, if the method employed does not specify how success can most appropriately be judged or how the government's role can be isolated from the many other factors that bear on complex social outcomes. Moreover, knowing a government's principal strengths and weaknesses does not necessarily reveal how effective it will be in meeting the needs of its people. There are so many qualities a government needs to have that efforts to evaluate it by assessing its "key capabilities" in a few sample situations are bound to be incomplete. Thus, it is possible that a government will respond well in a predetermined list of case studies, but still fail to achieve a variety of goals that matter to a majority of citizens.

9 "President Reagan's Inaugural Address," *New York Times* (January 21, 1981): B-1.
10 *New York Times* (January 24, 1996): A-10.
11 It should be noted that Mr. Reagan also stated in his inaugural address: "It is not my intention to do away with government. It is, rather, to make it work." "President Reagan's Inaugural Address," *New York Times* (January 21, 1981).
12 Ladd and Bowman, *What's Wrong*, p. 75.
13 Albert H. and Susan D. Cantril, *Reading Mixed Signals: Ambivalence in American Public Opinion about Government* (1999), p. 14.

Part II

1 President Clinton, Speech to Congress, September 22, 1993, reprinted in Erik Eckholm (ed.), *Solving America's Health Care Crisis* (1993), pp. 301–314.
2 Quoted in Theda Skocpol, *Boomerang: Clinton's Health Security Effort and the Turn against Government in U.S. Politics* (1996), p. 5.

3 Robert J. Blendon et al., "The Beliefs and Values Shaping Today's Health Reform Debate," *Health Affairs,* 13 (1994): 274.

4 See Daniel Yankelovich, "The Debate That Wasn't: The Public and the Clinton Health Plan," in Henry J. Aaron (ed.), *The Problem That Won't Go Away: Reforming U.S. Health Care Financing* (1996).

5 Tom Hamburger, Theodore Marmor, and Jon Meacham, "What the Death of Reform Teaches Us about the Press," *Washington Monthly* (November 1994); Kathleen Hall Jamieson and Joseph Cappella, "Newspaper and Television Coverage of the Health Care Reform Debate," Paper for the Annenberg Public Policy Center, Philadelphia, Pa. (1994).

3. The Usual Suspects

1 David S. Broder, "Where Did Our Government Go? Politicians, Special Interests and the Media Get the Blame for Disconnecting the People," *Washington Post,* National Weekly Edition (July 19–26, 1999): 37.

2 Post Modernity Project, University of Virginia, *The State of Disunion: 1996 Survey of American Political Culture,* Executive Summary (1996), pp. 5–6; "Americans Rate Their Society and Chart Its Values," *Public Perspective,* 8 (February–March 1997): 36.

3 Roper Center for Public Opinion Research, University of Connecticut at Storrs, *Roper Organization Poll, 1992.*

4 See, generally, Gary Wills, *Certain Trumpets: The Call of Leaders* (1994); Bruce Miroff, *Icons of Democracy* (1993).

5 Alexis de Tocqueville, *Democracy in America* (rpt. 1948; original French ed., 1835), vol. 1, p. 204.

6 See Allan G. Bogue et al., "Members of the House of Representatives and the Processes of Modernization, 1789–1960," *Journal of American History,* 63 (1976): 275.

7 Allen D. Hertzke and Ronald M. Peters, Jr., *The Atomistic Congress: An Interpretation of Congressional Changes* (1992), p. 38.

8 Adam Clymer, "The Body Politic: Nonvoting Americans and Calls for Reform Are Drawn into Sharp Focus in 2000 Races," *New York Times* (January 2, 2000): 1, 20.

9 See Linda Fowler, *Candidates, Congress and the American Democracy* (1993), p. 106.

10 This supposition is borne out by experience in "open" congressional races in which no incumbent is seeking reelection. In such elections, the proportion of candidates with political experience is considerably

higher, especially in districts where both parties have a reasonable chance of winning. Gary Jacobson, *The Politics of Congressional Elections,* 3rd ed. (1992), p. 5.

11 Ibid., p. 91.

12 A 1998 poll revealed that 49 percent of members of Congress were dissatisfied with their ability to attend to their personal life, while 42 percent were satisfied. Pew Research Center for the People and the Press, *Washington Leaders Wary of Public Opinion* (1998), p. 15.

13 Ibid., p. 8.

14 Ibid., p. 14.

15 This assessment has been made to me privately by several current and past members of Congress, from both parties. The point is echoed by Warren B. Rudman, *Combat: Twelve Years in the U.S. Senate* (1996), p. 254.

16 Although more than a few members of Congress worry that the quality of new members has begun to decline, this view is not universally shared. According to the author of a recent study: "We saw . . . little evidence that ambition for a House seat is diminishing. . . . The personal costs of running—family sacrifices, occupational tradeoffs, hard-fought and expensive campaigns—seem not to be driving a large number of potential candidates out of the electoral arena." Thomas A. Kazee, *Who Runs for Congress: Ambition, Context, and Candidate Emergence* (1994), p. 180.

17 This theme is developed in great detail in Alan Ehrenhalt, *The United States of Ambition: Politicians, Power, and the Pursuit of Office* (1991). See also Burdett Loomis, *The New American Politician: Ambition, Entrepreneurship and the Changing Face of Political Life* (1988).

18 At times, the link between political and advertising campaigns becomes explicit. In anticipation of the 2000 presidential campaign, for example, Republican candidate Steve Forbes hired an advertising executive, William Eisner, to craft a multi-million-dollar TV effort to "spruce up" his image. In Mr. Eisner's words, "We're trying to resuscitate brands all the time that lost their luster with customers. We're doing the same with Steve." Richard L. Berke, "Fitting Forbes for Oval Office Is Advertising Man's Assignment," *New York Times* (May 30, 1999): 1.

19 John Bartlett., *Bartlett's Familiar Quotations,* 16th ed., ed. Justin Kaplan (1992), p. 343.

20 Paul Leicester Ford (ed.), *The Writings of Thomas Jefferson,* 10 vols. (1892–1899), vol. 10, p. 90.

21 Ibid., vol. 9, pp. 451–452.

22 Harwood Group, *Journalism Credibility: Landscape Report,* Report prepared for the American Society of Newspaper Editors (1998), p. 3.

23 E.g., David S. Broder, "A New Assignment for the Press," Lecture delivered at University of California, Riverside, February 12, 1991; James Fallows, *Breaking the News: How the Media Undermine American Democracy* (1996).

24 See Norman R. Luttbeg and Michael M. Gant, *American Electoral Behavior, 1952–1992,* 2nd ed. (1992), pp. 48–59; Martin P. Wattenberg, *The Decline of American Political Parties, 1952–1992* (1994), especially p. 19.

25 See, e.g., Robert Lichter, "Consistently Liberal: But Does It Matter?" *Mediacritic* (1996): 26.

26 See, e.g., Doris Graber, *Mass Media and American Politics,* 5th ed. (1997), p. 263. At the same time, researchers have found that TV can affect how viewers evaluate news stories by the way the stories are presented. For example, airing a report as the lead story increases the subject's importance in the minds of many viewers. Moreover, presenting a story about poverty by presenting facts and statistics will tend to cause viewers to think of the problem as a product of economic forces, while presenting the same story by showing the plight of particular families will lead many viewers to conceive of poverty primarily as a matter of personal responsibility. See, e.g., Shanto Iyengar, "Framing Responsibility for Political Issues," *Annals of the American Academy of Political and Social Science* (July 1990): 59; more generally, see Stephan Ansolabehere, Roy Behr, and Shanto Iyengar, *The Media Game: American Politics in the Television Age* (1993). Effects of this kind seem inevitable under any conceivable system of presenting the news. Unless there were evidence that the media deliberately chose lead stories and framed their presentations to manipulate the public in particular ways, there is no apparent reason for being alarmed about these findings.

27 See Ben Bagdikian, *The Media Monopoly,* 3rd ed. (1990); Leo Bogart, *Commercial Culture: The Media System and the Public Interest* (1995).

28 Thomas Patterson, *Out of Order* (1993).

29 Ibid., p. 20.

30 Ibid.

31 S. Robert Lichter and Daniel R. Amundson, "Less News Is Worse News: Television News Coverage of Congress, 1972–1992," in Thomas E. Mann and Norman J. Ornstein (eds.), *Congress, the Press and the Public* (1994), pp. 131, 137.

32 Joseph N. Cappella and Kathleen H. Jamieson, "News Frames, Political Cynicism, and Media Cynicism," *Annals of the American Academy of Political and Social Science* (July 1996): 71.

33 This discussion is based in part on the work of Steven Voss, who studied correlations between readership (or viewership) and answers to questions in the same opinion poll measuring distrust or lack of confidence in government. To the same effect, see John R. Hibbing and Elizabeth Theiss-Morse, "The Media's Role in Public Negativity toward Congress: Distinguishing Emotional Responses and Cognitive Evaluations," *American Journal of Political Science,* 42 (1998): 475. Even Cappella and Jamieson, who have done the most to establish a link between cynicism and the media, admit: "We do not believe that the news media are the only or even the primary source of public cynicism about institutions." "News Frames, Political Cynicism, and Media Cynicism," p. 71. See, generally, Pippa Norris, *A Virtuous Circle* (2000).

34 See, e.g., Kenneth Auletta, *Three Blind Mice: How the TV Networks Lost Their Way* (1991).

35 See John H. McManus, *Market-Driven Journalism: Let the Buyer Beware* (1994), p. 2.

36 Ibid., p. 187.

37 One researcher studied fifty-seven stations in nineteen different markets and found that the amount of time allotted to covering murders did not change in accordance with the incidence of murder, nor did the emphasis on rape vary with the number of rapes. Rather, violent crime appeared to be used as a marketing device to appeal to younger, especially male audiences. James T. Hamilton, *Channeling Violence: The Economic Market for Violent Television Programming* (1998).

38 Doug Underwood, *When MBAs Rule the Newsroom: How the Marketers and Managers Are Reshaping Today's Media* (1993), p. 20.

39 Ibid., p. 19.

40 Harwood Group, *Journalism Credibility,* p. 9.

41 Ibid.

42 *Boston Globe* (June 22, 1997): A-25.

43 Two-thirds of all reporters claim that they are free to write as they choose, but the numbers have been dropping for some time. David H. Weaver and G. Cleveland Wilhoit, *The American Journalist: A Portrait of U.S. News People and Their Work,* 2nd ed. (1991), p. 75.

44 James D. Squires, *Read All About It: The Corporate Takeover of America's Newspapers* (1993), p. 216.

45 McManus, *Market-Driven Journalism,* p. 3.

46 Judith Valente, "Do You Believe What Newspeople Tell You?" *Parade Magazine, Boston Sunday Globe* (March 2, 1997): 4.

47 William P. Welch, "Campaign Contributions and Dairy Price Supports," *Western Political Quarterly,* 35 (1982): 478; John C. Wright, "PACs, Contributions, and Roll Calls: An Organizational Perspective," *American Political Science Review,* 79 (1985): 400. For a different (journalistic) view, see Philip M. Stern, *The Best Congress Money Can Buy* (1988).

48 See, e.g., Marie Hojnack and David C. Kimball, "Organized Interests and the Decision of Whom to Lobby," *American Political Science Review,* 92 (1998): 775.

49 E.g., Janet M. Grenzke, "Shopping in the Congressional Supermarket: The Currency Is Complex," *American Journal of Political Science,* 33 (1989): 1. Still other investigators have studied the voting records of lawmakers *after* they have announced their intention to retire permanently from Congress. If campaign contributions truly made an important difference, one might expect retiring legislators to change their voting patterns, at least to some degree, once they no longer needed to collect money for another election campaign. Yet the evidence shows that lawmakers continue to cast their votes exactly as before.

50 E.g., Wright, "PACs, Contributions, and Roll Calls:," p. 400.

51 Richard A. Smith, "Interest Group Influence in the U.S. Congress," *Legislative Studies Quarterly,* 20 (1995): 89.

52 Richard L. Hall and Frank W. Wayman, "Buying Time: Moneyed Interests and the Mobilization of Bias in Congressional Committees," *American Political Science Review,* 84 (1990): 727.

53 Gary C. Jacobson, "The Misallocation of Resources in House Campaigns," in Lawrence C. Dodd and Bruce I. Oppenheimer (eds.), *Congress Reconsidered,* 5th ed. (1993), p. 123.

54 Leslie Wayne, "If No Guarantee of Victory, Money Sure Makes It Easier," *New York Times* (November 6, 1998): A23.

55 James Q. Wilson, *American Government: Institutions and Policies,* 5th ed. (1992), p. 277.

56 "Hard Figures about Soft Money," *Boston Globe* (June 9, 1998): 45.

57 See, e.g., Raymond L. Hoewing, "Why Grassroots," in Wesley Pedersen (ed.), *Winning at the Grassroots: How to Succeed in the Legislative Arena by Mobilizing Employees and Other Allies* (1989), p. 3. Grassroots lobbying is not new. More than seventy-five years ago, the Anti-Saloon League reportedly built a mailing list of more than

500,000 supporters at a time when the country was far less populous than it is today.

58 Ken Kollman, *Outside Lobbying: Public Opinion and Interest Group Strategies* (1998), p. 155.

59 John F. Persinos, "Has the Christian Right Taken Over the Republican Party?" *Campaigns and Elections* (September 1994): 22. See also Mark J. Rozell and Clyde Wilcox (eds.), *God at the Grassroots: The Christian Right in the 1994 Elections* (1995); and Justin Watson, *The Christian Coalition: Dreams of Restoration, Demands for Recognition* (1997).

60 Haynes Johnson and David S. Broder, *The System: The American Way of Politics at the Breaking Point* (1996), p. 224.

61 See Burdett Loomis, *The Contemporary Congress* (1988), p. 35.

62 Quoted in Peter Levine, *The New Progressive Era: Toward a Fair and Deliberative Democracy* (2000), p. 117.

63 Jeffrey M. Berry, *The New Liberalism: The Rising Power of Citizens Groups* (1999).

64 See Jeffrey M. Berry, "The Rise of Citizen Groups," in Theda Skocpol and Morris P. Fiorina (eds.), *Civic Engagement in American Democracy* (1999), p. 367.

65 Ibid., pp. 120–127. The growth of so many new advocacy groups seems to have weakened the influence of the more traditional private-sector lobbies over the past thirty years. Surveys of high-level civil servants show that the proportion who believe that interest groups wield "a great deal of influence" declined from 33 percent in 1970 to only 14 percent in 1986–1987. Lobbyists for business groups report surprisingly modest results in some surveys, with representatives of citizens and nonprofit groups claiming higher rates of success than their counterparts from for-profit organizations. Paul S. Herrnson, Ronald G. Shaiko, and Clyde Wilcox, *The Interest Group Connection: Electioneering, Lobbying and Policymaking in Washington* (1988), pp. 150–151. Jeffrey Berry made his own calculation of legislative victories and concluded that business and professional groups still enjoyed the highest rates of success, but that their margin over citizen advocacy groups had narrowed greatly since the 1960s. Ibid., p. 85.

66 Quoted in Jack L. Walker, Jr., *Mobilizing Interest Groups in America: Patrons, Professions, and Social Movements* (1991), p. 2.

67 Jonathan Rauch, *Demosclerosis: The Silent Killer of American Government* (1994), p. 148. Rauch's analysis draws heavily on Mancur Olson, *The Rise and Decline of Nations: Economic Growth, Stagflation, and Social Rigidities* (1982).

68 Walker, *Mobilizing Interest Groups in America.*

69 Sidney Verba, Kay L. Schlozman, and Henry E. Brady, *Voice and Equality: Civic Voluntarism in American Politics* (1995), p. 190.

70 Lester M. Salamon, *America's Nonprofit Sector: A Primer,* 2nd ed. (1999), p. 137.

71 E.g., Raymond Bauer et al., *American Business and Public Policy* (1963); John P. Heinz et al., *The Hollow Core: Private Interests in National Policy Making* (1993).

72 Gary Mucciaroni, *Reversals of Fortune: Public Policy and Private Interests* (1995).

73 Ibid., p. 181.

74 See, e.g., Clive Thomas, *First World Interest Groups: A Comparative Perspective* (1993), p. 48.

4. What Do We Need to Explain?

1 Ronald Brickman, Sheila Jasanoff, and Thomas Ilgen, *Controlling Chemicals: The Politics of Regulation in Europe and the United States* (1985), p. 72.

2 James Day, *The Vanishing Vision: The Inside Story of Public Television* (1995), p. 5.

3 Ibid., p. 355.

4 E.g., National Commission on the Environment, *Choosing a Sustainable Future* (1993), p. 53. For similar comments on the Food and Drug Administration, see Peter B. Hutt, "Philosophy of Regulation under the Federal Food, Drug, and Cosmetic Administration," *Food and Drug Law Journal,* 50 (1995): 101, 103.

5 Carnegie Task Force on Meeting the Needs of Young Children, *Starting Points: Meeting the Needs of Our Youngest Children* (1994), p. 66.

6 Derek Bok, *The State of the Nation: Government and the Quest for a Better Society* (1996), ch. 12.

7 Tammy Tengs and John D. Graham, "The Opportunity Costs of Haphazard Societal Investments in Life-Saving," in Robert H. Hahn (ed.), *Risk Management: From Theory to Practice* (1997), p. 167.

8 Pew Research Center for the People and the Press, *Deconstructing Distrust: How Americans View Government* (1998), p. 124; idem, *Retro-Politics* (1999), p. 140; Everett C. Ladd and Karlyn H. Bowman, *What's Wrong: A Survey of American Satisfaction and Complaint* (1998), p. 101.

9 Benjamin I. Page and Robert Y. Shapiro, *The Rational Public: Fifty Years of Trends in Americans' Policy Preferences* (1992), pp. 143–144.

10 See, e.g., Marver Bernstein, *Regulating Business by Independent Commission* (1955).

11 E.g., Murray Weidenbaum, *Business, Government, and the Public* (1977).

12 Tengs and Graham, "The Opportunity Costs of Haphazard Societal Investments in Life-Saving."

13 Ibid.

14 Thomas O. McGarity and Sidney A. Shapiro, *Workers at Risk: The Failed Promise of the Occupational Safety and Health Administration* (1993).

15 See Bok, *The State of the Nation,* pp. 121–124.

16 Thomas Burke, "On the Rights Track: The Americans with Disabilities Act," in Pietro Nivola (ed.), *Comparative Disadvantages? Social Regulation and the Global Economy* (1997), pp. 242, 280.

17 John D. Graham, *Auto Safety: Assessing America's Performance* (1989); Jerry Mashaw and David C. Harfst, *The Struggle for Auto Safety* (1990).

18 Susan Rose-Ackerman, *Controlling Environmental Policy: The Limits of Public Law in Germany and the United States* (1995).

19 David Vogel, *National Styles and Regulation: Environmental Policy in Great Britain and the United States* (1986), p. 21. See also idem, *Kindred Strangers: The Uneasy Relationship between Politics and Business in America* (1996), pp. 79–80.

20 Robert A. Kagan and Lee Axelrod, *Regulatory Encounters: Multinational Corporations and American Adversarial Legalism* (forthcoming).

21 Bok, *The State of the Nation,* pp. 121–124, 259–260.

22 1988 Gallup Study of Public Knowledge and Opinion Concerning the Labor Movement, quoted in Richard B. Freeman and Joel Rogers, *Who Speaks for Us? Employee Representation in a Non-Union Labor Market,* (1992), exhibit 4.

23 Quoted in Nicholas Lemann, "The New American Consensus: Government Of, By and For the Comfortable," *New York Times Magazine* (November 1, 1998): 41. See also Richard B. Freeman and Joel Rogers, *What Workers Want* (1999), p. 130, showing that large majorities of workers feel they have too little protection against being fired arbitrarily, laid off, or forced into conflicts between job and family responsibilities.

24 Commonwealth Fund, *Can't Afford to Get Sick: A Reality for Millions of Working Americans* (1999), p. 2; Lawrence Mishel, Jared Bernstein,

and John Schmitt, *The State of Working America, 1998–99* (1999), p. 9.

25 Margaret Weir reports that in 1992 only 28.4 percent of family heads who had not completed high school received employer health benefits, whereas 81 percent of heads who had completed college received such benefits. Margaret Weir (ed.), *The Social Divide: Political Parties and the Future of Activist Government* (1998), p. 233.

26 Commonwealth Fund, *Can't Afford to Get Sick,* p. 6.

27 "Millions of Working Americans Can't Afford to Get Sick," *Commonwealth Fund Quarterly* (Fall 1999): 1.

28 Annette Bernhardt et al., *Summary of Findings: Work and Opportunity in the Post-Industrial Labor Market,* Report to the Russell Sage and Rockefeller Foundations (1998), p. 1.

29 Paul Osterman, *Securing Prosperity* (1999), p. 80.

30 Lawrence Mishel et al., *The State of Working America,* p. 239.

31 One writer estimates that up to 1 million workers are fired unjustifiably every year. David I. Levine, *Reinventing the Workplace: How Business and Employees Can Both Win* (1995), p. 9.. Another source places the total number of employees fired unjustifiably each year at 3 million; see William B. Gould IV, "Job Security in the United States: Some Reflections on Unfair Dismissal and Plant Closure Legislation from a Comparative Perspective," *Nebraska Law Review,* 67 (1988): 28, 30–32. Obviously, such estimates must be viewed with caution.

32 See Bok, *The State of the Nation,* pp. 263–267.

33 Ibid., p. 266.

34 Thomas Geoghegan, "Tampering with the Time Clock," *New York Times* (January 24, 1999), section 4, p. 15.

35 See Bok, *The State of the Nation,* ch. 8.

36 U.S. Department of Labor and U.S. Department of Commerce, Commission on the Future of Worker-Management Relations, "Fact-Finding Report" (May 1994), p. 70.

37 Times Mirror Center for the People and the Press, "Voter Anxiety Dividing GOP: Energized Democrats Backing Clinton" (November 14, 1995), p. 94.

38 Pew Research Center for the People and the Press, *Retro-Politics* (1999), p. 133. Many Americans are also concerned about having adequate health care under the insurance plans in which they are enrolled. In 1997, 40 percent "worried a great deal" that they would be denied a necessary medical procedure, and 40 percent were concerned that they would not be able to receive needed specialty care. Stuart H. Altman,

Uwe E. Reinhardt, and David Schactman, *Regulating Managed Care: Theory, Practice, and Future Options* (2000), p. 138.

39 Mishel et al., *The State of Working America*, p. 8.

40 McKinsey Global Institute, *Employment Performance* (1994), ch. 2, p. 15.

41 "The primary conclusion is ... that while the design of social programs affects employer and worker behavior, these programs do not create major inflexibilities in the labor market." Rebecca Blank, "Does a Larger Social Safety Net Mean Less Economic Flexibility?" in Richard Freeman (ed.), *Working under Different Rules* (1994), p. 158. "It seems clear that the broad case against labor market policy is weak": Paul Osterman, *Securing Prosperity* (1999), p. 122; see also p. 187.

42 Roper Center on Public Opinion, "American Public Opinion in the 1990s," *Public Perspective*, 9 (1998): 34.

43 See Linda Bennett and Stephen Bennett, *Living with Leviathan: Americans Coming to Terms with Big Government* (1990), p. 93.

44 Times-Mirror Center for the People and the Press, *The New Political Landscape* (1994), p. 152.

45 See Table 2 in Chapter 1, above.

46 Bok, *State of the Nation*, ch. 8.

47 Ibid., ch. 14.

48 Urban Institute, "Hunger and Food Insecurity among the Elderly," *Policy and Research Report* (Fall 1993): 4–5.

49 See, e.g., Michael B. Katz, *The Undeserving Poor: From the War on Poverty to the War on Welfare* (1989).

50 *Food Stamp Program: A Demographic Analysis of Participation and Nonparticipation*, GAO-PEMD 90-8 (1990).

51 See, e.g., James J. Heckman, "Doing It Right: Job Training and Education," *Public Interest* (Spring 1999): 86, 104.

5. Why Legislation Is Often Badly Designed

1 Henry Aaron and Harvey Galper, *Assessing Tax Reform* (1986), p. 1.

2 Ibid.

3 Sarah A. Binder and Steven S. Smith, *Politics or Principle? Filibustering in the United States Senate* (1997), pp. 9–13.

4 Lawrence C. Dodd and Bruce I. Oppenheimer (eds.), *Congress Reconsidered*, 6th ed. (1997), p. 240.

5 Gary W. Cox and Mathew D. McCubbins, *Legislative Leviathan: Party Government in the House* (1993).

6 See R. Douglas Arnold, "Legislators, Bureaucrats, and Locational Decisions," in Mathew McCubbins and Terry Sullivan (eds.), *Congress:
   Structure and Policy* (1987), p. 523.

7 Eric Uslaner, *The Decline of Comity in Congress* (1993); Steven S.
   Smith, *Call to Order: Floor Politics in the House and Senate* (1989).

8 This statement was made to me personally in November 1995 during
   an interview with the representative in question.

9 Terry Moe, "The Politics of Bureaucratic Structure," in John Chubb
   and Paul E. Peterson, *Can the Government Govern?* (1989).

10 Robert A. Katzman, *Institutional Disability: The Saga of Transportation Policy for the Disabled* (1980).

11 Joseph A. Califano, Jr., *Governing America: An Insider's View from the
   White House and the Cabinet* (1981), p. 259.

12 John J. DiIulio and Donald Kettl, *Fine Print: The Contract with
   America, Devolution and the Realities of American Federalism*
   (1995), p. 18; Richard P. Nathan, *Turning Promises into Performance*
   (1993).

13 See, e.g., Paul E. Peterson, Barry Rabe, and Kenneth Wong, *When Federalism Works* (1986).

14 Office of Public Health, Department of Health, State of New York,
   "Love Canal: Public Health Time Bomb," Special Report to the Governor and Legislature... (September 1978).

15 This report was prepared by Dante Picciano of the Biogenics Corporation for the Office of Research and Development of the Environmental
   Protection Agency, May 1980.

16 State of New York, "Report of the Governor's Panel to Review Scientific Studies and the Development of Public Policy on Problems Resulting from Hazardous Waste" (October 8, 1980).

17 The entire Love Canal controversy is recounted in Adeline G. Levine,
   Love Canal: Science, Politics, and People (1982).

18 Written response of Thomas C. Jorling, Assistant Administrator, Water
   and Waste Management, Environmental Protection Agency (1979),
   quoted in John A. Hird, *Superfund: The Political Economy of Environmental Risk* (1994), pp. 184–185.

19 Ibid., p. 121.

20 Quoted ibid., p. 184.

21 U.S. Senate, Committee on Environment and Public Works, *A Legislative History of the Comprehensive Environmental Response, Compensation, and Liability Act of 1980,* vol. 1, serial. 97-14 (1983), p. 153.

22 U.S. Senate, "Environmental Emergency Response Act, Report of the Committee on Environment and Public Works," Senate Report 96-848 (July 11, 1980), pp. 71–72.

23 Hird, *Superfund,* p. 186.

24 Andrew Lohof, "The Cleanup of Inactive Hazardous Waste Sites in Selected Industrialized Countries," Discussion Paper 069, American Petroleum Institute (August 1991).

25 Thomas W. Church and Robert T. Nakamura, *Cleaning Up the Mess: Implementation Strategies in Superfund* (1993), pp. 7–8.

26 Lloyd S. Dixon, *Fixing Superfund: The Effect of the Proposed Superfund Reform Act of 1994 on Transaction Costs* (1994), p. xvi. For international comparisons, see Lohof, "The Cleanup of Inactive Hazardous Waste Sites."

27 See, e.g., the EPA's own reports: "Reducing Risk: Setting Priorities and Strategies for Environmental Protection" (September 1990); and "Unfinished Business: A Comparative Assessment of Environmental Priorities" (1988).

28 This account draws heavily on. Hird, *Superfund;* and on Marc K. Landy, Marc J. Roberts, and Stephen R. Thomas, *The Environmental Protection Agency: Asking the Wrong Questions, from Nixon to Clinton,* expanded edition (1994), ch. 5, p. 133.

29 E.g., Charles E. Lindblom, *The Intelligence of Democracy* (1965); idem, "The Science of Muddling Through," *Public Administration Review,* 19 (1959): 79.

6. Why Regulation Makes So Many People Angry

1 Philip Howard, *The Death of Common Sense: How Law Is Suffocating America* (1994).

2 Seymour Martin Lipset, *American Exceptionalism: A Double-Edged Sword* (1996), pp. 49–50.

3 Derek Bok, *The State of the Nation: Government and the Quest for a Better Society* (1996), chs. 6 and 13.

4 James T. Hamilton and W. Kip Viscusi, "The Costly Is Clean? An Analysis of the Benefits and Costs of Superfund Remediations," *Journal of Policy Analysis and Management,* 18 (1999): 2.

5 John D. Graham, "Making Sure of Risk: An Agenda for Congress," in Robert W. Hahn (ed.), *Risks, Costs, and Lives Saved: Getting Better Results from Regulation* (1990), p. 183; Tammy Tengs and John D. Graham, "The Opportunity Costs of Haphazard Societal Investments

in Life-Saving," in Robert H. Hahn (ed.), *Risk Management: From Theory to Practice* (1997).

6 See, e.g., Howard Margolis, *Dealing with Risks: Why the Public and the Experts Disagree on Environmental Issues* (1996).

7 This episode is recounted in detail by Bruce T. Ackerman and William T. Hassler, *Clean Coal / Dirty Air* (1981).

8 Hamilton and Viscusi, "The Costly Is Clean?" p. 2.

9 E.g., Robert W. Hahn, *Reviving Regulatory Reform* (1998).

10 These reasons are discussed in great detail by Lisa Heinzerling, "Regulatory Costs of Mythic Proportions," *Yale Law Journal*, 107 (1998): 1981. See also Thomas O. McGarity and Sidney A. Shapiro, "OSHA's Critics and Regulatory Reform," *Wake Forest Law Review*, 33 (1996): 587.

11 See, e.g., John D. Graham, *Auto Safety: Assessing America's Performance* (1989): 232–233.

12 See John Scholz, "Comparative Regulatory Enforcement and the Politics of Administrative Effectiveness," *American Political Science Review*, 85 (1991): 115.

13 Quoted in Eugene Bardach and Robert A. Kagan, *Going by the Book: The Problem of Regulatory Unreasonableness* (1982), p. 44.

14 See Robert A. Kagan, "Adversarial Legalism and American Government," in Marc K. Landy and Martin A. Levin (eds.), *The New Politics of Public Policy* (1995), p. 88.

15 Robert Kagan and Lee Axelrod, "Adversarial Legalism: An International Perspective," in Pietro Nivola (ed.), *Comparative Disadvantages: Social Regulations and the Global Economy* (1997), pp. 146, 167–169.

16 Ronald Brickman, Sheila Jasanoff, and Thomas Ilgen, *Controlling Chemicals: The Politics of Regulation in Europe and the United States* (1985), p. 181.

17 Robert A. Kagan, "Adversarial Legalism and American Government," in Landy and Levin, *The New Politics of Public Policy*.

18 Brickman, Jasanoff, and Ilgen, *Controlling Chemicals*, p. 72.

19 Terry Moe, "The Politics of Bureaucratic Structure," in John Chubb and Paul E. Peterson (eds.), *Can the Government Govern?* (1989), p. 267.

20 Thomas Geoghegan, "Tampering with the Time Clock," *New York Times* (January 24, 1999), section 4, p. 15.

21 Richard Wokutch, *Worker Protection, Japanese Style* (1992); Richard Wokutch and Josette McLaughlin, "The U.S. and Japanese

Work Injury and Illness Experience," *Monthly Labor Review* (April 1992): 3.

22 Bardach and Kagan, *Going by the Book.*

23 Jeremy Rabkin, *Judicial Compulsions: How Public Law Distorts Public Policy* (1989), pp. 228–229.

24 See, e.g., "Occupational Safety and Health: OSHA Action Needed to Improve Compliance with Hazard Communication Standard," GAO/HRD 92-8 (November 1991).

25 Tillinghast-Towers Perrin, *Tort Cost Trends: An International Perspective* (1995).

26 Warren E. Burger, "State of the Judiciary Address to the American Bar Association" (February 1984).

27 Troyen A. Brennan and Donald M. Berwick, *New Rules: Regulation, Markets and the Quality of American Health Care* (1996), p. 341.

28 Bill Brubaker, "NCAA's Academic Eligibility Rules Attacked," *Washington Post* (January 19, 1999): A1, A10.

29 Dan Dutcher, "NCAA Regulation of College Athletics," *Journal of College and University Law,* 22 (1995): 33.

30 Ibid., p. 34.

7. Why Working People and the Poor Do Badly

1 Hubert Humphrey, quoted in Curtis Wilkie, "Another Kinder, Gentler Bush," *Boston Globe* (April 25, 1998): 1.

2 See, e.g., Charles Noble, *Welfare as We Know It: A Political History of the American Welfare State* (1997).

3 Daniel Levine, *Poverty and Society: The Growth of the American Welfare State in International Comparison* (1988); Gaston Rimlinger, *Welfare Policy and Industrialization in Europe, America, and Russia* (1971).

4 See, e.g., Sven Steinmo, "American Exceptionalism Reconsidered: Culture or Institutions," in Lawrence Dodd and Calvin Jillson (eds.), *The Dynamics of American Politics: Approaches and Interpretations* (1994), p. 106.

5 Theda Skocpol, "State Formation and Social Policy in the United States," *American Behavioral Scientist,* 35 (1992): 559.

6 Lynne M. Casper and Loretta E. Bass, "Voting and Registration in Election of November 1996," *Current Population Reports,* P-20-504 (1998): 6.

7 Seymour Martin Lipset, "The Sources of the 'Radical Right' in 1955," in Daniel Bell (ed.), *The Radical Right* (1963), pp. 259, 265.

8 See, e.g., Charles Murray, *What It Means To Be a Libertarian* (1997), p. 14.

9 Robert J. Blendon et al., "The Beliefs and Values Shaping Today's Health Reform Debates," *Health Affairs* (Spring 1994): 274, 276–277.

10 Albert H. Cantril and Susan D. Cantril, *Reading Mixed Signals: Ambivalence in American Public Opinion about Government* (1999), p. 1.

11 Everett C. Ladd and Karlyn H. Bowman, *What's Wrong: A Survey of American Satisfaction and Complaint* (1998), p. 87.

12 See, generally, Paul Osterman, *Securing Prosperity* (1999).

13 Quoted in Julie Kosterlitz, "Beefing Up Food Stamps," *National Journal* (February 17, 1990): 391.

14 "Report of the President's Task Force on Food Assistance" (January 1984), p. 2.

15 Robert Shapiro et al., "The Polls: Public Assistance," *Public Opinion Quarterly*, 51 (1987): 128.

16 Peter K. Eisinger, *Toward an End to Hunger in America* (1998), p. 137.

17 United States Department of Agriculture, *Household Food Security in the United States in 1995: Summary Report of the Food Security and Measurement Project* (1997).

18 Raymond Wolfinger and Steven Rosenstone, *Who Votes?* (1980), pp. 102, 114.

19 Stephen E. Bennett and David Resnick, "The Implications of Nonvoting for Democracy in the United States," *American Journal of Political Science*, 34 (1990): 771.

20 Kim Q. Hill and Jan E. Leighley, "The Policy Consequences of Class Bias in State Electorates," *American Journal of Political Science*, 36 (1992): 351. See, generally, Kim Q. Hill, *Democracy in the Fifty States* (1994).

21 Hill and Leighley, "The Policy Consequences of Class Bias," p. 363.

22 Paul E. Peterson, "An Immodest Proposal," Occasional Paper 92-3 (July 1992), Center for American Political Studies, Harvard University.

23 Quoted in Lisbeth Schorr, *Common Purposes: Strengthening Families and Neighborhoods to Rebuild America* (1997), p. 183.

24 Robert Greenstein, Richard Kogan, and Marion Nichols, "Bearing Most of the Burden: How Deficit Reduction During the 104th Congress Concentrated on Programs for the Poor," Center on Budget and Policy Priorities (December 3, 1996).

25 One can legitimately ask whether many of these cuts resulted not from a lack of political organization, but from a growing public reaction against subsidizing idle mothers who should be able to earn their living.

Without doubt, sentiments of this kind played a role. But Congress did not restrict its welfare cuts to unemployed mothers. Working families earning less than a poverty wage saw their food stamps trimmed by more than $350 per year. Programs for disabled children were heavily reduced. Nutrition programs for youngsters were slashed. If Congress had truly been concerned merely with putting idle women to work, it would presumably have appropriated enough money for childcare, transportation, job training, and other expenses required to ensure the transition from welfare to employment. But the Congressional Budget Office estimated that, over the following six years, the final Welfare Reform Bill fell $12 billion short of providing the money required to help welfare mothers get jobs, and even this estimate did not include the extra funds required to meet the additional childcare needs of working parents. Overall, therefore, the actions of Congress resembled a wholesale effort to cut expenditures for a politically feeble group, rather than a carefully targeted attempt to force indolent mothers to go to work.

26 Fay Lomax Cook and Edith J. Barrett, *Support for the American Welfare State: The Views of Congress and the Public* (1992).

27 Ladd, *The American Ideology,* p. 34.

28 Pew Research Center for the People and the Press, *Deconstructing Distrust: How Americans View Government* (1998), p. 48.

29 Ibid., p. 46.

30 Martin Gilens, "'Race Coding' and White Opposition to Welfare," *American Political Science Review,* 90 (1996): 593.

31 Ibid.

32 Ibid.

33 This statement is based on the work of a Harvard University research assistant, Steve Voss, who analyzed the relationship between answers to questions regarding attitudes toward spending on various programs and answers to questions in the same survey regarding cynicism and distrust toward government.

34 Ladd, *The American Ideology,* p. A22. See also Everett C. Ladd and Karlyn H. Bowman, *What's Wrong: A Survey of American Satisfaction and Complaint* (1998), p. 87.

35 Ladd, *The American Ideology,* p. A27.

36 Ibid., p. A26.

37 E.g., Charles Murray, *Losing Ground* (1984). For a more complex analysis, see Lawrence M. Mead, *The New Politics of Poverty* (1992). See, generally, Steven M. Teles, *Whose Welfare? AFDC and Elite Politics* (1998), especially pp. 60–74.

38 See Nadine Lefraucheur, "French Policies toward Lone Parents: Social Categories and Social Policies," in Katherine McFate, Roger Lawson, and William Julius Wilson (eds.), *Poverty, Inequality and the Future of Social Policy: Western States in the New World Order* (1995), p. 257; Sid Gustaffson, "Single Mothers in Sweden: Why Is Poverty Less Severe?" ibid., p. 291.

39 Teles, *Whose Welfare?*

40 Martin Gilens, *Why Americans Hate Welfare: Race, Media, and the Politics of Anti-Poverty Policy* (1999), p. 187.

41 See David Ellwood, "Welfare Reform as I Knew It," *American Prospect* (May–June 1996): 22.

42 Lawrence Mishel, Jared Bernstein, and John Schmitt, *The State of Working America, 1998–99* (1999), p. 368.

43 Christopher Jencks and Kathryn Edin, "The Real Welfare Problem," *American Prospect* (Spring 1990): 31; Christopher Jencks and Kathryn Edin, "Do Poor Women Have a Right to Bear Children?" *American Prospect* (Winter 1995): 43.

44 Derek Bok, "Emerging Issues in Social Legislation: Social Security," *Harvard Law Review,* 80 (1967): 717.

45 Quoted in Martha Derthick, *Policymaking for Social Security* (1979), p. 186.

46 See, e.g., Peter Peterson, *Facing Up: Paying Our Nation's Debt and Saving Our Children's Future* (1994).

47 See Theda Skocpol, *The Missing Middle: Working Families and the Future of American Social Policy* (2000), p. 27.

48 Gilens, *Why Americans Hate Welfare,* p. 187.

49 Quoted in Schorr, *Common Purpose,* p. 183.

8. Bringing Government Closer to the People

1 See Mark Katches and Daniel Weintraub, "The Tremors of Term Limits," *State Legislatures,* 23 (1997): 21; Stanley M. Caress, "The Impact of Term Limits on Legislative Behavior: An Examination of a Transitional Legislature," *P.S. Political Science and Politics,* 29 (1996): 671.

2 See John R. Alford and John R. Hibbing, "Increased Incumbency in the House of Representatives," *Journal of Politics,* 43 (1981): 1042. There is evidence that long-serving legislators tend to visit their districts less often, apparently because they are more involved with legislative activity. John R. Hibbing, *Congressional Careers: Contours of Life in the U.S. House of Representatives* (1991).

3 Hibbing, *Congressional Careers,* pp. 108ff.

4 E.g., Peter Schrag, "The Populist Road to Hell: Term Limits in California," *American Prospect* (Winter 1996): 24.

5 Ibid., p. 29. Schrag quotes a former state legislator and San Francisco mayor who declared: "No one will be in office long enough to touch the bureaucrats. . . . They tell us . . . 'We be here when you come and we be here after you're gone.'"

6 See Alford and Hibbing, "Increased Incumbency in the House of Representatives," p. 1042.

7 Roper Center, "American Public Opinion in the 1990s," *Public Perspective,* 9 (1998): 45. Apparently, this has been true for some time. See David B. Magleby, *Direct Legislation: Voting on Ballot Initiatives in the United States* (1984), p. 13.

8 John Naisbitt, *Megatrends* (1982), p. 160.

9 E.g., Benjamin Barber, *Strong Democracy: Participatory Politics for a New Age* (1984), pp. 281–289; Ian Budge, *The New Challenge of Direct Democracy* (1996).

10 "Full Democracy Survey: It Means Government by the People, and We Are the People," *Economist* (December 21, 1996): 3.

11 Ibid.

12 See, e.g., study carried out in New York in 1978, described in Thomas E. Cronin, *Direct Democracy: The Politics of Initiative, Referendum and Recall* (1989), pp. 72–73.

13 Albert H. Cantril (ed.), *Polling on the Issues* (1980), p. 170. One reason for this favorable verdict is that voters who do not feel fully informed on the issue tend to be cautious and conservative rather than impulsive in deciding whether to support ballot initiatives. In fact, only 36 percent of all initiatives are passed. Even when citizens are presented with propositions that appeal to their immediate self-interest, they are reluctant to vote in favor. Since it is rarely manifestly silly to stick with the status quo, a citizenry that opposes most of the proposals put before it is unlikely to seem terribly rash or hasty in its judgments.

14 Peter Schrag, *Paradise Lost: California's Experience, America's Future* (1998). For another critical account of ballot initiatives, see David S. Broder, *Democracy Derailed: Initiative Campaigns and the Value of Money* (2000).

15 Michael X. Delli Carpini and Scott Keeter, *What Americans Know about Politics and Why It Matters* (1996); Delli Carpini and Keeter, "Stability and Change in the U.S. Public's Knowledge of Politics," *Public Opinion Quarterly,* 55 (1991): 581.

16 Delli Carpini and Keeter, *What Americans Know about Politics and Why It Matters,* ch. 8.

17 See, generally, David B. Magleby, *Direct Legislation: Voting on Ballot Propositions in the United States* (1984), pp. 139–141, 144.

18 Ibid., p. 134.

19 See, e.g., Shawn Bowler and Todd Donovan, *Demanding Choices: Opinion Voting and Direct Democracy* (1998). See also Elisabeth R. Gerber, *The Populist Paradox: Interest Group Influence and the Promise of Direct Legislation* (2000).

20 Jerry L. Mashaw, *Greed, Chaos and Governance: Using Public Choice to Improve Public Law* (1997), pp. 41–45.

21 Noting these problems, a few commentators have argued that propositions on the ballot should be limited to measures already passed by the legislature. E.g., Ian Budge, "Direct Democracy: Setting Appropriate Terms of Debate," in David Held (ed.), *Prospects for Democracy: North, South, East, West* (1993), p. 136. In this way, citizens will vote only after lawmakers have deliberated and tried to arrive at constructive compromises. At the same time, legislators, knowing that their handiwork may well have to be approved by the voters, will arguably pay closer attention to the wishes of their constituents instead of drafting laws to satisfy the desires of special interests. With these advantages in mind, more than twenty states now permit this type of referendum.

   While this process preserves the deliberative role of the legislature in developing the propositions placed on the ballot, it does not cure the other defects of direct democracy. It does little to heighten the interest of voters; on the contrary, the record shows that even fewer people vote for proposals passed by the legislature than for initiatives placed directly on the ballot by citizen petition. (See David B. Magleby, *Direct Legislation: Voting on Ballot Initiatives in the United States* [1984], pp. 98–99.) Moreover, many laws are far too long and complicated to allow voters to make an informed decision. Who could ever read, let alone understand, measures such as farm bills or the latest Clean Air act, which run to hundreds of pages of mind-numbing text? Money and interest groups will also play an important role in expensive campaigns for or against ballot propositions, whether they take the form of initiatives or referenda. Worst of all, restricting what is on the ballot to laws already passed by the legislature removes one of the greatest advantages of direct democracy: the chance for voters to approve proposals, such as campaign finance reform, that have been bottled up in committee for selfish political reasons. All in all, therefore, efforts to salvage direct democracy by limiting its use in this way do not represent a clear improvement over the ordinary ballot initiative.

22 Magleby, *Direct Legislation*, p. 147.

23 Betty H. Zisk, *Money, Media and the Grassroots: State Ballot Issues and the Electoral Process* (1987).

24 Magleby, *Direct Legislation*, ch. 5; see also David H. Everson, "The Effects of Initiatives on Voter Turnout: A Comparative State Analysis," *Western Political Quarterly*, 34 (1981): 415, 418–419. In another study, Howard D. Hamilton found that turnouts were lower in elections where only initiatives, not candidates, were on the ballot. Hamilton, "Direct Legislation: Some Implications of Open Housing Referenda," *American Political Science Review*, 64 (1970): 126.

25 Magleby, *Direct Legislation*, ch. 6.

26 See James Fishkin, *Democracy and Deliberation: New Directions for Democratic Reform* (1991); Robert A. Dahl, *Democracy and Its Critics* (1989), pp. 338–341.

27 See, e.g., the comments of scientist M. Granger Morton in Adam M. Finkel and Dominic Golding (eds.), *Worst Things First? The Debate over National Environmental Priorities* (1994), p. 143.

28 James L. Sundquist, *Back to Gridlock? Governance in the Clinton Years* (1995), p. 99, reporting polls showing that 75 percent of the public favors giving the states more power over programs administered at the federal level.

29 Alice Rivlin, *Revising the American Dream: The Economy, the States, and the Federal Government* (1992), p. 9.

30 Ibid., p. 118.

31 Quoted in Theda Skocpol, "The Tocqueville Problem: Civic Engagement in American Democracy," Presidential Address, Annual Meeting of Social Science History Association, New Orleans, October 12, 1996, p. 6.

32 Paul E. Peterson, *The Price of Federalism* (1995).

33 See, e.g., John D. Donahue, *Disunited States* (1997).

34 Thomas R. Dye, *American Federalism: Competition among Governments* (1990).

35 Edward M. Gramlich and Deborah S. Laren, "Migration and Income Distribution Responsibilities," *Journal of Human Resources*, 19 (1984): 489. There is little chance, surely, that higher welfare payments will lead to tax increases sufficient to drive away well-to-do taxpayers. Gramlich and Laren have estimated that "a 30 percent increase in average AFDC benefit levels would raise the disposable income of AFDC re-

cipients approximately this amount but would reduce the disposable income of average income taxpayers by only one-third of 1 percent"—hardly enough to cause any rational person to leave the state.

Greater controversy persists over the effects of differing benefit levels on the migration of poor people. The most sophisticated recent studies find "little evidence that those women most likely to be candidates for AFDC move in a pattern consistent with the welfare magnet hypothesis." Philip Levine and Daniel J. Zimmerman, "An Empirical Analysis of the Welfare Magnet Debate Using the NLSY," Working Paper 5264, National Bureau of Economic Research (1995), p. 18. But other scholars disagree, claiming to have detected a tendency for welfare families to move to states with higher benefits. Peterson, *The Price of Federalism,* p. 121. In any case, they argue, even if poor people do *not* gravitate to more generous states, officials may *think* that they do and thus will strive to keep payments low.

36 Supporters of devolution insist that if competition truly produced a race to the bottom, benefit levels in the various states would gradually have become more equal. In fact, however, after more than fifty years of state discretion over the level of welfare payments, differences between states are no narrower than they were in 1940. Undaunted, opponents reply that all states may have lower benefits than they would if they did not worry about attracting more poor people. They add that the new welfare law may bring about even worse results because the federal government no longer offers matching funds but simply gives a block grant. Hence, states will have a greater incentive to lower benefits to save money and make certain that poor people will not find them attractive. This debate, with the arguments and studies on either side, is summarized in Jon K. Brueckner, "Welfare Reform and Interstate Welfare Competition: Theory and Evidence," Urban Institute, Occasional Paper 21 (1999).

37 Research has shown that welfare programs are significantly affected by voting rates, with benefit levels tending to be appreciably lower in states where fewer poor people go to the polls. Kim Q. Hill and Jan E. Leighly, "The Policy Consequences of Class Bias in State Electorates," *American Journal of Political Science,* 36 (1992): 351.

38 Lester M. Salamon, *America's Nonprofit Sector: A Primer,* 2nd ed. (1999), p. 22.

39 See John DiIulio and Donald Kettl, *Fine Print: The Contract with America, Devolution and the Administrative Realities of American Federalism* (1995).

40 See Peter L. Berger and John Neuhaus, *To Empower People: From State to Civil Society* (1996).

9. Reforming Bureaucracy

1 I am indebted for this story to Paul Streeten, "The Cheerful Pessimist: Gunnar Myrdal the Dissenter, 1898–1987," *World Development*, 26 (1998): 540.

2 Al Gore, *From Red Tape to Results: Creating a Government That Works Better and Costs Less* (1993).

3 See, e.g., Donald J. Savoie, *Thatcher, Reagan, Mulroney: In Search of a New Bureaucracy* (1994); Gerald E. Caiden, *Administrative Reform Comes of Age* (1991); Jonathan Boston, John Martin, June Pallot, and Pat Walsh, *Public Management: The New Zealand Model* (1996).

4 Boston et al., *Public Management*.

5 Jane E. Fountain, "Customer Service: An Institutional Perspective," paper prepared for American Political Science Association, Boston, September 4, 1998, pp. 2–4.

6 Niccolò Machiavelli, *The Prince*, ch. 6 (1532), quoted in John Bartlett, *Bartlett's Familiar Quotations* 16th ed., ed. Justin Kaplan (1992), p. 136.

7 *Leadership for America: Report of the National Commission on the Public Service* (1990). The National Commission on Public Service is commonly known as the Volcker Commission.

8 Paul C. Light, *The New Public Service* (1999), pp. 2, 4.

9 See, e.g., William Gormley, *Taming the Bureaucracy* (1989).

10 Light, *The New Public Service*.

11 G. Calvin Mackenzie, *The In-and-Outers: Presidential Appointees and the Transient Government in Washington* (1987).

12 Pew Research Center for the People and the Press, "Washington Leaders Wary of Public Opinion: Public Appetite for Government Misjudged" (April 17, 1998), p. 18.

13 Michel Crozier, *Crise de l'intelligence: Essai sur l'impuissance des élites à se réformer* (1995).

14 Quoted in Caiden, *Administrative Reform Comes of Age*, p. 233.

15 David Osborne and Peter Plastrik, *Banishing Bureaucracy: The Five Strategies for Reinventing Government* (1997), p. 52.

16 Not all analysts are convinced that the private sector is inherently more efficient than the public sector. See Kwong-leung Teng, "Efficiency of the Private Sector: A Critical Review of Empirical Evidence from Public

Services," *International Review of Administrative Sciences*, 4 (1997): 459.

17 Reason Foundation, *Privatization 1995* (1995), p. 2.

18 Jennifer R. Wolch, *The Shadow State: Government and Voluntary Sector in Transition* (1990), p. 59.

19 Donald F. Kettl, *Sharing Power: Public Governance and Private Markets* (1993), p. 166.

20 Ibid., p. 160.

21 Donald F. Kettl and John J. DiIulio, *Cutting Government: A Report of the Brookings Center for Public Management* (1995). See also Donald F. Kettl and John J. DiIulio (eds.), *Inside the Reinvention Machine: Appraising Governmental Reform* (1995).

22 Patrick J. Wolff, "Why Must We Reinvent the Federal Government? Putting Historical Developmental Claims to the Test," *Journal of Public Administration Research and Theory*, 7 (1997): 353, 375.

23 Paul C. Light, *Thickening Government: Federal Hierarchy and the Diffusion of Accountability* (1995).

24 Paul C. Light, *The True Size of Government* (1999), pp. 70–72.

25 See Kettl and DiIulio, *Cutting Government*, p. 29.

26 Ibid.

27 Kettl and DiIulio, *Inside the Reinvention Machine*, p. 82.

28 Donald F. Kettl, "Reinventing Government: A Fifth-Year Report Card" (September 1998), p. 17.

29 John P. Kotter and James L. Heskett, *Corporate Culture and Performance* (1992), pp. 104–105.

30 See Robert Kuttner, "Government's Happy Customers," *Boston Globe* (December 19, 1999): C7. More generally, see Daniel Katz, Barbara A. Gutek, Robert L. Kahn, and Eugenia Barton, *Bureaucratic Encounters* (1975).

31 See James Q. Wilson, Bureaucracy: What Government Agencies Do and Why They Do It (1989), pp. 318–319.

10. Campaign Finance Reform

1 Quoted by Stephen Breyer, "Reforming Regulation," *Tulane Law Review*, 59 (1984): 4.

2 *Buckley v. Valeo*, 424 U.S. 1 (1976).

3 *Colorado Republican Federal Campaign Committee v. Federal Election Commission*, 116 S.Ct. 2309 (1990).

4 *New York Times* poll, cited by Donald J. Simon, Testimony before the House Administration Committee, July 22, 1999, p. 3. According

to a 1997 Gallup Poll, 77 percent of the public believed that "elected officials in Washington are mostly influenced by the pressure they receive on issues from major campaign contributors," and that elections are not generally won by the best candidate but "are generally for sale to the candidate who can raise the most money." Gallup Poll, October 3–5, 1997, quoted in *A Government to Trust and Respect: Rebuilding Citizen-Government Relations for the Twenty-First Century,* Report by the Panel on Civic Trust and Citizen Responsibility, National Academy of Public Administration (1998), p. A-15.

5 Pew Research Center for the People and the Press, "Washington Leaders Wary of Public Opinion: Public Appetite for Government Misjudged" (April 17, 1998), p. 8.

6 Ibid.

7 See, generally, Anthony Corrado et al. (eds.), *Campaign Finance Reform: A Sourcebook* (1997).

8 Bradley A. Smith, "Faulty Assumptions and Undemocratic Consequences of Campaign Finance Reform," *Yale Law Journal,* 105 (1996): 1049.

9 See Chapter 3, above.

10 Thomas Gais, *Improper Influence: Campaign Finance Law, Political Interest Groups, and the Problem of Equality* (1996).

11 See Russell Feingold, "Modest Reform?" *Boston Review* (April–May 1997): 9.

12 See, e.g., John M. Hansen, "Individuals, Institutions, and Public Preferences over Public Finance," *American Political Science Review,* 92 (1998): 513, 526–527.

13 Ellen S. Miller, "Clean Elections, How To," *American Prospect* (January–February 1997): 56; David Donnelly, Janice Fine, and Ellen Miller, "Going Public," *Boston Review* (April–May 1997): 3.

14 Ellen Miller ("Clean Elections, How To") cites findings from several polls showing wide support for public financing.

15 Simon, Testimony before the House Administration Committee, p. 28.

16 Bruce Ackerman, "Crediting the Voters: A New Beginning for Campaign Finance," *American Prospect* (Spring 1993): 71.

17 Ibid., p. 74.

18 Donnelly et al., "Going Public," pp. 3, 6–7.

19 See Zach Polett, "Empower Citizens," *Boston Review,* 22 (April–May 1997): 12.

11. *Toward More Coherent Legislation*

1 Morris P. Fiorina, "The Decline of Collective Responsibility in American Politics," *Daedalus,* 109 (1980): 44.

2 See, e.g., Nelson W. Polsby, *Consequences of Party Reform* (1983); Martin Wattenberg, *The Decline of American Political Parties* (1990).

3 John K. White and Jerome M. Mileur, *Challenges to Party Control* (1992).

4 For a contrary view from a former member of the Republican top leadership team in the House of Representatives, see Mickey Edwards, "The Case against the Line-Item Veto," *Notre Dame Journal of Law, Ethics, and Public Policy,* 1 (1985): 191.

5 James A. Deerden and Thomas A. Husted, "Do Governors Get What They Want? An Alternative Examination of the Line-Item Veto," *Public Choice,* 77 (1993): 707; Louis Fisher and Neal Devins, "How Successfully Can the States' Item Veto Be Transferred to the President?" *Georgetown Law Journal,* 75 (1986): 159, 189.

6 *Clinton v. City of New York,* 118 S.Ct. 2091 (1998).

7 Susan Rose-Ackerman, *Rethinking the Progressive Agenda: The Reform of the American Regulatory State* (1992), p. 63.

8 Ibid., p. 43.

9 Quoted in Walter J. Oleszek, *Congressional Procedures and the Policy Process,* 4th ed. (1996), p. 18.

10 Lawrence C. Dodd and Bruce I. Oppenheimer (eds.), *Congress Reconsidered,* 6th ed. (1997), p. 24.

11 See Thomas E. Mann and Norman T. Ornstein, *A First Report on the Renewing Congress Project* (1992), pp. 17–19.

12 Pew Center for the People and the Press, "Washington Leaders Wary of Public Opinion: Public Appetite for Government Misjudged" (April 17, 1998), p. 8.

13 See Eric Uslaner, *The Decline of Comity in Congress* (1993).

14 Robert A. Katzman, *Courts and Congress* (1997).

15 As James Q. Wilson has remarked, "Given the fact that the views of both liberal and conservative elites are out of step with those of the average American, do we wish further to empower elites?" Quoted in Marc K. Landy and Martin A. Levin, *The New Politics of Public Policy* (1995), p. 266.

12. *Improving Regulation*

1 For useful discussions of the pros and cons of risk analysis, see Adam M. Finkel and Dominic Golding (eds.), *Worst Things First? The Debate over National Environmental Priorities* (1994). See also Stephen Breyer, *Breaking the Vicious Circle: Toward Effective Risk Regulation* (1993).

2 E.g., Robert W. Crandall et al., *An Agenda for Federal Regulatory Reform* (1997); Robert W. Hahn (ed.), *Risks, Costs, and Lives Saved: Getting Better Results from Regulation* (1996), pp. 202–203.

3 See Lisa Heinzerling, "Regulatory Costs of Mythic Proportions," *Yale Law Journal*, 107 (1998): 1981; Thomas O. McGarity, "A Cost Benefit State," *Administrative Law Review*, 50 (1998): 7.

4 See, e.g., remarks by scientist M. Granger Morton in Adam M. Finkel and Dominic Golding, *Worst Things First?* p. 143.

5 Jerry L. Mashaw and David C. Harfst, *The Struggle for Auto Safety* (1990).

6 See, e.g., Jeremy Rabkin, *Judicial Compulsion: How Public Law Distorts Public Policy* (1989).

7 See, e.g., "Occupational Safety and Health: OSHA Action Needed to Improve Compliance with Hazard Communication Standard," GAO/HRD 92-8 (November 1991); Commission on the Future of Worker-Management Relations, "Report and Recommendations" (December 1994), p. 49.

8 This experiment was described to me orally by Roland Droitch, Deputy Assistant Secretary of Labor, U.S. Department of Labor. For an earlier experiment, see General Accounting Office, "Regulatory Burden: Measurement Challenges and Concerns Raised by Selected Companies," GAO/GGD 97-2 (November 1996).

9 See, e.g., Philip J. Harter, "Negotiating Regulations: A Cure for Malaise," *Georgetown Law Journal* (1982): 1; Harry H. Perritt, Jr., "Administrative Alternative Dispute Resolution: The Development of Negotiated Rulemaking and Other Processes," *Pepperdine Law Review*, 14 (1987): 865.

10 Cary Coglianese, "Assessing Consensus: The Promise and Performance of Negotiated Rulemaking," *Duke Law Journal*, 46 (1997): 1255. For a contrary view, see Philip J. Harter, "Fear of Commitment: An Affliction of Adolescents," *Duke Law Journal*, 46 (1997): 1389.

11 Marcus Stanley, "OSHA and the Move to Cooperative Regulation," Unpublished paper, Kennedy School of Government, Harvard University (1996).

12 See, e.g., Joseph Rees, *Reforming the Workplace: A Study of Self-Regulation in Occupational Safety* (1988).

13 When OSHA invited companies to join the plan and develop their own safety programs with their employees, several business associations brought suit; they alleged that participation was not truly voluntary, since OSHA induced firms to comply by promising them relief from onerous agency inspections. Thus, argued the associations, the program was coercive and amounted to adopting a rule without following the elaborate procedures prescribed by law. In April 1999, the District of Columbia Court of Appeals handed down an opinion agreeing with the associations, placing the entire program in jeopardy. See *Chamber of Commerce of U.S. v. U.S. Department of Labor,* 174 F.3d 206 (1999).

This is not the only legal hurdle that collaborative health and safety plans can expect to meet. It is far from clear that judges will defer to private safety agreements if the agreements are challenged in court under the Occupational Health and Safety Act. After all, federal judges are charged with interpreting the will of Congress. They are unlikely to agree that private arrangements can ignore requirements imposed by law, unless Congress expressly allows such a result. See Patricia M. Wald, "Negotiation of Environmental Disputes: A New Role for the Courts?" *Columbia Journal of Environmental Law* (1985): 1.

14 See, e.g., Paul C. Weiler and Guy Mundlak, "New Directions for the Law of the Workplace," *Yale Law Journal,* 102 (1993): 1907.

15 1988 Gallup Study of Public Knowledge and Opinion Concerning the Labor Movement, quoted in Richard B. Freeman and Joel Rogers, *Who Speaks for Us? Employee Representation in a Non-Union Labor Market* (1992), exhibit 6. For a detailed study of employee attitudes toward representation in the workplace, see Richard B. Freeman and Joel Rogers, *What Workers Want* (1999).

16 Freeman and Rogers, *What Workers Want,* pp. 56–60.

17 Ibid., p. 142.

18 Ibid.

19 See Thomas E. Caballero, "Project XL: Making It Legal, Making It Work," *Stanford Law Journal,* 17 (1998): 399.

20 See, e.g., Nathaniel O. Keohane, Richard L. Revesz, and Robert N. Stavins, "The Positive Political Economy of Instrument Choice in Environmental Policy," *Harvard Environmental Law Review* (1998): 313.

21 E.g., Richard Schmalensee et al., "An Interim Evaluation of Sulfur Dioxide Emissions Trading," *Journal of Economic Perspectives,* 12 (1998): 53, 66.

22 Jeremy B. Hockenstein, Robert N. Stavins, and Bradley W. Whitehead, "Crafting the Next Generation of Market-Based Environmental Tools," *Environment,* 39 (May 1997): 16–17.

23 Robert N. Stavins, "Economic Incentives for Environmental Regulation," Faculty Research Working Paper Series, John F. Kennedy School of Government (April 1997), p. 12.

24 See, generally, Keohane et al., "The Positive Political Economy of Instrument Choice in Environmental Policy."

25 Even state officials will sometimes undercut the EPA's efforts to create a viable system of permits. For example, state public-utility commissions typically allow companies to include the cost of antipollution technology in their rate bases and thus pass the burden along to the consumer. But the same officials are not so keen on allowing utilities to treat the cost of permits in a similar fashion. For obvious reasons, then, utilities find it more advantageous to continue investing in expensive technology to meet emissions limits.

26 Stuart H. Altman, Uwe Reinhardt, and David Schactman, *Regulating Managed Care: Theory, Practice, and Future Options* (2000).

27 See Troyen Brennan and Donald M. Berwick, *New Roles: Regulation, Markets and the Quality of American Health Care* (1996).

28 See Paul C. Weiler et al., *A Measure of Malpractice: Medical Injury, Malpractice Litigation, and Patient Compensation* (1991). Weiler is a senior author of a massive empirical study of medical malpractice, "Harvard Medical Malpractice Study: Patients, Doctors, and Lawyers: Medical Injury, Malpractice Litigation, and Patient Compensation in New York," Report by the Harvard Medical Practice Study to the State of New York, Harvard College (1990).

29 Peter D. Jacobson, "Legal Challenges to Managed Care Cost Containment Programs: An Initial Assessment," *Health Affairs,* 18 (1999): 69.

30 Robert J. Blendon et al., "Understanding the Managed Care Backlash," *Health Affairs,* 17 (July–August 1998): 80, 83.

31 Institute for the Future, *Health and Health Care 2010: The Forecast, the Challenge* (2000), p. 134.

32 Blendon et al., "Understanding the Managed Care Backlash," p. 90.

33 Ibid., pp. 88–89.

34 In fact, choosing the appropriate party for purposes of liability can become quite complex. See Kenneth S. Abraham and Paul C. Weiler, "Enterprise Medical Liability and the Evolution of the American Health Care System," *Harvard Law Review,* 108 (1994): 381, especially pp. 415–420.

35 The most obvious alternative is some form of no-fault liability. Under such a system, claimants would not have the difficult task of proving that the provider acted negligently, but damages would be limited to actual out-of-pocket losses with no compensation for pain and suffering. Such liability would place the burden on those best suited to prevent the illness or injury and would ensure prompt recovery of essential losses for the patient. See Paul C. Weiler, "The Case for No-Fault Medical Liability," *Maryland Law Review,* 52 (1993): 908.

Despite these advantages, such a reform would be fiercely resisted by HMOs and hospitals. So few injured patients currently bring malpractice suits that no one can predict how many claims would result under a no-fault plan or what the total costs would be. Moreover, while claims would be resolved without the difficulty and expense of having to prove negligence, complicated issues could still arise over whether the injury or illness in question was actually caused by the HMO's treatment.

Problems such as these have led other countries that have tried this approach, notably Sweden and New Zealand, to draw back after a time and allow recovery only for "avoidable" illnesses and injuries—a standard falling somewhere between negligence and no-fault liability. This alternative would permit more patients to recover damages than the traditional fault-based system allows but would still leave some difficult issues to be resolved through costly, time-consuming litigation. Another possibility would be to let patients sue but allow the provider to offer to settle by paying the patient's out-of-pocket costs plus reasonable compensation for the time actually spent on the case by the lawyer. The claimant would then be required either to accept the settlement or to prove gross negligence by clear evidence in order to receive any punitive damages or recompense for pain and suffering. Jeffrey O'Connell and James F. Neale, "HMOs, Cost Containment, and Early Offers: New Malpractice Threats and a Proposed Reform," *Journal of Contemporary Health Law and Policy,* 14 (1998): 287, 310. By encouraging such settlements, this procedure would make it somewhat easier for more worthy claimants to obtain prompt relief while limiting their awards and avoiding the long delays and huge legal costs and fees that mar the current malpractice system. Moreover, as in the no-fault schemes, liability would rest squarely on those in the best position to determine the quality of care.

36 See William F. Benson, "The Long-Term Care Ombudsman Program," in Altman, Reinhardt, and Schactman (eds.), *Regulating Managed Care,* p. 117.

37 Ibid., p. 123.

13. Engaging Citizens of Modest Means

1 Robert A. Dahl, *Democracy and Its Critics* (1989), p. 333.

2 Lynne M. Casper and Loretta E. Bass, "Voting and Registration in the Election of November 1996," *Current Population Reports,* P20-504 (1998): 6. Compare with *Current Population Reports,* Series P20, Nos. 344, 405, 440, 464. The gap in voting rates between the wealthiest 20 percent of the population and the poorest 20 percent increased from approximately 31 percentage points in 1980 to 38 points in 1996.

3 Kim Q. Hill and Jan E. Leighley, "The Policy Consequences of Class Bias in State Electorates," *American Journal of Political Science,* 36 (1992): 351.

4 See Sidney Verba, Kay L. Schlozman, and Henry E. Brady, *Voice and Equality: Civic Voluntarism in American Politics* (1995), p. 190.

5 See, e.g., Stephen Knack, "Civic Norms, Social Sanctions, and Voter Turnout," *Rationality and Society,* 4 (1992): 133.

6 Frances Fox Piven and Richard Cloward, *Why Americans Don't Vote* (1988).

7 Marshall Ganz, "Motor-Voter or Motivated Voter?" *American Prospect* (September–October, 1996): 41–49.

8 Marshall Ganz, "Voters in the Crosshairs," *American Prospect* (Winter 1994): 100.

9 Steven Rosenstone and John M. Hansen, *Mobilization, Participation, and Democracy in America* (1993), p. 215.

10 Herbert F. Weisberg, "The Demographics of the New Voting Gap: Marital Differences in American Voting," *Public Opinion Quarterly,* 51 (1987): 335. But see Warren E. Miller and J. Merrill Shanks, *The New American Voter* (1996), pp. 589–590.

11 Rosenstone and Hansen, *Mobilization, Participation, and Democracy in America,* p. 219.

12 Richard Topf, "Electoral Participation," in Hans-Dieter Klingemann and Dieter Fuchs (eds.), *Citizens and the State* (1995), p. 49.

13 Mark N. Franklin, "Electoral Participation," in Lawrence LeDuc, Richard G. Niemi, and Pippa Norris (eds.), *Comparing Democracies: Elections and Voting in Global Perspective* (1996), pp. 216, 226.

14 Ibid.

15 See, e.g., Ruy Teixeira, *The Disappearing American Voter* (1992). For a contrary view, see Franklin, "Electoral Participation."

16 See Arend Lijphart, "Unequal Participation: Democracy's Unresolved Dilemma," *American Political Science Review,* 91 (1997): 1.

17 Ibid., p. 9.

18 Richard B. Freeman and Joel Rogers, *Who Speaks for Us? Employee Representation in a Non-Union Labor Market,* (1992), exhibit 6.

19 See, e.g., Edward S. Greenberg, *Workplace Democracy: The Political Effects of Participation* (1980); William M. Lafferty, "Work as a Source of Political Learning among Wage-Laborers and Lower-Level Employees," in Roberta S. Sigel (ed.), *Political Learning in Adulthood: A Sourcebook of Theory and Research* (1989).

20 Mary Beth Rogers, *Cold Anger: A Story of Faith and Power Politics* (1990).

21 Dennis Shirley, *Community Organizing for Urban School Reform* (1997).

22 See, e.g., Lisbeth Schorr, *Common Purpose: Strengthening Families and Neighborhoods to Rebuild America* (1997).

23 Bennett Harrison, *Building Bridges: Community Development Corporations and the World of Employment Training* (1993).

24 Robert J. Sampson, Stephen Raudenbush, and Felton Earls, "Neighborhood Crime: A Multilevel Study of Collective Efficacy," *Science,* 277 (August 15, 19997): 918.

25 Quoted in Harry C. Boyte and Nancy N. Kari, *Building America: The Democratic Promise of Public Work* (1996), p. 162.

26 Steven R. Smith and Michael Lipsky, *Nonprofits for Hire: The Welfare State in the Age of Contracting* (1993).

27 See, e.g., Walter A. Rosenbaum, "Public Involvement as Reform and Ritual: The Development of Federal Participation Programs," in Stuart Langton (ed.), *Citizen Participation in America: Essays on the State of the Art* (1978), p. 81.

28 Walter Dean Burnham, *Critical Elections and the Mainsprings of American Politics* (1990), p. 133.

29 See Michael McGerr, *The Decline of Party Politics: The American North, 1865–1928* (1986).

30 Quoted in William Crotty, *The Party Game* (1985), p. 121.

31 William Crotty, *Political Parties in Local Areas* (1986); Paul A. Beck, *Party Politics in America,* 8th ed. (1997).

32 Even in talking with voters, most activists act in ways that parallel trends in the media, discussing the character and personality of candidates more than talking about the issues in the campaign and criticizing opponents and condemning their ideas instead of promoting the views of their own candidate. Paul A. Beck, *Party Politics in America,* p. 135.

33 Charley Reese, "An Ignorant Army of Uninformed Voters," *Orlando Sentinel* (November 3, 1998): A-13.

34 Thomas R. Dye and L. Harmon Ziegler, *The Irony of Democracy* (1975), p. 18; see also Bernard Berelson, "Democratic Theory and Public Opinion," *Public Opinion Quarterly* (1952): 313.

35 John Stuart Mill, *Considerations on Representative Government* (Oxford: Blackwell, 1946; orig. pub. 1861), ch. 8.

36 See Michael X. Delli Carpini and Scott Keeter, *What Americans Know about Politics and Why It Matters* (1996).

37 Marshall Cohen (ed.), *The Philosophy of J. S. Mill: Ethical, Political and Religious* (1961), pp. 408–409.

38 See Samuel Bowles and Herbert Gintis, "Is Equality Passé? *Homo Reciproceus* and the Future of Egalitarian Politics," *Boston Review,* 23 (December–January 1998–1999): 4, 9.

39 See, generally, Robert A. Dahl, *Democracy and Its Critics* (1989).

40 These conclusions are based on data contained in Kathleen D. Morgan and Scott Morgan (eds.), *State Rankings, 1999* (1999), pp. v and 96. States in which turnouts for high-income residents were 80 percent or more above those of low-income residents were compared with states in which high-income turnouts were only 30 percent or less above low-income turnouts. See Hill and Leighley, "The Policy Consequences of Class Bias in State Electorates," p. 351.

14. How Much Influence Do Citizens Have?

1 See David Matthews, *Politics for People: Finding a Reasonable Public Voice* (1994).

2 Ibid., p. 15.

3 Pew Research Center for the People and the Press, *Deconstructing Distrust* (1998), p. 4.

4 "American Public Opinion in the 1990s," *Public Perspective,* 9 (February–March, 1998): 44.

5 Alan D. Monroe, "Consistency between Policy Preferences and National Policy Decisions," *American Politics Quarterly,* 7 (1979): 3.

6 Alan D. Monroe, "Public Opinion and Public Policy, 1980–1993," *Public Opinion Quarterly,* 62 (1998): 6. Using a somewhat different method of analysis, Lawrence Jacobs, in *The Health of Nations: Public Opinion and the Making of American and British Health Policy* (1993), has traced the substantial effect of public opinion on the evolution of health legislation in the United States.

7 Benjamin I. Page and Robert Y. Shapiro, "The Effects of Public Opinion on Policy," *American Political Science Review,* 77 (1983): 175.

8 James Madison, Alexander Hamilton, and John Jay, *The Federalist Papers,* ed. Isaac Krannick (1987), p. 371.

9 Ibid., pp. 409–410.

10 John R. Hibbing and Elizabeth Theiss-Morse, *Congress as Public Enemy: Public Attitudes toward American Political Institutions* (1995), p. 66.

11 George F. Will, *Restoration: Congress, Term Limits and the Recovery of Deliberative Democracy* (1992).

12 See, e.g., John Kingdon, *Congressmen's Voting Decisions,* 3rd ed. (1992).

13 Ibid.

14 Gerald C. Wright, Jr., Robert S. Erikson, and John P. McIver, "Public Opinion and Policy Liberalism in the American States," *American Journal of Political Science,* 31 (1987): 980.

15 Robert Erikson, Gerald Wright, Jr., and John P. McIver, *State House Democracy: Public Opinion and Policy in the American States* (1993), p. 247.

16 James A. Stimson, Michael MacKuen, and Robert S. Erikson, *Dynamic Representation* (1995), pp. 559–560.

17 Anthony King, *Running Scared: Why America's Politicians Campaign Too Much and Govern Too Little* (1997), p. 73.

18 Thomas Mann and Norman Ornstein, *The New Congress* (1981), p. 112.

19 Dick Morris, *The New Prince: Machiavelli Updated for the Twenty-First Century* (1999), p. 71.

20 Haynes Johnson and David S. Broder, *The System: The American Way of Politics at the Breaking Point* (1996).

21 Quoted in Robert Entman, *Democracy without Citizens: Media and the Decay of American Politics* (1989), p. 127.

22 "Perot Proves Public Is Suffering from Cult of Leadership," *Arizona Republic* (June 1, 1992): A11.

23 William Greider, *Who Will Tell the People? The Betrayal of American Democracy* (1992).

24 E. J. Dionne, *Why Americans Hate Politics* (1991).

25 James McCann has documented this tendency by comparing the degrees of liberalism and conservatism among four groups of Democrats and Republicans: rank-and-file partisans, partisans who attended a political caucus, caucus participants who were also campaign activists, and state party delegates. The liberalism ratings among the four groups of Democrats on a scale of 1 to 100 were 38, 50, 62, and 68, while the corresponding conservative ratings of Republicans were 65, 80, 87, and 91. "Presidential Nomination Activists and Political Representation: A View from the Active Minority Studies," in William G. Mayer (ed.), *In Pursuit of the White House: How We Choose Our Presidential Nominees* (1996).

26 Ibid.

27 Testimony of Donald J. Simon before the House Administration Committee, July 22, 1999, p. 11.

28 Morris, *The New Prince*, p. 75.

15. How Capable Are Americans of Self-Government?

1 Pew Research Center for the People and the Press, *That Year: A Look Back at 1998* (1999), p. 8.

2 Ibid.

3 Max Farrand (ed.), *The Records of the Federal Convention of 1787*, vol. 1 (1966), pp. 48, 132.

4 Walter Lippmann, *The Phantom Public* (1925).

5 Ibid. The statement is quoted in Michael Schudson, *The Power of News* (1995), p. 206.

6 Joseph A. Schumpeter, *Capitalism, Socialism and Democracy* (1942), p. 262.

7 "American Public Opinion in the 1990s," *Public Perspective,* 9 (February–March, 1998): 43.

8 Derek Bok, *The State of the Nation: Government and the Quest for a Better Society* (1996), pp. 9–16.

9 Richard W. Waterman, Hank C. Jenkins-Smith, and Carol L. Silva, "The Expectations Gap: Public Attitudes toward an Incumbent President," *Journal of Politics,* 61 (1999): 944.

10 "American Public Opinion in the 1990s," p. 31.

11 Times-Mirror Center for the People and the Press, *The New Political Landscape* (1994), p. 27.

12 Pew Research Center for the People and the Press, *Deconstructing Distrust: How Americans View Government* (1998), p. 33.

13 Ibid.

14 Everett Carll Ladd, *The American Ideology: An Exploration of the Origins, Meaning, and Role of "American Values"* (February 1992), pp. A-22, A-24, A-26, A-27. It is possible that Americans want more in services and benefits from the federal government than they are prepared to pay for. As long as anyone can remember, the United States has had lower taxes (even counting state and local levies) than other leading democracies such as Canada, Australia, and the major countries of Europe. (Bok, *State of the Nation,* p. 398.) Yet Americans expect their government to take care of a formidable array of problems. By large majorities, they believe that Congress should be doing more to help the poor, clean up the environment, provide health insurance for everyone, and address a series of other needs. (Pew Research Center for the People and the Press, *Deconstructing Distrust: How Americans View Government* [1998], pp. 95–96.) By equally large majorities, however, they complain that their taxes are already too high. See, e.g., William G. Mayer, *The Changing American Mind: How and Why American Public Opinion Changed between 1960 and 1988* (1992), p. 444.

Up to a point, the public can explain this seeming contradiction by pointing to waste in government. In fact, if the public were correct in its long-standing belief that the federal government squanders approximately half of every tax dollar it receives, Congress could satisfy all of the public's desires without raising taxes simply by cutting the fat out of federal programs. But there is no convincing evidence that waste exists on anything like the scale the public believes. Nor is it practical to think that any mortal officials can succeed in eliminating anything close to all wasteful or unnecessary programs.

There is also evidence that Americans would fund domestic-spending increases by cutting defense expenditures. Whether it would be possible to make such cuts in order to offset all the increases in domestic spending needed to meet the public's desires is a matter of opinion. The sudden reappearance of budget surpluses and the uncertainty over their likely size and duration make it doubly difficult to evaluate how consistent or realistic the public is in wanting more programs and lower taxes.

15 John R. Hibbing and Elizabeth Theiss-Morse, *Congress as Public Enemy: Public Attitudes toward American Public Institutions* (1995), p. 147.

16 See, e.g., David C. Kimball and Samuel C. Patterson, "Living Up to Expectations: Public Attitudes toward Congress," *Journal of Politics, 59* (1997): 701.

17 Benjamin I. Page and Robert Y. Shapiro, *The Rational Public: Fifty Years of Trends in Americans' Policy Preferences* (1992), p. 393.

18 Anthony Downs, "Up and Down with Ecology: The Issue-Attention Cycle," *Public Interest, 28* (1972): 28.

19 Robert J. Blendon and John M. Benson, "Editorial: Whatever Happened to Politicians' Concerns about the Nation's Uninsured?" *American Journal of Public Health, 88* (1998): 345.

20 For a more detailed summary of the public's tendency to err in evaluating risks, see Stephen G. Breyer, *Breaking the Vicious Circle: Toward Effective Risk Regulation* (1993).

21 Page and Shapiro, *The Rational Public.*

22 Lawrence Jacobs, *The Health of Nations: Public Opinion and the Making of American and British Health Policy* (1993).

23 Paul Burstein, *Discrimination, Jobs and Politics: The Struggle for Equal Employment Opportunity in the United States since the New Deal* (1985).

24 Steven M. Teles, *Whose Welfare: AFDC and Elite Politics* (1998).

25 Robert S. Blendon et al., "Bridging the Gap between the Public's and the Economists' View of the Economy," *Journal of Economic Perspectives, 11* (1997): 105.

26 Ibid.

27 Ibid.

28 Ibid.

29 *Washington Post*—Kaiser Family Foundation—Harvard University Survey Project, *Why Don't Americans Trust the Government?* (1996), pp. 4–5.

30 Donald F. Kettl, "Reinventing Government: A Fifth-Year Report Card" (September 1998), p. 36.

31 Walter Lippmann, *Public Opinion* (rpt. 1965), p. 229.

32 Ibid.

33 Robert S. Blendon et al., "What Happened to Americans' Support for the Clinton Health Plan?" *Health Affairs, 14* (1995): 7.

34 "Trust in Government" Survey, conducted September 25–October 31, 1997, by Princeton Survey Research Associates for the Pew Research Center for the People and the Press.

35 Robert S. Blendon et al., "Public Ambivalence and Knowledge about Health Care Reform," unpublished paper (1993), p. 10. This paper reports the results of a survey conducted March 18–25, 1993, by the Harvard School of Public Health and the Boston-based polling firm Marttila and Kiley.

36 Theda Skocpol, *Boomerang: Clinton's Health Security Effort and the Turn against Government in U.S. Politics* (1996), p. 125.

37 Daniel Yankelovich, "The Debate That Wasn't: The Public and the Clinton Health Plan," *Brookings Review* (Summer 1995).

38 Page and Shapiro, *The Rational Public,* p. 14.

39 Benjamin I. Page, *Who Deliberates? Mass Media in Modern Democracy* (1996), p. 124.

40 See, e.g., Max Kaase and Kenneth Newton, *Beliefs in Government* (1995), p. 85.

41 These results were obtained with the help of a Harvard graduate student, Steve Voss, using data contained in the *Washington Post* poll.

42 In a study of South Dakota initiatives, James A. Meader concluded: "The voters are capable of taking a long-range outlook when they consider initiatives on the ballot. Rather than opt for a short-range financial benefit, the voters showed a stronger concern for maintaining . . . [what] will enhance the quality of life in South Dakota into the future." Quoted in Lawrence K. Grossman, *The Electronic Public: Reshaping Democracy in the Information Age* (1995), p. 67. To the same effect, see, e.g., Max Radin in Albert H. Cantril (ed.), *Polling on the Issues* (1980), p. 170.

43 See, e.g., Arthur Lupia and Mathew D. McCubbins, *The Democratic Dilemma: Can Citizens Learn What They Need to Know?* (1998); Arthur Lupia, "Shortcuts versus Encyclopedias: Information and Voting Behavior in California Insurance Reform Elections," *American Political Science Review,* 88 (1994): 63.

44 Larry M. Bartels, "Uninformed Votes: Information Effects in Presidential Elections," *American Journal of Political Science,* 40 (1996): 194. The author says of voters: "The fact of the matter, it seems, is that they do significantly better than they would by chance but significantly less well than they would with complete information, despite the availability of cues and shortcuts." Ibid., p. 217.

45 See, e.g., Peter Schrag, *Paradise Lost: California's Experience, America's Future* (1998).
46 The differences between people's initial opinions and their considered judgment are discussed in great detail in Daniel Yankelovich, *Coming to Public Judgment: Making Democracy Work in a Complex World* (1991).

16. The Ambitions and Realities of Civic Participation

1 David S. Broder, *Democracy Derailed: Initiative Campaigns and the Value of Money* (2000), p. 228.
2 Dick Morris, *The New Prince: Machiavelli Updated for the Twenty-First Century* (1999), p. 250.
3 Mark N. Franklin, "Electoral Participation," in Lawrence Le Duc, Richard G. Niemi, and Pippa Norris (eds.), *Comparing Democracies: Elections and Voting in Global Perspective* (1996), p. 216.
4 See also National Commission on Civic Renewal, *A Nation of Spectators: How Civic Disengagement Weakens America and What We Can Do about It* (1998), p. 28. Reports of decline in political activity have been challenged by Everett C. Ladd, *The Ladd Report* (1999), p. 105. Ladd's figures are based on findings from the Roper Organization in 1981, 1990, and 1997. What Ladd appears to have done, however, is to select quite arbitrarily a single monthly result from each of these years. When all of the monthly Roper results are plotted from these and other years from 1993 to 1994, the trend is unmistakably down, resulting in the figures shown in the text. Other sources dispute the decline in letters written to members of Congress. See, e.g., Michael Schudson, *The Good Citizen: A History of American Civic Life* (1998), p. 300. Measuring such correspondence and establishing meaningful trends are particularly difficult in view of the massive growth of grassroots lobbying in which large organizations go to great lengths to engineer communications of this kind.
5 See Richard Topf, "Beyond Electoral Participation," in Hans Dieter Klingemann and Dieter Fuchs (eds.), *Citizens and the State* (1995), p. 78.
6 Peter Levine, *The New Progressive Era: Toward a Fair and Deliberative Democracy* (2000), p. 95.
7 See, generally, Robert D. Putnam, *Bowling Alone: The Challenge and Revival of American Community* (2000).
8 Ibid., pp. 183–287.

9 Eric L. Dey, Alexander W. Astin, and William S. Korn, *The American Freshman: Twenty-Five-Year Trends, 1966–1990* (1991). See also individual reports for 1991–1998 by the Higher Education Research Institute at the University of California, Los Angeles.

10 Robert D. Putnam and Steven Yonish, "New Evidence on Trends in American Social Capital and Civic Engagement: Are We Really Bowling Alone?" unpublished paper (January 1, 1998), pp. 38–39. See also Putnam, *Bowling Alone*, p. 252.

11 Times Mirror Center for the People and the Press, "The Age of Indifference: A Study of Young Americans and How They View the News" (June 28, 1990).

12 Ibid.

13 Elizabeth Crowley, "Young Turn from Politics to Community Service," *Wall Street Journal Interactive Edition* (June 16, 1999), http://interactive.wsj.com.

14 Wendy M. Rahm and John E. Transue, "Social Trust and Value Change: The Decline of Social Capital in American Youth, 1976–1995," *Political Psychology,* 19 (1998): 545.

15 Alexis de Tocqueville, *Democracy in America* (1969; original French ed., 1835), p. 540.

16 David Matthews, *Politics for People: Finding a Reasonable Public Voice* (1994), p. 15. "This sense of being pushed out of the political process goes to the core of how Americans view politics."

17 David B. Magleby, *Direct Legislation: Voting on Ballot Legislation in the United States* (1984).

18 Everett C. Ladd, *The Ladd Report* (1999), p. 154.

19 Ibid.

20 Heinz Eulau, "The Politics of Happiness," *Antioch Review,* 16 (1956): 259.

21 Michael Schudson, *The Good Citizen: A History of American Civic Life* (1998).

22 Ibid., p. 311. Gabriel Almond and Sidney Verba describe the role of the citizen in somewhat similar terms in their classic work, *The Civic Culture: Political Attitudes and Democracy in Five Nations* (1963), ch. 15.

23 David Whitman, *The Optimism Gap: The "I'm OK—They're Not" Syndrome and the Myth of American Decline* (1998), pp. 16–21.

24 As V. O. Key remarked, "If politicians perceive the electorate as responsive to father images, they will give it father images. If they see voters as most certainly responsive to nonsense, they will give them nonsense. If

they see voters susceptible to delusion they will delude them. If they see an electorate receptive to the cold, hard realities, they will give it the cold, hard realities." Key, *The Responsible Electorate: Rationality in Presidential Voting, 1936–1960* (1966), p. 6.

25 Nelson W. Polsby, *Consequences of Party Reform* (1983).

26 George F. Will, *Restoration: Congress, Term Limits, and the Recovery of Deliberative Democracy* (1992).

27 George Kennan, *Around the Cragged Hill* (1993), pp. 232–249. See also Stephen Breyer, *Breaking the Vicious Circle: Toward Effective Risk Regulation* (1993), pp. 59–80.

28 See, e.g., Thomas R. Wolanin, *Presidential Advisory Commissions: Truman to Nixon* (1975); Daniel A. Smith, Kevin M. Leyden, and Stephen A. Borrelli, "Predicting the Outcome of Presidential Commissions: Evidence from the Johnson and Nixon Years," *Presidential Studies Quarterly*, 28 (1998): 269.

17. Building Citizenship

1 Quoted in Michael J. Sandel, *Democracy's Discontent: America in Search of a Public Philosophy* (1996), p. 218.

2 Ibid.

3 The following discussion and the preceding chapter owe an intellectual debt to earlier works on participation in democracy. See, particularly, Carol Pateman, *Participation and Democratic Theory* (1970); and Benjamin Barber, *Strong Democracy: Participatory Politics for a New Age* (1984). But there are significant differences. The earlier works affirm the value of citizen participation as a necessary means of achieving each author's conception of a good democracy, whereas this book is concerned with the more practical task of giving a systematic account of why an active, engaged citizenry is important if our government is to achieve the goals which its citizens support. Much of the earlier work—notably Pateman's book and, before that, G. D. H. Cole, *Social Theory* (1920)—look almost exclusively to worker participation in companies rather than considering other ways of encouraging citizens to participate, such as improving civic education, increasing access to relevant public-affairs information, fostering public deliberation, and easing barriers to voting. Barber's work comes closer to the theme developed in these pages, but even he does not give a systematic account of the practical effects of apathy on the functioning of democratic institutions and politics in America. Moreover, his policy recommendations vary substantially from mine—for example, he supports establishing local

citizens' councils, distributing local offices by lot, instituting compulsory national service, and providing for national ballot initiatives. More generally, his ultimate goal is to substitute participatory democracy for representative government, an idea that I do not consider practical or even desirable.

4 See Point 28 in Washington's farewell address, quoted in Matthew Spalding and Patrick J. Garrity, *A Sacred Union of Citizens: George Washington's Farewell Address and the American Character* (1996), p. 183.

5 Quoted in Ralph Ketcham, "The Liberal Arts, Civic Education, and Good Government: Some Jeffersonian Reflections," *Southern Humanities Review,* 23 (1989): 321.

6 See Margaret S. Branson, "The Role of Civic Education: Education Position Paper," prepared for the Educational Policy Task Force of the Communitarian Network (1998), p. 19.

7 The only mention of citizenship is in the following sentence of Goal 3: "Every school in America will ensure that all students learn to use their minds well, so that they may be prepared for responsible citizenship, further learning, and productive employment in our modern economy." Quoted in National Educational Goals Panel, *The National Education Goals Report: Building a Nation of Learners* (1998), p. vi.

8 Kenneth J. Cooper, "Most Students Have Little Understanding of Civics," *Washington Post* (November 19, 1999): A16; Chris Hedges, "35 Percent of School Seniors Fail National Civics Test," *New York Times* (November 21, 1999): 16. The results of the 1998 survey cannot be compared with earlier surveys because the questions for students were too dissimilar.

9 National Assessment Government Board, "NAEP Civics: Civics Framework for the 1998 National Assessment of Educational Progress" (1998), p. 9.

10 The decline of civic education is described in detail by Morris Janowitz, *The Reconstruction of Patriotism: Education for Civic Consciousness* (1983). Janowitz describes the decline in national assessment results from 1969 to 1976 on pp. 152–155.

11 See, e.g., Ernest Boyer, "Civic Education for Responsible Citizens," *Educational Leadership* (November 1990): 4; James D. Carroll et al., *We the People: A Review of U.S. Government and Civic Textbooks* (1987).

12 M. Kent Jennings and Richard G. Niemi, *The Political Character of Adolescence: The Influence of Families and Schools* (1974); John Miller, *Effective Participation: A Standard for Social Studies Education*

(1985). See also James Youniss, Jeffrey A. McLellan, and Miranda Yates, "What We Know about Engendering Civic Identity," *American Behavioral Scientist,* 40 (1997): 620.

13 E.g., David Denver and Gordon Hands, "Does Studying Politics Make a Difference? The Political Knowledge, Attitudes, and Perceptions of School Students," *British Journal of Political Science,* 20 (1990): 263. Gregory B. Markus, Jeffrey P. F. Howard, and David C. King, "Integrating Community Service and Classroom Instruction Enhances Learning: Results from an Experiment," *Educational Evaluation and Policy Analysis,* 15 (1993): 410.

14 Michael McDevitt and Steven H. Chafee, "Second-Chance Political Socialization: 'Trickle-Up Effects' of Children on Parents," in Thomas J. Johnson, Carol E. Hays, and Scott P. Hays (eds.), *Engaging the Public: How Government and the Media Can Reinvigorate American Democracy* (1998), p. 57.

15 Alan Melchior, Center for Human Resources, Brandeis University, "National Evaluation of Learn and Serve America: School and Community-Based Programs," Interim Report (April 1997); see also Maryann Jacobi et al., Rand Corporation, "Evaluation of Learn and Serve America, Higher Education: First-Year Report, Volume I" (May 1996).

16 Youniss et al., "What We Know about Engendering Civic Identity." More than half of American high school students engaged in some sort of community service during 1999, but only 30 percent of students are involved in programs that link service to classroom learning and discussion. National Center for Educational Statistics, *Youth Service Learning and Community Service among Sixth- through Twelfth-Grade Students in the United States* (1999).

17 Carole L. Hahn, *Becoming Political: Comparative Perspectives on Citizenship Education* (1998), pp. 75–78; Connie Flanagan et al., "Adolescents and the Social Contract: Developmental Roots of Citizenship in Seven Countries," in Miranda Yates and James Youniss (eds.), *Roots of Civic Identity: International Perspectives on Community Service and Activism in Youth* (1999), pp. 135, 147.

18 Ernest T. Pascarella and Patrick T. Terenzini, *How College Affects Students: Findings and Insights from Twenty Years of Research* (1991), p. 278.

19 Mellman Group, "National Study of College Students" (January 11, 2000), p. 5.

20 William James, "The Moral Equivalent of War," *International Conciliation,* 27 (1910).

21 See, e.g., Charles C. Moskos, *A Call to Civic Service: National Service for Country and Community* (1988); William M. Evers, *National Service: Pro and Con* (1990).

22 Robert D. Putnam and Steven Yonish, "New Evidence on Trends in American Social Capital and Civic Engagement: Are We Really 'Bowling Alone'?" unpublished paper (January 4, 1998), p. 19.

23 Robert D. Putnam, *Making Democracy Work: Civic Traditions in Modern Italy* (1993); see also Sidney Verba, Kay L. Schlozman, and Henry E. Brady, *Voice and Equality: Civic Voluntarism in American Politics* (1995), p. 144.

24 See Robert D. Putnam, *Bowling Alone: The Collapse and Revival of American Community* (2000), pp. 296–349.

25 Jay Rosen, *Getting the Connections Right: Public Journalism and the Troubles in the Press* (1996); see also Michael Schudson, "The Public Journalism Movement and Its Problems," in Doris Graber, Denis McQuail, and Pippa Norris (eds.), *The Politics of News: The News of Politics* (1998).

26 James Day, *The Vanishing Vision: The Inside Story of Public Television* (1995), p. 361.

27 Peter Levine, *The New Progressive Era: Toward a Fair and Deliberative Democracy* (2000), p. 95.

28 Nina Eliasoph, *Avoiding Politics: How Americans Produce Apathy in Everyday Life* (1998).

29 Quoted in Thucydides, *History of the Peloponnesian War,* trans. Rex Warner (1954), p. 147.

30 Quoted in Thomas Ferguson and Joel Rogers (eds.), *The Hidden Election: Politics and Economics in the 1980 Campaign* (1981), p. 4.

31 Michael J. Avery, *The Demobilization of American Voters: A Comprehensive Theory of Voter Turnout* (1989), p. 89, citing a study by Lutz Erbring, Norman Nie, and Edward Hamberg.

32 Seymour Martin Lipset, *American Exceptionalism: A Double-Edged Sword* (1996), p. 51.

33 Ibid., pp. 278–279.

34 "American Public Opinion in the 1990s," *Public Perspective,* 9 (February–March 1998): 13.

35 See e.g., Robert A. Dahl, "The Problem of Civic Competence," *Journal of Democracy,* 3 (1992): 45.

INDEX